J.K. LASSER'S ™

Tax Deductions for Your Small Business

Fourth Edition

Barbara Weltman

IDG Books Worldwide, Inc.

1633 Broadway
New York, NY 10019-6785

IDG Books Worldwide, Inc. books may be purchased for business or sales promotional use. For information please write: Special Markets Department, IDG Books Worldwide, Inc., 1633 Broadway, New York, NY 10019.

J.K. Lasser and the J.K. Lasser Institute are trademarks of IDG Books Worldwide, Inc.

Publisher's Note: *J.K. Lasser's Tax Deductions for Your Small Business* is published in recognition of the great need for useful information regarding the income tax laws for the millions of men and women who must fill out returns. We believe the research and interpretation by the J.K. Lasser Institute™ of the nation's tax laws to be authoritative and of help to taxpayers. Reasonable care has been taken in the preparation of the text. Taxpayers are cautioned, however, that this book is sold with the understanding that the publisher and the contributors are not engaged in rendering legal, accounting, or other professional services herein. Taxpayers with specific tax problems are urged to seek the professional advice of a tax accountant, lawyer, or preparer.

The publisher and contributors to this book specifically disclaim any responsibility for any liability, loss, or risk (financial, personal, or otherwise) that may be claimed or incurred as a consequence, directly or indirectly, of the use and/or application of any of the contents of this book.

J.K. Lasser Editorial and Production
Elliott Eiss, Member of the New York Bar, Editorial Director of the J.K. Lasser Institute™
Kathy Nebenhaus, Publisher, Lifestyle Publishing Group
Cindy Kitchel, Associate Publisher, Lifestyle Publishing Group
Brice Gosnell, Managing Editor
Michelle Patterson, Marketing Manager
Rebecca Cremonese, Book Coordinator
George McKeon, Cover Designer
designLab and Holly Wittenberg, Interior Designers
Debra Kincaid, Layout
John Sleeva, Indexer

Library of Congress Cataloging-in-Publication Data
Weltman, Barbara
J.K. Lasser's tax deductions for your small business / Barbara Weltman.
ISBN 0-02-863690-2
1. Small business—Taxation—Law and legislation—United States. 2. Income tax deduction—United States. 3. Tax returns—United States. I. J.K. Lasser Tax Institute. II. Title.

Manufactured in the United States of America

10 9 8 7 6 5 4 3 2 1

Contents

Introduction

S mall business is big news today. The IRS estimates that already 24 million small businesses are in operation. As part of the IRS's reorganization mandated by the IRS Restructuring and Reform Act of 1998, there will be a new Small Business Division just to handle businesses with assets under $5 million; this division expects to service approximately 40 million tax filers (accounting for about 40 percent of the total revenues collected). The Small Business Administration is teaming up with the IRS to provide small business owners with help on tax issues.

The numbers and types of small business are growing impressively. Women and minority small business ownership has more than doubled in recent years, providing jobs for millions of Americans. Technology has spawned new business, small and large. Many people still working as employees are also starting up sideline businesses to augment their income and provide job security. And a survey by the Small Business Administration says that about 30 percent of all Americans are currently thinking about starting their own business, so expect to see the ranks of small business continue to grow.

As a small business owner, you work, try to grow your business, and hope to make a profit. What you can keep from that profit depends in part on the income tax you pay. The income tax applies to your net income rather than to your gross income or gross receipts. You are not taxed on all the income you bring in by way of sales, fees, commissions, or other payments. Instead, you are essentially taxed on what you keep after paying off the expenses of providing the services or making the sales that are the crux of your business. Deductions for these expenses operate to fix the amount of income that will be subject to tax. So deductions, in effect, help to determine the tax you pay and the profits you keep.

What is the legal authority for claiming deductions? Deductions are a legal way to reduce the amount of your business income subject to tax. But there is no constitutional right to tax deductions. Instead, deductions are a matter of "legislative grace"; if Congress chooses to allow a particular deduction, so be it. Therefore, deductions are carefully spelled out in the Internal Revenue Code (the Code).

The language of the Code in many instances is rather general. It may describe a category of deductions without getting into specifics. For example, the Code contains a general deduction for all "ordinary and necessary" business expenses, without explaining what constitutes ordinary and necessary business expenses. Over the years the IRS and the courts have worked to flesh out what business expenses are ordinary and necessary. Often the IRS and the courts reach different conclusions, leaving the taxpayer in a somewhat difficult position. If the taxpayer uses a more favorable court position to claim a deduction, the IRS may very well attack the deduction in the event that the return is examined. This puts the taxpayer in the position of having to incur legal expenses to bring the matter to court. On the other hand, if the taxpayer simply follows the IRS approach, a good opportunity to reduce business income by means of a deduction will have been missed. Throughout this book, whenever unresolved questions remain about a particular deduction, both sides have been explained. The choice is up to you and your tax adviser.

Sometimes the Code is very specific about a deduction, such as an employer's right to deduct employment taxes. Still, even where the Code is specific and there is less need for clarification, disputes about applicability or terminology may still arise. Again, the IRS and the courts may differ on the proper conclusion. It will remain for you and your tax adviser to review the different authorities for the positions stated and to reach your own conclusions based on the strength of the different positions and the amount of tax savings at stake.

A word about authorities for the deductions discussed in this book: There are a number of sources for these write-offs in addition to the Internal Revenue Code. These sources include court decisions from the U.S. Tax Court, the U.S. district courts and courts of appeal, the U.S. Court of Federal Claims, and the U.S. Supreme Court. There are also regulations issued by the Treasury Department to explain sections of the Internal Revenue Code. The IRS issues a number of pronouncements, including Revenue Rulings, Revenue Procedures, Notices, Announcements, and News Releases. The department also issues private letter rulings, determination letters, and technical advice memoranda. While these private types of pronouncements cannot be cited as authority by a taxpayer other than the one for whom the pronouncement was made, they are important nonetheless. They serve as an indication of IRS thinking on a particular topic, and it is often the case that private letter rulings on topics of general interest later get restated in revenue rulings.

What is a tax deduction worth to you?   The answer depends on the tax bracket you are in. The tax bracket is dependent on the way you organize your business. If you are self-employed and in the top tax bracket of 39.6 percent, then each dollar of deduction will save you 39.6 cents. Had you not claimed this deduction, you would have had to pay 39.6 cents of tax on that dollar of income that was offset by the deduction. If you have a personal service corporation, a special type of corporation for most professionals, the corporation pays tax at a flat rate of 35 percent. This means that the corporation is in the 35-percent tax bracket. Thus, each deduction claimed saves 35 cents of tax on the corporation's income. Deductions are even more valuable if your business is in a state that imposes income tax. The impact of state income tax and special rules for state income taxes are not discussed in this book. However, you should explore the tax rules in your state and ascertain their impact on your business income.

When do you claim deductions?   The timing of deductions—when to claim them—is determined by your tax year and method of accounting. Your form of business organization affects your choice of tax year and your accounting method.

Even where expenses are deductible, there may be limits on the timing of those deductions. Most common expenses are currently deductible in full. However, some expenses must be capitalized or amortized, or you must choose between current deductibility and capitalization. Capitalization generally means that expenses can be written off ratably as amortized expenses or depreciated over a period of time. Amortized expenses include, for example, fees to incorporate a business and expenses to organize a new business. Certain capitalized costs may not be deductible at all but are treated as an additional cost of an asset ("basis").

Credit versus deduction.   Not all write-offs of business expenses are treated as deductions. Some can be claimed as tax credits. A tax credit is worth more than a deduction since it reduces your taxes dollar for dollar. Like deductions, tax credits are available only to the extent that Congress allows. In a couple of instances, you have a choice between treating certain expenses as a deduction or a credit. In most cases, however, tax credits can be claimed for certain expenses for which no tax deduction is provided. Business-related tax credits, as well as personal credits related to working or running a business, are included in this book.

HOW TO USE THIS BOOK

The purpose of this book is to make you acutely aware of how your actions in business can affect your bottom line from a tax perspective. The way you organize your business, the accounting method you select, and the types of payments you make all have an impact on when and the extent to which you can take deductions. This book is not designed to make you a tax expert. It is strongly suggested that you consult with a tax adviser before making certain important decisions that will affect your ability to claim tax deductions. I hope that the insight you gain from this book will allow you to ask your adviser key questions to benefit your business.

In Part I you will find topics of interest to all businesses. First, there is an overview of the various forms of organization for running a business and an explanation of how these forms of organization affect tax deductions. The most common forms of business organization include independent contractors, sole proprietors, and sole practitioners—individuals who work for themselves and do not have any partners. If self-employed individuals join with others to form a business, they become partners in a partnership. Sometimes businesses incorporate. A business can be incorporated with only one owner or with many owners. A corporation can be a regular corporation, called a C corporation, or it can be a small business corporation, called an S corporation. The difference between the C and S corporations is the way in which income of the business is taxed to the owner (which is explained in detail in Part I). There is also a relatively new form of business organization called a limited liability company, or LLC. LLCs generally are taxed like partnerships even though their owners enjoy protection from personal liability. The important thing to note is that each form of business organization will affect what deductions can be claimed and where to claim them. Part I also explains tax years and accounting methods that businesses can select.

Part I contains two additional topics of general interest to all businesses. First, it discusses certain limits on deducting losses. Your business may have many deductions, more deductions than the income generated by the business. You may be limited in how much of those deductions can be claimed. Second, Part I covers important recordkeeping requirements and suggestions to help you audit-proof your return and protect your deductions and tax credits. You may incur certain expenses, but unless you have specific proof of those expenses, you may not be able to claim a deduction or credit. Learn how to keep the necessary records to back up your write-offs in the event your return is questioned by the IRS.

Part II focuses on specific deductions. It will provide you with guidance on the various types of deductions you can use to reduce your business income. Each type of deduction is explained in detail. Related tax credits are also explained in each deduction chapter. In the first part of each chapter, you will learn what the deduction is all about and any dollar limits or other special requirements that may apply. Then scan the second part of each chapter, which explains where on the tax return you can claim the write-off. The answer depends on your form of business organization. You simply look for your form of business organization to learn where on the return to claim the deduction. The portion of the appropriate tax form or schedule is highlighted in certain instances. For your convenience, key tax forms for claiming these deductions have been included. While the forms and schedules are designed for the 1998 returns, they serve as an example for future years.

In Chapter 19, on miscellaneous deductions, you will find checklists that serve as handy reference guides on all the business deductions. The checklists are organized according to your status: self-employed, employee, or small corporation. You will also find a checklist of deductions that have not been allowed.

Several forms and excerpts from forms have been included throughout the book to illustrate reporting rules. These forms are not to be used to file your return. (In many cases, the appropriate forms were not available when this book was published, and older or draft versions of the forms were included.) You can obtain the forms you need off the Internet from the IRS Web site at http://www.irs.ustreas.gov.

The final chapter in Part II contains some special tax deduction strategies that you can use for your business. It also highlights the most common mistakes that taxpayers make in their returns when claiming deductions. This information will enable you to avoid making the same mistakes and losing out on tax-saving opportunities.

Recently many favorable tax changes have been made for small business owners. These rules take effect in 1998 and later years. This book, in its third edition, has been revised to include all of these new deduction rules and ways you can best take advantage of them. Upcoming changes are also noted to help you plan for the future. Finally, it is important to stay alert to future changes. Pending or possible changes are noted throughout the book. Be sure to check on any final action before you complete your tax return or take any steps that could be affected by these changes.

I would like to thank Sidney Kess for his valuable suggestions in the preparation of this book and Elliott Eiss for his expertise and constant assistance with this and other projects.

PART I

Organization

CHAPTER 1

Business Organization

The form of your business controls how deductions are taken. If you have a great idea for a product or a business and are eager to get started, do not let your enthusiasm get you off on the wrong foot. Take a while to consider how you will organize your business. Sometimes you have a choice of types of business organization; other times your circumstances limit your choices. Where you have not yet set up your business and do have a choice, this discussion may influence your decision on business organization. Where you have already set up your business, you may want to change to another form of organization. In this chapter you will learn about:

- Sole proprietorships (including independent contractors)
- Partnerships and limited liability companies
- S corporations and their shareholder-employees
- C corporations and their shareholder-employees
- Employees
- Factors in choosing your form of business organization
- Comparison of forms of business organization
- Changing your form of business

For a further discussion on worker classification, see IRS Publication 15-A, Employer's Supplemental Tax Guide.

SOLE PROPRIETORSHIPS

If you go into business for yourself and do not have any partners, you are considered a sole proprietor. You may think that the term "proprietor" connotes a storekeeper. For purposes of tax treatment, "proprietor" means any unincorporated business owned entirely by one person. Thus, the category includes individuals in professional practice, such as doctors, lawyers, accountants, and architects. Former employees who are expert in an area, such as engineering, public relations, or computers, may set up consulting businesses that fall into the category of sole proprietor. The designation also applies to independent contractors.

There are no formalities required to become a sole proprietor; you simply conduct business. (You may have to register your business with your city, town, or county government by filing a simple form stating that you are "doing business as" the "Quality Dry Cleaners" or some other business name. This is sometimes referred to as a DBA.)

From a legal standpoint, as a sole proprietor, you are personally liable for any debts your business incurs. For example, if you borrow money and default on a loan, the lender can look not only to your business equipment and other business property but also to your personal stocks, bonds, and other property. Some states may give your house homestead protection; state or federal law may protect your pensions and even IRAs. Other than that, your only protection for personal assets is having adequate insurance against accidents for your business and other liabilities and paying your debts in full.

Independent Contractors

One type of sole proprietor is the independent contractor. To illustrate this term, suppose you used to work for Corporation X. You have retired, but X gives you a consulting contract under which you provide occasional services to X. In your retirement you decide to provide consulting services not only to X but to other customers as well. You have now become a consultant. You are an independent contractor to each of the companies for which you provide services.

More precisely, an independent contractor is an individual who provides services to others outside an employment context. The providing of services becomes a business, an independent calling. In terms of claiming business deductions, classification as an independent contractor is generally more favorable than classification as an employee. (See "Tax Treatment of Deductions in General," below.) Therefore, many individuals whose employment status is not clear may wish to claim independent contractor status. Also, from the employer's perspective, hiring independent contractors is more favorable because the employer is not liable for employment taxes and need not provide employee benefits. Federal employment taxes include Social Security and Medicare taxes (FICA) and unemployment taxes (FUTA).

You should be aware that the IRS aggressively tries to reclassify workers as employees in order to collect employment taxes from employers. It has provided its agents with a special audit manual designed to help the agents reclassify a worker as an employee if appropriate. The key to worker classification is "control." In order to prove independent contractor status, you, as the worker, must show that you have the right to control the details and means by which your work is to be accomplished. You may also want to show that you have an economic stake in your work (that you stand to make a profit or loss depending on how your work turns out). It is helpful in this regard to supply your own tools and place of work, although working from your home, using your own computer, and even setting your own hours (flex time) are not conclusive factors that preclude an employee classification. Various behavioral, financial, and other factors can be brought to bear on the issue of whether you are under someone else's control. You can learn more about worker classification in IRS Publication 15-A, Employer's Supplemental Tax Guide.

There is a distinction that needs to be made between the classification of a worker for income tax purposes and the classification of a worker for employment tax purposes. Certain employees are treated as independent contractors for employment taxes even though they continue to be treated as employees for income taxes. Other employees are treated as employees for employment taxes even though they are independent contractors for income taxes.

Two categories of employees are, by statute, treated as nonemployees for purposes of federal employment taxes. Instead, they are treated as independent contractors (the ramifications of which are discussed later in this chapter). These two categories are real estate salespersons and direct sellers of consumer goods. Such workers are treated as independent contractors if at least 90 percent of their compensation is determined by their output. In other words, they are independent contractors if they are paid by commission as opposed to a fixed salary. Also, they must perform their services under a written contract that specifies they will not be treated as employees for federal employment tax purposes.

Statutory Employees

Some individuals who consider themselves to be in business for themselves may still be treated as employees for purposes of employment taxes. As such, Social Security and Medicare taxes (FICA) are withheld from their compensation. These individuals include:

- Corporate officers

- Agent-drivers or commission-drivers engaged in the distribution of meat products, bakery products, produce, beverages other than milk, laundry, or dry-cleaning services

- Full-time life insurance salespersons

- Homeworkers who personally perform services according to specifications provided by the service recipient

- Traveling or city salespersons engaged on a full-time basis in the solicitation of orders from wholesalers, retailers, contractors, or operators of hotels, restaurants, or other similar businesses

Full-time life insurance salespersons, homeworkers, and traveling or city salespersons are exempt from FICA if they have made a substantial investment in the facilities used in connection with the performance of services.

Tax Treatment of Deductions in General

Sole proprietors, including independent contractors and statutory employees, report their income and deductions on Schedule C, Profit and Loss from Business. The net amount (profit or loss after offsetting income with deductions) is then reported as gross income on page 1 of Form 1040. Such individuals may be able to use a simplified form for reporting business income and deductions: Schedule C-EZ, Net Profit from Business. Individuals engaged in farming activities report business income and deductions on Schedule F. Individuals who are considered employees cannot use Schedule C to claim deductions. See pages 21–22 for the tax treatment of deductions by employees.

PARTNERSHIPS AND LIMITED LIABILITY COMPANIES

If you go into business with others, then you cannot be a sole proprietor. You are treated as being in a partnership if you join together to share the profits from the business. Owners of a partnership are called partners.

There are two types of partnerships: general partnerships and limited partnerships. In general partnerships all of the partners are personally liable for the debts of the business. Creditors of the business can go after the personal assets of any and all of the partners to satisfy partnership debts. In limited partnerships only the general partners are personally liable for the debts of the business. Limited partners are liable only to the extent of their investments in the business plus their share of recourse debts and obligations to make future investments.

EXAMPLE: If a partnership incurs debts of $10,000 (none of which are recourse), a general partner is liable for the full $10,000. A limited partner who initially contributed $1,000 to the limited partnership is liable only to that extent. He or she can lose the $1,000 investment, but creditors cannot go after personal assets.

General partners are "jointly and severally liable" for the business's debts. This means that a creditor can go after any one partner for the full amount of the debt. Then that partner can seek to recoup a proportional share of the debt from other partner(s).

Partnerships can be informal agreements to share profits and losses of a business venture. More typically, however, they are organized with formal partnership agreements. These agreements detail how income, deductions, gains, losses, and credits are to be split (if there are any special allocations to be made) and what happens on the retirement, disability, bankruptcy, or death of a partner. A limited partnership must have a partnership agreement that complies with state law requirements.

Another form of organization that can be used by those joining together for business is a limited liability company (LLC). This is a type of business organization formed under state law in which all owners are given limited liability. Owners of limited liability companies are called members. These companies are rather new but have attracted great interest across the country. Every state now has limited liability company statutes to permit the formation of a limited liability company within its

Deduction Portion of Schedule C

Part II   **Expenses.** Enter expenses for business use of your home **only** on line 30.

8	Advertising	8		19 Pension and profit-sharing plans	19
9	Bad debts from sales or services (see page C-3) . .	9		20 Rent or lease (see page C-5):	
				a Vehicles, machinery, and equipment .	20a
10	Car and truck expenses (see page C-3)	10		b Other business property . .	20b
11	Commissions and fees . . .	11		21 Repairs and maintenance . .	21
12	Depletion	12		22 Supplies (not included in Part III) .	22
13	Depreciation and section 179 expense deduction (not included in Part III) (see page C-4) . .	13		23 Taxes and licenses	23
				24 Travel, meals, and entertainment:	
				a Travel	24a
14	Employee benefit programs (other than on line 19) . . .	14		b Meals and entertainment .	
15	Insurance (other than health) .	15		c Enter 50% of line 24b subject to limitations (see page C-6) .	
16	Interest:				
a	Mortgage (paid to banks, etc.) .	16a		d Subtract line 24c from line 24b .	24d
b	Other	16b		25 Utilities	25
17	Legal and professional services	17		26 Wages (less employment credits) .	26
18	Office expense	18		27 Other expenses (from line 48 on page 2)	27

28	**Total expenses** before expenses for business use of home. Add lines 8 through 27 in columns . ▶	28	
29	Tentative profit (loss). Subtract line 28 from line 7	29	
30	Expenses for business use of your home. Attach **Form 8829**	30	
31	**Net profit or (loss).** Subtract line 30 from line 29.		

31   **Net profit or (loss).** Subtract line 30 from line 29.
 • If a profit, enter on **Form 1040, line 12,** and ALSO on **Schedule SE, line 2** (statutory employees, see page C-6). Estates and trusts, enter on Form 1041, line 3.   } **31**
 • If a loss, you MUST go on to line 32.

32   If you have a loss, check the box that describes your investment in this activity (see page C-6).
 • If you checked 32a, enter the loss on **Form 1040, line 12,** and ALSO on **Schedule SE, line 2**   **32a**   All investment is at risk.
 (statutory employees, see page C-6). Estates and trusts, enter on Form 1041, line 3.   **32b**   Some investment is not
 • If you checked 32b, you MUST attach **Form 6198.**   at risk.

For Paperwork Reduction Act Notice, see Form 1040 instructions.   Cat. No. 11334P   Schedule C (Form 1040) 1999

Part V   **Other Expenses.** List below business expenses not included on lines 8–26 or line 30.

....	
....	
....	
....	
....	
....	
....	
....	
48 **Total other expenses.** Enter here and on page 1, line 27	48

Deduction Portion of Schedule C-EZ

Part III	**Information on Your Vehicle.** Complete this part **ONLY** if you are claiming car or truck expenses on line 2.

4 When did you place your vehicle in service for business purposes? (month, day, year) ▶ ..../........./....... .

5 Of the total number of miles you drove your vehicle during 1999, enter the number of miles you used your vehicle for:

a Business .... **b** Commuting .... **c** Other ....

6 Do you (or your spouse) have another vehicle available for personal use? . . . . ☐ Yes ☐ No

7 Was your vehicle available for use during off-duty hours? . . . . ☐ Yes ☐ No

8a Do you have evidence to support your deduction? . . . . ☐ Yes ☐ No

b If "Yes," is the evidence written? . . . . ☐ Yes ☐ No

For Paperwork Reduction Act Notice, see Form 1040 instructions.   Cat. No. 14374D   **Schedule C-EZ (Form 1040) 1999**

---

boundaries. (The majority of states also permit limited liability partnerships, or LLPs–LLCs for accountants, attorneys, doctors, and other professionals.) At present, state law is evolving to determine the treatment of limited liability companies formed in one state but doing business in another.

As the name suggests, the creditors of limited liability companies can look only to the assets of the company to satisfy debts; creditors cannot go after members and hope to recover their personal assets. For federal income tax purposes, limited liability companies are treated as partnerships unless the members elect to have the LLCs taxed as corporations. Tax experts have yet to come up with any compelling reason for LLCs to choose corporate tax treatment, but if it is desired, the businesses just "check the box" on a special form (IRS Form 8832). For purposes of our discussion throughout the book, it will be assumed that limited liability companies have not chosen corporate tax treatment and so are taxed in the same way as partnerships. In states that permit one-member limited liability companies, the LLC is treated like a sole proprietor if it is owned by an individual who reports the company's income and expenses on his or her Schedule C.

Tax Treatment of Deductions in General

Partnerships and limited liability companies are "pass-through" entities. They are not separate taxpaying entities; instead, they pass through to their owners income, deductions, gains, losses, and tax credits. The owners then report these amounts on their individual returns. While the entity does not pay taxes, it must file an information return with the IRS—Form 1065, U.S. Partnership Return of Income—to report the total pass-through amounts. (Even though the return is called a partnership return, it is the same return filed by limited liability companies with two or more owners.) The entity also completes Schedule K-1 of Form 1065, a copy of which is given to each owner. The K-1 tells the owner his or her allocable share of partnership/LLC amounts.

Two types of items pass through to an owner: trade or business income or loss and separately stated items. A partner's or member's share is called the distributive share. Trade or business income or loss takes into account most ordinary deductions of the business—compensation, rent, taxes, interest, and so forth. Guaranteed payments to an owner are also taken into account in determining ordinary income or loss. From an owner's perspective, deductions net out against income from the business, and the owner's allocable share of the net amount is then reported on the owner's Schedule E.

Separately stated items are stand-alone items that pass through to owners apart from the net amount of trade or business income. These are items that are subject to limitations on an individual's own tax return and so must be segregated from the net amount of trade or business income. They are reported along with similar items on the owner's own tax return.

EXAMPLE: A charitable contribution deduction made by a partnership passes through separately as a charitable contribution. The partner then adds the amount of the pass-through charitable contribution to his or her other charitable contributions. Since an individual's cash contributions are deductible only to the extent of 50 percent of adjusted gross income, the partner's allocable share of the partnership's charitable contribution is subject to his or her individual adjusted gross income limit.

Other items that pass through separately to owners include capital gains and losses, Section 179 first-year expense deductions, investment interest deductions, and tax credits.

Where a partnership or limited liability company has substantial expenses that exceed its operating income, a loss is passed through to owners. The owner may not be able to claim the entire loss. A number of different rules operate to limit a loss deduction. The loss is limited by the owner's "basis" in the interest in the partnership. Basis is the amount of cash and property contributed to the partnership.

EXAMPLE: You contributed $2,000 to the AB Partnership. In 1999 the partnership had sizable expenses and only a small amount of revenue. Your allocable share of partnership loss is $3,000. You may deduct only $2,000 in 1999, the amount of your basis in your partnership interest. You may deduct that additional $1,000 of loss when you have additional basis to offset it.

There may be additional limits on your write-offs from partnerships and limited liability companies. If you are a passive investor—a silent partner—in these businesses, your loss deduction is further limited by the passive activity loss rules. In general, these rules limit a current deduction for losses from passive activities to the extent of income from passive activities. Additionally, losses are limited by the amount of an individual's economic risk in the business. This limit is called the at-risk rule. The passive activity loss and at-risk rules are discussed in Chapter 3. For a further discussion of the passive activity loss rules, see IRS Publication 925, Passive Activity and At-Risk Rules.

S CORPORATIONS AND THEIR SHAREHOLDER-EMPLOYEES

S corporations are like regular corporations (called C corporations) for business law purposes. They are separate entities in the eyes of the law and have their own existence independent from their owners. For example, if an owner dies, the S corporation's existence goes on. S corporations are formed under state law in the same way as other corporations. The only difference between S corporations and other corporations is their tax treatment for federal income tax purposes.

Schedule K-1 for Partners and Members

SCHEDULE K-1 **(Form 1065)** Department of the Treasury Internal Revenue Service	**Partner's Share of Income, Credits, Deductions, etc.** ▶ See separate instructions. For calendar year 1999 or tax year beginning , 1999, and ending ,	OMB No. 1545-0099 19**99**

Partner's identifying number ▶ | **Partnership's identifying number ▶**

Partner's name, address, and ZIP code | Partnership's name, address, and ZIP code

A This partner is a ☐ general partner   ☐ limited partner
   ☐ limited liability company member
B What type of entity is this partner? ▶ ....
C Is this partner▶ ☐ domestic or ▶☐ foreign partner?
D Enter partner's percentage of: (i) Before change or termination   (ii) End of year
   Profit sharing . . . . % .... %
   Loss sharing . . . . % .... %
   Ownership of capital . . . . % .... %
E IRS Center where partnership filed return:

F Partner's share of liabilities (see instructions):
   Nonrecourse . . . . $ ....
   Qualified nonrecourse financing . $ ....
   Other . . . . $ ....
G Tax shelter registration number . ▶ ....
H Check here if this partnership is a publicly traded partnership as defined in section 469(k)(2) . . . . . ☐
I Check applicable boxes: **(1)** ☐ Final K-1 **(2)** ☐ Amended K-1

J Analysis of partner's capital account:

(a) Capital account at beginning of year	(b) Capital contributed during year	(c) Partner's share of lines 3, 4, and 7, Form 1065, Schedule M-2	(d) Withdrawals and distributions	(e) Capital account at end of year (combine columns (a) through (d))
		( )	( )	

	(a) Distributive share item		(b) Amount	(c) 1040 filers enter the amount in column (b) on:
Income (Loss)	**1** Ordinary income (loss) from trade or business activities . . .	**1**		See page 6 of Partner's Instructions for Schedule K-1 (Form 1065).
	2 Net income (loss) from rental real estate activities	**2**		
	3 Net income (loss) from other rental activities	**3**		
	4 Portfolio income (loss):			
	a Interest	**4a**		Sch. B, Part I, line 1
	b Ordinary dividends	**4b**		Sch. B, Part II, line 5
	c Royalties	**4c**		Sch. E, Part I, line 4
	d Net short-term capital gain (loss)	**4d**		Sch. D, line 5, col. (f)
	e Net long-term capital gain (loss):			
	(1) 28% rate gain (loss)	**e(1)**		Sch. D, line 12, col. (g)
	(2) Total for year.	**e(2)**		Sch. D, line 12, col. (f)
	f Other portfolio income (loss) *(attach schedule)*	**4f**		Enter on applicable line of your return.
	5 Guaranteed payments to partner	**5**		See page 6 of Partner's Instructions for Schedule K-1 (Form 1065).
	6 Net section 1231 gain (loss) (other than due to casualty or theft) .	**6**		
	7 Other income (loss) *(attach schedule)*	**7**		Enter on applicable line of your return.
Deduc-tions	**8** Charitable contributions (see instructions) *(attach schedule)* . .	**8**		Sch. A, line 15 or 16
	9 Section 179 expense deduction	**9**		See pages 7 and 8 of Partner's Instructions for Schedule K-1 (Form 1065).
	10 Deductions related to portfolio income *(attach schedule)* . . .	**10**		
	11 Other deductions *(attach schedule)*.	**11**		
Credits	**12a** Low-income housing credit:			
	(1) From section 42(j)(5) partnerships for property placed in service before 1990	**a(1)**		Form 8586, line 5
	(2) Other than on line 12a(1) for property placed in service before 1990	**a(2)**		
	(3) From section 42(j)(5) partnerships for property placed in service after 1989	**a(3)**		
	(4) Other than on line 12a(3) for property placed in service after 1989	**a(4)**		
	b Qualified rehabilitation expenditures related to rental real estate activities	**12b**		See page 8 of Partner's Instructions for Schedule K-1 (Form 1065).
	c Credits (other than credits shown on lines 12a and 12b) related to rental real estate activities.	**12c**		
	d Credits related to other rental activities	**12d**		
	13 Other credits	**13**		

For Paperwork Reduction Act Notice, see Instructions for Form 1065.   Cat. No. 11394R   **Schedule K-1 (Form 1065) 1999**

Schedule K-1 (Form 1065) 1999   Page **2**

		(a) Distributive share item	(b) Amount	(c) 1040 filers enter the amount in column (b) on:
Investment Interest	**14a**	Interest expense on investment debts **14a**		Form 4952, line 1
	b	(1) Investment income included on lines 4a, 4b, 4c, and 4f . . **b(1)**		See page 9 of Partner's Instructions for Schedule K-1 (Form 1065).
		(2) Investment expenses included on line 10 . . . . **b(2)**		
Self-employment	**15a**	Net earnings (loss) from self-employment **15a**		Sch. SE, Section A or B
	b	Gross farming or fishing income **15b**		See page 9 of Partner's Instructions for Schedule K-1 (Form 1065).
	c	Gross nonfarm income **15c**		
Adjustments and Tax Preference Items	**16a**	Depreciation adjustment on property placed in service after 1986 **16a**		
	b	Adjusted gain or loss **16b**		See page 9 of Partner's Instructions for Schedule K-1 (Form 1065) and Instructions for Form 6251.
	c	Depletion (other than oil and gas) **16c**		
	d	(1) Gross income from oil, gas, and geothermal properties . . **d(1)**		
		(2) Deductions allocable to oil, gas, and geothermal properties **d(2)**		
	e	Other adjustments and tax preference items (attach schedule) **16e**		
Foreign Taxes	**17a**	Type of income ▶		Form 1116, check boxes
	b	Name of foreign country or possession ▶		
	c	Total gross income from sources outside the United States (attach schedule) **17c**		Form 1116, Part I
	d	Total applicable deductions and losses (attach schedule) . . **17d**		
	e	Total foreign taxes (check one): ▶ ☐ Paid ☐ Accrued . . . **17e**		Form 1116, Part II
	f	Reduction in taxes available for credit (attach schedule) . . . **17f**		Form 1116, Part III
	g	Other foreign tax information (attach schedule) **17g**		See Instructions for Form 1116.
Other	**18**	Section 59(e)(2) expenditures: **a** Type ▶		See page 9 of Partner's Instructions for Schedule K-1 (Form 1065).
	b	Amount **18b**		
	19	Tax-exempt interest income **19**		Form 1040, line 8b
	20	Other tax-exempt income **20**		See pages 9 and 10 of Partner's Instructions for Schedule K-1 (Form 1065).
	21	Nondeductible expenses **21**		
	22	Distributions of money (cash and marketable securities) . . . **22**		
	23	Distributions of property other than money **23**		
	24	Recapture of low-income housing credit:		
	a	From section 42(j)(5) partnerships **24a**		Form 8611, line 8
	b	Other than on line 24a **24b**		

Supplemental Information

25 Supplemental information required to be reported separately to each partner (attach additional schedules if more space is needed):

....

....

....

....

....

....

....

....

....

....

....

....

....

....

Portion of Schedule E Used by Partners, Members, and S Corporation Shareholders to Report Their Allocable Share of Company Income or Loss

Schedule E (Form 1040) 1999	Attachment Sequence No. **13**	Page **2**
Name(s) shown on return. Do not enter name and social security number if shown on other side.	**Your social security number**	

Note: *If you report amounts from farming or fishing on Schedule E, you must enter your gross income from those activities on line 41 below. Real estate professionals must complete line 42 below.*

Part II   **Income or Loss From Partnerships and S Corporations**   Note: *If you report a loss from an at-risk activity, you MUST check either column (e) or (f) on line 27 to describe your investment in the activity. See page E-5. If you check column (f), you must attach Form 6198.*

27	(a) Name	(b) Enter P for partnership; S for S corporation	(c) Check if foreign partnership	(d) Employer identification number	Investment At Risk? (e) All is at risk	(f) Some is not at risk
A						
B						
C						
D						
E						

	Passive Income and Loss		Nonpassive Income and Loss		
	(g) Passive loss allowed (attach **Form 8582** if required)	(h) Passive income from **Schedule K–1**	(i) Nonpassive loss from **Schedule K–1**	(j) Section 179 expense deduction from **Form 4562**	(k) Nonpassive income from **Schedule K–1**
A					
B					
C					
D					
E					
28a Totals					
b Totals					

29	Add columns (h) and (k) of line 28a .	29
30	Add columns (g), (i), and (j) of line 28b .	30 ( )
31	Total partnership and S corporation income or (loss). Combine lines 29 and 30. Enter the result here and include in the total on line 40 below .	31

For the most part, S corporations are treated as pass-through entities for federal income tax purposes. This means that, as with partnerships and limited liability companies, the income and loss pass through to owners, and their allocable share is reported by S corporation shareholders on their individual income tax returns. The tax treatment of S corporations is discussed more fully later in this chapter. (Note: State laws vary on the tax treatment of S corporations for state income tax purposes. Be sure to check the laws of your state as well as any state in which you do business.)

S corporation status is not automatic. A corporation must elect S status in a timely manner. This election is made on Form 2553, Election by Small Business Corporations to Tax Corporate Income Directly to Shareholders. It must be filed with the Internal Revenue Service no later than the fifteenth day of the third month of the corporation's tax year.

EXAMPLE: A corporation on a calendar year wanted to elect S status. It had to file an election no later than March 15, 1999 to be effective for its 1999 tax year.

If an S election is filed after the fifteenth day of the third month of the corporation's tax year, it is automatically effective for the following year. A corporation can simply decide to make a prospective election by filing at any time during the year prior to that for which the election is to be effective.

EXAMPLE: A corporation on a calendar year wants to elect S status for its 2000 tax year. It can file an election at any time during 1999.

An election cannot be made before the corporation is formed. The board of directors of the corporation must agree to the election and should indicate this assent in the minutes of a board of directors meeting.

Remember, if state law also allows S status, a separate election may have to be filed with the state. Check with state law requirements.

Tax Treatment of Deductions in General

For the most part, S corporations, like partnerships and limited liability companies, are "pass-through" entities. They generally are not separate taxpaying entities. Instead, they pass through to their shareholders income, deductions, gains, losses, and tax credits. The shareholders then report these amounts on their individual returns. The S corporation files a return with the IRS—Form 1120S, U.S. Income Tax Return for S Corporation—to report the total pass-through amounts. The S corporation also completes Schedule K-1 of Form 1120S, a copy of which is given to each shareholder. The K-1 tells the shareholder his or her allocable share of S corporation amounts.

Unlike partnerships and limited liability companies, however, S corporations may themselves become taxpayers if they have certain types of income. There are only three types of income that result in a tax on the S corporation.

The first is built-in gains, which are gains related to appreciation on assets held by a C corporation that converts to S status. Thus, if a corporation is formed and immediately elects S status, there will never be any built-in gains to worry about.

The second type of item that results in a tax on the S corporation is passive investment income of a corporation that has earnings and profits from a time when it was a C corporation and this passive investment income exceeds 25 percent of gross receipts. Again, if a corporation is formed and immediately elects S status, or if a corporation that converted to S status did not have any earnings and profits at the time of conversion, then there will never be any tax from this source.

The third item that results in a tax on the S corporation is recapture from LIFO inventory. Where a C corporation using LIFO to report inventory converts to S status, there may be recapture income that is taken into account partly on the final return of the C corporation but also on the S return. Again, if a corporation is formed and immediately elects S status, there will not be any recapture income on which the S corporation must pay tax. These three items cannot be reduced by any deductions.

To sum this up, if a corporation is formed and immediately elects S status, the corporation will always be solely a pass-through entity and there will never be any tax at the corporate level. If the S corporation was, at one time, a C corporation, there may be some tax at the corporate level.

C CORPORATIONS AND THEIR SHAREHOLDER-EMPLOYEES

A C corporation is an entity separate and apart from its owners. It has its own legal existence. Though formed under state law, it need not be formed in the state in which the business operates. Many corporations, for example, are formed in Delaware or Nevada because the laws in these states favor the corporation, as opposed to investors (shareholders). However, state law for the state in which the business operates may still require the corporation to make some formal notification of doing business in the state. And the corporation may be subject to tax on income generated in that state.

For federal tax purposes, a C corporation is a separate taxpaying entity. It files its own return, Form 1120, Corporate Income Tax Return, to report its income or losses (or Form 1120-A, U.S. Corporation Short-Form Income Tax Return, for corporations with gross receipts under $500,000). Shareholders do not report their share of the corporation's income. The tax treatment of C corporations is explained more fully later in this chapter.

Personal Service Corporations (PSCs)

Certain professionals who incorporate their practices are a special type of C corporation called personal service corporations (PSCs).

Schedule K-1 for S Corporation Shareholders

SCHEDULE K-1 (Form 1120S) Department of the Treasury Internal Revenue Service	**Shareholder's Share of Income, Credits, Deductions, etc.** ▶ See separate instructions. For calendar year 1999 or tax year beginning _____ , 1999, and ending _____ ,	OMB No. 1545-0130 19**99**
Shareholder's identifying number ▶		**Corporation's identifying number** ▶
Shareholder's name, address, and ZIP code		Corporation's name, address, and ZIP code

A Shareholder's percentage of stock ownership for tax year (see instructions for Schedule K-1) . . . . ▶ _____ %
B Internal Revenue Service Center where corporation filed its return ▶ ....
C Tax shelter registration number (see instructions for Schedule K-1) . . . . ▶ ....
D Check applicable boxes: **(1)** ☐ Final K-1 **(2)** ☐ Amended K-1

		(a) Pro rata share items		**(b)** Amount	**(c)** Form 1040 filers enter the amount in column (b) on:
Income (Loss)	1	Ordinary income (loss) from trade or business activities . . .	1		See pages 4 and 5 of the Shareholder's Instructions for Schedule K-1 (Form 1120S).
	2	Net income (loss) from rental real estate activities	2		
	3	Net income (loss) from other rental activities	3		
	4	Portfolio income (loss):			
	a	Interest	4a		Sch. B, Part I, line 1
	b	Ordinary dividends	4b		Sch. B, Part II, line 5
	c	Royalties	4c		Sch. E, Part I, line 4
	d	Net short-term capital gain (loss)	4d		Sch. D, line 5, col. (f)
	e	Net long-term capital gain (loss):			
		(1) 28% rate gain (loss)	e(1)		Sch. D, line 12, col. (g)
		(2) Total for year	e(2)		Sch. D, line 12, col. (f)
	f	Other portfolio income (loss) *(attach schedule)*	4f		(Enter on applicable line of your return.)
	5	Net section 1231 gain (loss) (other than due to casualty or theft)	5		See Shareholder's Instructions for Schedule K-1 (Form 1120S).
	6	Other income (loss) *(attach schedule)*	6		(Enter on applicable line of your return.)
Deductions	7	Charitable contributions *(attach schedule)*	7		Sch. A, line 15 or 16
	8	Section 179 expense deduction	8		See page 6 of the Shareholder's Instructions for Schedule K-1 (Form 1120S).
	9	Deductions related to portfolio income (loss) *(attach schedule)* .	9		
	10	Other deductions *(attach schedule)*	10		
Investment Interest	11a	Interest expense on investment debts	11a		Form 4952, line 1
	b	**(1)** Investment income included on lines 4a, 4b, 4c, and 4f above	b(1)		See Shareholder's Instructions for Schedule K-1 (Form 1120S).
		(2) Investment expenses included on line 9 above	b(2)		
Credits	12a	Credit for alcohol used as fuel	12a		Form 6478, line 10
	b	Low-income housing credit:			
		(1) From section 42(j)(5) partnerships for property placed in service before 1990 .	b(1)		Form 8586, line 5
		(2) Other than on line 12b(1) for property placed in service before 1990	b(2)		
		(3) From section 42(j)(5) partnerships for property placed in service after 1989	b(3)		
		(4) Other than on line 12b(3) for property placed in service after 1989	b(4)		
	c	Qualified rehabilitation expenditures related to rental real estate activities	12c		
	d	Credits (other than credits shown on lines 12b and 12c) related to rental real estate activities	12d		See page 7 of the Shareholder's Instructions for Schedule K-1 (Form 1120S).
	e	Credits related to other rental activities	12e		
	13	Other credits	13		

For Paperwork Reduction Act Notice, see the Instructions for Form 1120S.   Cat. No. 11520D   **Schedule K-1 (Form 1120S) 1999**

Schedule K-1 (Form 1120S) (1999)   Page **2**

	(a) Pro rata share items		(b) Amount	(c) Form 1040 filers enter the amount in column (b) on:
Adjustments and Tax Preference Items	**14a** Depreciation adjustment on property placed in service after 1986	14a		See page 7 of the Shareholder's Instructions for Schedule K-1 (Form 1120S) and Instructions for Form 6251
	b Adjusted gain or loss	14b		
	c Depletion (other than oil and gas)	14c		
	d **(1)** Gross income from oil, gas, or geothermal properties . .	d(1)		
	(2) Deductions allocable to oil, gas, or geothermal properties	d(2)		
	e Other adjustments and tax preference items *(attach schedule)* .	14e		
Foreign Taxes	**15a** Type of income ▶			Form 1116, Check boxes
	b Name of foreign country or U.S. possession ▶			
	c Total gross income from sources outside the United States *(attach schedule)*	15c		⎫ Form 1116, Part I
	d Total applicable deductions and losses *(attach schedule)* . . .	15d		
	e Total foreign taxes (check one): ▶ ☐ Paid ☐ Accrued	15e		Form 1116, Part II
	f Reduction in taxes available for credit *(attach schedule)* . .	15f		Form 1116, Part III
	g Other foreign tax information *(attach schedule)*	15g		See Instructions for Form 1116
Other	**16** Section 59(e)(2) expenditures: **a** Type ▶			See Shareholder's Instructions for Schedule K-1 (Form 1120S).
	b Amount	16b		
	17 Tax-exempt interest income	17		Form 1040, line 8b
	18 Other tax-exempt income	18		
	19 Nondeductible expenses	19		⎫ See pages 7 and 8 of the Shareholder's Instructions for Schedule K-1 (Form 1120S).
	20 Property distributions (including cash) other than dividend distributions reported to you on Form 1099-DIV	20		
	21 Amount of loan repayments for "Loans From Shareholders" . .	21		
	22 Recapture of low-income housing credit:			
	a From section 42(j)(5) partnerships	22a		⎫ Form 8611, line 8
	b Other than on line 22a	22b		

Supplemental Information	**23** Supplemental information required to be reported separately to each shareholder *(attach additional schedules if more space is needed)*:

⊛

Income Tax Return for C Corporations

Form **1120**	**U.S. Corporation Income Tax Return**	OMB No. 1545-0123
Department of the Treasury Internal Revenue Service	For calendar year 1999 or tax year beginning ...., 1999, ending ...., ... ▶ Instructions are separate. See page 1 for Paperwork Reduction Act Notice.	**1999**

A Check if a:	Use IRS label. Other-wise, print or type.	Name	**B** Employer identification number
1 Consolidated return (attach Form 851) ☐			
2 Personal holding co. (attach Sch. PH) ☐		Number, street, and room or suite no. (If a P.O. box, see page 5 of instructions.)	**C** Date incorporated
3 Personal service corp. (as defined in Temporary Regs. sec. 1.441-4T— see instructions) ☐		City or town, state, and ZIP code	**D** Total assets (see page 5 of instructions)

E Check applicable boxes: (1) ☐ Initial return (2) ☐ Final return (3) ☐ Change of address $ _____

Income

	Gross receipts or sales _____ **b** Less returns and allowances _____ **c** Bal ▶	**1c**	
2	Cost of goods sold (Schedule A, line 8)	**2**	
3	Gross profit. Subtract line 2 from line 1c	**3**	
4	Dividends (Schedule C, line 19)	**4**	
5	Interest	**5**	
6	Gross rents	**6**	
7	Gross royalties	**7**	
8	Capital gain net income (attach Schedule D (Form 1120))	**8**	
9	Net gain or (loss) from Form 4797, Part II, line 18 (attach Form 4797)	**9**	
10	Other income (see page 6 of instructions—attach schedule)	**10**	
11	**Total income.** Add lines 3 through 10 . . . . ▶	**11**	

Deductions (See instructions for limitations on deductions.)

12	Compensation of officers (Schedule E, line 4)		**12**	
13	Salaries and wages (less employment credits)		**13**	
14	Repairs and maintenance		**14**	
15	Bad debts		**15**	
16	Rents		**16**	
17	Taxes and licenses		**17**	
18	Interest		**18**	
19	Charitable contributions (see page 8 of instructions for 10% limitation)		**19**	
20	Depreciation (attach Form 4562)	**20**		
21	Less depreciation claimed on Schedule A and elsewhere on return . . .	**21a**	**21b**	
22	Depletion		**22**	
23	Advertising		**23**	
24	Pension, profit-sharing, etc., plans		**24**	
25	Employee benefit programs		**25**	
26	Other deductions (attach schedule)		**26**	
27	**Total deductions.** Add lines 12 through 26 . . . . ▶		**27**	
28	Taxable income before net operating loss deduction and special deductions. Subtract line 27 from line 11		**28**	
29	**Less:** **a** Net operating loss (NOL) deduction (see page 9 of instructions)	**29a**		
	b Special deductions (Schedule C, line 20)	**29b**	**29c**	

Tax and Payments

30	**Taxable income.** Subtract line 29c from line 28		**30**	
31	Total tax (Schedule J, line 12)		**31**	
32	**Payments: a** 1998 overpayment credited to 1999	**32a**		
b	1999 estimated tax payments . .	**32b**		
c	Less 1999 refund applied for on Form 4466	**32c** ( ) **d** Bal ▶	**32d**	
e	Tax deposited with Form 7004		**32e**	
f	Credit for tax paid on undistributed capital gains (attach Form 2439) . .	**32f**		
g	Credit for Federal tax on fuels (attach Form 4136). See instructions	**32g**	**32h**	
33	Estimated tax penalty (see page 10 of instructions). Check if Form 2220 is attached . . . ▶ ☐		**33**	
34	**Tax due.** If line 32h is smaller than the total of lines 31 and 33, enter amount owed		**34**	
35	**Overpayment.** If line 32h is larger than the total of lines 31 and 33, enter amount overpaid		**35**	
36	Enter amount of line 35 you want: **Credited to 2000 estimated tax** ▶ _____ **Refunded** ▶		**36**	

Sign Here ▶

Under penalties of perjury, I declare that I have examined this return, including accompanying schedules and statements, and to the best of my knowledge and belief, it is true, correct, and complete. Declaration of preparer (other than taxpayer) is based on all information of which preparer has any knowledge.

▶ Signature of officer	Date	▶ Title

Paid Preparer's Use Only

Preparer's signature ▶	Date	Check if self-employed ☐	Preparer's SSN or PTIN
Firm's name (or yours if self-employed) and address ▶		EIN ▶	
		ZIP code ▶	

Cat. No. 11450Q

> **Definition**   Personal service corporation   A C corporation that performs personal services in the fields of health, law, accounting, engineering, architecture, actuarial science, performing arts, or consulting and meets certain ownership and service tests.

PSCs are subject to special rules in the tax law. Some of the special rules are beneficial; other are not:

- PSCs cannot use graduated corporate tax rates. Instead, they are subject to a flat tax rate of 35 percent.

- PSCs generally are required to use the same tax year as that of their owners. Typically, individuals report their income on a calendar year basis (explained more fully in Chapter 2), so their PSCs must also use a calendar year. However, there is a special election that can be made to use a fiscal year.

- PSCs can use the cash method of accounting. Other C corporations generally cannot use the cash method and instead must use the accrual method (explained more fully in Chapter 2).

- PSCs are subject to the passive loss limitation rules (explained in Chapter 3).

- PSCs can have their income and deductions reallocated by the IRS between the corporation and the shareholders if it more correctly reflects the economics of the situation.

- PSCs have a smaller exemption from the accumulated earnings penalty than other C corporations. This penalty imposes an additional tax on corporations that accumulate their income above and beyond the reasonable needs of the business instead of distributing income to shareholders.

Tax Treatment of Deductions in General

The C corporation claims its own deductions as offsets to its income on Form 1120, U.S. Corporation Income Tax Return. Shareholders in C corporations do not have to report any income of the corporation (and cannot claim any deductions of the corporation). Instead, distributions from the C corporation to shareholders are personal items for the shareholders. For example, if a shareholder works for his or her C corporation and receives a salary, the corporation deducts that salary. The shareholder reports the salary as income on his or her individual income tax return. If the corporation distributes a dividend to the shareholder, again, the shareholder reports the dividend as income on his or her individual income tax return. In the case of dividends, however, the corporation cannot claim a deduction. This, then, creates a two-tier tax system, commonly referred to as double taxation. First, earnings are taxed at the corporate level. Then, when they are distributed to shareholders as dividends, they are taxed again, this time at the shareholder level. There has been sentiment in Congress over the years to eliminate the double taxation, but as of yet no legislation has been introduced to accomplish this end.

EMPLOYEES

If you do not own any interest in a business but are employed by one, you may still have business expenses to account for. Your salary or other compensation is reported as gross income on page 1 of Form 1040. Your deductions (with a few exceptions), however, can be claimed only as miscellaneous itemized deductions on Schedule A. These deductions are subject to two limitations. First, the total is deductible only to the extent it exceeds 2 percent of adjusted gross income. Second, high-income taxpayers have an overall reduction of itemized deductions when adjusted gross income exceeds a threshold amount.

Under the 2-percent rule, only the portion of total miscellaneous deductions in excess of 2 percent of adjusted gross income is deductible on Schedule A. Adjusted gross income is the tax term for your total income subject to tax (gross income) minus business expenses (other than employee business expenses), capital losses, and certain other expenses that are deductible even if you do not claim itemized deductions, such as qualifying IRA contributions or alimony. By completing the Income and Adjusted Gross Income sections on page 1 of Form 1040, you arrive at your adjusted gross income.

EXAMPLE: You have business travel expenses that your employer does not pay for and other miscellaneous expenses (such as tax preparation fees) totaling $2,000. Your adjusted gross income is $80,000. Only $400 of the $2,000 expenses is deductible on Schedule A. The amount up to the 2-percent floor, or $1,600 (2 percent of $80,000), is disallowed.

The second deduction limitation applies to higher-income taxpayers whose adjusted gross income exceeds a threshold amount that is adjusted annually for inflation. For example, for 1999 returns the limitation applies to taxpayers with adjusted gross income over $126,600, or over $63,300 if married and filing separately. If the limitation applies, itemized deductions other than medical expenses, investment interest, casualty or theft losses, and gambling losses are generally reduced by 3 percent of the excess of adjusted gross income over the annual threshold ($126,600 or $63,300 for 1999 returns). A worksheet included in the IRS instruction booklet is used to calculate the reduction.

If you fall into a special category of employee called a statutory employee, you can deduct your business expenses on Schedule C instead of Schedule A. Statutory employees were discussed earlier in this chapter.

FACTORS IN CHOOSING YOUR FORM OF BUSINESS ORGANIZATION

In deciding on which form of business organization to choose, many factors come into play. Throughout this chapter, the differences in how deductions are claimed have been explained. But these differences are not the only reasons for choosing a form of business organization.

Personal Liability

If your business owes money to another party, are your personal assets—your home, your car, your investment—at risk? The answer depends on your form of business organization. You have personal liability—your personal assets are at risk—if you are a sole proprietor or a general partner in a partnership. In all other cases, you do not have personal liability. Thus, for example, if you are a shareholder in an S corporation, you do not have personal liability for the debts of your corporation.

Of course, you can protect against personal liability for some types of occurrences by having adequate insurance coverage. For example, if you are a sole proprietor who runs a store, be sure that you have adequate liability coverage in the event someone is injured on your premises and sues you.

Even if your form of business organization provides personal liability protection, you can become personally liable if you agree to it in a contract. For example, some banks may not be willing to lend money to a small corporation unless you, as a principal shareholder, agree to guarantee the corporation's debt. In this case, you are personally liable to the extent of the loan to the corporation. If the corporation does not or cannot repay the loan, then the bank can look to you, and your personal assets, for repayment.

There is another instance in which corporate or limited liability company status will not provide you with personal protection. Even if you have a corporation or limited liability company, you can be personally liable for failing to withhold and deposit payroll taxes to the IRS. This liability is explained in Chapter 5.

Fringe Benefits

The tax law gives employees of corporations the opportunity to enjoy special fringe benefits on a tax-free basis. They can receive employer-provided group term life insurance up to $50,000, health insurance coverage, dependent care assistance up to $5,000, education assistance up to $5,250, adoption assistance, and more. They can also be covered by medicalreimbursement plans. This same opportunity is not extended to sole proprietors. Remember that sole proprietors are not employees, so they cannot get the benefits given only to employees. Similarly partners, limited liability company members, and even S corporation shareholders who own more than 2 percent of the stock in their corporations are not considered employees for purposes of these fringe benefits.

Where the business can afford to provide these benefits, the form of business becomes important. All forms of business can offer tax-favored retirement plans.

Nature and Number of Owners

With whom you go into business affects your choice of business organization. For example, if you have any foreign investors, you cannot use an S corporation, because foreign individuals are not permitted to own S corporation stock directly. An S corporation also cannot be used if shareholders are to be partnerships or corporations. In other words, in order to use an S corporation, all shareholders must be individuals who are not nonresident aliens (there are exceptions for estates, certain trusts, and certain exempt organizations).

The number of owners also presents limits on your choice of business organization. If you are the only owner, then your choices are limited to a sole proprietorship or a corporation (either C or S). (Some states may allow one-member limited liability companies.) If you have a more than one owner, you can set up the business in just about any way you choose. S corporations cannot have more than 75 shareholders, but this number provides great leeway for small businesses.

If you have a business already formed as a C corporation and want to start another corporation, you must take into consideration the impact of special tax rules for multiple corporations. These rules apply regardless of the size of the business, the number of employees you have, and the profit the businesses make. Multiple corporations are corporations under common control, meaning they are essentially owned by the same parties. The tax law limits a number of tax breaks in the case of multiple corporations. Instead of each corporation enjoying a full tax benefit, the benefit must be shared among all of the corporations in the group. For example, the tax brackets for corporations are graduated. In the case of certain multiple corporations, however, the benefit of the graduated rates must be shared. In effect, each corporation pays a slightly higher tax because it is part of a group of multiple corporations. If you want to avoid restrictions on multiple corporations, you may want to look to limited liability companies or some other form of business organization.

Tax Rates

Both individuals and C corporations (other than personal service corporations) can enjoy graduated income tax rates. The top tax rate paid by sole proprietors and owners of other pass-through businesses is 39.6 percent. The top corporate tax rate imposed on C corporations is 35 percent. (Personal service corporations are subject to a flat tax rate of 35 percent.) This is almost a 5-percent differential. But remember, even though the C corporation has a lower top tax rate, there is a two-tier tax structure with which to contend if earnings are paid out to you—tax at the corporate level and again at the shareholder level. And capital gains of C corporations are not subject to special tax rates (they are taxed the same as ordinary business income), while owners of other types of businesses may pay tax on the business's capital gains at only 20 percent (or as low as 10 percent if they are in the 15-percent tax bracket on their other income). Tax rates alone should not be the determining factor in selecting your form of business organization.

Social Security and Medicare Taxes

Owners of businesses organized any way other than as a corporation (C or S) are not employees of their businesses. As such, they are personally responsible for paying Social Security and Medicare taxes (called "self-employment taxes" for owners of unincorporated businesses). This tax is made up of the employer and employee shares of Social Security and Medicare taxes. (The deduction for one-half of self-employment taxes is explained in Chapter 11.)

However, owners of corporations have these taxes applied only against salary actually paid to them. Owners of unincorporated businesses pay self-employment tax on net earnings from self-employment. This essentially means profits, whether they are distributed to the owners or reinvested in the business. The result: Owners of unincorporated businesses can wind up paying higher Social Security and Medicare taxes than comparable owners who work for their corporations. On the other hand, in unprofitable businesses, owners of unincorporated businesses may not be able to earn any Social Security credits, while corporate owners can have salary paid to them on which Social Security credits can be generated.

Restrictions on Accounting Periods and Accounting Methods

As you will see in Chapter 2, the tax law limits the use of fiscal years and the cash method of accounting for certain types of business organizations. For example, partnerships and S corporations in general are required to use a calendar year to report income. Also, C corporations generally are required to use the accrual method of accounting to report income. There are exceptions to both of these rules. However, as you can see, accounting period and accounting methods are important considerations in choosing your form of business organization.

Audit Chances

Each year the IRS publishes statistics on the number and type of audits it conducts. The chances of being audited vary with the type of business organization, the amount of income generated by the business, and the geographic location of the business. While the chance of audit is not a very significant reason for choosing one form of business organization over another, it is helpful to keep these statistics in mind.

The following table provides some light on your chances of being audited, based on the most recently available statistics.

PERCENTAGE OF RETURNS AUDITED

	1997*	1996
Sole proprietors—based on gross receipts		
Under $25,000	3.19%	4.21%
$25,000 to under $100,000	2.57	2.85
$100,000 and over	4.13	4.09
Partnerships	0.59	0.49
S corporations	1.04	0.92
C corporations—based on assets		
Under $250,000	1.19	1.04
$250,000 to under $1 million	3.52	2.76
$1 million to under $5 million	7.79	6.54

The most recent year for which statistics are available.

COMPARISON OF FORMS OF BUSINESS ORGANIZATION

Throughout this chapter you have learned about the various forms of business organization. Which form is right for your business? The answer is really a judgment call based on all the factors previously discussed. You can, of course, use different forms of business organization for your different business activities. For example, you may have a C corporation and personally own the building in which it operates—directly or through a limited liability company. Or you may be in partnership for your professional activities, while running a sideline business as an S corporation.

The following chart summarizes for you two important considerations: how the type of business organization is formed, and what effect the form of business organization has on where deductions are claimed.

COMPARISON OF FORMS OF BUSINESS ORGANIZATION

Type of business	How it is formed	Where deductions are claimed
Sole proprietorship	No special requirements	On owner's Schedule C or C-EZ (Schedule F for farming)
Partnership	No special requirements (but generally have partnership agreement)	Some taken into account in figuring trade or business income directly on Form 1065 (allocable amount claimed on partner's Schedule E); separately stated items passed through to partners and claimed in various places on partner's tax return
Limited partnership	Special partnership under state law	Some taken into account in figuring trade or business income directly on Form 1065 (allocable amount claimed on partner's Schedule E); separately stated items passed through to partners and claimed in various places on partner's tax return
Limited liability company	Organized as such under state law	Some taken into account in figuring trade or business income directly on Form 1065 (allocable amount claimed on member's Schedule E); separately stated items passed through to members and claimed in various places on member's tax return
Limited liability partnership	Organized as such under state law	Some taken into account in figuring trade or business income directly on Form 1065 (allocable amount claimed on member's Schedule E); separately stated items passed through to members and claimed in various places on member's tax return

continued on next page

COMPARISON OF FORMS OF BUSINESS ORGANIZATION

Type of business	How it is formed	Where deductions are claimed
S corporation	Formed as corporation under state law; tax status elected by filing with IRS	Some taken into account in figuring trade or business income directly on Form 1120S (allocable amount claimed on shareholder's Schedule E); separately stated items passed through to shareholders and claimed in various places on shareholder's tax return
C corporation	Formed under state law	Claimed by corporation in figuring its trade or business income on Form 1120 or 1120-A
Employee	No ownership interest	As itemized deductions on Schedule A (certain expenses first figured on Form 2106)
Independent contractor	No ownership interest in a business	Claimed on individual's Schedule C

CHANGING YOUR FORM OF BUSINESS

Suppose you have a business you have been running as a sole proprietorship. Now you want to make a change. Your new choice of business organization is dictated by the reason for the change. If you were taking in a partner, you would consider these alternatives: partnership, limited liability company, S corporation, or C corporation. If you were not taking in a partner but want to obtain limited personal liability, you would consider a limited liability company (if your state permits a one-person limited liability company), S corporation, or C corporation. If you were looking to take advantage of certain fringe benefits, such as medical reimbursement plans, you would consider only a C corporation.

Whatever your reason, changing from a sole proprietorship to another type of business organization generally does not entail tax costs on making the changeover. You can set up a partnership or corporation, transfer your business assets to it, obtain an ownership interest in the new entity, and do all this on a tax-free basis. You may, however, have some tax consequences if you transfer your business liabilities to the new entity.

But what if you now have a corporation or partnership and want to change your form of business organization? This change may not be so simple. Suppose you have an S corporation or C corporation. If you liquidate the corporation to change to another form of business organization, you may have to report gain on the liquidation. In fact, gain may have to be reported both by the business and by you as owner. Before changing your form of business organization it is important to review your particular situation with a tax professional.

In making any change in business, consider the legal and accounting costs involved.

CHAPTER 2

Tax Year and Accounting Methods

Once you select your form of business organization, you must decide how you will report your income. There are two key decisions you must make: the time frame for calculating your income and deductions (called the tax year or accounting period) and the rules you will follow to calculate your income and deductions (called the accounting method). In some cases, as you will see, your form of business organization restricts you to an accounting period or accounting method. In other cases, however, you can choose which method is best for your business.

In this chapter you will learn about:

- Accounting periods

- Accounting methods

- Uniform capitalization rules

For a further discussion on tax years and accounting methods, see IRS Publication 538, Accounting Periods and Methods.

ACCOUNTING PERIODS

You account for your expenses on an annual basis. This period is called your tax year. There are two methods for fixing your tax year. Under the calendar year, you use a 12-month period ending on December 31. Under the fiscal year, you use a 12-month period ending at the end of any month other than December.

You select your tax year when you first begin your business. You do not need any IRS approval for your tax year; you simply use it to govern when you must file your first return. You then continue to use the same tax year thereafter. When you commence your business in the middle of the tax year you have selected, your first tax year will be short.

EXAMPLE: You start your S corporation in May 1999. It uses a calendar year to report expenses. The corporation will have a short tax year ending December 31, 1999, for its first tax year. Then, for 2000, it will have a full 12-month tax year.

In the first or final year of business, you may have a short period (less than 12 full months). For example, you open your doors on May 1, 1999, and select a calendar year. Your first tax year is a short period because it is only seven months. You do not have to apportion or prorate deductions for this short period because the business was not in existence for the entire year. (Different rules apply if a short period results from a change in accounting period.)

Seasonal Businesses

Seasonal businesses should use special care in selecting their tax year. It is often advisable to select a tax year that will include both the period in which most of the expenses as well as most of the income is realized. For example, if a business expects to retail its products primarily in the spring and incurs most of its expenses in the fall, it may be best to select a fiscal year ending just after the selling season, such as July or August. In this way, the expenses and the income that are related to each other will be reported on the same return.

Limits on Use of the Fiscal Year

C corporations other than personal service corporations can choose a calendar year or a fiscal year, whichever is more advantageous. Other entities, however, cannot simply choose a fiscal year even though it offers tax advantages to its owners. In general, partnerships, limited liability companies, S corporations, and personal service corporations must use a "required year."

> **Definition** *Required year* For S corporations, this is a calendar year; for partnerships and LLCs, it is the same year as the tax year of the entity's owners. When owners have different tax years, special rules determine which owner's tax year governs.

Since individuals typically use a calendar year, their partnership or LLC must also use a calendar year.

Business Purpose for Fiscal Year

The entity can use a fiscal year even though its owners use a calendar year if it can be established to the satisfaction of the IRS that there is a business purpose for the fiscal year. The fact that the use of a fiscal year defers income for its owners is not considered to be a valid business purpose warranting a tax year other than a required tax year.

> **Definition** *Business purpose* This can be shown if the fiscal year is the natural business year of the entity. For a personal service corporation, for example, a fiscal year is treated as a natural business year if, for three consecutive years, 25 percent or more of its gross receipts for the 12-month period ending on the fiscal year end are received within the last two months of the year.

Section 444 Election for Fiscal Year

If an entity wants to use a fiscal year that is not its natural business year, it can do so by making a "Section 444 election." The only acceptable tax years under this election are those ending September 30, October 31, and November 30. Use of these fiscal years means that at most there can be a three-month deferral for the owners. The election is made by filing Form 8716, Election to Have a Tax Year Other Than a Required Tax Year, by the earlier of the due date of the return for the new tax year (without regard to extensions) or the fifteenth day of the sixth month of the tax year for which the election will be effective.

If the election is made, then partnerships, limited liability companies, and S corporations must make certain "required payments." These essentially are designed to give to the federal government the tax that has been deferred by reason of the special tax year. This payment can be thought of as simply a deposit, since it does not serve to increase the tax that is otherwise due. The payment is calculated using the highest individual income tax rate plus 1 percent. Therefore the current rate is 40.6 percent. The required payment is made by filing Form 8752, Required Payment or Refund Under Section 7519 for Partnerships and S Corporations, by May 15 of the calendar year following the calendar year in which the election begins. For example, if the election begins on October 1, 1999, the required payment must be made no later than May 15, 2000. In view of the high required payment and the complications involved in making and maintaining a Section 444 election, most of these entities use a calendar year.

Personal service corporations that make a Section 444 election need not make a required payment. Instead, these corporations must make "required distributions." They must distribute certain amounts to employee-owners by December 31 of each year for which an election is in effect. The reason for the required elections: to ensure that amounts will be taxed to owner-employees as soon as possible and will not be deferred simply because the corporation uses a fiscal year. Required distributions are figured on Part I of Schedule H of Form 1120, Section 280H limitations for a Personal Service Corporation.

Pass-Through Business on a Fiscal Year; Owners on a Calendar Year

Owners in pass-through entities report their share of the business's income, deductions, gains, losses, and credits from the entity's tax year that ends in the owners' tax year.

EXAMPLE: You are a partner in a partnership that uses a fiscal year ending October 31. The partnership's items for its 1999 fiscal year ending October 31, 1999, are reported on your 1999 return. The portion of the partnership's income and deductions from the period November 1, 1999, through December 31, 1999, are part of its 2000 fiscal year, which will be reported on your 2000 return.

Change in Tax Year

If your business has been using a particular tax year and you want to change to a different one, you must obtain IRS approval to do so. Depending on the reason for the change, approval may be automatic or discretionary. You can request a change in your tax year by filing Form 1128, Application to Adopt, Change, or Retain a Tax Year. You must also include a user fee (an amount set by the IRS) for this request.

ACCOUNTING METHODS

There are two principal methods of accounting: cash basis and accrual basis. Use of a particular method determines when a deduction can be claimed. However, restrictions apply for both methods of accounting. Also, the form of business organization may preclude the use of the cash method of accounting even though it may be the method of choice.

Cash Method

This is the simpler accounting method. Under this method of accounting, a deduction generally can be claimed when and to the extent the expense is paid.

EXAMPLE: You are a consultant. You buy business cards and stationery. You can deduct this expense when you pay for the supplies.

You may not be able to deduct all expenses when they are paid, because there are some limitations that come into play. Generally, you cannot deduct advance payments (so-called prepaid expenses) that relate to periods beyond the current tax year.

EXAMPLE: You take out a three-year subscription to a business journal and pay the three-year subscription price this year. You can deduct only one-third of the payment—the amount that relates to the current year. You can deduct another one-third next year and the final third the following year.

Prepayments may occur for a number of expenses. You may prepay rent, insurance premiums, or interest. In the case of rent prepayments, there is a difference of opinion between the IRS and one appellate court on when to claim the deduction. According to the IRS, if in November you prepay rent for one full year, you can deduct only two-twelfths of the payments, the portion that relates to November and December. The appellate court, however, says you can deduct the entire prepayment amount, since it does not cover a period beyond one year. The IRS applies the same reasoning to advance payments of insurance premiums.

In the case of interest, no deduction is allowed for prepayments by businesses. For example, if you are required to pay "points" to obtain a mortgage on your office building, these points are considered to be prepaid interest. You must deduct the points ratably over the term of the loan.

EXAMPLE: If the mortgage on the office building runs for 30 years (or 360 months) and you pay the points on July 1, you can deduct 6/360 of the points in the first year. In each succeeding year you would deduct 12/360 of the points. In the final year, you would again deduct 6/360.

If you pay off the mortgage before the end of the term (you sell the property or refinance the loan), you can then write off any points you still have not deducted.

Restrictions on the Use of the Cash Method

You cannot use the cash method of accounting if you maintain inventory. In this instance, you must use the accrual method.

Also, certain types of business organizations generally cannot use the cash method of accounting. These include:

- Corporations other than S corporations

- Partnerships that have a corporation (other than an S corporation) as a partner

- Tax shelters

However, there are exceptions under which some of these businesses can still use the cash method of accounting.

Farming exception   A farming business with gross receipts of $25 million or less can use the cash method. A farming business includes any business that operates a nursery or sod farm or that raises or harvests trees bearing fruit, nuts, or other crops and ornamental trees.

PSC exception   A qualified personal service corporation (PSC) can use the cash method of accounting.

> **Definition**   *Qualified personal service corporation*   This is a corporation (other than an S corporation) with a substantial amount of activities involving the performance of personal services in the fields of medicine, law, accounting, architecture, actuarial sciences, performing arts, or consulting by someone who owns stock in the corporation (or who is retired or the executor of the estate of a deceased former employee).

Small business exception   Corporations other than S corporations and partnerships that have a corporation (other than an S corporation) as a partner can use the cash method of accounting if they are considered to be a "small business." A small business for this purpose is one that has average annual gross receipts of $5 million or less in at least one of three prior taxable years. In view of the gross receipt rule, you can see that a business may be able to use the cash method for one year but be precluded from using it in the following year. As a practical matter, if a business gets big enough to approach $5 million in gross receipts, it may have outgrown the cash method and may prefer to change permanently to the accrual method to avoid changes dependent upon gross receipts.

> **Definition**   *Gross receipts*   This is all the income taken in by the business without offsets for expenses. For example, if a consultant receives fees of $25,000 for the year and has expenses of $10,000, gross receipts are $25,000.

Accrual Method of Accounting

Under this method, you deduct expenses when they are incurred rather than when they are paid. There are two tests to determine whether an expense is treated as having been "incurred" for tax purposes.

All events test   All events that set the liability must have occurred. Also, you must be able to determine the amount of the expense with reasonable accuracy.

Economic performance test   In order to deduct an expense, economic performance must occur. In most cases, this is rather obvious. If goods or services are provided to you, economic performance occurs when the goods or services are provided. Thus, for example, if you buy office supplies, economic performance occurs when the purchase is made and the bill is tendered. You can accrue the expense at that date even though you do not pay the bill until some later date.

There is an exception to the economic performance test for certain recurring items (items that are repeated on a regular basis). A deduction for these items can be accrued even though economic performance has not occurred.

There is a special rule for real estate taxes. An election can be made to ratably accrue real property taxes that are related to a definite period of time over that period of time.

EXAMPLE: You own a building in which you conduct your business. Real property taxes for the fiscal year ending June 30 are $12,000. You are an accrual method taxpayer on a calendar year of reporting. You can elect to ratably accrue the taxes. If the election is made, you deduct $6,000 in the current year, the amount of taxes that relate to the period for your tax year. The balance of the taxes is deductible next year.

Any real property taxes that would normally be deductible for the tax year that apply to periods prior to your election are deductible in the year of the election.

The election must be made for the first tax year in which real property taxes are incurred. It is made simply by attaching a statement to the return for that tax year. The return must be filed on time (including any extensions) in order for the election to be valid. Include on the statement the businesses to which the election applies and their methods of accounting, the period of time to which the taxes relate, and the computation of the real property tax deduction for the first year of the election.

Once you make this election, it continues indefinitely unless you revoke it. To revoke your election you must obtain the consent of the IRS. However, there is an automatic procedure rule that allows you to elect or revoke an election by attaching a statement to your return. Under this method you may assume you have IRS consent; you do not have to request it and wait for a reply. This automatic procedure rule is detailed in Revenue Procedure 94-32.

If you have been accruing real property taxes under the general rule for accrual, you must file for a change in accounting method. To do this, you must file Form 3115 during the year for which the change is to be effective. See the instructions to Form 3115, Application for Change in Accounting Method, for further details.

You can make an election to ratably accrue real property taxes over the period to which they relate for each separate business.

Two-and-a-half-month rule   If you pay salary, interest, or other expenses to an unrelated party, you can accrue the expense only if it is paid within two and a half months after the close of the tax year.

EXAMPLE: You declare a year-end bonus for your manager (who is not related to you under the rules discussed below). You are on the calendar year. You can accrue the bonus in the year in which you declare it if you actually pay it no later than March 15.

Related persons   If expenses are paid to related persons, a special rule applies. This rule, in effect, puts an accrual taxpayer on the cash basis so that payments are not deductible until *actually* paid. Related persons include:

- Members of an immediate family (spouses, children, brothers and sisters of whole or half blood, grandchildren, and grandparents).

- An individual and a C corporation (other than a personal service corporation) in which he or she owns more than 50 percent of the corporation's outstanding stock (based on the stock's value). Stock ownership may be direct or indirect. Direct means that the individual holds the stock in his or her name. Indirect ownership means the stock is owned by a member of the individual's immediate family (see who is considered immediate family, above) or by a corporation, partnership, estate, or trust owned in full or in part by the individual. If the individual has only a partial ownership interest, that same proportion of stock owned by the entity is treated as owned by the individual. For example, if an individual owns 75 percent of stock in Corporation X and X owns 100 percent of the stock in Corporation Y, the individual is treated as owning 75 percent of the stock in Y for purposes of this accrual method limitation.

- An individual and an S corporation in which he or she owns any of the corporation's outstanding stock.

- A personal service corporation and any owner-employee (regardless of the amount of stock ownership). Thus, if an individual owns 10 percent of the stock in Corporation X (a personal service corporation), and X owns 100 percent of the stock in Y, the individual is treated as owning 100 percent of the stock in Y.

- Other categories of related parties.

If you fall under this related party rule, you cannot deduct the expense until payment is actually made and the related party includes the payment in his or her income.

EXAMPLE: You have an accrual business in which your child is an employee. Your business is on the calendar year. On December 31, 1999, you declare a year-end bonus of $5,000 for your child. You may not accrue the bonus until you pay the $5,000 to your child and your child includes the payment income. Suppose you write a check on January 15, 2000, for the bonus and your child cashes it that day. You can accrue the expense in 2000.

Other Accounting Methods

The cash and accrual methods of accounting are the most commonly used methods. There are, however, other accounting methods. For example, if you sell property and receive payments over time, you generally can account for your gain on the installment method. This method can be used by taxpayers who report other income and expenses on the cash or accrual method.

LEGISLATIVE ALERT

Congress was considering prohibiting the use of the installment method by accrual basis taxpayers. If enacted, this change could affect certain installment sales made in 1999.

The installment method applies only to gains on certain sales; it does not have any application to accounting for expenses. It cannot be used by dealers in personal property or for real estate held for resale to customers.

UNIFORM CAPITALIZATION RULES

Regardless of your method of accounting, special tax rules limit your ability to claim a current deduction for certain expenses. These are called the uniform capitalization rules, sometimes referred to as the UNICAP rules for short. The uniform capitalization rules are a form of accounting method that operates in coordination with the accrual method but overrides it. In essence, these rules require you to add to the cost of property certain expenses instead of currently deducting them. The cost of these expenses, in effect, are recovered through depreciation or amortization, or as part of the costs of goods sold when you use, sell, or otherwise dispose of the property. The uniform capitalization rules are very complex. The important things to recognize are whether you may be subject to them and that expenses discussed throughout this book may not be currently deductible because of the application of the uniform capitalization rules.

Capitalization Required

Unless one of the exceptions discussed below is applicable, you must use the uniform capitalization rules and add certain expenses to the basis of property if you:

- Produce real property or tangible personal property for use in your business or for sale to customers ("producers"), or

- Acquire property for resale ("resellers").

Exceptions to the UNICAP rules   There are a large number of exceptions to the uniform capitalization rules. Many small businesses may be able to escape application of the uniform capitalization rules by relying on one of these exceptions:

- You do not have to capitalize costs if the property you produce is for your personal or nonbusiness use.

- You do not have to capitalize costs if you acquire property for resale and your average annual gross receipts do not exceed $10 million ("small reseller exception"). If a reseller has been in business for less than three years, application of the exception is determined by annual gross receipts for the shorter period.

- Creative expenses incurred by freelance authors, photographers, and artists are not subject to the uniform capitalization rules. According to the IRS, this exception does not apply to a musician's demo tape or other sound recording.

- There is a "de minimis" exception for certain producers who use a simplified method and whose total indirect costs are $200,000 or less.

- There are other exceptions as well for certain farming businesses and other types of businesses.

Capitalized costs   If you are subject to the uniform capitalization rules, you capitalize all direct costs of your production or resale activities. You also capitalize a portion of indirect costs.

Direct costs for producers include direct material costs and direct labor costs. Direct costs for resellers mean acquisition costs.

Indirect costs for producers and resellers include costs of purchasing, handling, and storage, as well as taxes, interest, rent, insurance, utilities, repairs, engineering and design costs, quality control, tools and equipment, licensing, and more.

CHAPTER 3

Limits on Deducting Losses

Y ou might think that because an item is called a deduction it is deductible. This is not necessarily so. All the deductions you will learn about throughout this book may not necessarily be deductible if your deductions exceed your business income. Three important limitations may operate to disallow or delay your deductions in excess of income. In this chapter you will learn about:

- Hobby losses

- At-risk rules

- Passive activity loss rules

For a further discussion of hobby losses, see IRS Publication 535, Business Expenses. For a further discussion of the at-risk rules and the passive activity loss rules, see IRS Publication 925, Passive Activity and At-Risk Rules.

HOBBY LOSSES

If your business sustains losses year after year, you may not be able to deduct the losses in excess of your business income unless you can show that you have undertaken the business in order to make a profit. This limitation on losses is called the hobby loss rule, because it is designed to prevent individuals who collect coins and stamps, breed dogs or cats, or carry on other hobby activities from deducting what the tax law views as personal expenses. Any activity you do mainly for recreation, sport, or personal enjoyment is suspect. But the hobby loss rule is not limited to these types of activities. It can apply to any activity—even investment activities intended to produce only tax losses for investors. In fact, the IRS even tried to apply the hobby loss rule to a young attorney just starting her practice. The IRS argued that the losses she sustained were not deductible because of the hobby loss rule. The attorney was able to show a profit motive (proof of a profit motive is explained below) and was allowed to deduct her losses.

Impact of Hobby Classification

If your business is classified as a hobby, then any year in which you make a profit you must pay taxes on your entire profit. Any year you have losses (expenses exceeding income), you cannot deduct them. What is more, you cannot carry over the unused losses to claim them in another year. You lose the deduction for your losses forever.

Proving a Profit Motive

There is no hard and fast way for proving that you have a profit motive. Rather, a profit motive is something that is inferred on the basis of various factors. The burden of proof is on you, the taxpayer. No single factor is determinative. Some or all of the following factors may apply:

- Whether you carry on the activity in a businesslike manner. Operating in a businesslike manner means that you keep good books and records separate and apart from your personal records and have a business bank account, telephone, stationery, and other indices of a business.

- Whether the time and effort you put into the activity shows that you intend to make a profit. If you spend only a small amount of time on it, this may show that there is no realistic way in which you can make a profit.

- Whether you depend on the income from the activity for your livelihood. If you do, then obviously you hope to make a profit to live on.

- Whether you change methods of operation to improve profitability. If you get the advice of experts, this shows you want to make a profit.

- Whether the activity is profitable in some years, and how much profit is realized in those years. Certainly an activity may not always be profitable, but if there has already been a profit in some years and that profit is substantial, this shows an expectation of continued profit.

- Whether you or your advisers have the know-how needed to carry on your business at a profit. If you undertake some activity that you enjoy but know nothing about, this may indicate a lack of profit motive.

- Whether you can expect to see a profit from the appreciation of the assets used in the activity. You may not necessarily realize profit from the operations of the business, but its assets may prove to be profitable. A realistic expectation of this profit from the appreciation of business assets shows profit motive.

Presumption of a Profit Motive

Your business may not be profitable, particularly in the early or start-up years. The tax law gives you a special presumption on which you can rely to show a profit motive (and delay an IRS inquiry into your activity). An activity is presumed to be engaged in for profit if you have a profit in at least three out of five years. If the activity is breeding, training, showing, or racing horses, the presumption period is two out of seven years. If you meet this presumption, then the hobby loss rules do not apply and your losses in the off years can be claimed in excess of your income from the activity.

You can rely on this presumption and avoid having the IRS question your losses by filing Form 5213, Election to Postpone Determination with Respect to the Presumption that an Activity Is Engaged in for Profit. In effect, the form asks the IRS to delay a determination of your profit motive until the end of the five-year (or seven-year) period.

Generally, you must file Form 5213 within three years of the due date of the return for the year in which you first carry on the activity. You should know within this time whether you can reasonably expect to be profitable and avoid the hobby loss rules or whether you need to rely on the presumption to gain additional time for the business to make a profit.

The downside to filing this form to raise the presumption of profit is that it extends the statute of limitations (the period in which the IRS can question your return and assess additional taxes). In this case, the statute of limitations is extended to two years after the due date of the return for the last year of the presumption period. However, it is extended only for deductions from the activity and any related deductions. Other items on your return, such as your personal itemized deductions, are not affected by this extension of the statute of limitations.

Is it a good idea to file Form 5213 and raise the presumption? Doing so is almost a guarantee that the IRS will look closely at your return. Should you not show a profit in the required number of years during the presumption period, you will be forced to argue that you have a profit motive despite recurrent losses. Thus you are no better off than if you had not filed the form.

How Your Choice of Business Organization Affects Application of the Hobby Loss Rule

The hobby loss rule applies to individuals (including partners and LLC members) and S corporations. It does not apply to C corporations.

For partnerships, LLCs, and S corporations whose business losses pass through to owners, the determination of whether there is a profit motive is made at the business level rather than at the owner level. In other words, the business itself must have a reasonable expectation of making a profit. The fact that an individual owner has a profit motive does not transform a hobby loss into a deductible loss if the business does not reasonably have a profit motive.

AT-RISK RULES

In the past it was not uncommon for someone to invest in a business by contributing a small sum of cash and a large note on which there was no personal liability. The note increased the investor's "basis" against which tax write-offs could be claimed. If the business prospered, all was well and good. If the business failed, the individual lost only the small amount of cash invested. Congress felt this arrangement was unreasonably beneficial to investors and created the at-risk rules. The at-risk rules operate to limit your losses to the extent of your at-risk amounts in the activity. Your at-risk amounts are, in effect, your economic investment in the activity. This is the cash you put into a business. It also includes the adjusted basis of other property you contribute and any debts secured by your property or for which you are personally liable for repayment.

EXAMPLE: You invest in a partnership to distribute a motion picture. You invest $1,000 cash and sign a promissory note for $9,000. The note is non-recourse (you are not personally liable for the debt). Your at-risk amount is $1,000, the cash you invested. You cannot deduct losses from this activity in excess of $1,000.

You are not considered at risk if you have an agreement or arrangement that limits your risk.

As a practical matter, if you set up and conduct an active business operation, you probably do not have to be concerned with the at-risk rules. First, you may qualify for an exception to the at-risk rules for closely held C corporations (discussed below). Also, in all probability your investment is what has started and sustained the business. But if you are an investor, your contribution may be limited, and your losses limited as well.

If you are subject to the at-risk rules, you do not lose your deductions to the extent they exceed your at-risk amounts; you simply cannot claim them currently. The losses can be carried forward and used in subsequent years if your at-risk amount increases. There is no limit on the carryover period. If the activity is sold, your gain from the disposition of property is treated as income from the activity and you can then offset the gain by the amount of your carried-over losses.

The at-risk rules do not apply to investments in closely held C corporations that meet active business tests and that do not engage in equipment leasing or any business involving master sound recording, films, videotapes, or other artistic, literary, or musical property.

Calculating Your At-Risk Limitation

Your at-risk amounts—cash, adjusted basis of property contributed to the activity, and recourse loans—form your at-risk basis. It is this basis that is used to limit your losses. Your at-risk basis is calculated at the end of the year. Losses allowed reduce your at-risk basis. Thus, once you have offset your entire at-risk basis, you cannot claim further losses from the activity until you increase your at-risk basis.

Partners and LLC members are treated as at risk to the extent that basis in the entity is increased by their share of the entity's income. If the partnership or LLC makes distributions of income, the amount distributed reduces the partner's or LLC member's at-risk amount.

If you are subject to the at-risk rules, you must file Form 6198, At-Risk Limitations, to determine the amount of loss you can claim in the current year. You file a separate form for each activity. If you have an interest in a partnership or an LLC or S corporation that has more than one investment in any of the four categories listed below, you can aggregate these activities. For example, if your S corporation distributes films and videotapes, you can aggregate these activities and treat them as one activity. The four categories subject to these aggregation rules are:

- Holding, producing, or distributing motion picture films or videotapes
- Exploring for or exploiting oil and gas properties
- Exploring for or exploiting geothermal deposits
- Farming (but not forestry)

In addition, all leased depreciable business equipment is treated as one activity for purposes of the at-risk rules.

You may also aggregate activities that you actively manage. This allows you to use losses from one activity as long as there is sufficient at-risk basis from another. If you invest in a partnership, LLC, or S corporation, the activities of the entity can be aggregated if 65 percent or more of the losses for the year are allocable to persons who actively participate in the management of the entity.

Special Rule for Real Estate Financing

You can treat nonrecourse financing from commercial lenders or government agencies as being at risk if the financing is secured by the real estate. This special rule does not apply to financing from related parties, seller financing, or financing from promoters. This special rule applies to real property placed in service after 1986. However, if you acquire an interest in a partnership, LLC, or S corporation after 1986, you can use this special rule regardless of when the entity placed the realty in service.

PASSIVE ACTIVITY LOSS RULES

If you work for your business full time, you need not be concerned with the passive activity loss rules. These rules apply only to a business in which you have an ownership interest but do not work in the day-to-day operations or management.

> **Definition**   *Passive activity*   Any activity involving the conduct of a business in which you do not materially participate and all rental activities.

These rules operate to limit a current deduction for losses from these activities unless certain exceptions, discussed later in this chapter, apply.

> **Definition**   *Material participation*   Participation in a passive activity that satisfies one of seven tests set forth in the tax law. The basic test requires a minimum of 500 hours of participation during the year. Material participation may be allowed for as little as 100 hours of participation during the year if no other owner in the activity participates more.

The seven tests for proving material participation include:

1. You participate in the activity for more than 500 hours. You need only participate for a mere 10 hours a week for 50 weeks in the year to satisfy this test.

2. Your participation is substantially all of the participation in the activity of all individuals for the year, including the participation of individuals who did not own any interest in the activity. This means that if you are a sole proprietor and do not hire someone else to run the business, you meet this participation test, even if you work only five hours each week.

3. You participate in the activity for more than 100 hours during the tax year, and you participate at least as much as any other individual (including individuals who did not own any interest in the activity) for the year.

4. The activity is a "significant participation activity," and you participate in all significant participation activities for more than 500 hours. A significant participation activity is any business in which you participate for more than 100 hours during the year and in which you did not materially participate under any of the other material participation tests.

5. You materially participated in the activity for any five (whether or not consecutive) of the 10 preceding tax years. This rule can be useful to someone who retires from the business while continuing to own an interest but who materially participated prior to retirement.

6. The activity is a personal service activity in which you materially participated for any three (whether or not consecutive) preceding tax years.

7. Based on all the facts and circumstances, you participate in the activity on a regular, continuous, and substantial basis. At a minimum you must have participated during more than 100 hours. Managing the activity is not treated as participation if any person other than you received compensation for managing it or any individual spent more hours during the year managing the activity than you (regardless of whether such individual was compensated).

Rental Real Estate Exceptions
There are two special rules for rental real estate activities that may allow you to claim losses in excess of rental income.

Rule 1 allows a limited amount of loss in excess of income to be deducted if participation is considered to be active.

Definition *Active participation* Participation in a rental real estate activity that is less than the material participation standard. Participation in decision making may be sufficient. For example, if you set the rents, screen tenants, and review expenses, you may satisfy the active participation test. Having a managing agent to collect rents and see to property repairs does not prevent active participation by an owner.

This is called the $25,000 allowance and can be claimed by individuals whose adjusted gross income does not exceed $100,000. The allowance is phased out for those with adjusted gross income over $100,000 and is entirely eliminated when adjusted gross income is $150,000 or more. Married couples must file jointly to claim this allowance unless they lived apart for the entire year. In this case, up to $12,500 in losses can be deducted on a separate return (with a phase-out of the allowance for adjusted gross income over $50,000).

Rule 2 allows real estate professionals to escape the passive activity loss limitations altogether for purposes of deducting losses from their rental real estate activities. Individuals can be considered real estate professionals if they meet certain tests regarding their participation in real estate activities in general, including real estate construction, conversion, management, or brokerage activities, as well as rental real estate. If a qualifying real estate professional then meets material participation tests with respect to the rental real estate, losses from the rental real estate activity escape passive activity loss restrictions. Details of these rules are in the instructions to Form 8582.

The passive activity loss rules are very complicated. Determine whether you may be subject to the rules or whether you can ignore them. If you are subject to the rules, be sure you understand what impact that can have on deducting expenses of the activity.

If you run the business or work full time, you need not be concerned with the passive loss rules. You will certainly meet the tests for material participation. If you are a silent partner in a partnership, LLC, or S corporation, you should be concerned that you may be subject to the passive activity loss rules. However, you may be able to fall within an exception to the passive loss rules in order to deduct losses in excess of income from the activity. For example, you may be able to eke out enough participation to be considered a material participant. Keep a diary or log book noting the time you put into the business and the types of activities you perform for the business.

How the Passive Activity Loss Rules Limit Deductions for Expenses

If the rules apply, your losses from passive activities that exceed income from all other passive activities cannot be deducted in the current year. You can carry over your unused deductions to future years. These are called suspended losses, for which there is no limit on the carryover period.

You can claim all carryover deductions from an activity in the year in which you dispose of your entire interest in the activity. A disposition includes a sale to an unrelated party, abandonment of the business, or the business becoming completely worthless. Simply giving away your interest does not amount to a disposition that allows you to deduct your suspended losses.

The passive activity loss limitation for noncorporate taxpayers is computed on Form 8582, Passive Activity Loss Limitations. Closely held C corporations subject to the passive activity loss rules must file Form 8810, Corporate Passive Activity Loss and Credit Limitations. Similar rules apply to tax credits from passive activities. The limitation on tax credits from passive activities for noncorporate taxpayers is computed on Form 8582-CR, Passive Activity Credit Limitations.

Coordination with the At-Risk Rules

The at-risk rules are applied first. Any amounts that are deductible after applying your at-risk loss limitation are then subject to the passive activity loss rules. Complete Form 6198 first; then complete Form 8582.

CHAPTER 4

Recordkeeping for Business Deductions

Recordkeeping is a tiresome and time-consuming task. Still, you have little choice but to do it. As a general rule, you must be able to back up your deductions with certain proof, such as receipts, canceled checks, and other documentation. If you do not have this proof, your deductions may be disallowed. Certain deductions require specific evidence. Other deductions are based on more general means of proof. In this chapter you will learn about:

- Recordkeeping in general

- Specific substantiation requirements for certain expenses

- Records for depreciation, carryovers, and prepaid expenses

- How long you should you maintain records

This chapter is concerned with recordkeeping for tax deduction purposes. However, it is equally important to maintain good records to help you to manage your business efficiently and to apply for credit if you need it. For further information on recordkeeping, see IRS Publication 334, Tax Guide for Small Business (for Individuals Who File Schedule C or C-EZ); IRS Publication 552, Recordkeeping for Individuals; and IRS Publication 583, Starting a Business and Keeping Records.

RECORDKEEPING IN GENERAL

The tax law does not require you to maintain books and records in any particular way. It does, however, require you to keep an accurate and complete set of books for each business you operate. Statistics show that it is an awesome task for small business owners who spend, on average, 10 hours each week in maintaining business records (about 520 hours each year).

You set up your books when you begin your business. Your books are based on your choice of tax year and accounting method, as explained in Chapter 2. You also need to choose a bookkeeping method—single entry or double entry. If you are a service business, single-entry bookkeeping may be sufficient. However, if your business involves inventory or is complicated, double-entry should be used.

Your books should be set up in various accounts in order to group your income and expenses. The broad categories of accounts include income, expenses, assets, liabilities, and equity (or net worth). Within these accounts you can keep various sub-accounts. For example, in an account called "expenses" you can have sub-accounts for advertising, bad debts, interest expense, taxes, rents, repairs, and more. In fact, your sub-accounts should reflect the various deduction topics discussed throughout this book.

Keeping Records by Computer

With about two-thirds of small businesses already owning computers, more and more businesses are using their computers to maintain books and records rather than having bookkeepers make handwritten entries. Computer-generated records save time—an important commodity for the small business owner—and generally are more accurate than handwritten entries.

The IRS accepts computer-generated records if they are legible and provide all the necessary information. You are required to keep a description of the computerized portion of your accounting system. Your document should show:

- Applications being performed
- Procedures used in each application
- Controls used to ensure accurate and reliable processing
- Controls used to prevent the unauthorized addition, alteration, or deletion of retained records

You must keep this documentation as long as you keep the records themselves.

Your books alone do not entitle you to deductions; you need supporting evidence. This evidence includes sales slips, invoices, canceled checks, paid bills, time sheets for part-time help, duplicate deposit slips, brokerage statements on stock purchases and sales, and other documents that help to explain a particular entry in your books. Certain deductions—travel and entertainment expenses and charitable contributions—require specific types of supporting evidence, as explained later in this chapter. The IRS considers your own memoranda or sketchy records to be inadequate when claiming deductions.

Keep these records and documentation in an orderly fashion. Use files or other storage facilities to retain receipts and other evidence.

Keep your files in a safe place. For example, keep a copy of computer files off premises, and store paper files in a fireproof safe. If you lose files with receipts because they were not stored safely, you may lose deductions and face penalties as well. If you "lose" records before or during an audit, you may be charged with a hefty fraud penalty. If, despite your best efforts, files and records are lost or destroyed by a casualty (such as a fire, storm, earthquake, or flood), you may be permitted to reconstruct records if you can prove those records existed before the casualty. Of course, reconstruction takes considerable time, and it is probably impossible to reconstruct all of your expenses. Therefore, take special care to safeguard your records.

Electronic Imaging Systems

Storage of receipts and other records in paper form makes retrieval of wanted items difficult. This is especially so for large companies, but can be problematic for smaller businesses as well. Recognizing the problem, the IRS now allows books and records to be maintained by electronic imaging systems.

Definition *Electronic imaging system*   A system to prepare, record, transfer, index, store, preserve, retrieve, and reproduce books and records by electronically imaging hard copy to an electronic storage media or transferring computerized books and records to an electronic storage media using a technique such as COLD (computer output to laser disk). This technique allows books and records to be viewed or reproduced without the use of the original program.

If an electronic imaging system is used, it must ensure accurate and complete transfer of the hard copy or the computerized books and records. It must include:

- Reasonable controls to ensure the integrity, accuracy, and reliability of the system

- Reasonable controls to prevent and detect the unauthorized creation of, addition to, alteration of, deletion of, or deterioration of records

- An inspection and quality assurance program evidenced by regular evaluations of the electronic storage system

- A retrieval system that includes an indexing system

- The ability to reproduce legible hard copies of electronically stored books and records

While most small businesses probably do not want to undertake the expense of using an electronic imaging system for their books and records, you should be aware of this option when your business grows and your recordkeeping space requirements burgeon.

SPECIFIC SUBSTANTIATION REQUIREMENTS FOR CERTAIN EXPENSES

Travel and Entertainment Expenses

The tax law imposes special substantiation requirements for claiming travel and entertainment expenses. If you fail to satisfy these requirements, your deduction for these business expenses may be disallowed. There are two types of records you need in order to claim deductions for your travel and entertainment expenses: written substantiation in a diary, log book, or other notation system containing certain specific information and documentary evidence (receipts, canceled checks, or bills) to prove the amount of the expense. The IRS now accepts certain electronic or faxed information to be treated as documentary evidence (for example, a faxed statement attesting to a "ticketless" airline ticket is considered documentary evidence).

There are a number of elements to substantiate for each business expense. In general, to substantiate each item you must show the amount, time, place, and business purpose for the travel or entertainment expense or the business relationship with the person or persons you entertain or provide gifts to and, in some cases, a description of the item. The exact substantiation requirements depend on the type of business expense.

In all cases, you are strongly advised to use a daily log or diary to record expenses. As you will see, you need written proof of your expenses, and this proof must be recorded "contemporaneously" with the expenses—generally meaning at the time you incur the expense or as soon as is practical thereafter to record it. It may be helpful to use a separate credit card for business expenses. The monthly statement from the credit card company is also useful in substantiating these expenses.

Travel You must show the amount of each separate expense for travel, lodging, meals, and incidental expenses. You can total these items in any reasonable category. For example, you can simply keep track of meals in a category called daily meals. You must also note the dates you left for the trip and returned, as well as the days spent on the trip for business purposes. You must list the name of the city or other designation of the place of the travel, along with the reason for the trip or the business benefit gained or expected to be gained from it.

While this may sound like a great deal of recordkeeping, as a practical matter hotel receipts may provide you with much of the information necessary. For example, a hotel receipt typically shows the dates you arrived and departed, the name and location of the hotel and separate charges for lodging, meals, telephone calls, and other items. A sample log for travel expenses can be found in Chapter 6.

Entertainment Again, you must list each separate expense. Incidental expenses, such as taxis and telephone calls, may be totaled on a daily basis. You must list the date of the entertainment. For meals or entertainment directly before or after a business discussion, list the date and duration of the business discussion. Include the name and address or location of the place of entertainment, as well as the type of entertainment if it is not apparent from the name of the place. Also list the place where a business discussion was held if entertainment took place directly before or after the discussion. Again, state the business reason or the business benefit gained or anticipated and the nature of the business discussion. Include the names of the persons entertained, including their occupations or other identifying information, and the names of those who took part in the business discussion. If the deduction is for a business meal, you must note that you or your employer were present at the meal.

Again, a restaurant receipt typically supplies much of the information required. It shows the name and location of the restaurant, the number of people served, and the date and amount of the expense. As a practical matter, the back of American Express credit card slips provides the space necessary to enter all the elements for substantiating an entertainment deduction. It may be helpful to use this credit card when entertaining for business and to complete the back of the slip. Be sure to retain these slips as your proof. A sample log for entertainment expenses can be found in Chapter 6.

Gifts   Show the cost of the gift, the date it was given, and a description of the gift. Also show the business reason for the gift or the business benefit gained or expected to be gained from providing it. Include the name of the person receiving the gift, his or her occupation or other identifying information, and his or her business relationship to you.

A canceled check, along with a bill, generally establishes the cost of a business item. However, the check alone does not prove a business expense without other evidence of its business purpose.

If you do not have adequate records and your return is questioned, you may still be able to deduct an item if you can prove by your own statement or other supporting evidence an element of substantiation. Where receipts are destroyed, you may be able to reconstruct your expenses. You must, of course, show that you actually maintained records and how the records were destroyed (for example, in a fire, storm, or flood). The IRS may require additional information to prove the accuracy or reliability of the information contained in your records.

Car expenses   Show the number of miles driven for business purposes (starting and ending odometer readings), the destination, the purpose of the trip, and the name of the party visited (if relevant). Simply jot down the odometer reading on January 1 to start a good recordkeeping habit. Include notations of expenses for gas, oil, parking, tolls, and other expenses. A sample log for keeping track of car expenses can be found in Chapter 7.

Recordkeeping relief   You do not need receipts, canceled checks, bills, or other proof of the cost of an expense in the following situations:

- You use a standard rate (such as a standard mileage rate for car use or a per diem rate for meals and lodging). Per diem rates are explained in Chapter 6; the standard mileage rate is explained in Chapter 7.

- The expense is less than $75. However, you cannot use this exception for lodging (you must have documentary evidence for lodging regardless of amount).

- You have a transportation expense (such as a taxi fare) for which a receipt is not readily available.

The Cohan rule   While the IRS says that deductions will be disallowed if you do not have adequate substantiation, you may be able to rely on a special rule developed by the courts. The Cohan rule, named after noted songwriter/showman George M. Cohan, is based on approximation. A court may agree to approximate your travel and entertainment expenses if your records are inadequate to establish actual expenses and you have some way to show your approximate expenses. A court cannot be compelled to use the Cohan rule; it must be persuaded to do so because of special circumstances. The Cohan rule is only a last resort for claiming unsubstantiated travel and entertainment expenses.

Charitable Contributions

In the past, canceled checks were sufficient evidence to support charitable contributions by individuals and corporations alike. Now special substantiation rules apply.

If you make contributions up to $75, your canceled check is still considered to be adequate substantiation of your contributions. A receipt from the charity is also considered adequate substantiation.

If you make contributions over $75 but not more than $250, your canceled check or a receipt from the charity also remains sufficient. What is more, the charity will notify you in writing on a disclosure statement if you received any goods or services by virtue of your contribution (for example, your contribution entitles you to attend a charity dinner). The disclosure statement will state the amount of the benefit you are entitled to receive. You then subtract this benefit from your contribution and deduct only the net amount.

If you make donations of $250 or more, your canceled check is not considered to be adequate substantiation. You must get a written receipt or acknowledgment from the charity by the due date of your return (or the extended due date if you receive a filing extension) describing your contribution (the amount of cash contributed or a description of property contributed). Each payment to the same charity is treated as a separate payment unless you designed the payment plan to avoid this substantiation requirement.

EXAMPLE: If you gave a charity $100 in February, $100 in June, and $100 in November, your canceled check is considered adequate substantiation of the donation unless you arranged these contributions to avoid having to obtain a written receipt or acknowledgment.

If a property donation is valued at over $5,000, you may also be required to obtain an appraisal and keep a record of this appraisal.

RECORDS FOR DEPRECIATION, BASIS, CARRYOVERS, AND PREPAID EXPENSES

For some tax items you must keep a running account, because deductions will be claimed not only in the current year but also in years to come.

Depreciation

Depreciation allows you to recover the cost of property over the life of that property by deducting a portion of the cost each year. In order to claim your annual deductions, you must keep certain records:

- Cost and other information necessary to calculate your depreciation

- Capital improvements to depreciable assets

- Depreciation deductions already claimed

- Adjustments to basis as a result of depreciation deductions

This information not only is necessary for depreciation purposes but will also be needed to calculate gain or loss and any depreciation recapture on the sale or other disposition of a depreciable asset. For full details on claiming depreciation, see Chapter 12.

The same recordkeeping rules apply not only to depreciation but also to amortization and depletion deductions.

Basis

Basis is the cost of property or some other value assigned to property. Basis is used for several purposes. It is the amount on which depreciation deductions are based, as well as the amount used to determine gain or loss on the sale or other disposition of property.

The basis of property can vary from its basis upon acquisition. Some items increase basis; others decrease it. Keep track of changes in basis. These can result from:

- Depreciation deductions or first-year expensing
- Casualty deductions relating to the property
- Certain tax credits
- Capitalized costs

Carryovers

A number of deductions may be limited in a current year, but you may be able to carry over any unused portion to other years. In order to take advantage of carryover opportunities, you must keep records of deductions you have already taken and the years in which they are taken. What is more, you must maintain relevant records for the carryover periods. The following list details the types of carryovers for which records should be maintained and limits on the carryover period, if any:

- **At-risk losses.** Losses disallowed because of the application of the at-risk rules (see Chapter 3) can be carried over indefinitely.

- **Capital losses.** There is no limit on the carryover period for individuals. There is a five-year limit on carryover losses for corporations.

- **Charitable contributions.** Individuals who cannot fully use current charitable contributions because of adjusted gross income limits can carry over the unused deductions for a period of five years. C corporations that cannot fully use current charitable contributions because of the 10-percent-of-taxable-income limit can carry over the unused deductions for a period of five years. If the deductions cannot be used within that five-year period (there is insufficient taxable income to offset the deduction in the carryover years), the deductions are lost forever.

- **Home office deductions.** Individuals who maintain an office in their home and whose home office deductions are limited in the current year by gross income earned in the home office can carry forward unused deductions indefinitely. The unused deductions can be used in a future year if there is gross income from the home office activity to offset it.

- **Investment interest.** Individuals (including partners, LLC members, and S corporation shareholders) may be limited in their current deduction for investment interest by the amount of their net investment income. Excess investment interest can be carried forward indefinitely. There is no limitation on corporations, so there is no carryover.

- **Net operating losses.** The carryover period depends on the year in which the net operating loss arises. There is a three-year carryback period and a 15-year carryforward period for losses arising in tax years beginning before August 5, 1997. There is a two-year carryback (three years for certain disaster losses affecting small businesses, five years for farmers and ranchers, and 10 years for product liability) and 20-year carryforward for net operating losses arising in tax years beginning after August 5, 1997. Thus, a 1999 net operating loss can be carried back for two years and forward for up to 20 years. Alternatively, each year in which a net operating loss arises, you can elect to forgo the carryback period and just carry forward the net operating losses. The same carryover periods apply to individuals and corporations.

- **Passive activity losses.** Losses disallowed because of the application of the passive activity loss rules (called suspended losses) can be carried forward indefinitely. The same rules apply to credits from passive activities.

Depreciation and carryovers are not the only tax items that may run beyond the current tax year. If you are on the cash basis and prepay certain expenses, you may not be allowed a current deduction for your outlays. You may be required to deduct the expenses ratably over the period of time to which they relate. Some examples of prepaid expenses that are commonly prepaid and may have to be deducted ratably include:

- **Insurance premiums.** If your insurance premiums cover a period of more than one year, you may be required to deduct them over the term covered by the policy.

- **Prepaid interest.** If you pay points or other amounts treated as prepaid interest to obtain financing to acquire real estate for your business, you deduct the prepaid interest ratably over the term of the loan. If you dispose of the property or refinance the loan before the end of the term, you can then deduct any unused portion of the prepaid interest in that final year.

- **Rents.** If you prepay rents for a period of more than one year, you may be required to deduct the rents over the term of the lease.

- **Subscriptions.** If you pay for subscriptions running more than one year, you generally have to deduct the cost over the term of the subscriptions. For example, if you pay in full the cost of a three-year subscription to a business journal, you generally must deduct the cost over the same three-year period.

You need to keep a running record of Section 1231 losses. This is because of a special recapture rule that applies to net ordinary losses from Section 1231 property. A net Section 1231 gain is treated as ordinary income to the extent it does not exceed nonrecaptured net Section 1231 losses taken in prior years. Nonrecaptured losses are the total of net Section 1231 losses for the five most recent years that have not yet been applied (recaptured) against any net Section 1231 gains in those same years. In order to determine this recapture, you must retain information on Section 1231 gains and losses. Section 1231 losses are explained in more detail in Chapter 15.

Finally, you need to keep track of tax credits that are not completely used in the current year. Tax credits that are part of the general business credit (such as the work opportunity credit, welfare-to-work credit, research credit, empowerment zone credit, employer Social Security credit, and the disabled access credit) are subject to a carryback and carryforward period depending on the year in which the excess credits result. For credits arising in years beginning before January 1, 1998, the excess credits are carried back three years and forward for up to 15 years. For credits arising in years beginning after December 31, 1997, the excess credits are carried back one year and forward for up to 20 years. No election can be made to forgo the carryback period.

HOW LONG YOU SHOULD MAINTAIN RECORDS

Your books and records must be available at all times for inspection by the IRS. You should keep these books and records at least until the time when the IRS can question your deductions runs out. This time is called the statute of limitations. In general, the statute of limitations is either three years after the due date of your return or two years after the date the tax was paid—whatever is later.

Some records must be kept even longer. You need to keep records to support the basis in property owned by the business. You also need to keep records for depreciation and carryovers, as discussed above.

Tax Returns

Keep copies of tax returns to help you prepare future returns, as well as to help you if your return is questioned by the IRS. While you can obtain old returns from the IRS, this entails unnecessary time and expense.

Keep a record of the basis of property used in your business for as long as you own the property, plus the statute of limitations on filing the return for the year in which property is sold or otherwise disposed of. For example, if in 1999 you buy equipment that you will sell in 2001, keep records on the basis of the property until 2005 (three years from the due date of the return for the year in which the property was sold).

Employer Records

If you have employees, special recordkeeping rules apply. You are required to keep records on employment taxes for at least four years after the due date of the return or after the tax is paid, whichever is later. Your records should show your employer identification number. Every business—sole proprietorship, partnership, corporation—must have one if wages are paid. The employer identification number (EIN) is a nine-digit number assigned to each business and used to report the payment of employment taxes and to file certain returns.

If you are just starting your business and do not have an EIN, you can obtain one by filing Form SS-4, Application for Employer Identification Number, with the IRS service center in the area in which your business is located. Application by mail takes several weeks. (An SS-4 can be obtained by calling 1-800-829-1040.) Alternatively, you can obtain an EIN immediately by calling a special Tele-TIN phone number. (The number for your service center is listed in the instructions to Form SS-4.) A number is assigned over the phone, after which you must send or fax a signed SS-4 within 24 hours.

You should also keep copies of all returns you have filed and the dates and amount of tax deposits you have made.

Income Tax Withholding

You must keep records of each employee's name, address, and Social Security number, the amount of each wage payment, the amount of each payment subject to income tax withholding, and the amount of income tax withheld. You must also keep copies of all employees' withholding allowance certificates (Form W-4). Similarly, you must keep any earned income credit advance payment certificates (Form W-5) filed with you by low-income wage earners who want to receive an advance on their earned income credit.

Other Employment Taxes

Similar records must be kept for each employee for Social Security and Medicare taxes, as well as for federal unemployment taxes (FUTA).

PART II

Business Deductions

CHAPTER 5

Employee Compensation: Salary, Wages, and Employee Benefits

If you are an employee, you do not pay compensation to another. You can skip most of this chapter and go on to look at other deductible expenses. However, you might want to review the areas covered to understand your employer's burdens and responsibilities for the wages and benefits paid to you. You may also be interested in two tax credits to which you may be entitled by virtue of working.

If you hire someone to work for you, the compensation and benefits you pay to that person may be deductible. You may have additional costs associated with paying wages and providing employee benefits. In this chapter you will learn about:

- Deductible compensation
- Disallowance repayment agreements
- Employee benefits
- Nonstatutory fringe benefits
- Employment tax obligations
- Employment tax credits
- Where to deduct compensation costs

Also discussed in this chapter are the earned income credit and the dependent care credit. These are not business credits; rather, they are personal credits that arise by virtue of employment. The earned income credit is a refundable credit for low-income householders, and the dependent care credit is designed to offset the costs of baby-sitting and other dependent-related expenses incurred to allow parents to work.

Medical coverage is an important facet of employee compensation. It is also a necessary item for self-employed individuals. Medical coverage for you and your employees is explained in Chapter 18.

For further information about employee compensation, see IRS Publication 334, Tax Guide for Small Business, IRS Publication 15, Circular E, Employer's Tax Guide, and IRS Publication 15-A, Employer's Supplemental Tax Guide.

DEDUCTIBLE COMPENSATION

Compensation you pay to your employees can take many forms. In general, most types of compensation are fully deductible by you. Deductible compensation includes the more common forms, such as salary, wages, bonuses for services performed, vacation pay, sick pay (not otherwise paid by insurance), and fringe benefits, whether or not they are tax-free to your employee. The deduction for these items must be reduced, however, by any employment tax credits claimed. These tax credits are discussed later in this chapter.

Employees Versus Independent Contractors

Compensation discussed throughout this chapter means payments to employees. Payments made to independent contractors are not treated as compensation. These payments may be deductible, but not as compensation. The rules for deducting payments to independent contractors are discussed in Chapter 19.

Since payments to independent contractors are not treated as compensation, they are not subject to withholding and employment taxes (discussed later in this chapter). Whether someone who works for you is an employee or an independent contractor should be resolved at the commencement of work. The rules for making this determination are discussed in Chapter 1.

It is critical to note that the consequences for misclassifying workers can be dire for an employer. If you fail to treat a worker as an employee when you should do so, you are penalized for not withholding income taxes on wages and paying employment taxes. Penalties and interest in this regard can, in some instances, be enough to bankrupt your company. Misclassification can also wreak havoc with employee benefit plans, including retirement plans. If the IRS successfully reclassifies workers as employees, you will be required to provide back benefits (medical, retirement plan contributions, and other benefits you provided to your correctly classified employees).

You may be able to rely on some special rules to avoid employment tax penalties. As a minimum, if you want to treat workers as independent contractors, make sure you do so consistently and that you have a reasonable basis for doing so. The tax law considers these situations to be a reasonable basis:

- You relied on a court case about federal taxes or a ruling issued to you by the IRS.

- You have already gone through an IRS audit in which the issue of worker classification was raised and your workers were not reclassified.

- A significant segment of your industry treats such workers as independent contractors.

Also make sure you file the required information return for independent contractors (Form 1099-MISC) if the worker earned at least $600.

The IRS has a classification settlement program designed to resolve worker classification issues amicably (and with modest penalties and interest charges).

If the IRS questions your worker classification and you cannot prove your position on audit or resolve it through the classification settlement program, you can now bring your case to Tax Court for a determination. This means you do not have to pay the taxes up front to have your case reviewed in court.

General Rules for Deductibility of Compensation

To be deductible, compensation must meet certain tests. First, it must be an "ordinary and necessary" business expense.

> **Definition** *Ordinary and necessary business expense*   An ordinary expense is one that is common and accepted in your business. A necessary expense is one that is helpful and appropriate to your business.

The payments must be directly connected to the conduct of your business. They also must be necessary for you to carry on your business.

Second, the compensation must be reasonable. For most employees, this issue never comes up; it is assumed that pay to rank-and-file employees is reasonable. The question of reasonableness typically arises in connection with pay to owners and top executives. There are no absolute guidelines for determining what is reasonable—it depends on the individual facts and circumstances. Ask yourself: "Would another business pay the same compensation under your circumstances?" If you are confident that the answer is yes, most likely the compensation is reasonable.

The IRS uses a number of factors to determine whether compensation is reasonable. These factors include:

- **The job description of the employee.** What duties must the employee perform? How much responsibility does the employee shoulder? How much time is required to perform the job? How much business is handled by the employee?

- **The nature of the business.** What are the complexities of your business? What has been your pay policy for all employees? What is the pay to a particular employee as compared with the gross and net profit of the business and distributions to shareholders?

- **The general cost of living in your locality.** Formula-based compensation (such as a percentage of sales or some other fixed arrangement) may be reasonable if it is an industry-wide practice to use these formulas.

Courts have also used a "hypothetical independent investor" standard to test reasonableness. Under this test, courts decide whether a disinterested investor would approve the compensation level in light of the dividends and return on equity.

In determining reasonableness, you must look at the total compensation package and not merely the base salary. Also, each employee's pay package must be reasonable by itself. The fact that your total payroll is reasonable is not sufficient.

Remember, if compensation paid to an employee who is also an owner of the corporation is not reasonable, then it may be viewed as a "constructive" dividend to such owner-employee. As such, it is not deductible by the corporation even though it is fully taxable to the owner. However, the owner-employee and corporation can enter into a disallowance repayment agreement to preserve deductibility. Such agreements are discussed later in this chapter.

Generally, it is up to you to prove the reasonableness of compensation. However, if the issue goes to court, the burden of proof shifts to the IRS once you have presented credible evidence of reasonableness. Only small businesses (corporations and partnerships cannot have a net worth exceeding $7 million) can shift the burden of proof to the IRS.

A third test requires that the payment be for services actually performed. This issue does not generally arise for ordinary employees. However, in a family situation, the IRS may pay closer attention to see that work has actually been performed for the compensation paid. Thus, for example, if you employ your spouse, children, or parent, be sure to document their work hours and duties should your return be questioned. In one case, a parent was able to deduct salary paid to his seven-year-old son because he was able to show that the child performed meaningful tasks for his business. In several cases, a deduction for equal pay to both spouses was denied where one spouse was a professional (e.g., an engineer or a doctor) and the other performed only administrative and secretarial duties. The compensation to the professional might have been reasonable, but the same pay to the spouse clearly was not.

Guaranteed annual wages may be deductible as salary even though work is not performed. The deduction is limited to full-time guaranteed wages paid under a collective bargaining agreement.

A fourth test is that you must actually have paid the compensation if you are on the cash basis, or incurred the expense if you are on the accrual basis. Incurring the expense means that economic performance has occurred. For a complete discussion on economic performance, see Chapter 2.

Other Types of Deductible Compensation
Here are some less common, but equally deductible, compensation items:

- **Outplacement services provided to workers you have laid off.** The types of outplacement services that are deductible include career counseling, résumé assistance, skills assessment, and even the cost of renting equipment to facilitate these services.

- **Black Lung benefit trust contributions made by coal mine operators,** provided the contributions are paid no later than the filing of the return (including extensions). The contribution must be made in cash (check) or property; a note or other evidence of a promise to pay is not currently deductible.

- **Interest-free or below-market loans to employees.** The amount of interest not charged that is less than the applicable federal interest rate (a rate that changes monthly and depends on whether the loan is short-term, mid-term, or long-term) is treated as compensation. However, you must include in your income that same amount as taxable interest.

- **Severance pay.** If you are forced to downsize your work force or otherwise let employees go, you may offer some benefits package. The IRS has acknowledged that severance pay generally is deductible as an ordinary and necessary business expense even though an argument could be made that it provides some future benefit (which would suggest capitalizing the cost). However, if the severance pay is part of a plan, method, or arrangement deferring the receipt of income, then it is deductible only when it is included in the worker's income (whether or not the employer is on the cash or accrual method of reporting).

- **Salary continuation.** If you want to continue paying wages to an owner-employee who becomes disabled and claim a deduction for such payments, do so under a salary continuation plan that you set up for this purpose. Without such a plan in place, you risk having the IRS label the payments as dividends or withdrawals of capital, neither of which are deductible by the company.

- **Director's fees.** A corporation's payment of fees to its directors is deductible, but such fees are not treated as compensation. This is so even though the director is also an officer or other employee of the corporation. The fees are deductible as other business expenses and are discussed in Chapter 20.

- **Employment agency fees.** If you pay a fee to an employment agency or headhunter to hire an employee, you may deduct the cost as an "other business expense."

OTHER LIMITS ON DEDUCTING COMPENSATION

Besides the "reasonable compensation" and other tests discussed earlier, there are several limitations on deducting compensation. For example, if your employee agrees to defer compensation to some future date, you cannot claim a deduction until such time as the employee includes the compensation in his or her income. This is true for accrual method businesses as well as cash basis businesses.

Another form of compensation subject to limitation is prizes and awards. Only certain prizes and awards are deductible, and then dollar limits apply. A deduction may be taken for an "employee achievement award." This is tangible personal property given for an employee's length of service or safety achievement, awarded as part of a meaningful presentation and under conditions and circumstances that do not create a significant likelihood of disguising the award as compensation. An award is not considered a length-of-service award if it is made within the first five years of employment. An award is not considered a safety achievement award if it is given to a manager, administrator, clerical employee, or other professional employee, or if it is given to more than 10 percent of your employees (other than those just listed). Awards can be qualified or nonqualified. The only significant difference between the classifications is the dollar limit on deductibility. There is no dollar limit on qualified achievement awards. A qualified achievement award is one given under a written plan that does not discriminate in favor of highly compensated employees as to eligibility or benefits. Also, an award is not considered a qualified award if the average cost of all employee achievement awards during the year exceeds $400. In determining this average cost, you cannot take into account awards of very small value. There is a specific dollar limit on nonqualified achievement awards: The maximum deduction for awards to any one employee is $400 per year. Then, too, your total awards, both qualified and nonqualified, made to any one employee during the year cannot exceed $1,600.

Another form of compensation subject to limitation is vacation pay by accrual basis employers. Vacation pay earned by an employee is deductible in the current year only if you actually pay it out by the close of the year or within two and a half months of the close of the year. If you fail to pay it out within this time frame, it becomes deductible in the year it is actually paid out. Of course, for cash basis employers, vacation pay is deductible as wages when it is paid to an employee.

Noncash Payments

In some cases you may pay your employees with property instead of cash. What is the amount you deduct? Your cost for the property ("basis"), or its value at the time it is paid to employees? You can deduct only your basis in the property, even though its value is included in the employee's income as compensation.

EXAMPLE: You own a car with a basis (after depreciation deductions) of $8,000. The car is worth $12,000. You give the car to your top salesperson as a bonus. You may deduct $8,000, the basis of the car. On the employee's W-2 form you include $12,000 as compensation.

Restricted Property

If you transfer stock or other property that is subject to restrictions to an employee in payment for services, you generally cannot deduct the expense until such time as the stock or other property is no longer subject to restrictions. Restrictions include limits on transferring the stock or property. The term also covers property that is not "substantially vested" in the employee.

> **Definition** *Substantially vested* The person can transfer the property and is not subject to a risk of forfeiture (is not likely to be forced to give up rights in the future).

When and how much you can deduct for this type of compensation depends upon a number of factors, such as the kind of property transferred and when the property is included in the employee's gross income. In the past, an employer could deduct restricted property only when such property was subject to withholding. Sometimes this was impossible, because a worker was no longer in the employer's employment. The IRS has eased its position and has dropped the withholding requirement. The property must still be included in the worker's income in order for the employer to claim a deduction. According to the IRS, the worker will be deemed to have included the amount in income in the year for which an employer complies with W-2 reporting requirements.

DISALLOWANCE REPAYMENT AGREEMENTS

If you are an employee of a corporation you own and a portion of your salary is viewed as "unreasonable," the corporation loses its deduction for the payment. You are taxed on the payment in any event—either as compensation or as a constructive dividend. However, there is a way in which you can ensure that the corporation does not lose out if the IRS later characterizes its compensation deduction as partially unreasonable: You can enter into a disallowance repayment agreement.

The repayment agreement provides that if certain payments to you by the corporation are disallowed by the IRS, you are required to repay such amounts to your corporation. The agreement must be in writing and enforceable under local law. The agreement should be reflected not only in a separate written agreement between you and your corporation, such as part of your employment contract with the corporation, but also in the corporate minutes as a resolution of the board of directors. The bylaws of the corporation should also reflect the ability of the board to enforce the agreement.

Effect of the repayment agreement   The repayment agreement is a way for you to offset dividend income you are required to report if the IRS considers payments to you to be constructive dividends. By virtue of the repayment agreement you are entitled to deduct the amounts you are contractually required to repay to your corporation. However, some tax experts do not think that a repayment agreement is a good idea. Having one could be viewed as an admission that the corporation expects to pay an "unreasonable" salary.

EMPLOYEE BENEFITS

In General

In today's increasingly tight job market, employers may want to offer various fringe benefits (also called *perks*) as a way of attracting and retaining a good work force. Businesses may also want to provide these benefits because owners want such benefits for themselves as well.

If you pay certain expenses for an employee, you can claim a deduction. This is so even though the benefits may be excluded from the employee's gross income. If you are a sole proprietor, partner, or LLC member, you are not an employee and cannot receive these benefits on a tax-free basis. For purposes of this rule, employees who are more than 2-percent shareholders in their S corporations are treated the same as partners and cannot get these benefits on a tax-free basis. Limits on benefits for sole proprietors, partners, LLC members, and more-than-2-percent S corporation shareholders are discussed later in this chapter.

The benefits provided to an employee must be ordinary and necessary business expenses. The cost of the benefits must be reasonable in amount. And, in most cases, the benefits must be provided on a nondiscriminatory basis; they cannot be extended only to owner-employees and highly paid workers.

There are two main categories of employee benefits. The first is called statutory employee benefits. These benefits, specifically detailed in the Internal Revenue Code, include health and accident plans, group term life insurance, dependent care assistance, adoption assistance, medical savings accounts, and cafeteria plans.

The other broad category of benefits is called nonstatutory fringe benefits. These refer to specific sub-categories into which various miscellaneous benefits can fall. For example, if you provide your employees with a turkey at Christmas, this minimal benefit is classified as a "de minimis fringe." It is not included in the employee's gross income even though you can claim a deduction for your cost of providing the benefit. Nonstatutory fringe benefits are discussed in greater detail later in this chapter.

Statutory Employee Benefits

Certain types of plans or arrangements are treated as statutory employee benefits. The law details what constitutes a plan, which employees must be covered, the limits, if any, on the excludability of benefits, and other details.

Medical insurance   In general, medical insurance coverage, along with any reimbursements of medical expenses, are excluded from an employee's gross income. You deduct the cost of the medical insurance premiums. If you are self-insured (you reimburse employees for medical costs out of your operating expenses under a written medical reimbursement plan), you deduct reimbursements to the employees when and to the extent made. Medical coverage, including long-term care coverage and medical reimbursement plans, is discussed more fully in Chapter 18.

Dependent care assistance   Up to $5,000 may be excluded from an employee's gross income; your outlays are fully deductible.

Group term life insurance   You deduct the cost of providing this benefit, which is the cost of the premiums. Typical coverage runs two times or more of the annual salary of the employee. The cost for up to $50,000 of coverage is excludable from an employee's gross income. If coverage over $50,000 is provided, an "imputed income" amount for excess coverage is includible in the employee's gross income. The imputed income is calculated according to an age-based IRS table; it is not based on the actual cost of premiums. For 1999, two IRS tables apply: one for figuring the taxable amount of excess coverage from January 1, 1999 through June 30, 1999, and a new table effective on July 1, 1999 to be used in figuring the taxable amount of excess coverage to the end of the year. While you deduct the actual cost of providing this benefit, your employees will be pleased to learn that the new table greatly reduces their taxable income from excess coverage. The following is used to figure employee income from excess coverage that is reported on the employee's Form W-2. The amount shown is the cost per $1,000 of excess coverage *each month:*

Age	Coverage through June 30, 1999	Coverage from July 1, 1999
Under age 25	$0.08	$0.05
25–29	.08	.06
30–34	.09	.08
35–39	.11	.09
40–44	.17	.10
45–49	.29	.15
50–54	.48	.23
55–59	.75	.43
60–64	1.17	.66
65–69	2.10	1.27
70 and older	3.76	2.06

The cost for up to $2,000 of coverage for spouses and dependents is also excludable from an employee's gross income as a *de minimis* fringe benefit (see below). If a group insurance plan is considered to be discriminatory, key employees (owners and top executives) will have income from the coverage and will not be able to exclude the cost for the first $50,000 of coverage. In this instance, income to them is the greater of the actual cost of the coverage, or the imputed amount calculated according to the age-based IRS tables. Special insurance coverage arranged on an individual basis (for example, split-dollar life insurance) is discussed later in this chapter.

Educational expenses   If the courses are job related, your payments are deductible as noncompensatory business expenses. If the courses are not job related, your expenses are deductible as wages. If you lay off workers and pay for their retraining, you may also deduct your payments.

A special exclusion of up to $5,250 for employer-financed education assistance under a qualifying plan for courses below the graduate level. The exclusion is set to expire on May 31, 2000 (although Congress may extend it as it has done many times in the past). Amounts you pay for an employee under the plan can be excluded from the employee's income even if the courses are not job related. In that case, your payments under the plan would be deductible as noncompensatory business expenses. However, as a practical matter, it is generally not advisable for owners of small businesses to set up educational assistance plans, since no more than 5 percent of benefits can go to owner-employees or their spouses or dependents.

Adoption assistance   You may deduct the cost of adoption assistance you provide to your employees. If you set up a special assistance program (a separate written plan to provide adoption assistance), your employees can exclude up to $5,000 per child ($6,000 for a child with special needs). However, the exclusion is phased out for those with adjusted gross income between $75,000 and $115,000 (regardless of your filing status as married or single). The exclusion is set to expire for amounts paid or incurred after December 31, 2001, unless Congress extends this benefit.

However, as in the case of educational assistance plans, adoption assistance plans do not make sense for small employers, since no more than 5 percent of benefits can go to owner-employees.

Medical savings accounts (MSAs)   If you are a small employer (with an average of 50 or fewer employees during either of the prior two years) and maintain a "high deductible" medical plan for your employees, you can deduct limited contributions to medical savings accounts set up for their benefit. You report your contributions on your employees' Form W-2; they can exclude them from their income. Contributions must be made no later than the due date of your return (without extensions). MSAs are set to expire on December 31, 2000, unless Congress extends this benefit.

Note: MSAs can be set up by self-employed individuals for their own benefit. These plans are discussed more fully in Chapter 18.

Cafeteria plans and flexible spending arrangements If you make contributions to cafeteria plans or flexible spending arrangements, you can claim a deduction as an employee benefit expense. Cafeteria plans are designed to offer employees choices among benefits on a nondiscriminatory basis. Flexible spending accounts are also nondiscriminatory plans but are funded primarily with employee contributions. Flexible spending arrangements are intended to cover medical costs or dependent care costs on a pretax basis.

Other Employee Benefits

In addition to the various employee benefit plans just discussed, there are other types of benefits you may provide for employees for which you can claim a deduction for your expenses.

Supplemental unemployment benefits If you make contributions to a welfare benefit fund to provide supplemental unemployment benefits for your employees, you may deduct your contributions as ordinary and necessary business expenses. The deduction is claimed as an employee benefit expense, not as a compensation cost. Your deduction cannot exceed the fund's qualified cost for the year. Qualified cost is the amount you could have claimed had you provided the benefits directly and been on the cash basis, plus the amount estimated to be actuarially necessary to build the fund to cover claims incurred but not yet paid and administrative costs for such claims.

Meals and lodging In general, the costs of providing meals and lodging to your employees are deductible as an expense of operating your business. The costs may or may not be taxable to your employees. The tax treatment of this benefit to your employees affects the amount and how you claim a deduction.

Generally, you may deduct only 50 percent of the cost of providing meals.

EXAMPLE: You pay your employee's meal costs when your employee is out of town on a sales call. (Assume proper substantiation and reimbursement arrangements, as explained in Chapter 6.) The meal costs are not included in your employee's gross income. You deduct 50 percent of the meal costs.

The 50-percent limit on deducting meals does not apply if your employees must include the benefit in income. In this case, you may deduct 100 percent of the cost as compensation.

EXAMPLE: You give your employee a $200 meal allowance because of seniority. The $200 is included in your employee's gross income. You deduct 100 percent of the $200 meal allowance.

The 50-percent limit on deducting meals does not apply if you operate a restaurant or catering business and provide meals to your employees at your restaurant or work site. However, in this case, the full cost of the meals is not deductible as compensation. Instead, it is treated as part of the cost of goods sold.

The 50-percent limit on meals does not apply if you provide the meals as part of the expense of providing recreational or social activities. For example, the cost of a company picnic is fully deductible.

You may deduct the full amount of meal costs if your employees are able to exclude this amount from their gross income. They do this if the meals are furnished on your premises and for your convenience, or if the meals qualify as a de minimis fringe benefit (described below).

Note: Under a new safe harbor rule, meals provided to all your employees are treated as furnished for your convenience (and fully deductible) if more than half of the employees to whom such meals are provided are treated as having been furnished meals for your convenience.

Special rules apply for valuing the meals provided at an employer-operated eating facility. An employer-operated eating facility is a lunchroom or other facility that you own or lease and operate directly or by a contract with another to provide meals on or near your business premises during or immediately before or after your employees' workday.

- Meals provided at an eating facility on or near your business premises are treated as a de minimis fringe benefit. As such, they are excluded from your employee's income and you can claim a full deduction (you do not have to apply the 50-percent limit).

If you provide your employees with lodging on your premises (for example, if you run a motel, nursing home, or rental property and the employee must live on the premises in order to manage it), you may deduct your full expenses according to the particular expense involved. For example, you deduct the cost of heating and lighting as part of your utilities, the cost of bedding as part of your linen expenses, and the use of the room as a depreciation item.

Travel and entertainment costs   If you pay for travel and entertainment costs, you may deduct your outlays, subject to certain limits. These expenses are explained in Chapter 6.

Employee use of a company car   If you allow an employee to use a company car for personal purposes, you must value this personal use and include it in the employee's gross income. It is a noncash fringe benefit. There are several valuation methods for calculating personal use of a company car.

One is based on the actual fair market value (FMV) of the personal use. This is determined by looking at the cost of leasing a comparable car at a comparable price for a comparable period of time. The cost of the vehicle can be its FMV if the car was purchased in an arm's-length transaction. Under a safe harbor rule, you can use the manufacturer's invoice price (including the price for all options), plus 4 percent.

Another method is based on the car's annual lease value (ALV). The annual lease value is set by the IRS and depends on the fair market value of the car on the date the car is first used for personal purposes.

ANNUAL LEASE VALUE TABLE

Car's FMV	ALV
$0 to 999	$600
1,000 to 1,999	850
2,000 to 2,999	1,100
3,000 to 3,999	1,350
4,000 to 4,999	1,600

continued on next page

ANNUAL LEASE VALUE TABLE

Car's FMV	ALV
5,000 to 5,999	1,850
6,000 to 6,999	2,100
7,000 to 7,999	2,350
8,000 to 8,999	2,600
9,000 to 9,999	2,850
10,000 to 10,999	3,100
11,000 to 11,999	3,350
12,000 to 12,999	3,600
13,000 to 13,999	3,850
14,000 to 14,999	4,100
15,000 to 15,999	4,350
16,000 to 16,999	4,600
17,000 to 17,999	4,850
18,000 to 18,999	5,100
19,000 to 19,999	5,350
20,000 to 20,999	5,600
21,000 to 21,999	5,850
22,000 to 22,999	6,100
23,000 to 23,999	6,350
24,000 to 24,999	6,600
25,000 to 25,999	6,850
26,000 to 27,999	7,250
28,000 to 29,999	7,750
30,000 to 31,999	8,250
32,000 to 33,999	8,750
34,000 to 35,999	9,250
36,000 to 37,999	9,750

Car's FMV	ALV
38,000 to 39,999	10,250
40,000 to 41,999	10,750
42,000 to 43,999	11,250
44,000 to 45,999	11,750
46,000 to 47,999	12,250
48,000 to 49,999	12,750
50,000 to 51,999	13,250
52,000 to 53,999	13,750
54,000 to 55,999	14,250
56,000 to 57,999	14,750
58,000 to 59,999	15,250

For cars over $59,999, calculate the annual lease value (ALV) as follows: Multiply the fair market value of the car by 25 percent and add $500. The ALV figures apply for a four-year period starting with the year of the ALV election. Thereafter, the ALV for each subsequent four-year period is based on the car's then fair market value.

EXAMPLE: ALV election. During all of 1999 your employee uses a company car 50 percent of the time for personal purposes and 50 percent for business purposes. The fair market value of the car as of January 1, 1999, is $15,000. The ALV is $4,350. The amount included in the employee's gross income is $2,175 ($4,350 × 50%).

If the car is used continuously for personal purposes for at least 30 days but less than the entire year, you must prorate the value of personal use.

EXAMPLE: The situation is the same as above, except the employee uses the car only from May 1 through September 30. The $2,175 is prorated for the 153 days of personal use. The amount included in the employee's gross income is $911.71 ($2,175 × 153/365).

The ALV method already takes into account maintenance and insurance costs. Fuel provided by an employer is not included in the ALV. Fuel provided in kind can be valued at fair market value or 5.5 cents per mile for purposes of including it in the employee's gross income. If fuel is paid by a company credit card, the actual charges are used to compute personal use included in the employee's gross income.

An employer may choose to treat all use by an employee of a company-owned car as personal use and include an appropriate amount in the employee's gross income. In this case, it is up to the employee to maintain records substantiating business use and then deduct such business use on his or her individual income tax return. If personal use of a company car is de minimis, then nothing need be included in the employee's gross income.

Another valuation method for personal use of a company car is the cents-per-mile special rule. This rule can be used only for a car regularly used in the business (at least 50 percent of total annual mileage is for the business, or the car is used each workday to drive at least three employees to and from work in a carpool) or for a car driven by employees at least 10,000 miles during a calendar year. If the car is owned or leased for less than a full year, the 10,000 miles are prorated accordingly. The value of personal use is based on the standard mileage rate. For 1999 the standard mileage rate is 32.5 cents per mile for travel through March 31, and 31 cents per mile for travel from April 1, 1999 to December 31, 1999. The rate may be adjusted annually for inflation.

If you want to use the ALV method or the cents-per-mile method, you must elect to do so. This election must be made no later than the first pay period in which the company car is used for personal purposes. You need not inform the IRS of your election.

Commuting vehicles   If you allow your employees to use company cars to commute to and from work, a special valuation rule is used to determine the amount includable in the employee's gross income. The car must be owned or leased by the employer for use in the business, and the employer must have genuine noncompensatory business reasons for requiring an employee to commute in the vehicle. Also, the employer must have a written policy preventing use of the vehicle for personal purposes other than commuting (or de minimis personal use). The employee cannot be a "control employee"—an employee who is a board-appointed, shareholder-appointed, confirmed, or elected officer with compensation of at least $50,000, a director, a 1-percent or greater owner, or someone who receives compensation of $100,000 or more. If the special commuting vehicle rule is met, then the value of commuting is $1.50 each way ($3 round trip), regardless of the length of the commute. The same flat rate applies to each employee even if more than one employee commutes in the vehicle. While the commuting vehicle rule is optional at the employer's election, it must be used for valuing all commuting if it is used for valuing any commuting.

The deduction for car expenses—depreciation, insurance, gas, oil, and repairs—is explained in Chapter 7. This chapter covers only business use of a company car.

Flights on Employer-Provided Aircraft

Special rules are used to determine the value of personal use of flights provided on employer aircraft. A discussion of these rules is beyond the scope of this book.

Life Insurance Provided on an Individual Basis

Businesses may provide owners and other top employees with coverage on an individual basis. Because coverage is taxable to the individual (as explained below), such coverage does not have to be provided on a nondiscriminatory basis. Coverage may be arranged to shift the cost primarily to the employer.

Under a split-dollar life insurance plan, the business buys life insurance coverage on the life of the employee. The business pays the cost of the premiums each year to the extent of the annual increases in the cash surrender value of the policy. The employee pays the balance of the premium. On the employee's death, the business recoups its outlay of premiums from the proceeds, with the balance payable to the employee's beneficiary. The employee reports as income the one-year term cost. The business deducts this amount as compensation.

NONSTATUTORY FRINGE BENEFITS

There is a special category of fringe benefits that you may provide to your employees on a tax-deductible basis but which your employees need not include in their income. These are referred to as "nonstatutory fringe benefits." What is more, if they are excludable from the employee's gross income, they are not subject to employment taxes.

In general, these benefits must be provided on a nondiscriminatory basis. This means that benefits cannot be provided solely to owners and highly paid employees and not to rank-and-file employees.

Nonstatutory fringe benefits include:

- **No-additional-cost service.** You need not include in your employee's gross income the value of a service you offer to customers in the ordinary course of the business in which your employee works. For example, say you run a ferry line and allow employees to ride for free on scheduled runs. In the case of no-additional-cost service, you generally do not have any expense to deduct by virtue of providing the benefit to the employee. You have already deducted costs related to providing the service.

- **Qualified employee discount.** You need not include in your employee's gross income a price reduction you give on certain property or services you offer to customers in the ordinary course of your business in which the employee performs services. For example, say you own a clothing boutique and give your salespersons a 15-percent discount on your merchandise. A qualified employee discount does not include any discount on property that is more than your gross profit percent (total sales price of property less cost of property, divided by total sales price of property) times the price charged to customers, or for services, 20 percent of the price charged to customers. A qualified employee discount does not include any discount on real property. Here a deduction for the goods or services provided is not taken into account as a compensation expense but rather some other item. For example, goods provided to employees at a discount are part of the cost of goods sold.

- **Working condition fringe benefit.** You need not include in your employee's gross income a benefit provided to your employee if the employee could have claimed his or her own deduction had he or she paid for the benefit. For example, if you paid for a job-related course that would have been deductible by your employee had the employee paid for it, the course is a working condition fringe benefit. Other examples of working condition fringe benefits include employer-provided vehicles and outplacement services.

- **De minimis (minimal) fringe.** You need not include in your employee's gross income the value of any small or inconsequential benefit, such as the typing of a personal letter by a company secretary or the occasional use of the company copying machine for personal matters. Holiday gifts of nominal value, such as turkeys and hams, are considered de minimis fringes. However, cash of any amount is not a de minimis fringe and must be included in the employee's gross income. Other examples of de minimis fringes include group term life insurance for spouses and dependents up to $2,000, meals furnished at an eating facility on or near your premises, coffee or soft drinks furnished to employees, occasional tickets to sporting or entertainment events, occasional meal money or transportation fare for employees working overtime, and company events (such as parties or picnics) for employees and their guests.

- **Qualified transportation fringe benefit.** If you provide your employee with a transit pass for mass transit, transportation in a commuter highway vehicle, or qualified parking, you need not include the benefit in your employee's gross income. The 1999 limit on this exclusion is $65 per month for a transit pass or commuter highway vehicle. The 1999 limit on the exclusion for qualified parking is $175 per month. The value of parking is based on what a person would have to pay for space in an arm's-length transaction. If you provide parking space to employees that is primarily available to customers, then the parking has no value. If you give employees who carpool preferential parking, the value of the space must be taken into consideration. The dollar limits for qualified transportation fringe benefits are subject to annual adjustment for inflation. If the limits are exceeded, only the excess is includible in gross income. However, in the case of partners who are given public transit passes, if the monthly amount exceeds the dollar limit, then the entire cost of the ticket is includable in the partner's gross income. The entire value of parking provided to partners and more-than-2-percent S corporation shareholders is taxable to them, even if it is less than $175 per month. The fact that you offer your an employee a choice between a qualified transportation fringe benefit and cash does not make the benefit taxable if the employee chooses the benefit. The employee is, of course, taxed on cash received in lieu of the transportation fringe benefit.

- **Moving expenses,** whether paid directly to the mover or as an allowance to the employee. Payments to an employee for nondeductible moving expenses are deductible as wages and subject to employment taxes. Payments or reimbursements that would be deductible by the employee had the employee paid them are not treated as wages and are not subject to employment taxes. They are still deductible by you as noncompensatory business expenses. Moving expenses are explained in Chapter 19.

- **Certain athletic facilities.** You need not include in your employee's gross income the value of an on-site gym or other athletic facilities for use by employees, their spouses, and children. However, if you pay for a membership to an outside health club or athletic facility open to the general public, you must include the benefit in the employee's gross income. No deduction can be claimed for club dues (see Chapter 19).

Frequent flyer mileage   Some companies allow employees to use business-generated frequent flyer mileage for personal purposes. This benefit defies classification and, to date, the IRS has not figured out a way to tax it without causing an administrative nightmare.

Limits on fringe benefits paid for the benefit of sole proprietors, partners, LLC members, and more-than-2-percent S corporation shareholders   Fringe benefits that are otherwise excludable by rank-and-file employees are taxable to sole proprietors, partners, LLC members, and more-than-2-percent S corporation shareholders. For example, if the business pays their health insurance (which may include long-term care insurance), the coverage is taxable to them. The business can deduct the costs as guaranteed payments to partners or as compensation to S corporation shareholders. Owners can then deduct a percentage of the amount directly from gross income on page 1 of Form 1040. The deductible percentage is:

Year	Deductible Percentage
1999–2001	60%
2002	70
2003 and later	100

> **LEGISLATIVE ALERT**
>
> Congress is considering acceleration of the 100-percent deduction that would become effective starting in 2000.

The balance can be treated as a deductible medical expense, which is taken as an itemized deduction subject to a 7.5-percent floor. Medical coverage for these owners is discussed in Chapter 18.

If, in 1999, the business provides qualified parking, the benefit is taxable to the sole proprietor, partner, LLC member, or 2-percent S shareholder even though its value is less than $175 per month.

EMPLOYMENT TAX OBLIGATIONS

You may be liable for the payment of certain taxes with respect to the compensation you paid to your employees. As a small business owner, you need to know what taxes you are responsible for, where and when to deposit the taxes, and what returns you must file for employment taxes. The returns you must file are discussed at the end of this chapter. In this section you will learn about employment taxes and where to deposit them. The deductibility of these taxes is discussed in Chapter 11.

Employment Taxes

The Federal Insurance Contribution Act (FICA) set up a system to provide for old age, survivors, disability, and hospital insurance of workers. Both you, the employer, and your employees contribute to this system. The Federal Unemployment Tax Act (FUTA), together with state unemployment systems, provides payment to workers in the event of unemployment. Only employers pay this tax.

You must withhold from your employees' wages income tax and the employee portion of Social Security and Medicare tax (FICA). These taxes are referred to as "trust fund" amounts because you, as employer, are holding the funds in trust for your employees. You must pay over these amounts to the IRS. You must also pay the IRS the employer portion of Social Security and Medicare tax (FICA), which is the same amount that the employee paid, plus federal unemployment insurance (FUTA).

The tax rate for the Social Security portion of FICA is 6.2 percent of the first $72,600 of wages in 1999. This wage base is adjusted annually for inflation. This means that you must withhold from the employee's compensation this amount of tax. In addition, as an employer, you must also pay the same rate of tax. The tax rate for the Medicare portion of FICA is 1.45 percent on all compensation. There is no wage base ceiling for purposes of computing this tax. You must withhold this amount from the employee's compensation and pay a similar amount as the employer.

It is important to note that the definition of compensation is, in some instances, different for purposes of income taxes and employment taxes. For example, a salary reduction that is contributed to an employee's 401(k) plan or SIMPLE plan is not treated as compensation subject to income tax. However, the salary reduction is still subject to employment tax.

Employing family members   If you are self-employed and employ your child who is under age 18, his or her wages are not subject to FICA. Your child's wages are exempt from FUTA until he or she reaches age 21. If you employ your spouse in your business, his or her wages are fully subject to FICA. If you have a corporation that employs a child under age 18, his or her wages are still subject to FICA.

Caution: The IRS looks closely at family hiring. Make sure that the wages are reasonable for the work performed. Keep time sheets as proof of work performed by your relatives.

Leased employees   If you lease employees from a corporation that supplies workers for your business, the employees may be treated as in the employ of the corporation that does the leasing rather than as your employees. The leasing corporation, and not you, is responsible for the payment of employment taxes.

FUTA   The tax applies only to the first $7,000 of compensation for each employee. The FUTA tax rate is 0.8 percent of taxable wages. Different rates apply for state unemployment purposes.

Depositing Employment Taxes   When employment taxes must be paid to the IRS is determined in part by the size of the tax liability. More precisely, employment taxes are deposited with a federal depository (certain banks) along with a deposit coupon, Form 8109, Federal Tax Deposit Coupon. (Ask at your local bank to determine whether it is qualified to accept employment tax deposits on behalf of the IRS.) Deposit slips are furnished to you by the IRS. New employers can expect to receive a coupon book within five to six weeks after applying for an employer tax identification number (EIN). The federal depository then turns the funds over to the government. The reporting of these deposits is made quarterly for Social Security and Medicare tax and income tax withholding, and annually for FUTA tax.

Employers at very small businesses may be able to pay employment taxes directly to the IRS along with their quarterly tax returns. Employers of larger businesses (those with aggregate federal tax deposits over $200,000 in 1998) must pay employment taxes via electronic transfer under the Electronic Federal Tax Payment System (EFTPS) beginning January 1, 2000.

Although you are not required to pay your employment taxes by electronic transfer (unless your aggregate federal tax deposits for 1998 exceeded $200,000), you are permitted to do so. Many employers at small businesses find paying by electronic transfer convenient, which they activate with their computers or a telephone call to their bank. Over 1.5 million businesses, many of them small businesses, have already enrolled in EFTPS. If you wish to voluntarily enroll, call 1-800-945-8400 or 1-800-555-4477.

Unless you fall within the exceptions explained below, you must deposit income tax you withhold from your employee's compensation as well as both the employer and employee portion of Social Security and Medicare taxes. This is done by electronic transfer under EFTPS or by mailing or delivering the required amount to a Federal Reserve Bank or an authorized financial institution. Ask your local bank whether it is qualified to accept employment tax deposits on behalf of the IRS. You include a special deposit slip, Form 8109, Federal Tax Deposit Coupon, with your payment. Deposit slips will be furnished to you by the IRS. New employers can expect to receive a coupon book within five to six weeks after you apply for an employer tax identification number (EIN).

Deposit dates   Depending on the size of your payroll, you are put on one of two deposit schedules, monthly or semiweekly. The IRS notifies all employers each November of the schedule they will be on for the coming calendar year. The determination of your deposit schedule is based on your employment taxes during a lookback period (two years prior to the upcoming year). If your employment taxes were $50,000 or less in the lookback period, you are on a monthly deposit schedule. If your employment taxes exceeded $50,000 in the lookback period, you are on a semiweekly deposit schedule. It is important to note that even if you are put on a monthly deposit schedule, you need not file the quarterly employment tax return monthly or more frequently unless the IRS instructs you to file Form 941-M, Employer's Monthly Federal Tax Return. Remember, the amount of your employment taxes, not the time you pay your employees (i.e., weekly, semimonthly, monthly), determines your depositor status.

DEPOSIT SCHEDULE

Monthly deposit schedule	15th day of the following month
Semiweekly deposit schedule	
Payment on Wed., Thurs., and/or Fri.	Following Wed.
Payment on Sat., Sun., Mon., and/or Tues.	Following Fri.

If the bank is closed on the required deposit date, the deposit is made on the next banking day.

Payment with returns   Instead of depositing employment taxes, you can pay them directly to the IRS along with your return if your net tax liability for the quarterly return is less than $1,000 (starting January 1, 1999, the $1,000 threshold, instead of the old $500 threshold, applies to annual returns as well). Thus, for example, if you have one employee who earned only $2,500 for the quarter, employment taxes will be under $1,000, so you can pay them directly to the IRS when you file your return, Form 941. If you are not sure whether your quarterly employment taxes will cross the $1,000 threshold, it is advisable to deposit the taxes monthly in order to avoid a penalty.

Penalty for Failure to Pay Employment Taxes

As an employer, you are required to deduct and withhold income taxes and FICA from your employee's compensation. If you fail to do so, or if you withhold an insufficient amount, you are still liable for the correct amount.

There is a 100-percent penalty imposed on persons who are responsible for paying employment taxes but fail to do so. This penalty, called the trust fund recovery penalty (because an employer pays income tax withholding and the employee's share of Social Security and Medicare taxes into a trust fund maintained by the government for the employee's benefit), is a personal one against an owner, officer, or other "responsible person." Thus, for example, a shareholder in a corporation who serves as company president may be personally liable for this penalty even though a shareholder generally is not liable for corporate debts.

Even if there is more than one responsible person, the IRS can collect the entire tax and penalty from one person. Then it is up to that one person to try to recover a portion of the payment from other responsible persons. If you make a written request, the IRS must notify you of the name of the person that it has determined to be responsible and whether it has attempted to collect the penalty from other responsible persons. There is a federal right of contribution (to collect a share of the penalty by someone who has paid it from someone else who is also responsible) where there are multiple responsible persons.

Caution: In view of this substantial penalty, it is essential that employment taxes be paid. If you are experiencing a cash crunch, see that these taxes are paid before satisfying other creditors.

Penalty for delinquent deposits   Unless you can show reasonable cause for failing to deposit required amounts or paying deposits directly to the IRS instead of depositing the employment taxes, you will be subject to a penalty. The penalty schedule is designed to encourage employers to comply with deposit requirements as quickly as possible. Thus, the penalty is 2 percent if deposits are made from one to five days late; it increases to 5 percent for deposits six to 15 days late. The penalty jumps to 10 percent for deposits more than 15 days late, deposits made at unauthorized financial institutions or directly to the IRS, and amounts paid to the IRS within 10 days of a first notice asking for tax due. A 15-percent penalty applies to amounts outstanding more than 10 days after a first notice from the IRS of amounts due or the day on which you receive a notice and demand for immediate payment, whichever is earlier. However, you can designate the period for which payment is made to avoid cascading penalties.

State Employment Tax Obligations

The above discussion deals entirely with federal employment tax obligations. However, as an employer, you should check out your obligation, if any, for state employment taxes.

Special Rules for Self-Employed Individuals

Self-employed individuals—sole proprietors, general partners, and LLC members who are not treated as limited partners—are not employees of their businesses even though they may be compensated for their services. Thus, they are not subject to FICA. However, self-employed individuals bear the same tax burden as owners who work for their corporations. Self-employed individuals pay both the employee and employer portion of FICA, called self-employment tax (SECA). The rate for self-employment tax is 12.4 percent on net earnings from self-employment up to $72,600 in 1999 and 2.9 percent on all net earnings from self-employment tax. To more closely equate self-employed individuals with corporations, self-employed individuals may claim a deduction for one-half of self-employment tax (what amounts to the employer portion of FICA). However, they pay self-employment tax on more than just an amount that could be called a salary. Sole proprietors pay self-employment tax on the net income reported on Schedule C (or Schedule F for farming activities). This is so even if they do no work at all for their business and in fact hire someone else to run it. General partners and LLC members who are not treated as limited partners pay self-employment income on their distributive share of income from the partnership or LLC and on guaranteed payments to them.

Limited partners (and LLC members treated as limited partners) are not subject to self-employment tax on their distributive share of partnership income. They are viewed as mere investors. At the present time, there is no guidance on how to treat LLC members for purposes of self-employment tax. The IRS was prevented, by law, from issuing regulations on this issue before July 1, 1998. At the time this book was being prepared, the IRS had not given any indication of forthcoming regulations on this issue.

Unlike FICA, self-employment tax is not deposited with a Federal Reserve Bank or other authorized financial institution. Instead, it is paid along with income taxes. This means that self-employed individuals must ensure that quarterly estimated taxes cover not only their income tax obligations but also their self-employment tax for the year.

Self-employed individuals are not subject to FUTA. They cannot cover themselves for periods of no work because, by definition, self-employed persons are never employed.

EMPLOYMENT TAX CREDITS

Tax credits are even better than tax deductions. A tax deduction is worth only as much as the tax bracket you are in. For example, if you are in the top federal income tax bracket for individuals, 39.6 percent, a $100 deduction saves $39.60 in taxes. Tax credits reduce your taxes dollar-for-dollar. A $100 tax credit saves $100 in taxes.

Employer's Employment-Related Tax Credits

There are a number of tax credits related to the employment of workers. These tax credits reduce your deduction for compensation dollar-for-dollar. For example, if your deduction for compensation is $40,000 and you are entitled to claim a $2,000 employment tax credit, you may deduct only $38,000.

Employment-related tax credits reduce your deduction for wages paid to your employees. Employment-related tax credits are part of the general business credit and subject to limitation as explained in Chapter 4.

Work opportunity credit   A credit can be claimed for employing individuals from certain economically disadvantaged groups (such as AFDC recipients, food stamp recipients, ex-felons, and high-risk youths). The credit is 40 percent of the first $6,000 of wages ($3,000 of wages for summer youth) for those who work at least 400 hours. The top credit is $2,100 ($1,050 for summer youth). The credit is 25 percent of the first $6,000 of wages ($3,000 of wages for summer youth) for those who work between 120 and 400 hours. The top credit is $2,400 ($1,200 for summer youth). The credit applies only for those beginning work before July 1, 1999 (although it can be claimed for wages paid after this date as long as they are paid within one year of commencing employment). If you employ an eligible worker, be sure to obtain the necessary certification from your state employment security agency. This is done by completing IRS Form 8850, Pre-Screening Notice and Certification Request for the Work Opportunity and Welfare-to-Work Credits. Without it, you cannot claim the credit unless you submitted the request and all necessary paperwork but the state agency failed to act on your request.

LEGISLATIVE ALERT

Congress has extended this credit numerous times in the past and may again act to extend it retroactively (or make it permanent) from its expiration on June 30, 1999.

Welfare-to-work credit   This credit can be claimed for employing individuals who are considered to be long-term family assistance recipients. The credit is 35 percent of qualifying first-year wages up to $10,000, plus 50 percent of qualifying wages up to $10,000. Thus the maximum credit for the first two years of employment is $8,500 ($3,500 in year one and $5,000 in year two). As with the work opportunity credit, you must obtain the required certification (as explained above). You may find that your worker qualifies you to claim the work opportunity credit and also the welfare-to-work credit. You cannot take both credits with respect to wages paid to the same worker. You must make a choice. Choose the credit that provides you with the larger benefit. The welfare-to-work credit is set to expire for workers hired after June 30, 1999.

LEGISLATIVE ALERT

Congress may extend this credit retroactively (or make it permanent) from its expiration on June 30, 1999.

FICA on tips   Owners of restaurant and beverage establishments can claim a credit for the employer portion of FICA paid on tips related to the furnishing of food and beverages on or off the premises. This is 7.65 percent of tips in excess of those treated as wages for purposes of satisfying the minimum wage provisions of the Fair Labor Standards Act (FLSA).

Empowerment zone employment credit   The Departments of Housing and Urban Development and Agriculture have named six cities and three rural areas across the country as "empowerment zones" and are authorized to name 22 more. In addition, the District of Columbia is an enterprise zone through 2002, and employers in the zone are eligible for the empowerment zone employment credit. If you do business in one of these economically depressed zones and hire part-time or full-time employees who perform substantially all of their employment services within the zone, you may claim a credit based on their wages. The credit is 20 percent of the first $15,000 of qualified wages. The top credit is $3,000 per employee per year. There is no limit on the number of employees for which you may claim the credit. "Wages" for purposes of calculating the credit include not only salary and wages but also training and educational benefits.

Indian employment credit   You can claim a credit if you employ part-time or full-time workers who receive more than 50 percent of their wages from services performed on an Indian reservation. The employee must be an enrolled member of an Indian tribe or a spouse of an enrolled member. The employee must also live on or near the reservation on which the services are performed. The credit is 20 percent of the first $20,000 of "excess" wages and the cost of health insurance. Excess wages and health insurance costs are such costs over amounts paid or incurred during 1993.

Employment tax credits are part of the general business credit. As such, they not only reduce your deduction for wages but are also subject to special limitations. The general business credit is the sum of employment tax credits and certain other business-related credits. The general business credit cannot exceed your net tax liability (tax liability reduced by certain personal and other credits), reduced by the greater of:

- Tentative minimum tax (the alternative minimum tax before the foreign tax credit), or

- 25 percent of regular tax liability (without regard to personal credits) over $25,000

The amount of the general business credit in excess of this limit can be carried back for one year. Any additional excess amount can then be carried forward for up to 20 years. You cannot elect to forego the carryback. (For credits arising in tax years before 1998, the carryback period was three years and the carryforward period was 15 years.)

EXAMPLE: Your 1999 tax liability (without regard to personal credits) is $15,000 and you have no alternative minimum tax liability. Your general business credit is $17,000. In 1999, you can claim a general business credit of $15,000 (your net tax liability reduced by your tentative minimum tax liability of zero). The $2,000 unused credit is carried back to 1998. If it cannot be fully used on an amended 1998 return, it can be carried forward for up to 20 years starting on your 2000 return.

Employee's Employment-Related Tax Credits
An employee may be entitled to claim certain credits by virtue of working. These include the earned income credit and the dependent care credit. They are personal tax credits, not business credits. They are in addition to any

child tax credit to which a person may be entitled (in 1999, $500 for each child under age 17 if income is below a threshold amount).

Earned income credit   If you employ an individual whose income is below threshold amounts, the employee may be eligible to claim an earned income credit. This is a special type of credit because it can exceed tax liability. It is called a refundable credit, since it can be paid to a worker even though it more than offsets tax liability.

From an employer's perspective, it is important to realize that a portion of the credit can be given to the employee along with the salary check. In essence, the credit is advanced to the employee. This credit belongs to the employee, not the employer. If you think you may have an employee who would qualify for the credit, you are required to inform him or her of eligibility and offer the option of receiving an advanced credit. You must notify employees who have no income tax withheld (other than those who claim exemption from withholding). You are encouraged to notify employees who have a qualifying dependent and compensation of less than a set amount (in 1999, less than $30,580 and two or more qualifying children; less than $26,928 and one qualifying child). (A limited credit may be claimed by low earners without any qualifying dependent, but they cannot receive the credit on an advanced basis.) The IRS has provided notification guidance in Notice 797, Possible Federal Tax Refund Due to the Earned Income Credit, and Notice 1015, Employers—Have You Told Your Employees About the Earned Income Credit?

Dependent care credit   Whether you are an employee or a business owner, if you hire someone to look after your children under age 13 or a disabled spouse or child of any age so that you can go to work, you may claim a tax credit. This is a personal tax credit, not a business tax credit. You claim the credit on your individual tax return.

The credit is a sliding percentage based on your adjusted gross income (AGI). The top percentage is 30 percent; it scales back to 20 percent for AGI over $28,000. This is the AGI on a joint return if you are married and do not live apart from your spouse for the entire year.

The percentage is applied to certain employment-related expenses up to $2,400 per year, or $4,800 per year if you have two or more qualifying dependents. Employment-related expenses include household expenses to care for your dependent—housekeeper, baby-sitter, or nanny—and out-of-the-house expenses for the care of dependents, such as day-care centers, preschool and kindergarten, and day camps. Not treated as qualifying expenses are the costs of food, transportation, education, and clothing. Also, the cost of sleep-away camp does not qualify as an eligible expense.

If you are eligible for a credit, be sure to get the tax identification number of anyone who works for you and the day-care center or other organization to which you pay qualified expenses. The tax identification number of an individual is his or her Social Security number. You must include this information if you want to claim the credit.

If you hire someone to work in your home, be sure to pay the "nanny tax." This is the employment taxes (Social Security, Medicare, and FUTA taxes) on compensation you pay to your housekeeper, baby-sitter, or other in-home worker. You must pay Social Security and Medicare taxes if annual payments to a household worker in 1999 exceed $1,100. If you paid cash wages of $1,000 or more in any calendar quarter to a household employee during the current tax year or the previous year, you also must pay federal unemployment tax (FUTA) on the first $7,000 of wages. You do not pay these taxes separately but instead can report them on Schedule H and include them on your Form 1040. You should increase your withholding or estimated tax to cover your liability for them to avoid estimated tax penalties. You cannot deduct employment taxes on household workers as a business expense. However, the tax itself is treated as a qualifying expense for the dependent care credit.

WHERE TO DEDUCT COMPENSATION COSTS

Self-Employed (Including Independent Contractors and Statutory Employees)

Compensation paid to employees and employee benefits paid to them or provided for them are deductible on the appropriate lines of Schedule C. The deduction for wages must be reduced by any employment taxes paid. Self-employed farmers deduct compensation costs on Schedule F.

If you maintain a cafeteria plan for employees, you must file an information return, Form 5500, annually.

If you personally incur dependent care costs for which a credit can be claimed, you must file Form 2441, Dependent Care Credit. The credit is then entered on Form 1040.

Partnerships and LLCs

Compensation paid to employees and employee benefits paid or provided to them is a trade or business expense taken into account in determining the profit or loss of the partnership or LLC on Form 1065, U.S. Partnership Return of Income. Report these items on the specific lines provided on Form 1065. Be sure to offset them by employment tax credits. Salaries and wages paid to employees and employee benefits are not separately stated items passed through to partners and members. Partners and members in LLCs report their net income or loss from the business on Schedule E; they do not deduct compensation and employee benefit costs on their individual tax returns.

Guaranteed payments to partners are also taken into account in determining trade or business profit or loss. There is a specific line on Form 1065 for reporting guaranteed payments to partners. They are also reported on Schedule K-1 as a separately stated item passed through to partners and LLC members as net earnings from self-employment. This will allow the partners and LLC members to calculate their self-employment tax on the guaranteed payments.

If the partnership or LLC maintains a cafeteria plan for employees, the business must file an information return, Form 5500, annually.

Partners and LLC members who personally incur dependent care costs for which a credit can be claimed must file Form 2441.

S Corporations

Compensation paid to employees and employee benefits paid or provided to them are trade or business expenses that are taken into account in determining the profit or loss of the S corporation on Form 1120S, U.S. Income Tax Return for an S Corporation. They are not separately stated items passed through to shareholders. This applies as well to compensation paid to owners employed by the corporation. Note that compensation to officers is reported on a separate line on the return from salary and wages paid to nonofficers. Be sure to reduce salary and wages by employment tax credits.

Shareholders report their net income or loss from the business on Schedule E; they do not deduct compensation and employee benefit costs on their individual tax returns.

If the corporation maintains a cafeteria plan for employees, it must file an information return, Form 5500, annually.

Employment Tax Credits for All Businesses

Employment taxes are figured on separate forms, with the results entered on Form 3800, General Business Credit. Form 3800 need not be completed if you are claiming only one business credit, you have no carryback or carryover, and the credit is not from a passive activity.

The separate forms for employment taxes are the following:

- Empowerment zone credit: Form 8844

- Indian employment credit: Form 8845

- Social Security tax credit on certain tips: Form 8846

- Welfare-to-work credit: Form 8861

- Work opportunity credit: Form 5884

C Corporations

Compensation and employee benefits paid to employees are trade or business expenses taken into account in determining the profit or loss of the C corporation on Form 1120, U.S. Corporation Income Tax Return. Compensation paid to officers is segregated from salaries and wages paid to employees. Be sure to reduce salary and wages by employment tax credits. Total compensation exceeding $500,000 paid to officers of the corporation is explained in greater detail on Schedule E of Form 1120. Remember that the corporation then pays tax on its net profit or loss. Shareholders do not report any income (or loss) from the corporation.

If the corporation maintains a cafeteria plan for employees, it must file an information return, Form 5500, annually.

Employment Tax Filing for All Businesses

If you have employees (even if you are your corporation's only employee), you must report quarterly to the IRS. Use Form 941, Employer's Quarterly Federal Tax Return, to report any income tax withholding and FICA withholding and payments made during the quarter. More than three million small businesses are eligible to file their quarterly returns using the 941TeleFile system. Under this system, quarterly payroll returns are filed by telephone. This system automatically calculates the tax and tells you any balance that is owed. Potentially eligible small businesses were sent

941TeleFile packages. If you think you are eligible but did not receive one, contact the IRS.

You must also file an annual return to report the payment of federal unemployment insurance. Use Form 940, Employer's Annual Federal Unemployment (FUTA) Tax Return. Alternatively, you may be able to use a simplified form, Form 940-EZ, Employer's Annual Federal Unemployment (FUTA) Tax Return, if you meet the following tests:

- You paid unemployment contributions to only one state.

- You paid all state unemployment contributions by January 31.

- All wages for FUTA tax were also taxable for state unemployment tax purposes.

- All wages were paid in a state other than a credit reduction state.

Note that reporting for employment tax obligations is separate and apart from income tax reporting.

Special reporting for employing a worker in your home   If you are a sole proprietor and have a nanny or other household employee, as well as regular business employees, you can report the FICA and FUTA taxes for your household employee on Schedule H and pay the taxes with your Form 1040. Alternatively, you can report and pay the FICA taxes for your household employee with the quarterly reports for your regular business employees on Form 941, and you can pay the FUTA taxes on Form 940 or Form 940-EZ.

CHAPTER 6

Travel and Entertainment Expenses

Technology has enabled small business owners to market their goods and services in a manner similar to that of larger companies. For example, local radio advertising may expand the market for a small business beyond the general area in which its office is located. To service these expanding markets, you may have to travel to see clients, customers, vendors, suppliers, and others who are part of your business operations. If you travel on business or entertain clients, customers, or employees, you may be able to deduct a number of expenses. In this chapter you will learn about:

- Local transportation costs
- Travel within the United States
- Foreign travel
- Conventions
- Living away from home on temporary assignments
- Meal and entertainment expenses
- Business gifts
- Reimbursement arrangements
- Recordkeeping requirements
- Where to deduct travel and entertainment expenses

For further information about travel and entertainment costs, see IRS Publication 463, Travel, Entertainment, Gift, and Car Expenses. For a listing of per diem rates, see IRS Publication 1542.

Business use of your car for travel and entertainment purposes is discussed in Chapter 7.

LOCAL TRANSPORTATION COSTS

Do you travel from your office to see clients or customers? Do you have more than one business location? Do you have an office in your home but go into the field to transact business? If the answer to any of these questions is yes, you may be able to deduct local transportation costs. More specifically, local transportation costs include the cost of work-related travel within the area of your tax home.

> **Definition**   *Tax home*   In general, your tax home is the entire city or general area of your regular place of business. If you have more than one business interest, then it is the location of your main business interest based on the comparative time spent in each location and the income derived from each business interest. If you do not have a regular place of business, you are considered an itinerant without any tax home.

Deductible Costs

Local transportation costs include the cost of driving and maintaining your car (including tolls and parking) or the cost of taxis, bus fare, train fare, or airfare. Computing the cost of driving and maintaining your car is discussed in Chapter 7.

Commuting Costs

As a general rule, the costs of commuting between your home and workplace are not deductible. Thus, your bus or train fare, gas for your car, bridge and highway tolls, and parking fees are nondeductible. This rule does not change merely because the commute is unusually long or you do work on the way (for example, reading reports on the train, talking to clients on your car phone, or displaying advertising on your car). Commuting costs are considered nondeductible personal expenses.

However, there are a few exceptions that make certain commuting expenses deductible:

1. If you have one or more regular places of business but work at different locations on a temporary basis (as defined under 2, below), you can deduct the daily cost of travel between your home and the other work site.

   EXAMPLE: You have a medical practice with an office across the street from the hospital in which you practice. You sometimes stop to see patients in their homes before going to the office or the hospital. You can deduct the cost of travel from your home to the patients' homes, as well as the cost of travel from their homes to your office or the hospital.

2. If you travel from your home to a temporary work site *outside* the metropolitan area where you live and normally work, you can deduct the daily cost of travel between your home and the temporary work site, regardless of the distance. "Temporary" means that work is realistically expected to last for one year or less. If it turns out to last longer, the period up until the realistic expectation change is treated as temporary.

   EXAMPLE: You have an office downtown but work on a two-month project at a client's facilities in the next city. You can deduct the cost of travel from your home (which is in the same metropolitan area as your office) to the client's facilities (and back) each day.

Note: If you do not have a regular place of business but work at temporary work sites in the metropolitan area of your home, you cannot deduct your transportation costs. Thus, according to the IRS, a lumberjack who worked at a number of temporary cutting sites was not allowed to deduct the cost of transportation to those sites. The entire area of the cutting sites was considered his regular place of business. However, the Tax Court has allowed a deduction for transportation costs in this instance, so the issue is not yet settled.

If you travel outside your metropolitan area, both the IRS and courts agree that the costs of traveling between your home and a temporary work site outside your area are deductible.

> **Definition**   *Metropolitan area*   The area within a city and its surrounding suburbs.

3. If you have a home office that is the principal place of business for the activity conducted there, the cost of traveling from your home to your clients or customers or to other business locations is deductible.

   EXAMPLE: You run a tax return preparation business from your home and generally meet clients in your home office. Occasionally you go to clients' homes to do your work. You may deduct the cost of traveling between your home and the clients' homes and back again.

4. If you must haul tools or equipment to your job site and you use a trailer or have to make other special arrangements, the additional cost of commuting with the tools is deductible. The basic transportation costs are still treated as nondeductible commuting expenses.

   EXAMPLE: You rent a trailer to haul tools to and from home and business. You may not deduct the expenses of using your car; however, you can deduct the cost of renting the trailer that you haul with your car.

TRAVEL WITHIN THE UNITED STATES

If you travel on business away from home, you can deduct not only the cost of transportation but also personal costs, such as your food, lodging, and incidentals. You must be away from your "tax home" (see above) for more than the day. You must be required, because of the distance or the length of the business day, to get sleep or rest away from home in order to meet the demands of your work. This is called the "sleep or rest" rule. And your travel away from home must be considered "temporary."

> **Definition**   *Temporary*   Travel that is expected to last for no more than one year and does in fact last no more than one year. Travel expected to last for more than a year or that actually lasts for more than a year is considered to be "indefinite," not temporary.

Temporary travel is discussed in more detail later in this chapter.

EXAMPLE: You fly from New York to San Francisco to meet with a business client. You stay for five days, after which time you return to New York. In this case, your travel expenses are deductible.

Deductible Costs

Travel costs include transportation costs, lodging, meals, and other related expenses.

Transportation costs   The cost of a ticket to travel by air, train, or bus between your home and a business destination is deductible. However, if you receive the fare for free because of "frequent flyer" miles or otherwise, the cost is not deductible. The cost of travel by ship may not be fully deductible (see the section on Conventions later in this chapter).

Transportation costs also include local costs once you arrive at your business destination. Thus, the cost of taxi fare between the airport and your hotel is deductible. Local transportation costs at the business location, such as taxi fare from your hotel to the location of clients or customers, are also deductible. Other deductible local transportation costs include bus fare and limousine fare.

Transportation costs for personal travel—sightseeing, visiting relatives, shopping, and other nonbusiness activities—are not deductible.

If you use your car for travel, see Chapter 7. If you rent a car for travel to or at your business destination, the rental charges, as well as gas, parking, and tolls, are deductible. However, if the rental exceeds 30 days and the value of the car exceeds a dollar limit, there may be income to include, called an "inclusion amount." This concept is also explained in the same chapter.

Lodging costs   The cost of hotel, motel, or other accommodations is deductible if the nature of the business trip requires an overnight stay in order for you to sleep or properly perform your job.

Meals   The cost of your meals on a trip away from home is deductible (subject to a percent limit, explained below). The cost of meals includes food, beverages, taxes, and tips. However, if the meals are considered to be lavish or extravagant, the deductible portion is limited to the amount that is reasonable. What is considered reasonable is based on the facts and circumstances of the situation. "Lavish or extravagant" is not automatically the conclusion when the cost of meals exceeds the standard meal allowance rate (see below) or when meals are eaten in deluxe hotels, restaurants, night-clubs, or resorts.

You have a choice when deducting meal costs: (1) keep track of all costs and deduct these actual costs, or (2) use a standard meal allowance set by the IRS.

Note: Using the standard meal allowance does not eliminate the need for other recordkeeping, as explained later in this chapter.

The daily dollar amount of the standard meal allowance is fixed by the government and is adjusted each year for inflation. The dollar amount depends on where your business takes you. In most of the United States, the daily amount is $30 (in 1999). In certain areas designated by the IRS as "High-Cost Areas," the daily amount is slightly higher ($34, $38, $42, or $46). You take the daily amount based on the rate in effect for the area where you stop to sleep or rest.

Per Diem Meal Allowances

The standard meal allowance in 1999 is $30 a day for most areas within the continental United States. However, for places designated as high-cost areas, a higher rate may or may not apply (a higher rate applies for lodging that makes it a high-cost area even if the meal portion is the standard $30-a-day limit). The following figures apply for travel to high-cost areas on or after January 1, 1999. (The $30 per day rate applies to areas not listed below.) Be sure to note that these rates may be adjusted for future years.

City	County	Amount
ALABAMA		
Birmingham	Jefferson	$38
Gulf Shores	Baldwin	34
Huntsville	Madison	38
Mobile	Mobile	34
Montgomery	Montgomery	38
ARIZONA		
Casa Grande	Pinal	34

City	County	Amount
Chinle	Apache	34
Flagstaff	Coconino	34
Grand Canyon National Park	Coconino	42
Phoenix	Maricopa	38
Prescott	Yavapai	38
Scottsdale	Maricopa	42
Tucson	Pima; Davis-Monthan AFB	38
Yuma	Yuma	34
ARKANSAS		
Little Rock	Pulaski	34
CALIFORNIA		
Barstow	Barstow city limits	34
Bridgeport	Mono	42
Clearlake	Lake	38
Contra Costa County	Contra Costa	42
Death Valley	Inyo	46
Eureka	Humboldt	38
Fresno	Fresno	38
Los Angeles	Los Angeles, Kern, Orange, and Ventura; Edwards AFB; China Lake Naval Center	46
Madera	Madera	34
Mammoth Lakes/Bridgeport	Mono	46
Marin County	Marin County	42
Merced	Merced	38
Modesto	Stanislaus	34
Monterey	Monterey	42

continued on next page

City	County	Amount
Napa	Napa	42
Oakhurst	City limits	38
Oakland	Alameda	38
Ontario	San Bernadino (except Barstow)	38
Orange County	Orange County	46
Palm Springs	Riverside	42
Palo Alto	Santa Clara	42
Point Arena	Mendocino	38
Redding	Shasta	38
Redwood City	San Mateo	42
Sacramento	Sacramento	42
San Diego	San Diego	46
San Francisco	San Francisco	46
San Jose	Santa Clara	38
San Luis Obispo	San Luis Obispo	38
San Mateo	San Mateo	42
Santa Barbara	Santa Barbara	38
Santa Cruz	Santa Cruz	42
Santa Rosa	Sonoma	42
South Lake Tahoe	El Dorado	42
Stockton	San Joaquin	38
Sunnyvale	Sunnyvale city limits	42
Tahoe City	Placer	42
Ventura County	Ventura County	38
Victorville	Victorville city limits	34
Visalia	Tulare	38
Yosemite National Park	Mariposa	46

City	County	Amount
COLORADO		
Adams County	Adams County	38
Arapahoe County	Arapahoe County	38
Aspen	Pitkin	46
Boulder	Boulder	42
Colorado Springs	El Paso	38
Cortez	Montezuma	34
Denver	Denver	42
Durango	La Plata	38
Fort Collins	Larimer (except Loveland)	34
Glenwood Springs	Garfield	38
Gunnison	Gunnison	34
Jefferson County	Jefferson County 34Keystone/Silverthorne Summit	38
Montrose	Montrose	34
Pueblo	Pueblo	34
Steamboat Springs	Routt	38
Telluride	San Miguel	46
Vail	Eagle	46
CONNECTICUT		
Bridgeport	Bridgeport city limits	34
Danbury	Fairfield (except Bridgeport)	38
Hartford	Hartford, Middlesex	42
Lakeville	Litchfield	38
Middlesex County	Middlesex County	34
New Haven	New Haven	38

continued on next page

City	County	Amount
New London	New London city limits	34
Salisbury	Litchfield	46
Vernon	Tolland	34
DELAWARE		
Dover	Kent	34
Lewes	Sussex	42
Wilmington	New Castle	34
DISTRICT OF COLUMBIA		
Washington, D.C.	Virginia counties of:	46
	Arlington, Loudoun, and Fairfax AND the cities of Alexandria, Fairfax, and Falls Church	
	Maryland counties of:	
	Prince George and Montgomery	
FLORIDA		
Altamonte Springs	Seminole	38
Boca Raton	Boca Raton city limits	38
Bradenton	Manatee	34
Cocoa Beach	Brevard	34
Daytona Beach	Volusia	34
Delray Beach	Delray Beach city limits	42
Fort Lauderdale	Broward	42
Fort Myers	Lee	42
Fort Walton Beach	Okaloosa	38
Gainesville	Alachua	34
Gulf Breeze	Santa Rosa	38
Jacksonville	Duval; Naval Station, Mayport	34

City	County	Amount
Key West	Monroe	46
Kissimmee	Osceola	34
Lakeland	Polk	34
Miami	Dade	42
Naples	Collier	38
Orlando	Orange	42
Palm Beach	Palm Beach city limits	46
Palm Beach Gardens	Palm Beach city limits	38
Palm Beach Shores	Palm Beach	38
Panama City	Bay	38
Pensacola	Escambia	34
Punta Gorda	Charlotte	38
Saint Augustine	Saint Johns	38
Sarasota	Sarasota	38
Singer Island	Singer Island city limits	38
Stuart	Martin	38
Tallahassee	Leon	34
Tampa/St. Petersburg	Hillsborough, Pinellas	38
Vero Beach	Indian River	38
West Palm Beach	Palm Beach	38
GEORGIA		
Albany	Dougherty	34
Athens	Clarke	34
Atlanta	Fulton	38
Augusta	Richmond	38
Cobb County	Cobb County	34
Columbus	Muscogee	34

continued on next page

City	County	Amount
Conyers	Rockdale	34
DeKalb County	DeKalb County	34
Macon	Bibb	34
Savannah	Chatham	38
Warner Robins	Houston	34
IDAHO		
Boise	Ada	38
Coeur d'Alene	Kootenai	34
Ketchum/Sun Valley	Blaine	42
McCall	Valley	38
Stanley	Custer	38
ILLINOIS		
Champaign/Urbana	Champaign	34
Chicago	Cook	46
DeCatur	Macon	34
Du Page County	Du Page County	38
Lake County	Lake County	42
Peoria	Peoria	38
Rockford	Winnebago	34
Springfield	Sangamon	38
INDIANA		
Bloomington/Crane	Monroe, Martin	34
Carmel	Hamilton	38
Fort Wayne	Allen	34
Indianapolis	Marion; Fort Benjamin Harrison	42
Michigan City	La Porte	34
Muncie	Delaware	34
Nashville	Brown	38

City	County	Amount
South Bend	St. Joseph	34
Valparaiso/Burlington Beach	Porter	34
IOWA		
Bettendorf/Davenport	Scott	34
Cedar Rapids	Linn	34
Des Moines	Polk	34
KANSAS		
Overland Park	Johnson	38
Wichita	Sedgwick	38
KENTUCKY		
Covington	Kenton	38
Florence	Boone	34
Lexington	Fayette	34
Louisville	Jefferson	38
LOUISIANA		
Baton Rouge	East Baton Rouge	38
Bossier City	Bossier	34
Gonzales	Ascension	34
Lake Charles	Calcasieu	34
New Orleans	Jefferson, Orleans, Plaquemines, St. Bernard	42
Slidell	St. Tammany	34
St. Francisville	West Feliciana	38
MAINE		
Bar Harbor	Hancock	38
Bath	Sagadahoc	34
Kennebunk	York	38
Kittery	Portsmouth Naval Shipyard	34

continued on next page

City	County	Amount
Portland	Cumberland	38
Rockport	Knox	42
Wiscasset	Lincoln	38
MARYLAND		
Annapolis	Anne Arundel	42
Baltimore	Baltimore, Harford	42
Columbia	Howard	42
Easton	Talbot	34
Frederick	Frederick	38
Grasonville	Queen Annes	38
Hagerstown	Washington	34
Lexington Park/St. Inigoes/ Leonardtown	St. Marys	34
Montgomery County	Montgomery County	38
Ocean City	Worcester	46
Prince George County	Prince George County	38
Saint Michaels	Talbot	42
Salisbury	Wicomico	34
MASSACHUSETTS		
Andover	Essex	38
Boston	Suffolk	46
Cambridge	Middlesex	38
Falmouth	Falmouth city limits	38
Hyannis	Barnstable	38
Martha's Vineyard	Dukes	46
Nantucket	Nantucket	46
New Bedford	New Bedford city limits	34
Northampton	Hampshire	34

City	County	Amount
Pittsfield	Berkshire	38
Plymouth	Plymouth	34
Quincy	Norfolk	38
Springfield	Hampden	34
Worcester	Worcester	34
MICHIGAN		
Ann Arbor	Washtenaw	38
Auburn Hillsq	Oakland	38
Charlevoix	Charlevoix	38
Detroit	Wayne	46
East Lansing	Ingham	38
Flint	Genessee	34
Frankenmuth	Saginaw	34
Frankfort	Benzie	34
Gaylord	Otsego	38
Grand Rapids	Kent	34
Grayling	Crawford	34
Holland	Ottawa	34
Lansing	Ingham	34
Leland	Leelanau	34
Mackinac Island	Mackinac	46
Midland	Midland	34
Mount Pleasant	Isabella	34
Petoskey	Emmet	38
Pontiac	Oakland	34
Sault Ste. Marie	Chippewa	34
South Haven	Van Buren	34

continued on next page

City	County	Amount
Traverse City	Grand Traverse	42
Troy	Troy city limits	38
Warren	Macomb	34
MINNESOTA		
Anoka County	Anoka County	34
Dakota County	Dakota County	34
Duluth	St. Louis	42
Minneapolis/St. Paul	Ankoa, Hennepin, Ramsey; Detachment BRAVO at Fort Snelling, Rosemount	46
Rochester	Olmsted	34
MISSISSIPPI		
	Hancock	38
Bay St. Louis		
Biloxi	Biloxi city limits	38
Gulfport	Harrison	34
Jackson	Hinds	34
Pascagoula	Jackson	34
Ridgeland	Madison	38
Robinsonville	Tunica	34
Vicksburg	Warren	34
MISSOURI		
Branson	Taney	34
Cape Girandeau	Cape Girandeau	34
Jefferson City	Cole	34
Kansas City	Clay, Jackson, Platte	42
Lake Ozark	Miller	34
Osage Beach	Camden	34
Platte County	Platte County	34

City	County	Amount
St. Charles County	St. Charles County	34
St. Louis	St. Louis	46
MONTANA		
Polson/Kalispell	Flathead, Lake	34
West Yellowstone Park	Gallatin	34
NEBRASKA		
Lincoln	Lancaster	34
Omaha	Douglas	38
NEVADA		
Incline Village	Washoe	38
Las Vegas	Clark; Nellis AFB	38
Reno	Washoe	38
Stateline	Douglas	42
Winnemucca	Humboldt	34
NEW HAMPSHIRE		
Concord	Merrimack	34
Conway	Carroll	38
Hanover	Grafto; Sullivan	42
Laconia	Belknap	34
Manchester	Hillsborough	34
Portsmouth/Newington	Rockingham; Pease AFB	42
Sullivan County	Sullivan County	34
NEW JERSEY		
Atlantic City	Atlantic	42
Belle Mead	Somerset	38
Bergen County	Bergen County	38
Cape May	Cape May	42
Cherry Hill/Camden/Moorestown	Camden, Burlington	42

continued on next page

City	County	Amount
Eatontown	Monmouth	38
Edison	Middlesex	34
Flemington	Hunterdon	34
Freehold	Freehold city limits	34
Hudson County	Hudson County	38
Millville	Cumberland	38
Newark	Bergen, Essex, Hudson, Passaic, Union	42
Ocean City	Ocean City city limits	38
Parsippany/Dover	Morris; Picatinny Arsenal	38
Passaic County	Passaic County	38
Piscataway	Middlesex	38
Princeton	Princeton city limits	3842
Tom's River	Ocean	38
Trenton	Mercer	38
Union County	Union County	38
NEW MEXICO		
Albuquerque	Bernalillo	38
Los Alamos	Los Alamos	34
Santa Fe	Santa Fe	46
Taos	Taos	34
NEW YORK		
Albany	Albany	42
Batavia	Genesee	34
Binghampton	Broom	38
The Bronx	The Bronx	46
Brooklyn	Brooklyn	46
Buffalo	Erie	38

City	County	Amount
Corning	Steuben	38
Elmira	Chemung	34
Glens Falls	Warren	34
Great Neck	Nassau (part of)	42
Ithaca	Tompkins	34
Kingston	Ulster	38
Lake Placid	Essex	38
Manhattan	Manhattan	46
Nassau County	Nassau County (other than Great Neck)	46
Niagara Falls	Niagara	38
Nyack/Palisdades	Rockland	38
Plattsburgh	Clinton	34
Poughkeepsie	Dutchess	38
Queens Borough	Queens	46
Rochester	Monroe	42
Saratoga Springs	Saratoga	38
Schenectady	Schenectady	34
Staten Island	Richmond	42
Suffolk County	Suffolk County	38
Syracuse	Onondaga	34
Tarrytown/White Plains	Westchester	42
Utica	Oneida	34
Waterloo/Romulus	Seneca	34
Watkins Glen	Schuyler	34
West Point	Orange	34
NORTH CAROLINA		
Asheville	Buncombe	34

continued on next page

City	County	Amount
Chapel Hill	Orange	34
Charlotte	Mecklenburg	38
Durham/Research Triangle Park	Durham	42
Fayetteville	Cumberland	34
Greensboro	Guilford	38
Kill Devil/	Dare	34
New Bern/	Craven	34
Raleigh	Wake	38
Wilmington	New Hanover	34
Winston-Salem	Forsyth	38
NORTH DAKOTA		
All locations		30
OHIO		
Akron	Summit	38
Cambridge	Guernsey	34
Canton	Stark	34
Cincinnati	Hamilton	46
Cleveland	Cuyahoga	42
Columbus	Franklin	38
Dayton	Montgomery Wright-Patterson AFB	38
Elyria	Lorain	34
Fairborn	Greene	34
Geneva/Hamilton	Ashtabula/Butler	34
Lancaster	Fairfield	34
Port Clinton/Oakharbor	Ottawa	34
Sandusky	Erie	38
Springfield	Clark	34
Toledo	Lucas	38

City	County	Amount
OKLAHOMA		
Oklahoma City	Oklahoma	38
Tulsa	Tulsa	38
OREGON		
Ashland	Jackson	42
Beaverton	Washington	38
Bend	Deschutes	38
Clackamas	Clackamas	34
Coos Bay	Coos	34
Crater Lake	City of Crater Lake	38
Eugene	Lane	38
Florence	Florence city limits	34
Gold Beach	Curry	34
Lincoln City/Newport	Lincoln	34
Portland	Multnomah	38
Salem	Marion	34
Seaside	Clatsop	34
PENNSYLVANIA		
Allentown	Lehigh	38
Chester/Radnor/Essington	Delaware	34
Gettysburg	Adams	34
Harrisburg	Dauphin	42
Hersey	Hersey city limits	42
King of Prussia/Ft. Washington	Montgomery	42
Lancaster	Lancaster	38
Malvern/Downington/Valley Forge	Chester	38
Mechanicsburg	Cumberland	34
Philadelphia	Philadelphia	46

continued on next page

City	County	Amount
Pittsburgh	Allegheny	46
Reading	Berks	38
Warminster	Bucks; Naval Air Development Center	42
Wayne	Wayne city limits	42
RHODE ISLAND		
Block Island	Block Island only	42
East Greenwich	Kent; Naval Construction Center in Davisville	38
Newport	Newport	42
Providence	Providence	42
SOUTH CAROLINA		
Charleston	Charleston, Berkeley	42
Columbia	Richland	38
Greenville	Greenville	38
Hilton Head	Beaufort	42
Myrtle Beach	Horry; Myrtle Beach AFB	42
Spartanburg	Spartanburg	34
SOUTH DAKOTA		
Custer	Custer	34
Rapid City	Pennington	34
TENNESSEE		
Chattanooga	Hamilton	34
Gatlinburg	Sevier	38
Knoxville	Knox County, City of Oak Ridge	38
Memphis	Shelby	38
Nashville	Davidson	42
Townsend	Blount	34

City	County	Amount
TEXAS		
Arlington	Tarrant	34
Austin	Travis	38
Brownsville	Cameron	34
College Station	Brazos	34
Corpus Christi	Nueces	38
Dallas	Dallas	46
El Paso	El Paso	38
Fort Worth	Fort Worth city limits	38
Galveston	Galveston	42
Houston	Harris; LBJ Space Center; Ellington AFB	42
Laredo	Webb	34
Lubbock	Lubbock	34
McAllen	Hidalgo	34
Odessa	Ector	34
Plano	Collin	34
San Antonio	Bexar	42
South Padre Island	Cameron	38
Tyler	Smith	34
UTAH		
Cedar City	Iron	34
Layton/Ogden	Davis and Weber	34
Moab	Grand	34
Park City	Summit	46
Provo	Utah	38
Salt Lake City	Salt Lake Dugway Proving Ground; Tooele Army Depot	42

continued on next page

City	County	Amount
VERMONT		
Burlington/St. Albans	Chittenden and Franklin	38
Manchester	Bennington	42
Middlebury	Addison	38
Rutland	Rutland	34
White River Junction	Windsor	34
VIRGINIA		
Alexandria	Alexandria	42
Arlington	Arlington	42
Blacksburg	Montgomery	34
Charlottesville	Albemarle	42
Chesterfield County	Chesterfield County	38
Loudoun County	Loudoun County	38
Lynchburg	Campbell	38
Manassas	Prince William	34
Fairfax County	Fairfax County	42
Richmond	Chesterfield, Henrico; Defense Supply Center	38
Roanoke	Roanoke	34
Shenandoah County	Shenandoah County	34
Virginia Beach	Virginia Beach (Norfolk, Portsmouth, Chesapeake)	34
Wallops Island	Accomack	34
Williamsburg	Williamsburg	38
Wintergreen	Nelson	46
Woolbridge	Woolbridge city limits	38
WASHINGTON		
Anacortes	Skagit, Island	38
Bellingham	Whatcom	34

City	County	Amount
Bremerton	Kitsap	34
Everett	Snohomish	38
Friday Harbor	San Juan	42
Lynnwood	Snohomish	34
Ocean Shores	Grays Harbor	38
Olympia/Tumwater	Thurston	38
Port Angeles	Clallam	38
Port Townsend	Jefferson	34
Seattle	King	34
Sequim	Clallam	34
Spokane	Spokane	38
Tacoma	Pierce	38
Vancouver	Clark	38
WEST VIRGINIA		
Berkeley Springs	Morgan	34
Charleston	Kanawha	38
Harpers Ferry	Jefferson	34
Morgantown	Monongalia	34
Parkersburg	Wood	34
Sheperdstown	Sheperdstown city limits	38
Wheeling	Ohio	34
WISCONSIN		
Brookfield	Waukesha	38
Eau Claire	Eau Claire	34
Green Bay	Brown	34
Lake Geneva	Walworth	38
Madison	Dane	38

continued on next page

City	County	Amount
Milwaukee	Milwaukee	42
Oshkosh	Winnebago	34
Rhinelander/Minocqua	Oneida	38
Sturgeon Bay	Door	34
Wisconsin Dells	Columbia	38
WYOMING		
Jackson	Teton	42

The standard meal allowances are listed in IRS Publication 1542, Per Diem Rates, which can be found on the IRS web site at www.irs.ustreas.gov. Per diem travel rates are also listed at www.policyworks.gov. These standard meal allowances do not apply outside the continental United States. Thus, they do not apply to travel in Alaska, Hawaii, or any foreign countries. However, there is a standard federal rate for foreign travel that is published monthly in Maximum Travel Per Diem Allowances for Foreign Travel, which is available from the Superintendent of Documents (U.S. Government Printing Office, P.O. Box 371954, Pittsburgh, PA 15250-7954). Foreign rates can also be obtained from the U.S. State Department at www.state.gov/www.perdiems/index.html.

You cannot use the standard meal allowance if you are related to your employer. You are considered "related" if your employer is your brother, sister (half or whole), spouse, parent, grandparent, child, or grandchild. You are also considered related if you own, directly or indirectly, more than 10 percent of the value of your employer's stock. Indirect ownership arises when you have an interest in a corporation, partnership, trust, or estate that owns stock in your employer's corporation or if family members own stock in your employer's corporation. However, you can use the standard meal allowance if you are self-employed.

As mentioned above, there is a percentage limit applied to the deduction for meal costs. Generally, the deduction is limited to 50 percent of meal costs (but there is an exception for those who are subject to the hours of service limitations under the Department of Transportation, as explained later in this chapter). Thus, if you spend $100 on meals while traveling away from home (and you're not subject to DOT hours of service limits), only $50 is deductible. The 50-percent limit also applies to the standard meal allowance. You will see that this limit is taken into account on the forms you use for deducting meal costs. For example, self-employed individuals filing Schedule C will note that the total cost of meals is entered and then the 50-percent limit is applied so that only one-half of meal costs is deductible.

Other deductible travel costs While you are away from home on business, you may incur a number of miscellaneous or incidental travel expenses. These expenses are deductible in full. They include, for example, the reasonable cost of cleaning and laundering your clothes and tips you pay for services rendered in connection with any deductible expenses (such as a meal, a taxi ride, or a bellhop). You may also incur any number of miscellaneous expenses that are deductible—telephone charges to talk to your office, fees to send or receive a business fax, computer rental fees, or public stenographer's fees.

Travel with Another Person

If you take your spouse, child, or another person on a business trip, the costs related to that person generally are not deductible. The only way in which the costs are deductible is if that person works for you, there is a bona fide business reason for the travel, and the costs would have been deductible had they been incurred by someone who was not accompanying you. If the person provides only incidental services (such as typing notes or acting as assistant), his or her travel expenses are not deductible.

How do you distinguish between expenses that are yours, and deductible, from those of your companion, which are not deductible? Clearly, the full cost of the other person's travel fare and meals is not deductible. In the case of lodging costs, if you are sharing a room, you must determine what you would have paid for a single, rather than a double, accommodation. For the most part, this is not simply half the cost. You may be able to deduct two-thirds or more of the cost of lodging.

There is a way for a business to turn nondeductible spousal travel costs into deductible costs. If your corporation treats spousal travel costs as additional compensation to you as an employee, then the corporation can claim a deduction for the costs as compensation rather than as travel and entertainment costs. In most cases, this alternative does not make much sense from your perspective, since it only shifts the tax burden from your corporation to you. However, if your personal tax picture is such that additional compensation will not result in additional tax, consider this alternative.

Major and Minor Job Locations

Some individuals work in more than one location. They may, for example, have a major job in one city and conduct some minor business in another. The cost of travel between the two jobs is deductible.

EXAMPLE: An airline pilot based in Minneapolis also flew for the National Guard out of Sioux Falls, South Dakota. His family lived in Sioux Falls. The IRS disallowed his travel expenses from Minneapolis to Sioux Falls, but a district court allowed the deduction. The fact that he derived some pleasure from the trip to Sioux Falls was secondary to the business nature of the trip. He deducted travel costs to that city only when he was required to fly there for Guard Duty.

Part Business—Part Pleasure

If you combine business with pleasure, only part of your costs may be deductible. If your trip was primarily for business, then the portion of the travel costs related to business are deductible. This means that the full amount of airfare may be deductible. Meals and lodging for the days spent on business are also deductible.

EXAMPLE: You travel from New York to San Diego for five days of business. You spend two more days sightseeing at the zoo and other attractions before returning to New York. All of your airfare is deductible. Five-sevenths of your lodging and food costs are also deductible. Any incidental expenses related to business are deductible. The cost of sightseeing and other personal expenses are not deductible.

Whether the time spent is primarily for business is determined by the facts and circumstances. There is no hard-and-fast rule.

If you stay over on a Saturday at a business location in order to obtain a reduced airfare, the stay is treated as business and the cost of lodging for that stay is fully deductible. This is so even though you spend the time on personal matters.

If the trip is primarily for personal reasons but you do conduct some business, you can deduct the direct costs of the business activities but no part of the travel costs.

EXAMPLE: You spend a week at a resort location. One afternoon you make a business appointment and take a client out to lunch. None of your airfare to the resort or your lodging costs is deductible. You may, however, deduct the cost of the business lunch (assuming it meets general deductibility requirements).

FOREIGN TRAVEL

Entirely for Business

If you travel abroad entirely on business, all of your travel costs are deductible. (Meal and entertainment costs are still subject to the 50-percent limit.)

If your trip is considered to be entirely for business, then even if some time is spent sightseeing or on other personal activities, all of your transportation expenses are still deductible. There are special rules for determining whether your trip is considered to be "entirely" for business. You are treated as having spent your entire trip on business if you meet any of the following four rules:

1. You do not have substantial control over arranging your trip, so travel is presumed to be entirely for business. You do not have control if you are an employee who is reimbursed for travel and are not related to your employer nor a managing executive (someone whose actions are not subject to veto by another). As a small business owner, it is virtually impossible to satisfy this rule. However, you can still fall within one of other rules.

2. You are outside the United States for a week or less (seven or fewer consecutive days). In counting days, do not count the day you leave the United States, but do count the day of your return.

   EXAMPLE: You fly from Washington, D.C., to London on Sunday, arriving at Heathrow Airport on Monday morning. You work until Friday morning, then spend Friday and Saturday sightseeing and shopping. You fly out on Saturday night, arriving back in Washington on Sunday morning. You are considered to have been abroad for seven days (Monday through Sunday). All of your airfare is deductible. The cost of lodging, meals, and incidentals for the business days are also deductible, but meals are subject to the 50-percent limit.

3. You spend less than 25 percent of the time outside the United States on personal activities, regardless of the length of the stay abroad. In counting days for this rule, count both the day you leave and the day you return.

   EXAMPLE: You fly on Sunday from Chicago to Paris, where you spend 14 days on business and five days on personal matters. You spend one day flying in each direction. Your total time abroad is 21 days (14 days for business, five days for personal activities, and two days for travel). Since the time spent on nonbusiness activities is less than 25 percent of the total travel time abroad (five days personal/21 days total), you may treat the trip as entirely for business. Thus, the entire cost of the airfare is deductible. You may treat the days of travel as business days so that 16/21 of the lodging and meal costs (subject to the 50-percent limit on meals) are deductible.

4. You can show that a personal vacation or another personal reason was not the major consideration in arranging the trip. You can use this rule even though you do have substantial control over arranging the trip.

Primarily for Business

If your travel abroad is not treated as "entirely" for business (because you do not meet any of the four rules), you may still deduct some business expenses if the trip is "primarily" for business. There is no mechanical rule to establish that the trip is primarily for business. However, if you can show a valid business reason for the trip, you can deduct the portion of business expenses allocable to the business part of the trip, including the allocable portion of transportation costs.

EXAMPLE: You fly from Boston to Rome, where you spend 10 days on business and five days on personal matters. You spend one day flying in each direction. Your total time abroad is 17 days (10 days for business, five for personal activities, and two days travel time). You had substantial control over arranging your trip, spent more than a week abroad, more than 25 percent of your time on personal activities, and cannot establish that a personal vacation was not a major consideration. Thus, you cannot show the trip was "entirely" for business. However, you can show the trip was "primarily" for business. You spent the greater part of the time on business and arranged the trip accordingly. In this instance, 12/17 of the cost of the airfare and other expenses are deductible business costs; the balance is treated as nondeductible personal expenses.

Counting business days   In counting days for business when travel is primarily for that purpose, travel days are treated as business days. However, extra days of travel for personal activities, such as side trips, are not counted. You can also treat any day your presence is required at a business meeting or activity as a business day even if you spend the greater part of the day on personal activities. You can also treat as business days any days you wanted to spend on business but were prevented from doing so by circumstances beyond your control (such as weather, strikes, or civil unrest). Saturday, Sunday, and holidays are treated as business days if they fall between two business days. Thus, if you work on Friday and Monday, you count the weekend days as business days. Weekends following the close of your business activities are not treated as business days if you choose to stay on for personal purposes. However, overnight Saturday stays to obtain a reduced airfare are treated as business even when the time is spent on personal activities.

Primarily for Vacation

If you travel abroad primarily for vacation but attend some business or professional seminar, you may not deduct any portion of the trip as a business expense. You may, however, deduct the cost of the seminar (registration fees and other related expenses) as a business expense.

EXAMPLE: Your professional association sponsors a two-week trip abroad. It holds two three-hour seminars during the trip and awards a Certificate in Continuing Education to those who attend the seminars. The entire cost of the trip is a nondeductible personal expense, as it is viewed as primarily for vacation. However, the registration fees for the seminars are deductible.

Conventions

Travel expenses to conventions held within the United States are deductible if you can show that your attendance benefits your business. The fact that you are appointed or elected to be a delegate to the convention does not, by itself, mean you can deduct expenses; you must show that attendance is connected to your business. You can do this by showing that the convention agenda is related to the active conduct of your business. The same rule applies to both employees and self-employed persons.

Foreign Conventions

The expenses of attending a convention outside the North American area (see list below) are not deductible unless the meeting is directly related to your business and it is reasonable to hold it outside the North American area.

North American Area

American Samoa	Kingman Reef
Baker Island	Marshall Islands
Barbados	Mexico
Bermuda	Micronesia
Canada	Midway Islands
Costa Rica	Northern Mariana Islands
Dominica	Palau
Dominican Republic	Palmyra
Grenada	Puerto Rico
Guam	Saint Lucia
Honduras	Trinidad and Tobago
Howland Island	United States
Jamaica	U.S. Virgin Islands
Jarvis Island	Wake Island
Johnston Island	

A number of facts and circumstances are taken into account in showing that it is reasonable to hold the convention outside the North American area:

- The purpose of the meeting and the activities taking place at the meeting

- The purposes and activities of the sponsoring organizations or groups

- The residences of the active members of the sponsoring organization and the places at which the meetings of the sponsoring organizations or groups have been held or will be held

- Other relevant factors

Cruise Ships

The cost of business conventions or meetings held on a cruise ship is limited. The maximum deduction per year is $2,000. In order to get this deduction, a number of requirements must be met:

1. The meeting must be directly related to your business.

2. The cruise ship must be a vessel registered in the United States. (All ships that sail are considered cruise ships.)

3. All of the ship's ports of call must be located in the United States or in U.S. possessions.

4. You must attach a written statement to your return showing the days of the cruise, the number of hours devoted to business, and a program of scheduled business activities.

5. You must also attach a written statement to your return signed by an officer of the organization or group sponsoring the meeting that shows the schedule of the business activities of each day of the meeting and the number of hours you attended.

LIVING AWAY FROM HOME ON TEMPORARY ASSIGNMENTS

If you work in a location other than your regular place of business and are forced to live away from your home (because the distance is too great to reasonably expect that you would travel back and forth each day), then not only the cost of your transportation to the temporary assignment but also living expenses are deductible.

Definition   *Temporary assignment*   An assignment away from the area of your tax home that is realistically expected to last for no more than a year and does, in fact, end at that time.

An assignment that is expected to last for more than a year, or one that does in fact last for more than a year, is considered indefinite. Also, a series of short jobs in the same location that, taken together, last more than a year are considered an indefinite assignment. Probationary work is also treated as indefinite. Thus, for example, if you relocate with the understanding that your job will be permanent if your work is satisfactory, the job is considered indefinite. Transportation to the location of the indefinite assignment from your general area of your tax home is deductible; personal living expenses are not.

Change in Job Assignments

Suppose your assignment gets extended or shortened. How does this affect whether the assignment is treated as temporary or indefinite?

Situation 1   You are sent out of town on a job assignment expected to last for 10 months but is extended and in fact lasts for 14 months. As long as the initial expectation of 10 months was reasonable, your living expenses are deductible until the time that the expectation changed. Thus, if at the end of 10 months the assignment projection changed, expenses for the first 10 months are deductible. If, however, at the end of six months the assignment projection changed, only expenses for the first six months are deductible.

Situation 2   You are sent out of town on a job assignment expected to last 14 months but in fact is shortened and lasts only 10 months. Since the original expectation of the job length exceeded one year, no part of the living expenses is deductible. The entire assignment is treated as indefinite even though it did in fact end within a year.

Remember, you must have a tax home to be away from when deducting living expenses on temporary assignments. If all your assignments are away and you have no tax home, no living expenses will be allowed.

EXAMPLE: An engineering consultant in Florida took temporary engineering assignments for a period of three years in five states as well as in his home state. During this time he maintained a home office in his apartment, where he returned after each assignment for periods of four to six months at a time, and he continued to seek permanent employment there. The IRS argued that he was an itinerant, so his expenses were not deductible. The

Tax Court disagreed and found his Florida home to be his tax home. He needed to maintain a permanent address and business number to obtain consulting jobs. He always returned there between assignments and never stopped seeking permanent employment there.

What Expenses Are Deductible

If a job assignment is temporary, then personal living expenses—rent, utilities, food, and other expenses—are deductible. The reason for this rule: Congress recognized that if you are required to be away from home on a temporary basis, you will have to incur duplicative living expenses, since it would be unreasonable to expect you to relocate for that short period of time. However, if the job assignment is indefinite, it would be reasonable to expect you to relocate and there would be no need for duplicative living expenses. If you do move to a new location, the cost of moving expenses may be deductible (see Chapter 19). If you are on a temporary assignment and return home on weekends, holidays, or visits, the time at home is not treated as away from home and the cost of your lodging at home is not deductible. The cost of your lodging at the temporary work site, however, continues to be deductible. Thus, for example, if you are living away from home in a motel and return home on a weekend but must pay for the motel room anyway, that cost is deductible. The cost of meals on a return trip home is deductible only to the extent that the cost of meals away would have been deductible. The cost of travel from the temporary assignment home and the return trip is also deductible.

MEAL AND ENTERTAINMENT EXPENSES

If you entertain your client, customer, or employee, the cost of your expenses is deductible, subject to the 50-percent limit discussed below. Entertainment may be an important way for you to generate business, create goodwill, and thank employees for a job well done. You may spend a considerable amount of time and expense wining and dining. Be sure to understand the rules to make your costs deductible to the fullest extent possible. Keep in mind that the area of meals and entertainment expenses attracts particular attention from the IRS, but if you meet the requirements for deductibility, your deductions will withstand IRS scrutiny.

General Rules on Deducting Meal and Entertainment Expenses

In order to be deductible as a meal and entertainment expense, an expense must be:

1. An ordinary and necessary business expense, and

2. Able to qualify under a directly related test or an associated test discussed below.

> **Definition** *Ordinary and necessary business expense* An ordinary expense is one that is common and accepted in your business. A necessary expense is one that is helpful and appropriate to your business. To be necessary, an expense need not be indispensable.

The Directly Related Test

You satisfy the directly related test if you can show that the main purpose of the entertainment activity was the active conduct of business and that you did, in fact, engage in business during the entertainment period. You must have more than a general expectation of deriving income or some other business benefit from the activity at some future time. You need not devote more time to business than entertainment in order to satisfy this test. You simply have to demonstrate that all the facts, including the nature of the business transacted and the reasons for conducting business during an entertainment, support a business purpose. Nor do you need to show that business income or some other business benefit actually resulted from a specific entertainment event.

You will be presumed to have failed the directly related test if you are on a hunting, skiing, or fishing trip or on yachts or other pleasure boats unless you can show otherwise. Other locations that are presumed to have failed the directly related test include nightclubs, golf courses, theaters, and sporting events.

Entertainment in a clear business setting is presumed to meet the directly related test.

EXAMPLE: Entertainment in a hospitality room or suite at a convention where your business products are on display is in a clear business setting.

Goodwill is presumed to be created through this entertainment in a clear business setting.

EXAMPLE: A price rebate on the sale of your products can be entertainment provided in a clear business setting. Thus, if you own a restaurant and offer a free meal to a customer or supplier, this entertainment in a clear business setting is directly related to your business and is deductible.

EXAMPLE: Where the entertainment itself is of a clear business nature but there is no personal or social relationship between you and the person or persons entertained, the costs are treated as directly related to your business. For example, if you entertain business leaders at the opening of a shopping mall in order to gain publicity, the cost is treated as a deductible entertainment expense.

You bear a heavy burden of proof when the entertainment is held in a place where there are substantial distractions that prevent the possibility of actively conducting any business. The entertainment is presumed to fail the directly related test. Substantial distractions are present at nightclubs, theaters, sporting events, and social gatherings (cocktail parties or meetings that include persons other than business associates). You can, however, overcome the presumption by showing that you engaged in a substantial business discussion during the entertainment despite the distractions.

Associated Test

If you cannot meet the higher standard of "directly related," you may still be able to show that the entertainment is associated with the conduct of your business. This test requires showing that the expense is associated with your business and directly precedes or follows a substantial business discussion. You must have a clear business purpose for having the entertainment expense. This includes entertainment to get new business or encourage continued business with existing clients or customers.

How do you know if a business discussion is "substantial"? There is no quantitative way to show this. There is no prescribed amount of time you must spend meeting or discussing business, and you do not have to devote more time to business than to entertainment. You do not even have to discuss business during the entertainment itself. Whether the entertainment meets the associated test depends on the facts and circumstances of the situation. You must be able to show that you actually held a business discussion to get income or other business benefit. Goodwill entertainment is considered to satisfy the associated test.

If the entertainment is held on the same day as a business discussion, it is treated as held preceding or following a substantial business discussion.

EXAMPLE: During working hours, a customer visits your offices and you discuss business for some time. That evening after your office is closed, you take your customer to the theater. This satisfies the associated test, since you held a substantial business discussion preceding the entertainment.

Where the business discussion is not held on the same day as the entertainment, all the facts are taken into account in determining whether the associated test is met. Factors considered are the place, date, and duration of the business discussion. For example, if you or your customers are out of town, the dates of arrival and departure may affect entertainment expenses.

EXAMPLE: A customer flies in from out of town on Tuesday afternoon. You take her to the theater that evening and meet with her in your office on the following morning, at which time you hold a substantial business discussion. The associated test is met in this instance.

Other Requirements

In addition to meeting the directly related or associated test, you must show that the cost of the entertainment was not "lavish or extravagant." There are no dollar figures used in making this determination; rather, it is based on the facts and circumstances. However, no deduction is allowed for fees paid to scalpers, ticket agents, or ticket brokers for tickets to theater, sporting, or other events. Only the face value of the ticket is deductible. Also, the cost of skyboxes and other private luxury boxes at a sports arena is limited. These boxes generally are rented for a season or a series of events, such as playoff games or a World Series. Where the cost covers more than one event, you cannot deduct more than the total of the face values of nonluxury box seats times the number of seats in the box. Then the 50-percent limit applies (see below).

EXAMPLE: You pay $1,200 for a skybox for two playoff games. The skybox seats 10 people. The cost of a 10-seat nonluxury box seat for each game is $200. Your deductible amount is limited to $400 ($200 × 2 events). Then it is subject to the 50-percent limit. (Had the box been rented for only one event at a cost of $600, then the full cost of the skybox, subject to the 50-percent limit, would have been deductible.)

Food, beverages, and other separately stated charges related to the skyboxes are separately deductible (subject to the 50-percent limit discussed below).

Home Entertainment

If you entertain business associates, customers, or employees at your home, can you deduct your expenses? The answer depends on whether you discuss specific business during the course of the dinner or other entertainment event. Business dinners may be conducive to business discussions. Other types of social gatherings, such as pool parties, may not be as conducive to business discussions and may raise questions with the IRS. It may be helpful to keep the guest list to a minimum (no more than 12) in order to be able to hold discussions with all guests. If you have a larger group, it may be difficult to show that you had business discussions with each guest.

If you do entertain at home, do not combine business with pleasure. The presence of nonbusiness guests may support the conclusion that the gathering was not for business reasons and that business was not discussed. Taxpayers have not fared well in proving that parties for personal events, such as a child's wedding, birthday, or bar mitzvah, were held for business even though business guests attended.

Limit

There is no dollar limit on what you can spend for meal and entertainment expenses. (Remember, though, that there is a "lavish or extravagant" limit.) However, only a portion of your costs is deductible. Meals and entertainment expenses generally are deductible only to the extent of 50 percent of cost. The 50-percent limit applies to meals eaten while traveling away from home even if they are paid with a per diem reimbursement rate.

LEGISLATIVE ALERT

Congress is considering an increase in the percentage of deductible meal and entertainment expenses starting in 2005. If enacted, the deductible percentage would increase by 5 percent each year until it reached 80 percent by 2010.

The 50-percent limit does not necessarily apply to all business meals or entertainment. There are some important exceptions:

- Promotional activities.

  EXAMPLE: A real estate broker selling vacation property gave potential investors a free meal if they agreed to sit through a sales presentation. The IRS allowed the broker to deduct the full cost of the meals in this case, since they were made available to the general public as part of promotional activities.

- Meals paid for recreational, social, or similar activities primarily for the benefit of employees. This exception would apply, for example, to your cost of providing food at a company picnic.

- Food and beverages provided to employees as a tax-free de minimis fringe benefit. This exception would apply to your expenses of providing an employee cafeteria on your premises.

- For those in the transportation industry: Employees who are subject to Department of Transportation hours of service limitations are subject to an increased meal deduction for food and beverages consumed while away from home as follows:

Year	Deductible Percentage
1999	55%
2000–2001	60
2002–2003	65
2004–2005	70
2006–2007	75
2008 and later years	80

Impact of the 50-Percent Limit on Employees

The fact that the company cannot deduct 50 percent of its costs for meals and entertainment does not affect employees. Employees are not taxed on the nondeductible portion of meal and entertainment costs even though they receive a full reimbursement or an advance for these expenses.

Club Dues

You cannot deduct the cost of dues, including initiation fees, to clubs organized for pleasure, recreation, or other social purposes. For example, the cost of airline clubs is not deductible. However, dues to certain business, professional, and civic organizations continue to be deductible. These include:

- **Business organizations:** business leagues, trade associations, chambers of commerce, boards of trade and real estate boards, business lunch clubs

- **Professional organizations:** bar associations, medical associations

- **Civic organizations:** Kiwanis, Lions, Rotary, Civitan

If you pay club dues for an employee, you can turn what would otherwise be a nondeductible expense into a deductible one. You can treat the payment of club dues on behalf of an employee as additional compensation. In this way the business can claim a deduction for club dues as compensation, not as travel and entertainment costs.

This option applies only to club dues that would otherwise be deductible but for the ban on deductibility. Thus, it applies only if the club is used for business. For example, suppose a corporation pays the country club dues of an employee. The employee uses the club 100 percent for entertaining clients for business purposes. The corporation can elect to treat these dues as additional compensation to the employee. Of course, the employee cannot claim any offsetting deduction on his or her individual income tax return. If the country club is used solely for personal purposes, then the cost of dues is not subject to this election rule.

The election to treat club dues as additional compensation can be made on an employee-by-employee basis. Thus, if you own a corporation that pays club dues on behalf of yourself and other employees, the corporation can elect to treat the club dues as additional compensation to your other employees but not to yourself. If the corporation pays your club dues and elects to treat this as compensation to you, all you are really doing is shifting the tax burden from the corporation to you, something that may not have any net advantage. The corporation should weigh this election carefully before making it.

Spouses' Expenses

If you take your spouse or a friend with you on business entertainment or take a client's or customer's spouse along, are the spouse's expenses deductible? In general, the answer is no. However, if you can show that the purpose for including the spouse was clearly for business and not some social or personal purpose, the spouse's costs are deductible.

EXAMPLE: You entertain a business customer. Assume that the costs of entertaining the customer are clearly deductible. The customer's spouse joins you because it would be impractical to entertain the customer without the spouse. In this case, the cost of the spouse's entertainment is an ordinary and necessary business expense. If your spouse were to join the entertainment because the customer's spouse is along, your spouse's costs would also be deductible.

BUSINESS GIFTS

In the course of your business, you may give gifts to your dealers, distributors, customers, clients, and employees. The cost of business gifts is deductible, within limits. You may deduct only up to $25 per person per year. This rule applies to both direct and indirect gifts. An indirect gift includes a gift to a company that is intended for the eventual personal use of a particular person or a gift to a spouse or child of a business customer or client.

In using the $25 limit, do not count incidental costs, such as wrapping, insuring, or shipping the gifts. Also, do not count engraving on jewelry.

EXAMPLE: You give a $30 gift to client 1. You may deduct $25.

EXAMPLE: You give a $20 gift to client 2. You may deduct $20.

Exceptions

Certain gifts are not subject to the $25 limit. These include gifts of nominal value ($4 or less) with your company name imprinted on them that you distribute to a number of clients or customers. These gifts would include, for example, pens, plastic bags, kitchen magnets, and calendars. Thus, if you give a customer a $25 gift and also send a calendar, the value of the calendar (assuming it is below $4) is not taken into account. Both gifts are deductible. Another exception to the $25 rule includes signs, display racks, or other promotional material used on business premises. Thus, if you give a dealer a display rack to hold your items, the gift is a deductible business expense, regardless of cost.

When Is an Item an Entertainment Expense?

If you give an item that could be treated as either an entertainment expense or a business gift, how do you know how to classify it? The choice is yours. In making it, take into the fact that an entertainment expense is subject to a 50-percent limit, while a business gift is subject to the $25 limit. Thus, if you give tickets to the theater or a ball game and you do not go with the client or customer to the performance or event, you can choose to treat the cost as either an entertainment expense or a business gift.

EXAMPLE: You give your client two tickets to the ball game. The tickets cost $20 each. If you treat them as a business gift, you can deduct $25 ($40 business gift up to the $25 limit). However, if you treat the tickets as an entertainment expense, only $20 is deductible ($40 expense subject to the 50-percent limit).

If you treat an item as a business gift but want to change the treatment, you may do so within three years of the filing of your return by filing an amended return.

If you go with the client to the theater or sporting event, you must treat the cost of the tickets as an entertainment expense; you cannot treat it as a business gift. However, if the gift is one of food or beverage intended to be consumed by the client or customer at a later time, you must treat it as a business gift. Thus, if you give bottles of wine or liquor, they constitute business gifts.

REIMBURSEMENT ARRANGEMENTS

If an employer reimburses an employee for travel and entertainment expenses, how you arrange the reimbursement affects what the employer and employee can deduct.

No Reimbursement Arrangement

If an employee on salary has no reimbursement arrangement and is expected or required to pay for travel and entertainment costs by himself or herself, the employee can deduct the expenses on his or her individual income tax return. The business expenses are deductible as miscellaneous itemized deductions. This means that after applying all the limits discussed above, such as the 50-percent limit on meals and entertainment, costs are deductible only to the extent they exceed 2 percent of the employee's adjusted gross income. In this instance, the employee is responsible for recordkeeping of business expenses.

Accountable Plans

If an employer maintains an "accountable plan," the employee does not deduct any expenses. Instead, the employer pays for and deducts all costs. No reimbursements are reported as income to the employee.

A reimbursement arrangement is treated as an accountable plan if:

1. The expenses have a business connection.

2. The employee must adequately account to the employer for expenses. The employee must supply the employer with documentary evidence (canceled checks, receipts, or bills) of mileage, travel, and other business expenses, along with a statement of expense, an account book or diary, or a similar record in which expenses are entered at or near the time at which they were incurred. All amounts received from an employer must be documented. This includes not only cash advances but also amounts charged to an employer by credit card or other method. If you receive advances or reimbursements at per diem rates as discussed below, then you are considered to have adequately accounted for the amount of the expenses. You must still account for the time, place, and business purpose for the travel.

3. The employee must return to the employer within a reasonable period of time any excess reimbursements. Thus, for example, if an employer advances an employee $400 for a business trip and expenses totaled only $350, the employee must return the excess $50 within a reasonable period of time. A reasonable period of time depends on the facts and circumstances. However, it is automatically treated as reasonable if an advance is made within 30 days of the expense, adequate accounting of the expense is made to the employer within 60 days after it was paid or incurred, and any excess reimbursement is refunded to the employer within 120 days after the expense was paid or incurred. It is also automatically treated

as reasonable if an employer furnishes an employee with a periodic (at least quarterly) statement requesting reimbursement of excess amounts and reimbursement is in fact made within 120 days after receipt of the statement.

If the employer maintains an accountable plan but an employee does not meet all the rules (for example, the employee fails to return excess amounts or is reimbursed for nonbusiness expenses), then those expenses are treated as paid under a nonaccountable plan. The remaining expenses are treated as paid under an accountable plan.

EXAMPLE: An employer maintains an accountable plan. During the year, an employee is reimbursed for business travel expenses and also receives reimbursement for meals eaten while working late for the employer. The meals are nonbusiness expenses. The employer is treated as having two plans in this instance: an accountable plan for the travel expenses and a nonaccountable plan for the personal meal expenses (see below).

Reimbursement at Per Diem Rates

If an employer pays for business expenses using a per diem rate, special rules apply. If the rate used by the employer is the same as or lower than the federal per diem rate for the area of travel, reimbursements are not reported on an employee's form W-2. If an employee's actual expenses exceeded the reimbursement at or below the federal rate, the employee can deduct the excess expenses on his or her individual income tax return. However, if the rate used by the employer is higher than the federal rate, the amounts are reported on Form W-2. The amount of the federal rate is not included in an employee's gross income, though excess reimbursements are included in the employee's gross income. The employee can, however, claim business deductions for these excess amounts (subject to the 2-percent floor).

There are three acceptable federal rates that an employer can use to make reimbursements: federal per diem rate, high-low method, and standard meal allowance.

Federal Per Diem Rate

This is the highest per diem rate paid by the federal government to its employees for lodging, meals, and incidental expenses (or meals and incidental expenses only) while traveling away from home in a particular area.

Different per diem rates apply in different areas. The rates change annually. Employers can get these rates from IRS Publication 1542, Per Diem Rates.

"High-Low" Method

Instead of finding out about different rates for each area of travel, you can use a simplified method where only two different rates apply. So-called high-cost areas are assigned one rate for lodging, meals, and incidental expenses; all other areas within the continental United States are assigned another rate. For 1999 the high-cost per diem rate is $185; for all other areas within the continental United States, it is $115.

HIGH-COST AREAS FOR 1999

State—Key city	County and other defined location
ALABAMA	
Gulf Shores (May 1-September 30)	Baldwin
CALIFORNIA	
Gualala	City limits of Gualala
Palo Alto	City limits of Palo Alton
San Francisco	San Francisco
Sunnyvale	City limits of Sunnyvale
Yosemite Nal't Park (April 1-October 31)	Mariposa
COLORADO	
Aspen (June 1-March 31)	Pitkin
Telluride (November 1-March 31)	San Miguel
Vail (November 1-March 31)	Eagle
DISTRICT OF COLUMBIA	
Washington, D.C.	Washington, D.C.; the cities of Alexandria, Falls Church, and Fairfax and the counties of Arlington, Loudoun, and Fairfax in Virginia; the counties of Montgomery and Prince George in Maryland

State—Key city	County and other defined location
FLORIDA	
Delray Beach (November 1-March 31)	City limits of Delary Beach
Jupiter (January 1-April 30)	City limits of Jupiter
Key West (December 1-April 30)	Monroe
Palm Beach (January 1-April 30)	City limits of Palm Beach
Singer Island (January 1-April 30)	City limits of Singer Island
IDAHO	
Sun Valley	City limits of Sun Valley
ILLINOIS	
Chicago	Cook
Lake County	Lake County
MAINE	
Bar Harbor	Hancock
MARYLAND	
Baltimore	Baltimore
Montgomery County	Montgomery County
Ocean City (April 1-August 31)	Worcester
MASSACHUSETTS	
Boston	Suffolk
Cambridge	Middlesex
Martha's Vineyard (June 1-September 30)	Dukes
NEVADA	
Stateline	Douglas
NEW JERSEY	
Cape May (June 1-September 30)	Cape May (except Ocean City)
Ocean City (June 1-August 31)	City limits of Ocean City

continued on next page

HIGH-COST AREAS FOR 1998

State—Key city	County and other defined location
Piscataway	City limits of Piscataway
Union County	Union County
NEW YORK	
The Bronx	The Bronx
Brooklyn	Brooklyn
Manhattan	Manhattan
Queens	Borough of Queens
Saratoga (August 1-August 31)	Saratoga
Tarrytown/White Plains	Westchester
West Point	Orange
NORTH CAROLINA	
Kill DevilHills (May 1-August 31)	Dare
PENNSYLVANIA	
Hersey (May 1-October 31)	City limits of Hersey
Philadelphia	Philadelphia; city of Bala Cynwyd in Montgomery County
RHODE ISLAND	
Newport (June 1-September 30)	Newport
SOUTH CAROLINA	
Hilton Head (March 1-August 31)	Beaufort
Myrtle Beach (June 1-September 30)	Horry County; Myrtle Beach AFB
UTAH	
Park City (December 1-March 31)	Summit
VIRGINIA	
See District of Columbia	
Wintergreen (June 1-October 31)	Nelson
WASHINGTON	
Seattle	King

Where an employer does not reimburse for lodging but only for meals and incidental expenses (M&IE), the allowance for high-cost areas is $42; for all other localities it is $34.

The meals and incidental expense portion of the reimbursement under the high-low substantiation method is subject to the 50-percent limit on meals and entertainment. Thus, while the allowance for M&IE for a high-cost area is $42 per day, in actuality only $21 is deductible ($42 × 50% limit). Of the $34 per diem rate for non-high-cost areas, only $17 is deductible ($34 × 50%).

Remember: Both the high-low substantiation rates and the designation of high-cost areas are subject to change each year.

Standard Meal Allowance

The dollar amount depends on where your business takes you. In most of the United States, the daily amount is $30 (in 1999). In certain areas designated by the IRS as "high-cost areas," the daily amount is slightly higher. Please note that the high-cost areas for the meal allowance are not the same as the high-cost areas for the high-low method.

In using the standard meal allowance, you take the daily amount based on the rate in effect for the area where you stop to sleep or rest. The figures for 1999 can be found earlier in this chapter. These standard meal allowance rates do not apply outside the continental United States. Thus, they do not apply to travel in Alaska or Hawaii or in any foreign countries. However, there is a standard federal rate for foreign travel that is published monthly in Maximum Travel Per Diem Allowances for Foreign Travel, which is available from the Superintendent of Documents (U.S. Government Printing Office, P.O. Box 371954, Pittsburgh, PA 15250-7954, or IRS Publication 1542, Per Diem Rates). Foreign rates can also be obtained from the U.S. State Department at www.state.gov/www.perdiems/index.html. The daily dollar amount of the standard meal allowance is usually adjusted each year for inflation.

Partial Days of Travel

If the federal per diem rate or high-low method is used for any day of travel that does not include a full 24-hour period, the per diem amount must be prorated. The full rate is allocated on a quarterly basis for each six-hour period in the day (midnight to 6 A.M.; 6 A.M. to noon; noon to 6 P.M.; 6 P.M. to midnight).

Nonaccountable Plans

If an employer maintains a reimbursement arrangement but it does not qualify as an accountable plan (for example, excess reimbursements need not be returned or reimbursements cover nondeductible personal expenses), the plan is considered a nonaccountable plan. In this case, the employer must report the reimbursements on an employee's Form W-2. The employee then deducts the expenses on his or her individual income tax return, subject to the 2-percent-of-adjusted-gross-income floor.

Recordkeeping Requirements

Business expenses can be disallowed unless there is adequate substantiation for the expenses claimed. For travel and entertainment expenses, there are two main ways to prove costs: actual substantiation or reliance on a per diem rate. First look at actual substantiation; then consider how recordkeeping can be simplified with the use of per diem rates.

There are a number of elements to substantiate for each business expense. In general, to substantiate each item you must show the amount, the time, the place, the business purpose for the travel or the business relationship with the person or persons you entertain or provide gifts to, and, in some cases, a description of the item. The exact type of substantiation required depends on the item of business expense.

Travel

You must show the amount of each separate expense for travel, lodging, meals, and incidental expenses. You can total these items in any reasonable category. For example, you can simply keep track of meals in a category called daily meals. You must also note the dates you left for the trip and returned, as well as the days spent on the trip for business purposes. You must list the name of the city or other designation of the place of the travel, along with the reason for the travel or the business benefit gained or expected to be gained from it.

While this may sound like a great deal of recordkeeping, as a practical matter hotel receipts may provide you with much of the information necessary. For example, a hotel receipt typically shows the dates you arrived and departed; the name and location of the hotel; and separate charges for lodging, meals, telephone calls, and other items. The IRS says that a charge slip for hotel costs is no substitute for the hotel receipt itself. You must have documentary evidence for the cost of lodging. You do not need documentary evidence if the item (other than lodging) is less than $75 or, in the case of transportation costs, if a receipt is not readily available. Thus, if a cab ride is $9 and the driver does not provide you with a receipt, you are not required to show documentary evidence of this expense.

Meals and Entertainment

List expenses separately. Incidental expenses, such as taxis and telephone, may be totaled on a daily basis. List the date of the meal or entertainment. For meals or entertainment directly before or after a business discussion, list the date and duration of the business discussion. Include the name and address or location of the place for the entertainment and the type of entertainment if not apparent from the name of the place. Also list the place where a business discussion was held if entertainment was directly before or after the discussion. State the business reason or the business benefit gained or expected to be gained and the nature of the business discussion. Include the names of the persons entertained, including their occupations or other identifying information, and indicate who took part in the business discussion.

If the deduction is for a business meal, you must note that you or your employer was present at the meal. Again, a restaurant receipt typically will supply much of the information required. It will show the name and location of the restaurant, the number of people served, and the date and amount of the expense. Be sure to jot down the business aspect of the meal or entertainment, such as asking a client for a referral or trying to sell your services.

Gifts

Show the cost of the gift, the date given, and a description of the gift. Also show the business reason for the gift or the business benefit gained or expected to be gained from providing it. Indicate the name of the person receiving the gift, his or her occupation or other identifying information, and his or her business relationship to you.

A canceled check, along with a bill, generally establishes the cost of a business item. A canceled check alone does not prove a business expense without other evidence to show its business purpose.

Using a Diary or Log

Enter your expenses in a diary or log at or near the time of the event giving rise to the expenses. Be sure to include all the elements required for the expense (especially the business reason for it).

SAMPLE EXPENSE DIARY

Date	Description	Fares	Lodging	Meals	Entertainment	Other
1/10	Breakfast with Sue Smith, CEO, X Corp. Discussed sales.				$21.50	
1/11	Sales trip— Buyers in NYC	$408.00	$455.00	$105.00		$28.00
1/14	Lunch with Mark Hess after sales call				$38.75	
1/15	Gift for John Jones (boss)					$22.00

It is a good idea to total expenses on a monthly basis and then use a recap form to put annual figures together.

Missing, Lost, or Inadequate Records

If you do not have adequate records, you may still be able to deduct an item if you can prove by your own statement or other supporting evidence an element of substantiation. A court may even allow an estimation of expenses under certain circumstances. Where receipts have been destroyed, you may be able to reconstruct your expenses. You must, of course, show how the records were destroyed (fire, storm, flood). The IRS may require additional information to prove the accuracy or reliability of the information contained in your records.

Recordkeeping alternatives are discussed in more detail in Chapter 4.

Per Diem Rates

If you receive reimbursement using one of the per diem rates discussed earlier, you need not retain documentary evidence of the amount of an expense. The per diem rate is deemed to satisfy the proof of the amount of the expense. However, use of the per diem rate does not prove any of the other elements of substantiation. For example, if an employee is reimbursed for business travel using the high-low method, he or she still must show the time, place, and business purpose for business travel.

WHERE TO DEDUCT TRAVEL AND ENTERTAINMENT EXPENSES

Employees

You calculate your travel and entertainment expenses on Form 2106, Employee Business Expenses, or Form 2106-EZ, Unreimbursed Employee Business Expenses. You can use the EZ form, which is a simplified version of Form 2106, if you do not get reimbursed by your employer for any expenses and, if you are claiming expenses for a car, you own the car and are using the standard mileage rate (as explained in Chapter 7). Then you enter your total from Form 2106 or 2106-EZ on Schedule A, Itemized Deductions, as a miscellaneous itemized expense. These deductions are then limited to the amount they exceed 2 percent of adjusted gross income. If adjusted gross income exceeds a certain amount, the deductions may be further limited. (The threshold for the reduction in itemized deductions is adjusted annually for inflation.)

Disabled employees   If you have physical or mental disability, your impairment-related work expenses are deductible as an itemized deduction, but the 2-percent floor does not apply. Impairment-related work expenses include expenses for attendant care at your place of work and other expenses that are necessary to enable you to work. General medical expenses, however, are not impairment-related work expenses; they are simply personal medical expenses and are deductible as such.

Special rule for performing artists   If you meet certain requirements, you can deduct all of your car expenses as an adjustment to gross income on page 1 of Form 1040 instead of claiming them as miscellaneous itemized deductions on Schedule A. You are treated as a performing artist if you meet all of the following tests:

1. You perform services in the performing arts for at least two employers.

2. You receive at least $200 each from any two of these employers.

3. Your related performing arts business expenses are more than 10 percent of your adjusted gross income from the performance of such services.

4. Your adjusted gross income does not exceed $16,000 (before deducting business expenses from your performing arts).

5. If you are married, you file a joint return (unless you lived apart from your spouse for the entire year). You figure tests 1, 2, and 3 based on your separate experience. However, the adjusted gross income in test 4 is based on the combined adjusted gross income of you and your spouse.

If you meet these criteria, you deduct your performing arts business expenses as an adjustment to gross income on page 1 of Form 1040. Enter these expenses on the line used for totaling adjustments to gross income. Write "QPA" next to your expenses.

Self-Employed (Including Independent Contractor and Statutory Employee)

You enter your travel, meals, and entertainment expenses on Schedule C, Profit and Loss from Business, or Schedule C-EZ, Net Profit from Business. On Schedule C there are separate lines for travel, for meals and entertainment, and for determining the 50-percent limit on meals and entertainment. Business gifts are reported as "other expenses," which are explained on page 2 of Schedule C. Schedule C-EZ can be used only if total business expenses are no more than $2,500. You simply add your travel and entertainment expenses to your other deductible business expenses and enter the total on the appropriate line of Schedule C-EZ. You need not attach an itemized statement explaining the deduction. Be sure that when you total your expenses, you apply the 50-percent limit on meals and entertainment.

Self-employed farmers deduct travel, meals, and entertainment expenses on Schedule F.

Partnerships and LLCs

Travel, meals, and entertainment expenses are reported on Form 1065 and are taken into account in arriving at the business's ordinary income (or loss). They are entered in the category of "Other Deductions" on the form. A schedule is attached to the return explaining the deductions claimed in this category. Be sure to apply the 50-percent limit to meals and entertainment.

Travel, meals, and entertainment expenses are not separately stated items. An owner's share of these expenses is reported on Schedule K-1.

S Corporations

Travel, meals, and entertainment expenses are reported on Form 1120S and are taken into account in arriving at the corporation's ordinary income (or loss). They are entered in the category of "Other Deductions" on the form. A schedule is attached to the return explaining the deductions claimed in this category. Be sure to apply the 50-percent limit to meals and entertainment.

Travel, meals, and entertainment expenses are not separately stated items. A shareholder's share of these expenses is reported on Schedule K-1.

C Corporations

Travel, meals, and entertainment expenses are reported on Form 1120 and are taken into account in arriving at the corporation's taxable income (or loss). They are entered in the category of "Other Deductions" on the form. A schedule is attached to the return explaining the deductions claimed in this category. Be sure to apply the 50-percent limit on meals and entertainment.

CHAPTER 7

Car Expenses

Americans are highly mobile, and the car is the method of choice for transportation. If you use your car for business, you may write off various costs. There are two methods for deducting costs: the actual expense method and the standard mileage allowance. In this chapter you will learn about:

- Deducting car expenses in general
- Actual expense method
- Standard mileage allowance
- Leasing a car for business
- Arranging car ownership
- Employee use of an employer-provided car
- Tax credit for electric cars
- Reimbursement arrangements
- Recordkeeping for car expenses
- Where to deduct car expenses

For further information about deductions with respect to business use of your car, see IRS Publication 463, Travel, Entertainment, Gift, and Car Expenses.

DEDUCTING CAR EXPENSES IN GENERAL

The discussion in this chapter applies to cars used partly or entirely for business.

> **Definition** *Car* Any four-wheel vehicle made primarily for use on public streets, roads, and highways that has an unloaded gross vehicle weight of 6,000 pounds or less. A truck or van is treated as a car if its unloaded gross weight is 6,000 pounds or less. Excluded from the definition of "car" is any ambulance, hearse, or combination thereof used in business and any vehicle used in business for transporting people or for compensation or hire.

The law allows you to choose between two methods for deducting business-related expenses of a car: the actual expense method or the standard mileage allowance, both of which are detailed in this chapter.

Choosing Between the Actual Expense Method and the Standard Mileage Allowance

Read over the rules on the actual expense method and the standard mileage allowance. For the most part, the choice of method is yours. In some cases, however, you may not be able to use the standard mileage rate. Where you are not barred from using the standard mileage rate and can choose between the methods, which is better? Obviously, it is the one that produces the greater deduction. However, there is no easy way to determine which method will produce the greater deduction. Many factors will affect your decision, including the number of miles you drive each year and the extent of your actual expenses. Take this comparison:

EXAMPLE: You buy or lease a car for $15,000 and use it 100 percent for business. In 1999, the first year the car is in service, you drive 1,500 miles per month. If you use the standard mileage allowance, your car deduction for 1999 is $6,625 (4,500 miles × 32.5¢ + 13,500 miles × 31¢). If your actual costs exceed this amount, it may be advisable to use the actual expense method. If they are less than $6,625, the standard mileage allowance may be better.

In making your decision, bear in mind that the standard mileage allowance simplifies recordkeeping for business use of the car.

You should make the decision in the first year you own the car. This is because a choice of the actual expense method for the first year will forever bar the use of the standard mileage allowance in subsequent years. If you use the standard mileage rate, you can still use the actual expense method in later years. However, if the car has not yet been fully depreciated (using the deemed depreciation rates discussed below), then, for depreciation purposes, you must use the straight-line method over what you estimate to be the car's remaining useful life.

ACTUAL EXPENSE METHOD

The actual expense method allows you to deduct all of your out-of-pocket costs for operating your car for business, plus an allowance for depreciation if you own the car. Actual expenses include:

ACTUAL EXPENSES

Depreciation	Lease fees	Repairs
Garage rent	Licenses	Tires
Gas	Oil	Tolls
Insurance	Parking fees	Towing

For individuals, whether interest on a car loan is deductible depends upon employment status. If you are an employee who uses a car for business, you cannot deduct interest on a car loan; the interest is treated as nondeductible personal interest. However, if you are self-employed, the interest may be treated as business interest. For corporations, interest on a car loan is fully deductible.

If you pay personal property tax on a car used for business, the tax is deductible by an employee only as an itemized deduction. Personal property tax is not grouped with other car expenses. Instead, it is listed on an individual's Schedule A as a personal property tax.

If your car is damaged, destroyed, or stolen, the part of the loss not covered by insurance may be deductible. If the car was used entirely for business, the loss is treated as a fully deductible casualty or theft loss. If it was used partly for personal purposes, the loss may be treated as a casualty or theft loss, but the portion of the loss allocated to personal purposes is subject to certain limitations. See Chapter 16 for a discussion of casualty and theft losses.

Not all car-related expenses are deductible. Luxury and sales taxes cannot be separately deducted even if a car is used entirely for business. These taxes are treated as part of the cost of the car. They are added to the "basis" of the car for purposes of calculating depreciation, as well as gain or loss on the future sale of the car.

Fines for traffic violations, including parking violations, are not deductible even when they were incurred in the course of business-related travel.

Depreciation

If you own your car and use it for business, you may recoup part of the cost of the car through a deduction called "depreciation." The amount of depreciation depends on a great many factors. First, it depends on whether you use the depreciation allowance or claim a "Section 179 deduction." It also varies according to the year in which you begin to use your car for business, the cost of the car, and the amount of business mileage for the year as compared with the total mileage for the year.

Business Use Versus Personal or Investment Use

Whether you claim a depreciation allowance or a Section 179 deduction, you can do so only with respect to the portion of the car used for business. For example if you use your car 75 percent for business and 25 percent for personal purposes, you must allocate the cost of the car for purposes of calculating depreciation. The allocation is based on the number of miles driven for business as compared with the total number of miles driven for the year.

EXAMPLE: In 1999 you buy a car for $16,000 and drive it 20,000 miles. Of this mileage, 15,000 miles were business miles; 5,000 miles were personal miles. For purposes of depreciation, you must allocate $12,000 for business use. It is this amount on which you figure depreciation.

If you use a car for investment purposes, you can add the miles driven for investment purposes when making an allocation for depreciation.

Depreciation Allowance

Cars are treated as five-year property under MACRS, the depreciation system currently in effect, as discussed in Chapter 12. As such, you would think that the cost of the car could be recovered through depreciation deductions over a period of five years. However, this is generally not the case because of a number of different rules that come into play. These rules all operate to limit the amount of depreciation that can be claimed in any one year and to extend the number of years for claiming depreciation.

A depreciation allowance is simply a deduction calculated by applying a percentage to the basis of the car.

Definition   *Basis*   Generally, this is the original cost of the car. If a car is bought in part with the trade-in of an old car, the basis of the new car is the adjusted basis of the old car plus any cash payment you make. Basis is reduced by any first-year expense deduction (see below), any clean fuel vehicle deduction, and any qualified electric vehicle tax credit. It is adjusted downward for any depreciation deductions.

Depreciation can take several forms. There is accelerated depreciation under MACRS, which results in greater deductions in the early years of ownership and smaller deductions in the later years. There is straight-line depreciation, which spreads depreciation deductions evenly over the years the car is expected to last (the fixed number of years may, in fact, have no relation to the actual number of years the car is in operation). Tables below provide the percentage for depreciation under both methods. Also note that the first-year expense deduction discussed below is another form of depreciation. It takes the place of depreciation for the first year. Any part of the car not recovered through the first-year expense deduction can then be recovered through depreciation deductions in subsequent years.

Business Use

In order for you to claim an accelerated depreciation deduction, the car must be used more than 50 percent for business. Compare the miles driven during the year for business with the total miles driven. If more than 50 percent of the mileage represents business use, accelerated depreciation (or the first-year expense deduction below) can be claimed.

If you satisfy the 50-percent test, you may also add to business mileage any miles driven for investment purposes when calculating the depreciation deduction. You may not add investment mileage in order to determine whether you meet the 50-percent test.

If you fail the 50-percent test (you use the car 50 percent or less for business), you can deduct depreciation using only the straight-line method. Your deduction is limited to the rates listed in the section on "Conventions," below.

What if the percentage of business use changes from year to year? You may use your car 75 percent for business in one year but only 40 percent the next. Where business use in the year the car is placed in service is more than 50 percent but drops below 50 percent in a subsequent year, you must also change depreciation rates. Once business use drops to 50 percent or below, you can use only the straight-line method thereafter. The depreciation rate is taken from the table for the straight-line method as if the car had not qualified for accelerated depreciation in a prior year.

Where business use drops to 50 percent or less, you may have to include in income an amount called excess depreciation. This is the amount of depreciation (including the first-year expense deduction) claimed when the car was used more than 50 percent for business over the amount of depreciation that would have been allowable had the car not been used more than 50 percent in the year it was placed in service.

In addition to including "excess depreciation" in income, you must increase the basis of your car by the same amount.

EXAMPLE: In 1997 you placed in service a car costing $17,000. (Assume the car was used 100 percent for business, you did not elect first-year expensing, and the half-year convention described below applied.) In 1999 business use drops to 40 percent. The depreciation claimed for 1997 and 1998 totaled $8,160 using MACRS (subject to dollar limits). Had the straight-line method been used, depreciation would have been $5,100. Thus, the excess of $3,060 ($8,160 − $5,100) must be included in income. Your new adjusted basis for the car is $11,900 ($17,000 − $8,160 + $3,060). When calculating the 1999 depreciation deduction, you use the old basis, $17,000, and take the percentage of business use (40 percent). Your basis for depreciation in 1999 is $6,800 ($17,000 × 40%). The depreciation percentage for 1999 (taken from tables below) is 20 percent. The dollar limit must also be reduced to reflect the percentage of business use.

Conventions

There are special rules that operate to limit write-offs for depreciation. These are called conventions. Two conventions apply to depreciation for cars: the half-year convention and the mid-quarter convention.

The half-year convention, in effect, assumes that the car was placed in service in the second half of the year. Thus, in the first year you are allowed to claim only one-half the normal rate of depreciation, regardless of when in the year the car was placed in service. Thus, even if the car was placed in service on January 1, the half-year convention must still be used.

You can see in the table that follows how the half-year convention operates to limit depreciation in the first year. By the same token, the amount of depreciation denied in the first year will ultimately be allowed in the sixth year. Still, the half-year convention means that even though the car is classified as "five-year property," its cost will be recovered only over a period of six years. If the half-year convention applies to property used 50 percent or less for business, the depreciation rate is taken from the following table:

STRAIGHT-LINE HALF-YEAR CONVENTION*

Year	Rate
1	10%
2	20
3	20
4	20
5	20
6	10

*Depreciation may not exceed a dollar limit (see page 168).

If the half-year convention applies to property used more than 50 percent for business, the depreciation rate is taken from the following table:

MACRS HALF-YEAR CONVENTION*

Year	Rate
1	20.00%
2	32.00
3	19.20
4	11.52
5	11.52
6	5.76

*Depreciation may not exceed a dollar limit (see page 168).

The other convention, the mid-quarter convention, applies if more than 40 percent of all the depreciable property you place in service during the year is placed in service in the last quarter of the year.

EXAMPLE: In 1999 you place in service a computer costing $5,000 in January and a car costing $15,000 in December. In this case, the mid-quarter convention applies because more than 40 percent of the depreciable property you placed in service during the year was placed in service during the last quarter of the year ($15,000 is 75 percent of the total of $20,000 of depreciable property placed in service in 1999).

EXAMPLE: The circumstances are the same as above, except the car was placed in service in January and the computer was placed in service in December. In this instance, the mid-quarter convention does not apply because only 25 percent of the depreciable property was placed in service in the last quarter of the year ($5,000 is 25 percent of the total of $20,000 of depreciable property placed in service in 1999).

If the mid-quarter convention applies to property used 50 percent or less for business, the rate is taken from the following table:

STRAIGHT-LINE MID-QUARTER CONVENTION*

Car Placed in Service in —			
Year	1st quarter	2nd quarter	3rd quarter	4th quarter
---	---	---	---	---
1	17.5%	12.5%	7.5%	2.5%
2	20.0	20.0	20.0	20.0
3	20.0	20.0	20.0	20.0
4	20.0	20.0	20.0	20.0
5	20.0	20.0	20.0	20.0
6	2.5	7.5	12.5	17.5

Depreciation may not exceed a dollar limit (see page 168).

EXAMPLE: In December 1999 you place in service a car costing $14,000. You use the car 40 percent for business and 60 percent for personal purposes. Assume that this is the only depreciable property you place in service in 1999, so the mid-quarter convention applies. Your depreciation deduction for the first year is $140 (2.5 percent of $5,600 [40 percent of $14,000]).

If the mid-quarter convention applies to property used more than 50 percent for business, the rate is taken from the following table:

MACRS MID-QUARTER CONVENTION*

Car Placed in Service in —			
Year	1st quarter	2nd quarter	3rd quarter	4th quarter
---	---	---	---	---
1	35.00%	25.00%	15.00%	5.00%
2	26.00	30.00	34.00	38.00
3	15.60	18.00	20.40	22.80
4	11.01	11.37	12.24	13.68
5	11.01	11.37	11.30	10.94
6	1.38	4.26	7.06	9.58

Depreciation may not exceed a dollar limit (see page 168).

EXAMPLE: In December 1999 you place in service a car costing $14,000. You use the car 100 percent for business. Assume that this is the only depreciable property you place in service in 1999, so the mid-quarter convention applies. Your depreciation deduction for the first year is $700 (5 percent of $14,000).

Section 179 Deduction

This deduction, also called the first-year expense allowance, is a one-time write-off for the cost of the car. If you use the first-year expense deduction for the year in which you buy the car and place it in service, you cannot then use depreciation in subsequent years. The annual limit on the first-year expense deduction is:

Year	Section 179 deduction
1999	$19,000
2000	20,000
2001–2002	24,000
2003 and later	25,000

LEGISLATIVE ALERT

Congress is considering an increase in the Section 179 deduction to $30,000 that would be effective starting in 2000.

However, because of the dollar limits discussed below, the actual limit on the first-year expense deduction is the dollar limit.

Should you use the first-year expense deduction or depreciation? As a general rule, it is not advisable to use the first-year expense deduction because of the dollar limit. For example, say you buy a car for $15,000 that you use 100 percent for business. Ordinarily, under the rules for the first-year expense deduction, you would deduct the full $15,000. However, because of the dollar limit, you may be able to deduct only a few thousand dollars. What is more, if you buy other depreciable equipment—a computer, machinery, or other equipment—you may well use up your $19,000 expensing limit on the other equipment.

First-year expensing may be claimed only if the car is used more than 50 percent of the time for business. (The rules on determining business use were explained earlier in this chapter.)

Dollar Limit on Depreciation Deduction

The law sets a dollar limit on the amount of depreciation that can be claimed on a car used for business that was placed in service after June 18, 1984. (Before that date there was no dollar limit on depreciation.) The dollar limit is intended to limit depreciation to the amount that could be claimed on a nonluxury car. In essence, the government does not want to underwrite the cost of buying high-priced cars. However, in reality the dollar limits do not really correlate with "luxury" cars, since the average cost of an American car in 1999 was over $15,000. Most would be hard pressed to conclude that a car costing $20,000 or so is really a "luxury" car. Still, the dollar limits are a factor you must reckon with in calculating your deduction limit.

The dollar limit applies only to cars with a gross vehicle weight (loaded) of 6,000 pounds or less. Most cars fall into this category. However, some sport utility vehicles (such as the Chevrolet Suburban and Tahoe, GMC Yukon, Toyota Land Cruiser, Lexus LX 450, Land Rovers, AM General Hummer, and some models of the Mitsubishi Montero and Ford Expedition) are heavier. If you use a sport utility vehicle as your business car, check the manufacturer's specifications to see if the weight exceeds 6,000 pounds. If so, you can ignore this section on the dollar limit on depreciation.

If the dollar limit applies to your business car, the amount depends upon the year in which the car was placed in service and how long you have owned it. Over the years the dollar limits have been modified by law changes. For a number of years they have been adjusted for changes in the cost-of-living index.

DOLLAR LIMIT ON DEPRECIATION

Car Placed in Service in —					
	1995	1996	1997	1998	1999
Ceiling in:					
1995	$3,060				
1996	4,900	$3,060			

Car Placed in Service in —					
	1995	**1996**	**1997**	**1998**	**1999**
1997	2,950	4,900	$3,160		
1998	1,775	2,950	5,000	$3,160	
1999	1,775	1,775	3,050	5,000	$3,060
2000	1,775	1,775	1,775	2,950	5,000
2001	1,775	1,775	1,775	1,775	2,950
2002	1,775	1,775	1,775	1,775	1,775

EXAMPLE: In 1999 you place in service a car costing $20,000 that is used 100 percent for business. The dollar limit on depreciation for 1999 is $3,060. For 2000 it will be $5,000; for 2001 it will be $2,950, and for each year thereafter it will be $1,775 as long as you use the car for business, until the car is fully depreciated.

EXAMPLE: In 1999 you placed in service a car costing $20,000. For 1999 and all later years, your dollar limit is $1,775.

As a practical matter, most individuals will not get to fully depreciate their cars. They will have sold or traded them in long before the cost has been fully written off. This is because of the dollar limit. In the example above, where a $20,000 car was placed in service in 1996, the car will not be fully depreciated until its ninth or tenth year (depending upon whether MACRS or the straight-line method was used) because of the application of the dollar limit.

For cars placed in service before 1995, different dollar limits apply. There were no dollar limits on cars placed in service before June 19, 1984. For cars placed in service after June 18, 1984, but before 1985, the annual limit is $6,000. For cars placed in service after 1984 but before April 3, 1985, the annual dollar is $6,200. For cars placed in service after April 2, 1985, and before 1987, the annual dollar limit is $4,800. For cars placed in service in 1987, 1988, 1989, or 1999, the annual dollar limit continues to be $1,475. For cars placed in service in 1991, 1992, 1993, or 1994, the annual dollar amount continues to be $1,675.

These dollar amounts apply to cars used 100 percent for business. If you use your car for personal purposes as well as for business, you must allocate the dollar limit. The method for allocating this limit is the same method used for allocating the cost of the car for purposes of depreciation, as described above.

EXAMPLE: In 1999 you place in service a car costing $20,000 that is used 75 percent for business and 25 percent for personal purposes. The full dollar limit of $3,060 is allocated 75 percent for business. Thus the 1999 dollar limit for this car is $2,295 (75 percent of $3,060).

For cars propelled primarily by electricity, the dollar limits are tripled. This increased depreciation limit applies to cars placed in service after August 5, 1997, and before January 1, 2005. You may be entitled to a special tax credit for the purchase of an electric car, as explained later in this chapter. If such credit is claimed, then the basis of the car for purposes of depreciation is reduced by the amount of the credit.

Increase Your Dollar Limit

The dollar limit applies on a per-car basis. If you own two cars and use each for business, you may be able to increase your total dollar limit. Be sure to apply the percentage of business use for each car to the applicable dollar limit.

EXAMPLE: In 1999 you buy a car costing $15,000. Assume you drive 24,100 miles during the year, 90 percent of which (21,700 miles) is for business. Your dollar limit on depreciation is $2,754 (90 percent of $3,060).

Now, instead assume you own two cars, each costing $15,000, which you use for business. You drive car number one 22,200 miles, of which 20,000 miles is for business. Thus your use of car number one is 90 percent for business. You drive car number two 3,200 miles, of which 1,700 is for business. Thus your use of car number two is 53 percent for business. Your dollar limit for car number one is $2,754 ($3,060 × 90%). Your dollar limit for car number two is $1,622 ($3,060 × 53%). Your total depreciation deduction is $4,376. By using two cars instead of one, your depreciation limit is $1,622 greater than it would be if you used one car (assuming the same combined business mileage).

Dispositions of a Car

When you sell your car, trade it in for a new one, or lose it as the result of a casualty or theft, you have to calculate your tax consequences.

Sale If you sell your car, your gain or loss is the difference between what you receive for the car and your adjusted basis. Your adjusted basis is your original basis reduced by any depreciation. If the car has been fully depreciated, anything you receive for the car is all gain.

If you used the standard mileage allowance, you are considered to have claimed depreciation even though you did not have to figure a separate depreciation deduction. The standard mileage allowance automatically takes into account a deduction for depreciation. You figure your "deemed depreciation" according to the number of miles you drove the car for business each year and the years in which it was used.

DEEMED DEPRECIATION

Year	Rate per mile
1994–1999	12 cents
1992–1993	11.5
1989–1991	11
1988	10.5
1987	10
1986	9
1983–1985	8

EXAMPLE: You bought your car and placed it in service at the beginning of 1995. You drove the car 20,000 miles each year for business. You sell it at the end of 1999. You must adjust the basis of the car for purposes of determining gain or loss on the sale by deemed depreciation of $9,600 (80,000 miles × 12 cents per mile each year).

You reduce your original basis by the total of deemed depreciation but do not reduce the basis below zero.

If you use the actual expense method and sell the car before the end of its recovery period, you can claim a reduced depreciation deduction in the year of disposition. Calculate what the depreciation deduction would have been had you held the car for the full year. Then, if you originally placed your car in service in the first three-quarters of the year (January 1 through September 30), you can deduct 50 percent of the amount that would have been allowed. If you originally placed your car in service in the last quarter of the year (October 1 through December 31), you can deduct an amount calculated by applying the percentage in the table below to what would have been allowed.

DEPRECIATION IN YEAR OF SALE

Car Placed in Service Oct. 1–Dec. 31	
Month car sold*	**Percentage**
January, February, March	12.5%
April, May, June	37.5
July, August, September	62.5
October, November, December	87.5

Table is not for fiscal-year taxpayers.

Trade-in   Generally, no gain or loss is recognized if you trade in your car to buy another car for business. Such a trade is treated as a like-kind exchange. This nonrecognition rule applies even if you pay cash in addition to your trade-in or if you finance the purchase. However, if the dealer gives you money back (because the new car costs less than the trade-in), you may have gain to recognize. The gain recognized will not exceed the amount of cash you receive.

If you buy a car by trading in another car, your basis for purposes of determining depreciation on the new car may be less than the value of the new car. Your basis is the adjusted basis of the old car that you traded in, plus any additional payments you make.

EXAMPLE: You buy a new car costing $15,000 by paying $9,000 cash and receiving $6,000 for the trade-in of your old car. The adjusted basis of the old car is $5,000. Your basis for purposes of calculating depreciation is $14,000 ($5,000 adjusted basis of the old car, plus $9,000).

Sale or trade-in?   If your car is fully depreciated, a trade-in avoids what would otherwise be a taxable gain. But the price for this legal tax avoidance is the loss of future depreciation deductions on the new car you receive on the trade-in. This factor may not be significant if you use the standard mileage rate (discussed below) to deduct car expenses.

Casualty or theft   If your car was damaged or stolen and insurance or other reimbursements exceed the adjusted basis of the car, you have a tax gain. However, if you use the reimbursements to buy another car for business or to repair the old car within two years of the end of the year of the casualty or theft, then no gain is recognized. The basis of the new car for purposes of depreciation is its cost less any gain that is not recognized.

For a further discussion of depreciation, see Chapter 12.

STANDARD MILEAGE ALLOWANCE

Instead of keeping a record of all your expenses and having to calculate depreciation, you can use a standard mileage allowance to determine your deduction for business use of your car. You can use the standard mileage allowance in 1999 whether you own or lease the car (in prior years you could not use the standard mileage allowance if you leased your car). The cents-per-mile allowance takes the place of a deduction for gasoline, oil, insurance, maintenance and repairs, vehicle registration fees, and depreciation (if you own the car) or lease payments (if you lease the car). Towing charges for the car are separately deductible in addition to the standard mileage allowance. Parking fees and tolls are also allowed in addition to the standard mileage allowance. Deductible parking fees include those incurred by visiting clients and customers or while traveling away from home on business. Fees to park your car at home or at your place of work are nondeductible personal expenses.

In 1999 the standard mileage allowance for business use of a car is 32.5 cents per mile for travel from January 1, 1999 through March 31, 1999, and 31 cents per mile for travel from April 1, 1999 through December 31, 1999. (Rural letter carriers who use their cars to deliver mail can deduct the amount paid to them by the U.S. Postal Service as an equipment maintenance allowance.) This rate is adjusted annually for inflation.

SAMPLE DEDUCTIONS UNDER THE STANDARD MILEAGE ALLOWANCE FOR 1999*

Miles driven	Deduction	Miles driven	Deduction
5,000	$ 1,566	30,000	$ 9,168
10,000	3,137	35,000	10,981
15,000	4,706	40,000	12,550
20,000	6,275	45,000	14,119
25,000	7,843	50,000	15,687

*Assuming mileage is ratable each month

Standard Mileage Rate Barred

You cannot use the standard mileage rate in certain instances:

- You use the car for hire (such as a taxi).

- You operate two or more cars at the same time (such as in a fleet operation). This limit does not apply to the use of two or more cars on an alternate basis. For example, if you own a car and a van and alternate the use of these vehicles for business use, then you are not barred from using the standard mileage rate to account for the expenses of the business use for the vehicles.

- You have already claimed MACRS or a first-year expense deduction on the car.

Standard Mileage Rate or Actual Expense Method?

As discussed earlier in this chapter, which method is preferable for you depends on a number of variables. The most important variable is the number of business miles you drive each year. As a rule of thumb, those who drive a great number of miles each year frequently find the standard mileage rate offers the greater deduction. It is also important to note that the standard mileage rate is not dependent on the price of the car. Less expensive cars can claim the same deduction as more expensive cars, assuming each is driven the same number of business miles.

LEASING A CAR FOR BUSINESS

Today it is increasingly popular to lease a car rather than buy it. If you use the car entirely for business, the cost of leasing is fully deductible. If you make advance payments, you must spread these payments over the entire lease period and deduct them accordingly. You cannot depreciate a car you lease, because depreciation applies only to property that is owned. However, you can choose to deduct the standard mileage rate in lieu of actual expenses (including lease payments).

Lease with an Option to Buy

When you have this arrangement, are you leasing or buying the car? The answer depends on a number of factors:

- Intent of the parties to the transaction

- Whether any equity results from the arrangement

- Whether any interest is paid

- Whether the fair market value of the car is less than the "lease" payment or option payment when the option to buy is exercised

Where the factors support a finding that the arrangement is a lease, the payments are deductible. If, however, the factors support a finding that the arrangement is a purchase agreement, the payments are not deductible.

Inclusion Amount

If the car price exceeds a certain amount and you deduct your actual costs (you do not use the standard mileage rate), you may have to include in income an "inclusion amount." This is because the law seeks to equate buying with leasing. Since there is a dollar limit on the amount of depreciation that can be claimed on a "luxury" car that is owned, the law also requires an amount to be included in income as an offset to high lease payments on a car that is leased. In essence, the inclusion amount seeks to limit your deduction for lease payments to what it would be if you owned the car and claimed depreciation. The inclusion amount, which is simply an amount that you add to your other income, applies if a car is leased for more than 30 days and its value exceeds a certain amount (which is adjusted periodically for inflation). The inclusion amount is added to income only so long as you lease the car. It is based on the value of the car as of the first day of the lease term. If the capitalized cost of the car is specified in the lease agreement, that amount is considered to be the fair market value of the car. At the start of the lease, you can see what your inclusion amount will be for that year and for all subsequent years. The inclusion amount is based on a percentage of the fair market value of the car at the time the lease begins.

> **Definition** *Fair market value* This is the price that would be paid for the property where there is a willing buyer and seller (neither being required to buy or sell) and both have reasonable knowledge of all the necessary facts. Evidence of fair market value includes the price paid for similar property on or about the same date.

The inclusion amount applies only if the fair market value of the car when the lease began was more than the following:

Fair market value of car	For leases beginning in
$12,800	1987–1990
13,400	1991
13,700	1992
14,300	1993
14,600	1994
15,500	1995–1996
15,800	1997–1998
15,500	1999

The inclusion amount is taken from IRS tables. Inclusion amounts are adjusted annually for inflation. They can be found in the appendix to IRS Publication 463, Travel, Entertainment, Gift, and Car Expenses. The full amount in the table applies if the car is leased for the full year and used entirely for business. If the car is leased for less than the full year, or if it is used partly for personal purposes, the inclusion amount must be allocated to business use for the period of the year during which it was used. The allocation for part-year use is made on a day-by-day basis.

EXAMPLE: The inclusion amount for your car is $500. You used your car only six months of the year (a leap year). You must include in income $250 (183/366 of $500).

Remember that if you use your car for commuting or other nonbusiness purposes, you cannot deduct that allocable part of the lease; there is no inclusion amount for this portion.

INCLUSION AMOUNTS FOR CARS PLACED IN SERVICE IN 1999

Fair Market Value		Tax Year During Lease				
Over	Not over	1st	2nd	3rd	4th	Later
$15,500	$15,800	$2	$3	$4	$4	$6
15,800	16,100	4	7	10	13	14
16,100	16,400	6	11	17	22	23
16,400	16,700	8	15	23	28	32
16,700	17,000	10	20	29	35	41
17,000	17,500	13	25	38	45	53
17,500	18,000	16	32	48	58	68
18,000	18,500	19	39	59	71	82
18,500	19,000	22	47	69	83	96
19,000	19,500	26	53	80	96	111
19,500	20,000	29	61	90	108	126
20,000	20,500	32	68	101	121	140
20,500	21,000	35	75	111	134	155
21,000	21,500	39	82	122	146	169
21,500	22,000	42	89	132	160	183
22,000	23,000	47	100	148	178	206
23,000	24,000	53	114	169	204	235

continued on next page

INCLUSION AMOUNTS FOR CARS PLACED IN SERVICE IN 1999

Fair Market Value		Tax Year During Lease				
Over	Not over	1st	2nd	3rd	4th	Later
24,000	25,000	60	128	190	229	264
25,000	26,000	66	142	212	254	293
26,000	27,000	73	156	233	279	322
27,000	28,000	79	171	253	305	351
28,000	29,000	85	185	275	330	380
29,000	30,000	92	199	296	355	410
30,000	31,000	98	214	316	381	439
31,000	32,000	105	227	338	406	468
32,000	33,000	111	242	359	431	497
33,000	34,000	118	256	380	456	527
34,000	35,000	124	270	402	481	556
35,000	36,000	131	284	423	506	585
36,000	37,000	137	299	443	532	614
37,000	38,000	144	313	464	557	643
38,000	39,000	150	327	487	582	672
39,000	40,000	157	341	507	607	702
40,000	41,000	163	355	528	633	731
41,000	42,000	170	369	549	658	760
42,000	43,000	176	384	570	683	789
43,000	44,000	183	398	591	708	819
44,000	45,000	189	412	612	734	848
45,000	46,000	196	426	633	759	877
46,000	47,000	202	441	654	784	906
47,000	48,000	208	455	675	810	935

Fair Market Value		Tax Year During Lease				
Over	Not over	1st	2nd	3rd	4th	Later
48,000	49,000	215	469	696	835	964
49,000	50,000	221	483	718	860	993
50,000	51,000	228	497	739	885	1,023
51,000	52,000	234	512	759	911	1,052
52,000	53,000	241	526	780	936	1,081
53,000	54,000	247	540	802	961	1,110
54,000	55,000	254	554	823	986	1,140
55,000	56,000	260	569	843	1,012	1,169
56,000	57,000	267	582	865	1,037	1,198
57,000	58,000	273	597	886	1,062	1,227
58,000	59,000	280	611	907	1,087	1,256
59,000	60,000	286	625	928	1,113	1,285
60,000	62,000	296	646	960	1,151	1,329
62,000	64,000	309	675	1,002	1,201	1,387
64,000	66,000	322	702	1,044	1,252	1,446
66,000	68,000	335	732	1,086	1,302	1,504
68,000	70,000	348	760	1,128	1,353	1,563
70,000	72,000	361	788	1,171	1,403	1,621
72,000	74,000	374	817	1,212	1,454	1,679
74,000	76,000	387	845	1,255	1,504	1,738
76,000	78,000	399	874	1,297	1,555	1,796
78,000	80,000	412	902	1,339	2,606	1,854
80,000	85,000	435	952	1,413	1,694	1,956
85,000	90,000	467	1,023	1,518	1,821	2,102
90,000	95,000	500	1,094	1,623	1,947	2,248

continued on next page

INCLUSION AMOUNTS FOR CARS PLACED
IN SERVICE IN 1999

Fair Market Value		Tax Year During Lease				
Over	Not over	1st	2nd	3rd	4th	Later
95,000	100,000	532	1,165	1,729	2,073	2,394
100,000	110,000	581	1,217	1,887	2,263	2,612
110,000	120,000	645	1,414	2,097	2,516	2,904
120,000	130,000	710	1,556	2,308	2,768	3,196
130,000	140,000	775	1,697	2,519	3,021	3,488
140,000	150,000	840	1,839	2,730	3,274	3,779
150,000	160,000	904	1,982	2,940	3,526	4,072
160,000	170,000	969	2,124	3,151	3,779	4,363
170,000	180,000	1,034	2,265	3,362	4,032	4,655
180,000	190,000	1,099	2,407	3,573	4,284	4,947
190,000	200,000	1,163	2,550	3,783	4,537	5,238
200,000	210,000	1,228	2,692	3,994	4,789	5,530
210,000	220,000	1,293	2,833	4,205	5,043	5,822
220,000	230,000	1,358	2,975	4,416	5,295	6,114
230,000	240,000	1,422	3,118	4,626	5,548	6,405
240,000	250,000	1,487	3,260	4,837	5,800	6,697

A different table is used to determine the inclusion amount for electric cars first leased in 1999. The inclusion amount applies to electric cars costing $47,000 or more. This table can be found in IRS Publication 463, Travel, Entertainment, Gift, and Car Expenses.

Should You Lease or Buy?

The decision to lease or buy a car used for business is not an easy one. There are many financial advantages to leasing. Most important is the fact that you need not put forth more than a small amount of up-front cash to lease, whereas a purchase generally requires a significant down payment. However, as a practical matter, if a car is driven extensively (more than 15,000 miles per year), leasing may not make sense because of the annual mileage limit and the charge for excess mileage. In such case, owning rather than leasing may be preferable. Also take into consideration the fact that at the end of the lease term you own nothing, whereas at the end of the same period of time with a purchased car you own an asset that can be sold or traded in for a newer model.

Whether there are any tax advantages is difficult to say. With leasing, you deduct the entire lease charge; with a purchase, you deduct depreciation. Given the current dollar limits on depreciation, this may not be as great as the lease charge. While the inclusion amount is designed to offset this differential, it may not be sufficient to make leasing and depreciation equate.

The only way to know whether leasing or buying is more advantageous tax-wise is to run the numbers. Project what your deductible costs would be if you leased versus what your costs would be if you purchased the car.

ARRANGING CAR OWNERSHIP

If you have a corporation, should you or your corporation own the car you will use for business? From a tax standpoint, it is generally wise to have the corporation own the car. The reason: The corporation can fully deduct the expenses of the car (subject, of course, to the dollar limit on depreciation). If you own the car, your deductions can be claimed only as itemized deductions subject to a floor of 2 percent of your adjusted gross income. If your adjusted gross income is substantial, your deductions may be further limited by an overall reduction in itemized deductions. For insurance purposes, it may also be more advantageous to have the corporation own the car. If the corporation owns more than one vehicle, it can command better insurance rates than an individual who owns only one or two cars. Also, if the car is involved in an accident, the corporation's insurance rates are not affected. If you own the car and it is in an accident, your personal insurance rates will be increased. Finally, if there is a lawsuit involving the car, it generally is preferable to have the corporation sued rather than you personally, since a recovery against the corporation is limited by corporate assets.

EMPLOYEE USE OF AN EMPLOYER-PROVIDED CAR

If your employer gives you a car to use for business, you may be able to deduct certain expenses. Your deduction is limited to the actual expenses of operating the car that were not reimbursed by your employer. The amount of the deduction depends on the amount your employer includes in your income and the number of business and personal miles driven. Your personal use is reported annually on your Form W-2. If your employer owns the car you use, you cannot use the standard mileage allowance for car expenses.

What Is Included on Your W-2?

Your employer has a choice of what to report. The employer can either report the actual value of your personal use or assume that you used the car entirely for personal purposes and include 100 percent of the benefit in your income. This 100-percent amount is based on the annual lease value for the car (explained in Chapter 5). The full amount reported on your W-2 is income to you. Your W-2 will note whether the 100-percent annual lease value or actual personal use was reported. Even though you must include the full amount reported on your W-2, whatever it might be, you may be able to reduce your income tax. You can offset this income to the extent that what was reported as personal use was actually business use and you deduct your business expenses. Where to claim these business deductions is detailed at the end of this chapter.

If your employer reported 100 percent of personal use even though you used the car in part for business, you can deduct your actual expenses for business use that were not reimbursed by your employer. If your employer included only a portion of the use of the car designed to reflect your personal use, then you can deduct any actual expenses for business use that were not reimbursed by your employer.

TAX CREDIT FOR ELECTRIC CARS

The tax law encourages a certain alternative to the gas or diesel engine typically used in cars propelled by electricity. At present these cars are not widely available. Even where they are available, they have limited range, making them generally impractical for business use.

Still, if you bought an electric car and used it for business, you may be entitled to a tax credit. (If you leased instead of purchased an electric car, be sure to take the inclusion amount into account when figuring your car deductions.) This credit reduces your taxes dollar-for-dollar and generally is worth more to you than deductions.

The credit, called the credit for qualified electric vehicles, is 10 percent of the cost of the car, up to a maximum credit of $4,000.

> **Definition** *Qualified electric vehicle* Any motor vehicle that is powered primarily by an electric motor drawing current from rechargeable batteries, fuel cells, or other portable sources of electrical current.

You cannot claim a credit for any portion of the car for which a first-year expense deduction is claimed. You must reduce the basis of the car for purposes of depreciation and otherwise by the amount of the credit. The credit cannot exceed the amount of your tax liability, reduced by certain refundable credits.

To claim the credit, you must be the original owner of the car and must not have bought it for resale (you are not a car dealer). The credit is not limited to the portion of the car for business use. You may claim the credit for the portion of the car used for personal purposes.

After the year 2001, the credit for qualified electric vehicles begins to phase out, and no credit will be allowed for any electric vehicle placed in service after 2004.

The credit is computed on Form 8834, Qualified Electric Vehicle Credit.

REIMBURSEMENT ARRANGEMENTS

If your employer reimburses you for the business use of your car, you may or may not need to claim deductions. The answer depends on the reimbursement arrangement with your employer.

Accountable Plan

If your employer maintains a reimbursement arrangement that reimburses you for business-related use of the car, requires you to adequately account to the employer for these expenses, and also requires you to return within a reasonable time any advances or reimbursements in excess of these expenses, then the plan is treated as an accountable plan. (For details on adequate accounting under accountable plans and returning excess amounts within a reasonable time, see Chapter 6.) If your employer maintains an accountable plan for reimbursement of business expenses and the amount of reimbursement does not exceed the standard mileage allowance, the reimbursements are not reported on your W-2 and you do not deduct any expenses.

If the reimbursements exceed the standard mileage allowance, only the excess over the standard mileage allowance is included on your W-2. You may then deduct your actual expenses that exceed the standard mileage rate.

Nonaccountable Plan

Your employer must include on your W-2 form all reimbursements made under a nonaccountable plan.

RECORDKEEPING FOR CAR EXPENSES

Regardless of whether you use the actual expense method or the standard mileage allowance for your car (or a car that your employer provides you with), certain recordkeeping requirements apply. You must keep track of the number of miles you drive each year for business, as well as the total miles driven each year. You must also record the date of the business mileage, the designation of the business travel, and the business reason for the car expense. It is advisable to maintain a daily travel log or diary in which you record the date, the destination, the business purpose of the trip, and the number of miles driven (use the odometer readings at the start and end of the trip, and then total the miles for each trip). Be sure to note the odometer reading on January 1 each year.

If you use the actual expense method, you must also keep a record of the costs of operating the car. These include the cost of gasoline and oil, car insurance, interest on a car loan (if you are self-employed), licenses and taxes, and repairs and maintenance. Record these amounts in your expense log or diary.

If you lease a car, you must keep track of the amount of the lease payments, in addition to the number of miles driven (and the number of business miles), the dates of travel, the destinations, and the purpose for the travel.

Use a diary or log to keep track of your business mileage and other related costs. You can buy a car expense log in stationery and business supply stores. The following is modeled on an IRS sample daily business mileage and expense log:

SAMPLE LOG

Date	Destination	Business Purpose	Odometer Readings			Expenses	
			Start	Stop	Miles this trip	Type	Amount
5/4/99	Local—St. Louis	Sales calls	8,097	8,188	91	Gas	$18.00
5/5/99	Indianapolis	Sales calls	8,211	8,486	275	Parking	$5.00
5/6/99	Louisville	Bob Smith (potential client)	8,486	8,599	113	Gas, repair flat tire	$17.80 $10.00
5/7/99	Return to St. Louis		8,599	8,875	276	Gas	$18.25
5/8/99	Local—St. Louis	Sales calls	8,914	9,005	91		
Weekly total			8,097	9,005	846		$69.05
Total Year-to-date					5,883		$1,014.75

Proving Expenses with a Mileage Allowance

If your employer pays for car expenses with a mileage allowance, the mileage allowance generally is considered to be proof of the amount of expenses. The amount of expenses that can be proven by use of this allowance is limited to the standard mileage allowance or the amount of a fixed and variable rate (FAVR) allowance that is not included on your W-2. The FAVR allowance includes a combination of fixed and variable costs, such as a cents-per-mile rate to cover variable operating costs (gas, oil, routine maintenance, and repairs) and a flat amount to cover fixed costs (depreciation, insurance, registration and license fees, and personal property taxes). The FAVR allowance applies only if the car is used for certain employees. Thus, use of this allowance is the employer's choice, not the employee's.

It is essential that you keep a written record of the business use of your car. You must note on your tax return whether you have such a record. Remember that your return is signed under penalty of perjury.

WHERE TO DEDUCT CAR EXPENSES

Employees

You compute your car expenses on Form 2106 (Employee Business Expenses) or Form 2106-EZ (Unreimbursed Employee Business Expenses). Form 2106-EZ can be used only if:

1. You were not reimbursed by your employer for expenses or, if you were reimbursed, the reimbursements were included in your income on your W-2, and

2. You use the standard mileage rate for deducting your car expenses.

If you use the actual expense method to deduct your car expenses, you must use Form 2106.

You then enter your total on Schedule A, Itemized Deductions, as a miscellaneous itemized expense. These deductions are then limited to the amount they exceed 2 percent of adjusted gross income. If adjusted gross income exceeds a certain amount, the deductions may be further limited. (The threshold for the reduction in itemized deductions is adjusted annually for inflation.)

Disabled Employees

If you have a physical or mental disability, your impairment-related work expenses are deductible as an itemized deduction, but the 2-percent floor does not apply. Impairment-related work expenses include expenses for attendant care at your place of work and other expenses that are necessary to enable you to work (such as the cost of a driver to bring you to business locations). General medical expenses, however, are not impairment-related work expenses; they are simply personal medical expenses and are deductible as such.

Special Rule for Performing Artists

If you meet certain requirements, you can deduct all of your car expenses as an adjustment to gross income on page 1 of Form 1040 instead of claiming them as miscellaneous itemized deductions on Schedule A. You are treated as a performing artist if you meet all of the following tests:

1. You perform services in the performing arts for at least two employers.

2. You receive at least $200 each from any two of these employers.

3. Your related performing arts business expenses are more than 10 percent of your adjusted gross income from the performance of such services.

4. Your adjusted gross income does not exceed $16,000 (before deducting business expenses from your performing arts).

5. If you are married, you file a joint return (unless you lived apart from your spouse for the entire year).

You perform tests 1, 2, and 3 based on your separate experience. However, the adjusted gross income in test 4 is the combined adjusted gross income of you and your spouse.

If you meet these tests, you deduct your performing arts business expenses as an adjustment to gross income on page 1 of Form 1040. Enter these expenses on the line used for totaling adjustments to gross income. Write "QPA" next to your expenses.

Self-Employed

You enter your car expenses on Schedule C, Profit and Loss from Business, or Schedule C-EZ, Net Profit from Business. If you are not required to complete Form 4562, Depreciation and Amortization, because you did not place any depreciable or amortizable property in service in 1999, then use Part IV of Schedule C and Part III of Schedule C-EZ to report information on your car. They ask when the car was placed in service and the number of miles driven for business, commuting, or other purposes. They also ask whether there is another car available for personal use and whether your business car was available during off-duty hours. Finally, both forms ask whether you have evidence to support your deductions and whether this evidence is written. If you are otherwise required to complete Form 4562, then report the information about your car on this form and not on Schedule C or Schedule C-EZ.

Farmers who are self-employed deduct their car expenses on Schedule F. Also complete Part IV of Form 4562, Depreciation and Amortization, to provide information about car use.

Portion of Schedule C Used to Report Car Use

Part IV **Information on Your Vehicle.** Complete this part **ONLY** if you are claiming car or truck expenses on line 10 and are not required to file Form 4562 for this business. See the instructions for line 13 on page C-4 to find out if you must file.

43 When did you place your vehicle in service for business purposes? (month, day, year) ▶ ..../........./........ .

44 Of the total number of miles you drove your vehicle during 1999, enter the number of miles you used your vehicle for:

a Business .... **b** Commuting .... **c** Other ....

45 Do you (or your spouse) have another vehicle available for personal use? . . . . ☐ **Yes** ☐ **No**

46 Was your vehicle available for use during off-duty hours? . . . . ☐ **Yes** ☐ **No**

47a Do you have evidence to support your deduction? . . . . ☐ **Yes** ☐ **No**

b If "Yes," is the evidence written? . . . . ☐ **Yes** ☐ **No**

Portion of Schedule C-EZ Used to Report Car Use

Part III **Information on Your Vehicle.** Complete this part **ONLY** if you are claiming car or truck expenses on line 2.

4 When did you place your vehicle in service for business purposes? (month, day, year) ▶ ..../........./........ .

5 Of the total number of miles you drove your vehicle during 1999, enter the number of miles you used your vehicle for:

a Business .... **b** Commuting .... **c** Other ....

6 Do you (or your spouse) have another vehicle available for personal use? . . . . ☐ **Yes** ☐ **No**

7 Was your vehicle available for use during off-duty hours? . . . . ☐ **Yes** ☐ **No**

8a Do you have evidence to support your deduction? . . . . ☐ **Yes** ☐ **No**

b If "Yes," is the evidence written? . . . . ☐ **Yes** ☐ **No**

For Paperwork Reduction Act Notice, see Form 1040 instructions.   Cat. No. 14374D   **Schedule C-EZ (Form 1040) 1999**

Partnerships and LLCs

Expenses of business-owned cars are reported on the business's Form 1065 as part of the business's ordinary income (or loss). They are entered in the category of "Other Deductions." A schedule is attached to the return explaining the deductions claimed in this category. Car expenses are not separately stated items. Then the owner's share of ordinary income (or loss) is reported on Schedule K-1.

S Corporations

Car expenses of business-owned cars are reported on the corporation's Form 1120S as part of the S corporation's ordinary income (or loss). They are entered in the category of "Other Deductions." A schedule is attached to the return explaining the deductions claimed in this category. Car expenses are not separately stated items. Then the shareholder's share of ordinary income (or loss) is reported on Schedule K-1.

C Corporations

Car expenses are reported on the corporation's Form 1120 as part of its taxable income (or loss). They are entered in the category of "Other Deductions." A schedule is attached to the return explaining the deductions claimed in this category.

All Businesses

If you claim depreciation for a car used in business, you must complete Form 4562, Depreciation and Amortization. This form is filed for the year the car is placed in service. C corporations must continue to file this for each year thereafter. Other taxpayers need not file the form after the first year (unless other depreciable property is placed in service).

CHAPTER 8

Repairs and Maintenance

Property and equipment generally need constant repairs to keep them in working order. When your computer goes down, a service person is required to make repairs. When the air-conditioning system in your office building stops working, again, servicing is necessary. If you have property or equipment to which you make repairs, you can deduct these expenses. The only hitch is making sure that the expenses are not capital expenditures. Capital expenditures cannot be currently deducted but instead are added to the basis of property and recovered through depreciation or upon the disposition of the property. In this chapter you will learn about:

- Ordinary repairs
- Rehabilitation plans
- Special rules for improvements for the elderly and handicapped
- Deductible repairs and capital improvements
- Where to take deductions for repairs

For further information about deducting repairs, see IRS Publication 535, Business Expenses.

Ordinary Repairs

Deducting Incidental Repairs in General
The cost of repairing property and equipment used in your business is a deductible business expense. In contrast, expenditures that materially add

to the value of the property or prolong its life must be capitalized (added to the basis of the property and recovered through depreciation). In most cases, the distinction is clear. If you pay a repair person to service your copying machine because paper keeps getting jammed, the cost of the service call is a repair expense that is currently deductible. If you put a new roof on your office building, you must capitalize the expenditure and recover the cost through depreciation. Sometimes, however, the classification of an expense as a repair or a capital expenditure is not clear.

Guidelines on Distinguishing Between a Repair and a Capital Item

Repairs are expenses designed to keep property in good working condition. These include replacement of short-lived parts. Typically, the cost of repairs is small compared with the cost of the property itself. Capital items, on the other hand, are akin to original construction. They replace long-lived parts or enlarge or improve on the original property. Costs are usually substantial.

EXAMPLES OF REPAIRS VERSUS CAPITAL ITEMS

Repairs	Capital items
Painting the outside of office building	Vinyl siding the outside of office building
Replacing missing shingles on roof	Replacing entire roof
Replacing compressor for air conditioner	Adding air-conditioning system
Repairs	Capital items
Cleaning canopy over restaurant entrance	Adding canopy over restaurant entrance
Resurfacing office floor	Replacing office floor

The fact that certain repairs are necessitated by governmental directives does not change the character of the expense. If it is a required repair, it is currently deductible; if it substantially improves the property, it is a capital expenditure. For example, in one case, rewiring ordered by local fire prevention inspectors was a capital expenditure. The same is true for capital expenditures ordered by the U.S. Public Health Service and state sanitary or health laws.

Repairs made to property damaged by a casualty are deductible if they merely restore the property to its pre-casualty condition. This is so even if a deduction is also claimed for a casualty loss to the property.

EXAMPLE: Severe flooding destroyed a business owner's property. He was not compensated by insurance. The IRS, in a memorandum to a district counsel, allowed him to deduct the cost of repairs to the property where such repairs merely restored it to its pre-casualty condition. In addition, he claimed a casualty loss for the same property.

The cost of upgrading computers and software to handle the Year 2000 problem is discussed in Chapter 12.

EPA Compliance

If you are forced to take certain actions to comply with EPA requirements, such as encapsulating or removing asbestos, be sure to understand which expenses are currently deductible and which expenses must be capitalized. Environmental remediation costs can be currently deducted. These are costs of cleanups to comply with environmental laws. The cost of capital improvements to comply with environmental laws, however, must be capitalized.

EXAMPLE: The cost of encapsulating asbestos in a warehouse is currently deductible. The cost of removing asbestos from a boiler room must be capitalized. (The removal makes the property substantially more attractive to potential buyers.)

EXAMPLE: The cost of cleaning up contaminated soil where the contamination was caused by the taxpayer is currently deductible. The cost in this instance is for the removal of the contaminated soil and the replacement of it with clean soil. However, the cost of installing and operating groundwater treatment and monitoring facilities to avoid future contamination must be capitalized. (It is not clear whether a current deduction can be claimed for the cleanup of land bought with a contaminated condition. The IRS might argue that this is a substantial improvement that must be capitalized.)

For certain environmental cleanup expenditures, you can elect to deduct certain costs that would otherwise be capitalized. Since property that has been contaminated by hazardous substances has been referred to as "brownfields," you may see this expensing election referred to as a "brownfield deduction." Only expenses for cleanups in "targeted areas" qualify for this election. If the election is made, then expenses are treated in the same way as depreciation (explained in Chapter 12) so that they will be recaptured when the property that has been cleaned up is later sold or otherwise disposed of. The election is set to expire for expenses paid or incurred after December 31, 2000.

REHABILITATION PLANS

If you make repairs as part of a general plan to recondition or improve property—typically, office buildings, stores, and factories—then the expenses must be capitalized. This is so even though the expenses would have been deductible if made outside a general plan of repair. This rule is called the rehabilitation doctrine. For example, painting generally is treated as a currently deductible repair expense. However, if you add an extension to your office building, the cost of painting the extension upon completion is a capital item under the rehabilitation doctrine.

Protecting the Deduction for Repairs

With proper planning, you can make sure that repair costs are currently deductible even though you also undertake capital expenditures. Schedule repairs separately from capital improvements so they will not be treated as one rehabilitation plan, and get separate bills for the repairs.

Tax Credits for Rehabilitation

While rehabilitation costs generally must be capitalized, in special instances you can claim a tax credit for your expenditures. If you rehabilitate a nonresidential building that was built before 1936, you can claim a credit for 10 percent of your expenditures. If you rehabilitate a certified historic structure (a building that is listed in the National Register or located in a registered historic district), the credit is 20 percent of costs. The credit is claimed in the year the property is placed in service, not the year in which the expenditures are made. Thus, for example, if you undertake a two-year project beginning in 1999 and do not place the building in service until 2000, the credit is taken in 1999.

Rehabilitation requires that you make substantial improvements to the building but leave a substantial portion of it intact. A substantial portion means that within any two-year period you select, the rehabilitation expenditures exceed the adjusted basis of the building or $5,000, whichever is greater. In the case of a pre-1936 building, at least 75 percent of the external walls must be left intact and at least 50 percent of external walls must remain as external walls. The Secretary of the Interior must certify that the rehabilitation of certified historic structures will be in keeping with the building's historic status.

The credit is claimed on Form 3468, Computation of Investment Credit. For individuals and C corporations, it is part of the general business credit computed on Form 3800, General Business Credit. The credit may be limited by the passive loss rules explained in Chapter 3. The general business credit limitations are explained in Chapter 4.

Demolition Expenses

As a general rule, the costs of demolishing a building are not deductible. Instead, they are added to the basis of the new building (that is, the building put up in the place of the demolished building). However, the costs of demolishing only a part of a building may be currently deductible. According to the IRS, if 75 percent or more of the existing external walls and 75 percent or more of the existing internal framework are both retained, the costs of demolition need not be capitalized (added to basis) but instead can be currently deducted.

SPECIAL RULES FOR IMPROVEMENTS FOR THE ELDERLY AND HANDICAPPED

The Americans with Disabilities Act (ADA) may require you to make certain modifications to your office, store, or factory if you have not done so already. You may have to install ramps, widen doorways and lavatories to accommodate wheelchairs, add elevators, or make other similar changes to your facilities to render them more accessible to the elderly and handicapped as mandated in the ADA.

These modifications may be more in the nature of capital improvements than repairs. Still, the law provides two special tax incentives to which you may be entitled. One is a tax credit; the other is a special deduction. These incentives allow for a current benefit rather than requiring capitalization of expenditures that will be recovered over long periods of time.

Disabled Access Credit

Small business owners can claim a tax credit for expenditures to remove barriers on business property that impede the access of handicapped individuals and to supply special materials or assistance to visually or hearing-impaired persons.

Definition *Small business owners* Owners with gross receipts of no more than $1 million (after returns and allowances) and no more than 30 full-time employees. Full-time employees are those who work more than 30 hours per week for 20 or more calendar weeks in the year.

The credit cannot exceed 50 percent of expenditures over $250 but not over $10,250. The maximum credit is $5,000.

EXAMPLE: You, as a small business owner, spend $4,000 to install ramps in your strip mall. You may take a tax credit of $1,875 ($4,000 − $250 = $3,750 × 50%).

The dollar limit applies at both the partner and partnership levels. The same rule applies to shareholders and S corporations, as well as to members and LLCs.

Qualifying Expenditures

These are expenditures designed to meet the requirements of the ADA. Many of these requirements are set forth below in connection with the expense deduction for the removal of architectural and transportation barriers. However, eligible expenditures do not include those in connection with new construction. Thus, if you are in the process of building an office complex and you install special bathroom facilities to accommodate a wheelchair, you cannot claim the credit because this is new construction. If you claim the credit, you cannot also claim a deduction for the same expenditures, as discussed below.

Deduction for Removal of Architectural or Transportation Barriers

As you have seen throughout this chapter, expenditures that improve or prolong the life of property generally must be capitalized and the cost recovered through depreciation. You have already seen two special credits that can be claimed for expenditures that would otherwise have to be capitalized. There is one more important exception to this capitalization rule: You can elect to deduct the expenses of removing architectural or transportation barriers to the handicapped and elderly. The election is made simply by claiming the deduction on a timely filed tax return.

The maximum deduction in any one year is $15,000. If your expenditures for a removal project exceed this limit, you can deduct the first $15,000 of costs and capitalize (and then depreciate) the balance.

The dollar limit applies at both the partner and partnership levels. A partner must combine his or her distributive share of these expenditures from one partnership with any distributive share of such expenditures from any other partnerships. The partner may allocate the $15,000 limit among his or her own expenditures and the partner's distributive share of partnership expenditures in any manner. If the allocation results in all or a portion of the partner's distributive share of partnership's expenditures not being an allocable deduction, then the partnership can capitalize the unallowable portion.

EXAMPLE: A partner's distributive share of partnership expenditures (after application of the $15,000 limit at the partnership level) is $7,500. The partner also has a sole proprietorship that made $10,000 of expenditures. The partner can choose to allocate the $15,000 limitation as follows: $5,000 to his or her distributive share of the partnership's expenditures and $10,000 to individual expenditures. If the partner provides written proof of this allocation to the partnership, the partnership can then capitalize $2,500, the unused portion of the partner's distributive share of expenditures ($7,500 distributive share less $5,000 allocated as a deduction).

While the regulations on applying the dollar limits at both the partner and partnership levels do not specify other pass-through entities, presumably the same rules that apply to partners and partnerships apply as well to shareholders and S corporations.

If the election is made to expense these expenditures, then no disabled access credit can be claimed for the same expenses.

Qualifying Expenditures

These are expenses that conform a facility or public transportation vehicle to certain standards that make them accessible to persons over the age of 65 or those with physical or mental disability or impairment. It does not include any expense for the construction or comprehensive renovation of a facility or public transportation vehicle or the normal replacement of depreciable property.

GUIDANCE ON ACCEPTABLE STANDARDS FOR THE ELDERLY AND HANDICAPPED

Type of Expense	Requirements
Grading	The ground should be graded to attain a level with a normal entrance to make the facility accessible to individuals with physical disabilities.
Walks	A public walk should be at least 48 inches wide and have a gradient of no more than 5 percent.
	A walk should have a continuing common surface (not interrupted by steps or abrupt changes in level).
	A walk or driveway should have a nonslip surface.
Parking lots	At least one space that is accessible and proximate to the facility must be set aside and designated for the handicapped.
	The space must be open to one side to allow wheelchair access.
	For head-on parking, the space must be at least 12 feet wide.
Ramps	A ramp should not have a slope greater than a 1-inch rise in 12 inches.
	There must be a handrail 32 inches in height.
	A ramp should have a nonslip surface.
	A ramp should have a level surface at the top and bottom (if a door swings into the platform, the platform should be at least 5 by 5 feet).
	A ramp should have level platforms at least every 30 feet.
	A curb ramp should be provided at every intersection (the ramp should be 4 feet wide, with transition between two surfaces and a nonslip surface).

continued on next page

GUIDANCE ON ACCEPTABLE STANDARDS FOR THE ELDERLY AND HANDICAPPED

Type of Expense	Requirements
Entrances	A building should have at least one primary entrance wheelchair accessible and on a level accessible to an elevator.
Doors and doorways	A door should have an opening of at least 32 inches.
	The floor inside and outside the doorway should be level for at least 51 inches.
	The threshold should be level with the floor.
	The door closer should not impair the use of the door by someone who is handicapped.
Stairs	Stairs should have handrails at least 32 inches from the tread at the face of the riser.
	Steps should not have risers exceeding 7 inches.
Floors	Floors should have a nonslip surface.
Toilet rooms	The rooms should provide wheelchair access. At least one stall should be 66 inches wide by 60 feet deep, with 32-inch door space and handrails.
Water fountains	A water fountain or cooler should have up-front spouts and hand and foot controls.
	A water fountain should not be in an alcove unless there is 36 inches of space.
Public telephones	Each phone should be placed so the dial and headset can be reached by someone in a wheelchair.
	Coin slots should be not more than 48 inches from the floor.
	Public phones should be equipped for those with hearing impairments.
Elevators	An elevator should be on entry levels to buildings and in all areas normally used.
	Cab size should allow a wheelchair to turn.
	The door opening should be at least 32 inches.

Type of Expense	Requirements
Controls	Switches and controls for all essential uses (light, heat, ventilation, windows, draperies, fire alarms) should be within reach of a person in a wheelchair (no higher than 48 inches from the floor).
Identification	Raised letters or numbers should be used to identify rooms (letters or numbers placed on the left or right of the door at a height of 54 to 66 inches).
Warning signals	A visual seaming signal should be accompanied by an audible sound for the benefit of the blind.
Hazards	Hanging signs, ceiling lights, and similar objects and fixtures should be placed at a minimum height of 7 feet (measured from the floor).
International	Wheelchair-accessible entrances should be identified with the accessibility symbol.

Recordkeeping

If you elect to deduct these expenditures, you must maintain records and documentation, including architectural plans and blueprints, contracts, and building permits to support your claims. How long these records should be kept is discussed in Chapter 4.

LISTS OF DEDUCTIBLE REPAIRS AND CAPITAL IMPROVEMENTS

Over the years various expenditures have come under review by the IRS and the courts. The following lists, one of deductible repairs and the other of improvements that must be capitalized, are based on actual cases and rulings.

Deductible Repairs

- Altering building for street-widening program
- Caulking seams
- Replacing compressor for air conditioner

- Replacing copper sheeting for cornice (blown off by wind)
- Relining basement walls and floors with cement
- Cleaning a restaurant canopy
- Cutting and filling cracks in storage tanks
- Tuck pointing and cleaning exterior brick walls
- Adding timbers to support walkway over basement
- Mending plaster walls and ceilings
- Painting walls and ceiling over basement
- Papering walls
- Patching a leaking roof
- Relocating steam pipes and radiators
- Resurfacing floors
- Repairing sidewalks
- Shoring up building foundation
- Replacing retaining walls
- Repairing gutters

Capital Improvements

- Installing new doors
- Installing new windows
- Replacing a coal burner with an oil burner heating system
- Installing skylights
- Installing fire escapes
- Replacing a roof
- Adding new floor supports
- Replacing iron piping with brass piping in hot water system
- Raising, lowering, or building new floors

- Erecting permanent partitions

- Installing fire sprinklers

- Bricking up windows

- Installing an air-conditioning system

- Installing a ventilation system

- Rewiring or upgrading electrical service

- Replacing windows and doors

- Expanding a building (building an addition)

- Installing a burglar alarm system

- Blacktopping a driveway

- Improving a storefront

- Adding new plumbing fixtures

- Constructing a drainage system

WHERE TO TAKE DEDUCTIONS FOR REPAIRS

Employees

An employee can deduct repair costs as an itemized employee business expense on Schedule A, subject to the 2-percent rule and the reduction for higher-income taxpayers discussed in Chapter 1.

Self-Employed

Repair costs are deductible on Schedule C. This schedule contains a line specifically for "repairs and maintenance." Repair costs can also be deducted on Schedule C-EZ if total business expenses do not exceed $2,500. Farmers who are self-employed deduct repair costs on Schedule F.

Partnerships and LLCs

Repair costs are trade or business expenses that are taken into account in determining the profit or loss of the partnership or LLC on Form 1065. There is a specific line for deducting repair and maintenance costs. They are not separately stated items passed through to partners and members. Therefore partners and members in LLCs report their net income or loss from the business on Schedule E; they do not deduct repair costs on their individual tax returns.

An exception applies to expenditures for the removal of architectural and transportation barriers to the elderly and handicapped that are elected to be expensed. These items must be separately stated, since dollar limits apply at both the owner and entity levels.

S Corporations

Repair costs are trade or business expenses that are taken into account in determining the profit or loss of the S corporation on Form 1120S. There is a specific line for deducting repair and maintenance costs. They are not separately stated items passed through to shareholders. Therefore shareholders report their net income or loss from the business on Schedule E; they do not deduct repair costs on their individual tax returns.

An exception applies to expenditures for the removal of architectural and transportation barriers to the elderly and handicapped that are elected to be expensed. These items must be separately stated, since dollar limits apply at both the owner and entity levels.

C Corporations

Repair costs are trade or business expenses that are taken into account in determining the profit or loss of the C corporation on Form 1120. This form contains a separate line for deducting repairs and maintenance costs. Shareholders do not report any income (or loss) from the corporation.

Rehabilitation Credit for All Taxpayers

This credit is computed on Form 3468, Investment Tax Credit. It is part of the general business credit and is subject to the limitations on the general business credit (explained in Chapter 4), which is computed on Form 3800, General Business Credit filed with Form 1040 and Form 1120. (Partners and S corporation shareholders figure the general business credit limitation on their individual returns.)

Disabled Access Tax Credit for All Taxpayers

This credit is computed on Form 8826, Disabled Access Credit. It is part of the general business credit and is subject to the limitations on the general business credit, which is computed on Form 3800, General Business Credit filed with Form 1040 and Form 1120. (Partners and S corporation shareholders figure the general business credit limitation on their individual returns.)

CHAPTER 9

Bad Debts

No one thinks that the loans they make to others will go unpaid; otherwise, such loans would not be made in the first place. If, in the course of your business, you lend money or extend goods and services but fail to receive payment, you can take some comfort in the tax treatment for these transactions gone sour. You may be able to deduct your loss as a bad debt. In this chapter you will learn about:

- Bad debts in general
- Business versus nonbusiness bad debts
- Loans by shareholder-employees
- Guarantees that result in bad debts
- Special rules for accrual taxpayers
- Reporting bad debts on the tax return
- Where to deduct bad debts

For further information about deducting bad debts, see IRS Publication 535, Business Expenses.

BAD DEBTS IN GENERAL

If you cannot collect money that is owed to you in your business, your loss may be deductible. You must prove a number of factors in order to establish a bad debt. These factors include:

1. The debtor-creditor relationship
2. Worthlessness
3. Loss

The Debtor-Creditor Relationship

You must prove there is a debtor-creditor relationship. This means that there is a legal obligation on the part of the debtor to pay to the creditor a fixed or determinable sum of money.

If you lend money to a friend or relative, the relationship between you and the borrower is not always clear. You may, for example, lend the money with the expectation of receiving repayment but later forgive some or all of the payments. This forgiveness with a friend or relative transforms what might have been a bad debt into a gift. The law does not bar loans between relatives or friends, but be aware that the IRS gives special scrutiny to loan arrangements involving related parties.

The simplest way to prove a debtor-creditor relationship is to have a written note evidencing the loan arrangement. The note should state the following terms:

- The amount of the loan
- A stated rate of interest
- A fixed maturity date
- A repayment schedule

If you have a corporation to which you lend money, establishing the debtor-creditor relationship is crucial. Unless you can show that an advance to the corporation is intended to be a loan, it will be treated as a contribution to the capital of the corporation (which is not deductible). Make sure that not only do you have a written note but also that the corporation carries the advance as a loan on its books.

Worthlessness

You must also show that the debt has become worthless and will remain that way. You must be able to show that you took reasonable steps to collect the debt. It is not necessary that you actually go to court to collect if you can show that a judgment would remain uncollectible. If the borrower is in bankruptcy, this is a very good indication that the debt is worthless, at least in part. Generally, the debt is considered to be worthless as of the settlement date of the bankruptcy action, but facts can show that it was worthless before this time.

Whether a loan is fully or only partially worthless affects whether you can claim a deduction for the loss. Business bad debts are deductible whether they are fully or partially worthless. If the loss is a nonbusiness bad debt, it is deductible only if the debt is fully worthless. No partial deduction is allowed for nonbusiness bad debts.

Loss

You must show that you sustained a loss because of the debt. A loss results where an amount is included in income but the income is never received. This might happen, for example, where an accrual method taxpayer accrues income but later fails to collect it. If you sell goods on credit and fail to receive payment, you sustain an economic loss whether you are on the accrual method or the cash method of accounting. If you are on the cash basis and extend services but fail to collect, you cannot claim a bad debt deduction. You are not considered to have an economic loss even though you might argue that you put in your time and effort and were not justly compensated.

EXAMPLE: A cash basis accountant prepares an individual's tax return. The bill comes to $400. The accountant never receives payment. She cannot deduct the $400. The accountant never reported the $400 as income, so she is not considered to have suffered an economic loss, even though she extended services and invested her time and energy.

If you make payments to a supplier for future shipments and the supplier fails to deliver because of insolvency, you have a business bad debt, regardless of your method of accounting. Again, you have an economic loss (the money you advanced to the supplier) that gives rise to the bad debt deduction.

Collection of Bad Debts

Suppose you fully investigated a debt, made every effort to collect it, and finally concluded it was worthless. You claim a deduction; then, lo and behold, the debtor repays you a year or two later. You need not go back and amend your return to remove the bad debt deduction. Instead, include the recovery of the bad debt in income in the year you receive payment.

BUSINESS VERSUS NONBUSINESS BAD DEBTS

Business bad debts, as the term implies, arise in connection with a business. Nonbusiness bad debts are all other debts; they can arise in either a personal or investment context. Business bad debts are deductible as ordinary losses. Business debts of a C corporation are always bad debts. Nonbusiness bad debts are deductible by an individual only as short-term capital losses. As such, they are deductible only to offset your capital gains, and then up to $3,000 of ordinary income. Business bad debts are deductible if partially or wholly worthless. Nonbusiness bad debts must be wholly worthless to be deductible.

Business Bad Debts

Business bad debts are treated as ordinary losses that offset ordinary business income. To be treated as a business bad debt, the debt must be closely related to the activity of the business. There must have been a business reason for entering into the debtor-creditor relationship.

Business bad debts typically arise from credit sales to customers. They can also be the result of loans to suppliers, customers, employees, or distributors. Credit sales are generally reported on the books of the business as accounts receivable. Loans to suppliers, customers, employees, or distributors generally are reported on the books of the business as notes receivable. When accounts receivable or notes receivable become uncollectible, this results in a business bad debt.

Valuing a Bad Debt

Accounts receivable and notes receivable generally are carried on the books at fair market value. Thus, when they go bad, they are deductible at fair market value. This is so even where that value is less than the face value of the obligations.

Impact of Loans with Your Business or Associates

If you lend money to your corporation and the corporation later defaults, you cannot claim a bad debt deduction unless it was a true loan. If, as explained earlier, the advance to the corporation was in fact a contribution to its capital, then you cannot claim a bad debt deduction.

If you have a partnership that breaks up and there is money owing from the partnership, you may be forced to make payments if your partner or partners do not. This payment may be more than your share of the partnership's debts. In this case, you can claim a bad debt deduction if your partner or partners were insolvent and you were required to pay their share.

If you go out of business but still try to collect outstanding amounts owed to you, potential bad debt deductions are not lost. You can still claim them as business bad debts if the debts become worthless after you go out of business.

Nonbusiness Bad Debts

Loans made to protect investments or for personal reasons give rise to nonbusiness bad debts when they go bad.

EXAMPLE: An attorney lent money to a friend and is later unable to collect despite a number of attempts. Since the loan had nothing to do with the attorney's business, the failure to collect results in a nonbusiness bad debt if it is wholly worthless.

LOANS BY SHAREHOLDER-EMPLOYEES

When a shareholder who is also an employee of a corporation lends the corporation money but fails to receive repayment, or guarantees corporate debt and is called upon to make good on the guarantee, it is not always clear whether the resulting debt is a business bad debt or a nonbusiness bad debt.

A business bad debt must arise in the context of a business. A shareholder who lends money to the corporation is doing so to protect his or her investment. An employee who lends money to his or her corporation is doing so to protect his or her business of being an employee. In this instance, employment is treated as a business. When an individual is both a shareholder and an employee, which status governs?

According to the U.S. Supreme Court, the dominant motive for making the loan to the corporation is what makes a debt a business or nonbusiness bad debt. Where the dominant motive is to protect one's investment, then the bad debt is treated as a nonbusiness bad debt. Where the dominant motive is to protect one's employment status to ensure continued receipt of salary, then the bad debt is treated as a business bad debt. In making this assessment, several factors are taken into account:

The size of your investment in the corporation   If your investment is substantial, this indicates that a bad debt might be the result of a desire to protect this investment.

The size of your after-tax salary from the corporation   If your salary is minimal, this indicates that your real interest may be protecting your investment rather than your salary.

Other sources of income available to you   If the salary is an important source of income to you, then the debt may have been incurred to protect the income. Where the investment is large compared with the salary received and there are other sources of income available, this tends to support the view that the dominant motive was the protection of investment. On the other hand, where the investment is small compared with the salary received and there are no or only insubstantial other sources of income, then the dominant motive may be viewed as protection of salary.

A person's subjective intention in making a loan or guarantee is a factor to be considered, but it is not controlling. Rather, motive is deduced from all the facts and circumstances surrounding the making of the loan or guarantee.

EXAMPLE: A retired engineer formed a company of which he was the principal shareholder and CEO. When the company experienced cash flow problems, he lent it money and gave personal guarantees for third-party loans to the company. When the company went under, he lost $450,000 (besides his investment in the company). This $450,000 comprised the loans to the company and the guarantees he had to make good on when the company could not. He claimed a business bad debt deduction, which an appellate court allowed. He was a retiree who wanted to continue to work. In view of his age and background, forming his own company was the way to optimal employment. His guarantees in this case far exceeded his initial investment, which was minimal. Therefore his dominant motive in making the loans and guarantees was to protect his employment.

EXAMPLE: After being terminated from her job as president of a company and spending a year looking for another job, this individual formed her own company. She did not take salary for the first year; her salary thereafter was between $30,000 and $50,000. Her outside income was substantially more (over $1 million in the year she drew no salary). She guaranteed more than $1 million of loans to the company, which she was called upon to repay. But here her bad debt was treated as a nonbusiness bad debt. Her dominant motive was protection of her investment. She could not prove that her dominant motive was protection of salary, since it is not reasonable to believe someone would guarantee over $1 million in loans to protect a salary of $30,000.

GUARANTEES THAT RESULT IN BAD DEBTS

Banks and other lending institutions are well aware of the limitation on personal liability of owners in corporations. If corporations are in their infancy and do not have significant assets to use as collateral for loans, shareholders may be asked to extend their personal guarantees to induce the banks or other lending institutions to advance funds to the corporations.

Let's say you do not lend money directly to your business. However, you guarantee, endorse, or indemnify someone else's loan made to your business and are then called upon to make good on your guarantee, endorsement, or indemnity. How do you treat this payment?

If the dominant motive for making the guarantee was proximately related to your business (for example, you guaranteed a loan to the corporation for which you work), then you claim a business bad debt (see above).

If the dominant motive for making the guarantee was to protect an investment, you claim a nonbusiness bad debt (see above).

If the guarantee was made for a friend or relative without the receipt of consideration, no bad debt deduction can be claimed. The reason: You did not enter into the arrangement for profit or to protect an investment.

If there is more than one guarantor but only one co-guarantor pays the debt, the co-guarantor who pays the debt can claim only his or her proportional share of the obligation unless it can be proved that the other guarantors were unable to pay.

EXAMPLE: Three equal shareholders of Corporation X guarantee a bank loan made to the corporation. X defaults and one of the shareholders pays off the loan. That shareholder can deduct only one-third of the debt unless he can prove that the other two shareholders were unable to make any payment.

If you, as guarantor, give your own note to substitute or replace the note of the party for whom you became the guarantor, you cannot claim a bad debt deduction at that time. The deduction arises only when and to the extent you make payments on the notes.

When to Claim the Deduction

In general, a bad debt deduction in the case of a guarantee is claimed for the year in which payment is made by the guarantor. Suppose you guarantee a debt but have the right of subrogation or other right against the debtor to recoup your outlays. In this case, you claim your bad debt deduction only when the right against the debtor becomes worthless.

SPECIAL RULES FOR ACCRUAL TAXPAYERS

All taxpayers (other than certain financial institutions) use the "specific charge-off method" to account for bad debts. Under this method, business bad debts are deducted when and to the extent that they arise.

Nonaccrual-Experience Method

Taxpayers on the accrual basis have an alternative way to account for bad debts. Under this method, income that is not expected to be collected need not be accrued. If, based on prior experience, it is determined that certain receivables will not be collected, then they need not be included in gross income for the year. Since income is not taken into account, there is no need to then claim a bad debt deduction.

The nonaccrual-experience method applies only to accounts receivable for performing services. It cannot be used for amounts owed from activities such as lending money, selling goods, or acquiring receivables or the right to receive payments.

Nor can this method be used if interest or penalties are charged on late payments. However, merely offering a discount for early payment is not treated as charging interest or a late penalty if the full amount is accrued as gross income at the time the services are provided and the discount for early payment is treated as an adjustment to gross income in the year of payment.

The nonaccrual-experience method can be used under either a separate receivable system or a periodic system. The separate receivable system applies the nonaccrual-experience method separately to each account receivable; the periodic system applies it to the total of the qualified accounts receivable at the end of the year. This is a highly technical accounting rule that should be discussed with an experienced accountant.

The nonaccrual-experience method is explained more fully in IRS Publication 535, Business Expenses.

LEGISLATIVE ALERT

Congress is considering a law change that would limit the use of the nonaccrual-experience method to amounts received for the performance of qualified personal services. These would include services in the fields of health, law, engineering, architecture, accounting, actuarial science, performing arts, or consulting. If enacted, the change would apply for tax years starting in 2000.

REPORTING BAD DEBTS ON THE TAX RETURN

If you want to claim a bad debt deduction on your return, you must do more than simply enter your loss. You also must attach a statement to your return explaining each element of the bad debt. These elements include:

- A description of the debt

- The name of the debtor

- Your family or business relationship to the debtor

- The due date of the loan

- Your efforts to collect the debt

- How you decided the debt became worthless

There is no special IRS form required for making this statement.

This reporting requirement applies only to individuals who claim bad debts on Schedule A, C, E, or F. Partnerships, LLCs, S corporations, and C corporations need not attach a statement to their returns explaining their bad debt deductions.

WHERE TO DEDUCT BAD DEBTS

Employees

Nonbusiness bad debts are deducted on Schedule D as a short-term capital loss. On this schedule, enter the amount of the bad debt and "Statement Attached." Then include on an accompanying statement more information about the bad debt, as explained earlier in this chapter.

Nonbusiness bad debts are deductible only to the extent of an individual's capital gains, plus up to $3,000 of ordinary income. These capital loss limits are taken into account when completing Schedule D. Remember that unused capital losses can be carried forward indefinitely and used against future capital gains and up to $3,000 of ordinary income each year.

Business bad debts are deducted as ordinary losses on Schedule A as a miscellaneous itemized deduction subject to the 2-percent rule.

Self-Employed

Business bad debts are deducted from business income on Schedule C (or Schedule F in the case of farming operations). Schedule C contains a specific line for claiming bad debts from sales or services. Be sure to attach a statement to the return explaining the bad debts.

Nonbusiness bad debts are reported as short-term capital losses on Schedule D. Self-employed persons report nonbusiness bad debts in the same way as employees, discussed above.

Partnerships and LLCs

Partnerships and LLCs can deduct business bad debts on their return. Form 1065 contains a specific line for claiming bad debts. These bad debts reduce the partnerships' or LLCs' trade or business income. They are not passed through as separate items to partners or LLC members. Partnerships and LLCs need not attach a statement to the return explaining the bad debts.

To date there have been no cases or rulings in which bad debts of partnerships or LLCs have been treated as nonbusiness bad debts. However, should such debts occur, see the treatment of nonbusiness bad debts for S corporations, below.

S Corporations

Bad debts are usually business bad debts. Business bad debts are not separately stated items passed through separately to shareholders. Instead, they serve to reduce the amount of business income or loss that passes through to shareholders. They are entered on Form 1120S on the line specifically for bad debts. S corporations need not attach a statement to the return explaining the bad debts.

It should be noted that where the loss is considered a nonbusiness bad debt, it must be separately stated on Schedule K-1 and passed through to shareholders. In this way the short-term capital loss for the shareholder is subject to that shareholder's capital loss limits.

C Corporations

Bad debts are always business bad debts in the case of C corporations. They are reported on Form 1120 on the specific line provided for bad debts. Corporations need not attach a statement to the return explaining the bad debts.

CHAPTER 10

Rents

From a financial standpoint, it might make more sense in some cases to rent than to buy property and equipment. Renting may require a smaller cash outlay than buying. Also, the business may not as yet have established sufficient credit to make large purchases but can still gain the use of the property or equipment through renting. If you pay rent to use office space, a store, or other property for your business, or you pay to lease business equipment, you generally can deduct your outlays. In this chapter you will learn about:

- Deducting rent payments in general

- The cost of acquiring or canceling a lease

- Improvements you make to leased property

- Rental of a portion of your home for business

- Leasing a car

- Leveraged leases

- Where to deduct rent payments

DEDUCTING RENT PAYMENTS IN GENERAL

If you pay to use property for business that you do not own, the payments are rent. They may also be called lease payments. Rents paid for property used in a business are deductible business expenses. These include obligations you pay on behalf of your landlord. For example, if you are required by the terms of your lease to pay real estate taxes on the property, you can deduct these taxes as part of your rent payments.

The rents must be reasonable in amount. The issue of reasonableness generally does not arise where you and the landlord are at arm's length. However, the issue does come up when you and the landlord are related parties, such as family members or related companies. Rent paid to a related party is treated as reasonable if it is the same rent that would be paid to an unrelated party. A percentage rental is also considered reasonable if the rental paid is reasonable.

If the rent payments entitle you to receive equity in or title to the property at the end of some term, the payments are not rent. They may, however, be deductible in part as depreciation (see Chapter 12).

Rent to Your Corporation

If you rent property to your corporation, the corporation can claim a rental expense deduction, assuming the rents are reasonable. However, you cannot treat the rents as passive income that you could use to offset your losses from other passive activities. The law specifically prohibits you from arranging this type of rental for tax benefit.

If you rent a portion of your home to your employer, see the discussion on "Rental of a Portion of Your Home for Business" later in this chapter.

Rent with an Option to Buy

Sometimes it is not clear whether payments are to lease or purchase property. There are a number of factors used to make such a determination.

Nature of the document   If you have a lease, payments made thereunder generally are treated as rents. If you have a conditional sales contract, payments made thereunder are nondeductible purchase payments. A document is treated as a conditional sales contract if it provides that you will acquire title to or equity in the property upon completing a certain number or amount of payments.

Intent of the parties   How the parties to the agreement view the transaction affects whether it is a lease or a conditional sales contract. Intent can be inferred from certain objective factors. A conditional sales contract exists if any of the following are found:

- The agreement applies part of each payment toward an equity interest.

- The agreement provides for the transfer of title after payment of a stated amount.

- The amount of the payment to use the property for a short time is a large part of the amount paid to get title to the property.

- The payments exceed the current fair rental value of the property (based on comparisons with other similar properties).

- There is an option to buy the property at a nominal price as compared with the property's value at the time the option can be exercised.

- There is an option to buy the property at a nominal price as compared with the total amount required to be paid under the agreement.

- The agreement designates a part of the payments as "interest" or in some way makes part of the payments easily recognizable as interest.

EXAMPLE: You "lease" an office building for a period of two years. The lease agreement provides that at the end of that term you have the option of buying the property and all of the payments made to date will be applied toward the purchase price. In this case, your payments probably would be viewed as payments to purchase rather than payments to lease the property.

Advance Rents

Generally, rents are deductible in the year in which they are paid or accrued. What happens if you pay rent in advance? According to the IRS, you can deduct only the portion of the rent that applies to use of the rented property during the year.

EXAMPLE: You report income and expenses on the calendar-year basis and lease property for three years, beginning January 1999. The lease payment is $6,000 per year. You pay the entire amount ($18,000) in January 1999.

You can deduct only $6,000 in 1999. The balance is deductible at the rate of $6,000 in 2000.

EXAMPLE: You report on the calendar-year basis and lease property for five years, beginning July 1, 1999. You pay one year's rent on that date of $12,000. According to the IRS you may deduct only $6,000, the portion of the rent related to the last six months of the year covered by the lease.

However, one appellate court has allowed a deduction in the year of payment for rents that do not exceed one year.

EXAMPLE: In December 1999 you pay rent for the next 12 months (covering the period of December 1999 through November 2000). According to an appellate court, you may deduct the entire rent payment in 1999. It would seem that in the example above, this court would have allowed the full $12,000 deduction for 1999 even though part of the payments related to 2000, since the rent payment did not exceed a period of one year.

Gift-Leasebacks

If you own property you have already depreciated, you may want to create a tax deduction for your business by entering into a gift-leaseback transaction. Typically, the property is gifted to your spouse or children, to whom you then pay rent. In the past this type of arrangement was more popular, but the passive loss rules put a damper on deducting losses created by these arrangements. If you still want to shift income to your children (who presumably are in a lower tax bracket than you) while getting a tax deduction for your business, be sure that you meet these requirements:

1. You do not retain control over the property after the gift is given.

2. The leaseback is in writing and the rent charged is reasonable.

3. There must be a business purpose for the leaseback. For example, where a doctor transferred the property in which his practice was located to his children in fear of malpractice suits, this was a valid business reason for leasing rather than owning the property.

There are other factors to consider before entering into a gift-leaseback. Consider the impact of the "kiddie tax" if your children are under the age of 14. It is strongly suggested that you consult with a tax adviser before giving business property to your children and then leasing it back for use in your business.

Miscellaneous Rentals

Some payments for the use of property that you may not otherwise think of as rentals but that may be required by your business include:

- Safety deposit box rental fees
- Post office box rental fees

THE COST OF ACQUIRING OR CANCELING A LEASE

The Cost of Acquiring a Lease

Where you pay a premium to obtain immediate possession under a lease that does not extend beyond the tax year, the premium is deductible in full for the current year. Where the premium relates to a long-term lease, the cost of the premium is deductible over the term of the lease. The same amortization rule applies to commissions, bonuses, and other fees paid to obtain a lease on property you use in your business.

When the lease contains renewal options, what is the term of the lease for purposes of deducting lease acquisition premiums? The tax law provides a complicated method for making this determination. The term of the lease for amortization purposes includes all renewal option periods if less than 75 percent of the cost is attributable to the term of the lease remaining on the purchase date. Do not include any period for which the lease may be renewed, extended, or continued under an option exercisable by you, the lessee, in determining the term of the lease remaining on the purchase date.

EXAMPLE: You pay $10,000 to acquire a lease with 20 years remaining on it. The lease has two options to renew, for five years each. Of the $10,000, $7,000 is paid for the original lease and $3,000 for the renewal options. Since $7,000 is less than 75 percent of the total cost, you must amortize $10,000 over 30 years (the lease term plus the two renewal option periods).

EXAMPLE: The circumstances are the same as above, except $8,000 is allocable to the original lease. Since this is not less than 75 percent of the total cost, the entire $10,000 can be amortized over the original lease term of 20 years.

The Cost of Modifying a Lease

If you pay an additional rent to change a lease provision, you amortize this additional payment over the remaining term of the lease.

The Cost of Canceling a Lease

If you pay to get out of your lease before the end of its term, the cost generally is deductible in full in the year of payment. However, where a new lease is obtained, the cost of canceling the lease must be capitalized if the cancellation and new lease are viewed as part of the same transaction.

EXAMPLE: A company leased a computer system under a lease that was to run for five years. To upgrade its system, the company canceled the original lease and entered into a new one with the same lessor. Because the termination of the old lease was conditioned on obtaining a new lease, the cost of termination had to be capitalized (i.e., added to the cost of the new lease and deducted ratably over the term of the new lease).

IMPROVEMENTS YOU MAKE TO LEASED PROPERTY

If you add a building or make other permanent improvements to leased property, you can depreciate the cost of the improvements using MACRS depreciation. (For a further discussion of depreciation, see Chapter 12.) The improvements are depreciated over their recovery period, a time fixed by law. They are not depreciated over the remaining term of the lease.

EXAMPLE: You construct a building on land you lease. The recovery period of the building is 39 years. When the building construction is completed, there are 35 years remaining on the lease. You depreciate the building over its recovery period of 39 years, not over the 35 years remaining on the lease.

If you acquire a lease through an assignment and the lessee that assigns you the lease has made improvements to the property, the amount you pay for the assignment is a capital investment. Where the rental value of the leased land has increased since the beginning of the lease, part of the capital investment is for the increase in that value; the balance is for your investment in the permanent improvements. You amortize the part of the increased rental value of the leased land; you depreciate the part of the investment related to the improvements.

If you enter into a lease after August 5, 1997, for retail space for 15 years or less and you receive a construction allowance from the landlord to make additions or improvements to the space, you are not taxed on these payments provided they are fully used for the purpose intended.

RENTAL OF A PORTION OF YOUR HOME FOR BUSINESS

If you rent your home and use part of it for business, you may be able to deduct part of your rent as a business expense. This part of the rent is treated as a home office deduction if you meet certain requirements.

The Home Office

To claim a rental deduction, you must use the portion of your home as the principal place of business for the activity conducted at home; as a place for meeting or dealing with clients, customers, or patients in the ordinary course of your business; or as a separate structure not attached to your dwelling unit that is used in connection with your business. The principal place of business requirement is satisfied if the home office is used to conduct substantial administrative or managerial activities and there is no other fixed location for performing such activities.

If you are an employee, use of the home office must also be for the convenience of your employer. This is based on all the facts and circumstances. Use of a home office is not treated as for the convenience of an employer merely because it is appropriate and helpful.

The portion of the home used for business must be used regularly and exclusively for this purpose. Thus, even one room can be used in part for business if it is sectioned off and used only for business. (A deduction may also be allowed when the home is used for care of children or adults or when space is used to store inventory or samples from your business, even though that portion of the home is sometimes used for personal purposes.)

If you lease part of your home to your corporation, you cannot deduct any expenses (including the allocable portion of rent you pay to your landlord) related to that portion of your home in which you perform services as an employee. The corporation can still deduct its rental payments to you, and you must report such rental payments as income. Since you cannot offset this rental income by expenses, such a rental arrangement generally is not advisable.

Deduction Limit

The amount of your home office deduction, including a write-off for rent, cannot exceed gross income derived from your home office activity. Any deductions in excess of this limit can be carried forward and used in the following year to the extent there is sufficient gross income from the activity.

EXAMPLE: You rent a two-bedroom apartment and use one bedroom as an office for your consulting business. The annual rent attributable to this portion of your apartment is $2,400. (For purposes of this example, assume no other home office expenses.) Gross income from your business is $30,000. You may deduct all your rent allocated to the home office. But if your gross income from consulting was only $1,000, the deduction for rent allocated to the home office would be limited to $1,000; $1,400 would be carried forward to the next year and would be deductible if gross income from your consulting was sufficient to offset the carryforward.

The home office deduction is discussed more fully in Chapter 17.

LEASING A CAR

If you lease a car for business use, the treatment of the rental costs depends upon the term of the lease. If the term is less than 30 days, the entire cost of the rental is deductible. Thus, if you go out of town on business and rent a car for a week, your rental costs are deductible.

If the lease term exceeds 30 days, the lease payments are still deductible if you use the car entirely for business. If you use it for both business and personal purposes, you must allocate the lease payments and deduct only the business portion of the costs. However, depending on the value of the car at the time it is leased, you may be required to include an amount in gross income called an "inclusion amount" (explained below).

If you make advance payments, you must spread these payments over the entire lease period and deduct them accordingly. You cannot depreciate a car you lease, because depreciation applies only to property that is owned.

Lease with an Option to Buy

When you have this arrangement, are you leasing or buying the car? The answer depends on a number of factors:

1. Intent of the parties to the transaction

2. Whether any equity results from the arrangement

3. Whether any interest is paid

4. Whether the fair market value of the car is less than the "lease" payment or option payment when the option to buy is exercised

Where the factors support a finding that the arrangement is a lease, the payments are deductible. If, however, the factors support a finding that the arrangement is a purchase agreement, the payments are not deductible.

Inclusion Amount

Where the car price exceeds a certain amount and you do not use the standard mileage rate to account for expenses, you may have to include in income an amount called an "inclusion amount." This is because the law seeks to equate buying with leasing. Since there is a dollar limit on the amount of depreciation that can be claimed on a "luxury" car that is owned, the law also requires an amount to be included in income as an offset to high lease payments on a car that is leased. In essence, the inclusion amount seeks to limit your deduction for lease payments to what it would be if you owned the car and claimed depreciation.

The inclusion amount, which is simply an amount that you add to your other income, applies if a car is leased for more than 30 days and its value exceeds a certain amount (which is adjusted periodically for inflation). The inclusion amount is added to income only so long as you lease the car. Inclusion amounts are based on the value of the car as of the first day of the lease term. If the capitalized cost of the car is specified in the lease agreement, that amount is considered to be the car's fair market value. At the start of the lease, you can see what your inclusion amount will be for that year and for all subsequent years. The inclusion amount is based on a percentage of the fair market value of the car at the time the lease begins.

Definition *Fair market value* This is the price that would be paid for the property where there is a willing buyer and seller (neither being required to buy or sell) and both have reasonable knowledge of all the necessary facts. Evidence of fair market value includes the price paid for similar property on or about the same date.

The inclusion amount applies only if the fair market value of the car when the lease began was more than the following:

Fair market value of car	For leases beginning in
$12,800	1987–1990
13,400	1991
13,700	1992
14,300	1993
14,600	1994
15,500	1995–1996
15,800	1997–1998
15,500	1999

The inclusion amount is taken from IRS tables. The full amount in the table applies if the car is leased for the full year and used entirely for business. If the car is leased for less than the full year, or if it is used only partly for personal purposes, then the inclusion amount must be allocated to business use for the period of the year in which it was used. The allocation for part-year use is made on a day-by-day basis.

EXAMPLE: The inclusion amount for your car is $500. You used the car only six months of the year (a leap year). You must include in income $250 (183/366 of $500).

SAMPLE INCLUSION AMOUNTS* FOR CARS FIRST LEASED IN 1999

Fair Market Value		Year of Lease				
Over	Not over	1st	2nd	3rd	4th	5th/later
$15,500	$15,800	$2	$3	$4	$4	$6
17,000	17,500	13	25	38	45	53
19,500	20,000	29	61	90	108	126
22,000	23,000	47	100	148	178	206

continued on next page

SAMPLE INCLUSION AMOUNTS* FOR CARS
FIRST LEASED IN 1999

Fair Market Value		Year of Lease				
Over	Not over	1st	2nd	3rd	4th	5th/later
25,000	26,000	66	142	212	254	293
30,000	31,000	105	227	338	406	468
40,000	41,000	163	355	528	633	731
50,000	51,000	228	497	739	885	1,023

*Actual amounts for cars valued at amounts not listed in the table above may be found in Chapter 7.

Inclusion amounts are adjusted annually for inflation. Inclusion amounts for cars leased before 1999 can be found in IRS Publication 463, Travel, Entertainment, Gifts, and Car Expenses. Different inclusion amounts apply to electric cars costing more than $47,000 in 1999. The table for finding inclusion amounts for electric cars can also be found in this IRS publication.

Remember that if you use your car for commuting or other nonbusiness purposes, you cannot deduct that allocable part of the lease.

Car leasing, including the advisability of leasing versus buying a business car, is discussed more fully in Chapter 7.

LEVERAGED LEASES

If you are the lessee in a transaction referred to as a "leveraged lease," you generally can deduct your lease payments.

Definition *Leveraged lease* A three-party transaction in which the landlord (lessor) obtains financing from a third party and in which lease payments are sufficient to cover the cost of repaying the financing. Also, the lease term generally covers the useful life of the property.

It is important that the lessor, and not the lessee, be treated as the owner of the property if lease payments are to be deductible. The lessor is treated as the owner if he or she has a minimum amount at risk (at least 20 percent) during the entire term of the lease and the lessee does not have a contractual right to buy the property at its fair market value at the end of the lease term. Other factors necessary to show that the lessor and not the lessee is the owner of the property: The lessor has a profit motive (apart from tax benefits); the lessee does not lend money to the lessor; and the lessee does not invest in the property.

If you are about to become the lessee of a leveraged lease and want to be sure that you will not be treated as the owner (which would mean your rental expenses would not be deductible), you can ask the IRS for an advance ruling on the issue. There is a user fee for this service. It may be advisable to seek the assistance of a tax professional in obtaining the ruling.

However, the IRS will not issue an advance ruling on leveraged leases of so-called limited use property.

> **Definition** *Limited use property* Property not expected to be either useful to or usable by a lessor at the end of the lease term except for continued leasing or transfer to the lessee or a member of a lessee group.

Special rules apply to leases of tangible personal property over $250,000.

WHERE TO DEDUCT RENT PAYMENTS

Employees

Rent expenses are deductible as itemized expenses on Schedule A. If you lease a car for more than 30 days, you must complete Form 2106, Employee Business Expenses, to report the lease payments. (You cannot use the simplified form, 2106-EZ, if you lease rather than own your car.) The results of Form 2106 are then entered on Schedule A and are subject to the 2-percent-of-adjusted-gross-income floor discussed in Chapter 1.

If you rent your home and use part of it for business for the convenience of your employer, you can claim a home office deduction for that part of the rent. There is no special form that an employee is required to use for calculating his or her home office deduction. However, you may figure the deduction on a special worksheet for this purpose in IRS Publication 587. The deductible portion of your rent (along with other home office expenses) is entered on Schedule A as an itemized expense, which, again, is subject to the 2-percent floor.

Self-Employed

Rents are deductible on Schedule C. This schedule provides two separate lines for reporting rents and leases so that rents and leases for vehicles, machinery, and equipment are reported separately from those of other business property. If you lease a car for more than 30 days, you must complete Part IV of Schedule C if you are not otherwise required to file Form 4562, Depreciation and Amortization, or directly on this form if you placed in service any property in 1999 that is subject to depreciation or amortization.

Farmers who are self-employed deduct rents on Schedule F. Information about leased cars must be entered on Form 4562, Depreciation and Amortization.

If you rent your home and use part of it for business and file Schedule C, you can claim a home office deduction for that part of the rent. Home office expenses, including rent, are computed on Form 8829, Expenses for Business Use of Your Home. Then the deductible portion is entered on Schedule C. If you are a farmer who files Schedule F, figure your home office deduction on the worksheet found in IRS Publication 587. Then enter the deductible portion on Schedule F.

Partnerships and LLCs

Rent and lease payments are deducted by partnerships and LLCs on their returns as part of the entity's ordinary trade or business income, on Form 1065. The return contains a separate line for reporting rents. Rent and lease payments are not passed through to partners or LLC members as separate items.

If you rent your home and use part of it for the business of the partnership, you can claim a home office deduction for that part of the rent. There is no special form that a partner must use for calculating his or her home office deduction. However, you may figure the deduction on a special worksheet for this purpose in IRS Publication 587. The deductible portion of your rent (along with other home office expenses) is entered on Schedule E as part of your share of partnership income and expenses.

S Corporations

Rents and lease payments are deducted by the S corporation as part of its ordinary trade or business income on Form 1120S. The return contains a separate line for reporting rents. Rents and lease payments are not passed through to shareholders as separately stated items.

C Corporations

C corporations deduct rent and lease payments on Form 1120. The return contains a separate line for reporting rents.

CHAPTER 11

Taxes and Interest

Taxes and interest are two types of expenses that are hard to avoid. In the course of your business activities, you may pay various taxes and interest charges. In this chapter you will learn about:

- Deductible taxes

- Nondeductible taxes

- Deductible interest

- Nondeductible interest and other limitations on deductibility

- Where to deduct taxes and interest

For further information about deducting taxes and interest, see IRS Publication 535, Business Expenses.

DEDUCTIBLE TAXES

General Rules

In order for you to deduct taxes, they must be imposed on you. The tax must be owed by the party who pays it. Thus, if your corporation owns an office building, it is the party that owes the real property taxes. If, as part of your lease, you are obligated to pay your landlord's taxes, you can deduct your payment as an additional part of your rent; you do not claim a deduction for taxes, since you are not the owner of the property.

The taxes must be paid during the year if you are on a cash basis. If you pay taxes at year end by means of a check or even a credit card charge, the tax is deductible in the year the check is sent or delivered or the credit charge is made. This is so even though the check is not cashed until the following year or you do not pay the credit card bill until the following year. If you pay any tax by phone or through your computer, the tax is deductible on the date of payment reported on the statement issued by the financial institution through which the payment is made. If you contest a liability and do not pay it until the issue is settled, you cannot deduct the tax until it is actually paid. It may be advisable to settle a disputed liability in order to fix the amount and claim a deduction.

If you pay tax after the end of the year for a liability that relates to the prior year, you deduct the tax in the year of payment.

EXAMPLE: An S corporation on a calendar year, cash basis method pays its state franchise fee for 1999 in March 2000. The payment is deductible on the S corporation's 2000 income tax return, not on its 1999 return.

Real Estate Taxes

In general, real property taxes are deductible. Assessments made to real property for the repair or maintenance of some local benefit (such as streets, sidewalks, or sewers) are treated as deductible taxes.

If you acquire real property for resale to customers, you may be required under uniform capitalization rules to capitalize these taxes. The uniform capitalization rules are discussed in Chapter 2.

Special rules apply when real estate is sold during the year. Then real property taxes must be allocated between the buyer and seller according to the number of days in the real property tax year. The seller can deduct the taxes up to but not including the date of sale. The buyer can deduct the taxes from the date of sale onward.

Accrual basis taxpayers can deduct only taxes accruing on the date of sale. An accrual basis taxpayer can elect to accrue ratably real property taxes related to a definite period of time over that period of time.

EXAMPLE: X Corp., a calendar-year taxpayer on the accrual basis, owns an office building on which annual taxes are $1,200 for the fiscal year July 1, 1999, through June 30, 2000. If X elects to ratably accrue taxes, $600 of the taxes is deductible in 1999, the balance in 2000.

The election to accrue taxes ratably applies for each separate business. If one business owns two properties, an election covers both properties. The election is binding and can be revoked only with the consent of the IRS. You make the election by attaching a statement to your return for the first year that real property taxes are due on property. The statement should include the businesses for which the election is being made, the period of time to which the taxes relate, and a computation of the real property tax deduction for the first year of the election. The election must be filed with a timely filed income tax return (including extensions).

If you have already owned property for some time but want to switch to the ratable accrual method, you must obtain the consent of the IRS. To do so, file Form 3115, Change in Accounting Method, within the year for which the change is to be effective.

Construction Period Taxes and Interest

These costs cannot currently be deducted. They may be capitalized as construction costs. The costs can then be amortized.

State and Local Income Taxes

A corporation that pays state and local income taxes can deduct the taxes on its return. A self-employed individual who pays state and local taxes with respect to business income reported on Schedule C can deduct them only as an itemized deduction on Schedule A. Similarly, an employee who pays state and local taxes with respect to compensation from employment can deduct these taxes only on Schedule A. However, if a state tax is imposed on gross income (as opposed to net income) that is directly attributable to a business, the tax is treated as a business expense deductible on Schedule C for sole proprietors.

Self-Employment Tax

Businesses do not pay self-employment tax; individuals do. Sole proprietors, general partners (whether active or inactive), and certain LLC members pay self-employment tax on their net earnings from self-employment (amounts reported on Schedule C or as self-employment income on Schedule K). Limited partners do not pay self-employment tax on their share of income from the business. However, limited partners are subject to self-employment tax if they perform any services for the business or receive any guaranteed payments. LLC members who are like general partners pay self-employment tax; those like limited partners do not. The IRS was precluded from issuing regulations defining a limited partner before July 1, 1998. At the time this book was being prepared, the IRS had not issued any regulations nor given any indication when it would.

Those who pay self-employment tax are entitled to deduct one-half of the tax as an adjustment to gross income on their personal income tax returns. The deduction on page 1 of Form 1040 reduces your gross income and serves to lower the threshold for certain itemized deductions.

While S corporations are pass-through entities similar to partnerships and LLCs, owners of S corporations who work for their businesses are not treated the same as partners and LLC members for purposes of self-employment tax. Owners of S corporations who are also employees of their businesses do not pay self-employment tax on their compensation—they are employees of the corporation for purposes of employment tax. Their compensation is subject to FICA, not to self-employment tax. Individuals who both are self-employed and have an interest in an S corporation cannot use losses from the S corporation to reduce net earnings from self-employment.

Personal Property Tax

Personal property tax on any property used in a business is deductible. Personal property tax is an ad valorem tax—namely, a tax on the value of personal property. For example, a "floor tax" is a property tax levied on inventory sitting on the floor (or shelves) of your business. Registration fees for the right to use property within the state in your trade or business are deductible. Where the fees are based on the value of the property, they are considered a personal property tax.

Sales and Use Taxes

Sales tax to acquire a depreciable asset used in a trade or business is added to the basis of the asset and is recovered through depreciation. If sales tax is paid to acquire a nondepreciable asset, it is still treated as part of the cost of the asset and is deducted as part of the asset's expense. For example, sales tax on business stationery is part of the cost of the stationery and is deducted as part of that cost (not as a separate sales tax deduction). Sales tax paid on property acquired for resale is also treated as part of the cost of that property.

Sales tax you collect as a merchant or other business owner and turn over to the state is deductible only if you include it in your gross receipts. If not, the sales tax is not deductible.

Where sales tax is imposed on the seller or retailer and the seller or retailer can separately state the tax or pass it on to the consumer, then the consumer, rather than the seller or retailer, gets to deduct the tax. Where the consumer is in business, how the tax is treated depends on the asset acquired. See above for sales tax paid for depreciable property, nondepreciable property, and property held for sale or resale.

A compensating use tax is treated as a sales tax. This type of tax is imposed on the use, storage, or consumption of an item brought in from another taxing jurisdiction. Typically, it is imposed at the same percentage as a sale tax.

Luxury Tax

Like sale taxes, a luxury tax paid to acquire a depreciable asset is added to the basis of the asset; it is not separately deductible. Thus, for example, if you pay a luxury tax to acquire a high-priced car that you use for business, the amount of the tax becomes part of the car's basis for purposes of depreciation.

Employment Taxes

If you have employees and pay the employer portion of FICA for them, you can deduct this amount as a tax. FICA comprises a Social Security tax and a Medicare tax. The employer portion of the Social Security tax is 6.2 percent. This is applied to a wage base (up to $72,600 in 1999) that is adjusted annually for inflation. The employer portion of the Medicare tax is 1.45 percent. This is applied to all wages paid to an employee; there is no wage base limit. If you as an employer pay both the employer and employee portion of the tax, you may claim a deduction for your full payments.

You may also be liable for FUTA (federal unemployment tax) for your employees. The gross federal unemployment tax rate is 6.2 percent. This is applied to wages of an employee up to $7,000. However, you may claim a credit of up to 5.4 percent for state unemployment tax that you pay. If your state unemployment tax rate is 5.4 percent or more, then the net federal unemployment tax rate is 0.8 percent. Even if your state unemployment rate is less than 5.4 percent, you are permitted to claim a full reduction of 5.4 percent. However, if you are exempt from state unemployment tax, you must pay the full federal unemployment tax rate of 6.2 percent. FUTA tax payments are deductible by you as an employer.

A complete discussion of employment taxes can be found in Chapter 5.

State Benefit Funds

An employer who pays into a state unemployment insurance fund may deduct the payments as taxes. An employee who must contribute to the following state benefit funds can deduct the payments as state income taxes on Schedule A:

- California: Nonoccupational Disability Benefit Fund

- New Jersey: Nonoccupational Disability Benefit Fund

- New York: Nonoccupational Disability Benefit Fund

- Rhode Island: Nonoccupational Disability Benefit Fund

- Washington State: Supplemental Workmen's Compensation Fund

The deduction for these taxes is not subject to a 2-percent-of-adjusted-gross-income floor (see Chapter 1), as is the case with other employee business expenses.

Franchise Taxes

Corporate franchise taxes (which is another term that may be used for state corporate income taxes and has nothing to do with whether the corporation is a franchise) are a deductible business expense. Your state may or may not impose franchise taxes on S corporations; check with your state corporate tax department.

Excise Taxes

Excise taxes paid or incurred in a trade or business are deductible as operating expenses.

Fuel Taxes

Taxes on gas, diesel fuel, and other motor fuels used in your business are deductible. As a practical matter, they are included in the cost of the fuel and are not separately stated. Thus they are deducted as a fuel cost rather than as a tax.

You may be able to claim a tax credit for tax paid on fuels used for certain purposes. For further information on this credit, see IRS Publication 378, Fuel Tax Credits and Refunds.

Foreign Taxes

Income taxes paid to a foreign country or U.S. possession may be claimed as a deduction or a tax credit. To claim foreign income taxes as a tax credit, you must file Form 1116, Foreign Tax Credit (unless as an individual you have foreign tax of $300 or less, or $600 or less on a joint return). Corporations claim the foreign tax credit on Form 1118. The same rules apply for foreign real property taxes paid with respect to real property owned in a foreign country or U.S. possession.

Other Rules

Where a corporation pays a tax imposed on a shareholder and the shareholder does not reimburse the corporation, then the corporation, and not the shareholder, is entitled to claim the deduction for the payment of the tax.

NONDEDUCTIBLE TAXES

You may not deduct federal income taxes, even the amount paid with respect to your business income. These are nondeductible taxes.

Other nondeductible taxes include:

- Assessments on real property for local benefits that tend to add to the value of the property. Such assessments may be made, for example, to build sidewalks, streets, sewers, or parks. These assessments are added to the basis of the property. But assessments for maintenance purposes (such as for repairs to sidewalks, streets, and sewers) are deductible. Water bills, sewage, and other service charges are not treated as taxes. They are, however, deductible as business expenses.

- Employee contributions to private or voluntary disability plans.

- Fines imposed by a governmental authority. These are not deductible as a tax even if incurred in a trade or business. For example, if while traveling away from home on business you receive a fine for a speeding ticket, the fine is not deductible.

- Penalties imposed by the federal government on taxes or for failing to file returns. These are not deductible even though they may be computed with regard to the length of time the taxpayer has failed to comply with a tax law requirement.

- Occupational taxes.

DEDUCTIBLE INTEREST

General Rules

Interest paid or incurred on debts related to your business generally is fully deductible as business interest. Business interest is deductible without limitation, except where such interest is required to be capitalized. (Remember, for example, that construction period interest and taxes must be capitalized, as explained earlier in this chapter.) There is one main exception to the general deductibility rule for business interest: interest on life insurance policies. The limits on deducting interest with respect to life insurance policies are discussed in Chapter 19 in connection with insurance.

Interest characterized as personal interest is nondeductible (except to the extent of qualified home mortgage interest and a limited amount of student loan interest).

Interest characterized as investment interest is deductible only to the extent of net investment income.

Interest characterized as incurred in a passive activity is subject to the passive loss rules.

The characterization of interest depends on what the proceeds of the loan that generated the interest were used for. The characterization is not dependent on what type of property—business or personal—was used as collateral for the loan. Thus, if you borrow on your personal life insurance policy and use the proceeds to buy equipment for your business, you can deduct the interest as business interest. On the other hand, if you take a bank loan using your corporate stock as collateral, and use the proceeds to invest in the stock market, the interest is characterized as investment interest. One thorny issue is whether interest on a tax deficiency relating to

Schedules C, E, or F should be treated as deductible business interest or nondeductible personal interest. While the Tax Court has allowed a deduction for this interest, several appellate courts have sided with the IRS in denying a deduction for this interest.

Where the proceeds are used for more than one purpose, you must make an allocation based on the use of the loan's proceeds. When you repay a part of the loan, the repayments are treated as repaying the loan in this order:

- Amounts allocated to personal use

- Amounts allocated to investments and passive activities

- Amounts allocated to passive activities in connection with rental real estate in which you actively participate

- Amounts allocated to business use

As in the case of taxes discussed earlier, the interest obligation must be yours in order for you to claim an interest deduction. If you pay off someone else's loan, you cannot deduct the interest you pay. If you are contractually obligated to make the payment, you may be able to deduct your payment as some other expense item, but not as interest.

Debt Incurred to Buy an Interest in a Business

If you use loan proceeds to buy an interest in a partnership, LLC, or S corporation or to make a contribution to capital, this is treated as a "debt-financed acquisition." In this case, you must allocate the interest on the loan according to an allocation based on the assets of the pass-through business. The allocation can be based on book value, market value, or the adjusted bases of the assets.

EXAMPLE: You borrow $25,000 to buy an interest in an S corporation. The S corporation owns $90,000 of equipment and $10,000 of stocks (based on fair market value). In this case, nine-tenths of the interest on the loan is treated as business interest ($90,000/$100,000); one-tenth of the interest is treated as investment interest ($10,000/$100,000).

If you, as an S corporation shareholder, LLC member, or partner, receive proceeds from a debt, you must also allocate the debt proceeds. This is called debt-financed distributions. Under a general allocation rule, debt proceeds distributed to an owner of a pass-through entity are allocated to the owner's use of the proceeds. Thus, if the owner uses the proceeds for personal purposes, the pass-through entity must treat the interest as nondeductible personal interest. Under an optional allocation rule, the pass-through entity may allocate the proceeds (and related interest) to one or more of the entity's expenditures other than distributions. The expenditures to which the debt is allocated are those made in the same year as the allocation is made (see Notice 89-35 for allocations in pass-through entities).

If you borrow money to buy stock in a closely held C corporation, the Tax Court considers the interest to be investment interest. The reason: C corporation stock is, like any publicly traded stock, held for investment. This is so even if the corporation never pays out investment income (dividends) or the purchase of the stock is made to protect one's employment with the corporation.

Loans Between Shareholders and Their Corporations

Special care must be taken when shareholders lend money to their corporation, and vice versa, or when shareholders guarantee third-party loans made to their corporation.

Corporation's indebtedness to shareholders   If a corporation borrows from its shareholders, the corporation can deduct the interest it pays on the loan. The issue sometimes raised by the IRS in these types of loans is whether in fact there is any real indebtedness. Sometimes loans are used in place of dividends to transform nondeductible dividend payments into deductible interest. In order for a loan to withstand IRS scrutiny, be prepared to show a written instrument bearing a fixed maturity date for the repayment of the loan. The instrument should also state a fixed rate of interest. There should be a valid business reason for this borrowing arrangement (such as evidence that the corporation could not borrow from a commercial source at a reasonable rate of interest). If the loan is subordinated to the claims of corporate creditors, this tends to show that it is not a true debt, but other factors may prove otherwise. Also, where the corporation is heavily indebted to shareholders, the debt-to-equity ratio may indicate that the loans are not true loans but merely disguised equity.

When a corporation fails to repay a loan to a shareholder, this may give rise to a bad debt deduction for the shareholder. Bad debts are discussed in Chapter 9.

Shareholder guarantees of corporate debt   Often for small businesses, banks or other lenders may require personal guarantees by the corporation's principal shareholders as a condition for making loans to the corporation. This arrangement raises one of the basic rules for deducting interest discussed earlier: The obligation must be yours in order for you to deduct the interest.

EXAMPLE: A sole shareholder paid interest on a loan made by a third party to his corporation. He had agreed that he would pay any outstanding debt if the corporation failed to do so. He was not entitled to claim an interest deduction because it was the corporation, not he, who was primarily liable on the obligation. The shareholder was only a guarantor.

Below-Market and Above-Market Loans
When shareholders and their corporations arrange loans between themselves, they may set interest rates at less than or more than the going market rate of interest. This may be done for a number of reasons, including to ease the financial burden on a party to the loan or to create tax advantage. Whatever the reason, it is important to understand the consequences of the arrangement.

Below-market loans   If you receive an interest-free or below-market-interest loan, you may still be able to claim an interest deduction. You can claim an interest deduction equal to the sum of the interest you actually pay, plus the amount of interest that the lender is required to report as income under the below-market loan rules. The amount that the lender is required to report as income is fixed according to interest rates set monthly by the IRS. Rates are set for short-term, mid-term, and long-term loans. These rates are called the applicable federal rates. If a loan is payable on demand, the short-term rate applies. However, if the loan is outstanding for an entire year, you can use a blended annual rate provided by the IRS to simplify the computation of the taxable imputed interest.

EXAMPLE: On January 1, 1999, you borrowed $40,000 from your corporation for investments. You were not charged any interest by your corporation and the loan was payable on demand. The applicable federal rate for determining interest that the lender must report for 1999 is the blended rate of 4.94 percent for demand loans outstanding for the entire year. Thus, your interest deduction is $1,976 (subject to the limitation on deducting investment interest).

Whether you are required to report this amount as income (which would in effect offset the interest deduction) depends on the amount of the loan and the context in which it was made. If it was treated as compensation or a dividend, you have to include it in income; if it was considered a gift loan, you do not have additional income. Gift loans are loans up to $10,000 (as long as the loan is not made for tax avoidance purposes). From the corporate (lender) perspective, it must report the "interest" as income. If the loan is to an employee, an offsetting deduction can be taken for compensation. But if the loan is to a nonemployee, such as a shareholder who does not work for the corporation, no offsetting deduction can be taken.

Above-market loans   Instead of borrowing from a bank, your corporation may be able to borrow from a relative of yours, such as your child or parent, to whom you want to make gifts. You can turn the arrangement into a profitable one for both your corporation and your relative (the lender). Set the interest rate at more than what would be charged by the bank. Provided that the interest is still considered "reasonable" and the loan is an arm's-length transaction, your corporation deducts the interest and the lender receives it. If an unreasonably high rate of interest is charged and the arrangement is not at arm's length, however, the IRS will attack the arrangement and may disallow the interest as being a disguised dividend payment to you.

Home Mortgage Interest and Home Offices

If you are self-employed, use a portion of your home for business, and claim a home office deduction, you must allocate the home mortgage interest. The portion of the interest on the mortgage allocated to the business use is deducted on Form 8829, Home Office Expenses. The balance is treated as personal interest deductible as an itemized expense on Schedule A.

NONDEDUCTIBLE INTEREST AND OTHER LIMITATIONS ON DEDUCTIBILITY

If you borrow additional funds from the same lender to pay off a first loan for business, you cannot claim an interest deduction. Once you begin paying off the new loan, you can deduct interest on both the old and new loans. Payments are treated as being applied to the old loan first and then to the new loan. All interest payments are then deductible.

As in the case of taxes, if interest is paid to acquire a capital asset for resale, you must capitalize the interest expense. The interest is recovered when the asset is sold.

Commitment Fees

Fees paid to have business funds available for drawing on a standby basis are not treated as deductible interest payments. They may, however, be deductible as business expenses. Fees paid to obtain a loan may be treated as deductible interest. However, the fees are not immediately deductible; rather, they are deductible only over the term of the loan. If the loan falls through, the fees can be deducted as a loss.

Similarly, points paid to acquire a loan on business property are treated as prepaid interest. They are not currently deductible as such. Instead, they are deductible over the term of the loan.

EXAMPLE: Your business pays a $200 commitment fee for a $10,000 loan with a 10-year term. Each year the business may deduct $20 ($200 divided by 10 years).

If you pay off the loan before the end of the term (before you have fully deducted the prepaid interest), you can deduct the remaining balance of prepaid interest in the final year of payment.

Interest Paid on Income Tax Deficiencies by a Sole Proprietor, S Corporation Shareholder, Partner, or LLC Member

If you pay interest on a tax deficiency arising from business income from your sole proprietorship, S corporation, partnership, or LLC, can you deduct the interest on your individual return?

The IRS says no. According to temporary regulations, this interest is treated as nondeductible personal interest even though business income generated the deficiency. However, the Tax Court considers this temporary regulation to be invalid and has allowed an unincorporated business owner to deduct interest on a tax deficiency "allocable to a trade or business." Unfortunately, the Tax Court is not the only word on the question. Prior to this case, a federal appellate court concluded that such interest was nondeductible personal interest because the obligation to pay tax on business income is a personal obligation. If you pay interest on a tax deficiency relating to business items, weigh the risk of litigation against the potential tax savings from claiming the deduction. You may want to protect yourself from penalty by filing Form 8275-R, Regulation Disclosure Statement, to disclose a position that is contrary to the regulations. Of course, this clearly flags your return for examination and will probably mean you will have to litigate if you want to stick to your position.

While a C corporation can deduct interest it pays on any tax deficiency, no taxpayer can deduct tax penalties. This rule applies to both civil and criminal penalties. Amounts assessed for the delay of filing a return are considered penalties. Thus, estimated tax penalties, which are imposed because of a delay in payment, are not deductible even though they are calculated by application of an interest rate. Similarly, amounts owing because of the failure to deposit employment taxes are treated as penalties. Additions to tax contained in sections 6651 through 6658 of the Internal Revenue Code are considered penalties.

Interest Related to Tax-Exempt Income

No deduction is allowed for interest paid or incurred to buy or carry tax-exempt securities.

WHERE TO DEDUCT TAXES AND INTEREST

Employees

Taxes and interest are deductible only as miscellaneous business expenses reported on Schedule A and subject to the 2-percent-of-adjusted-gross-income floor. However, employees can elect to claim a credit on foreign taxes. See Chapter 1.

Self-Employed

Taxes and interest are deducted on Schedule C (or Schedule F in the case of farming operations). This form provides separate space for claiming deductions for mortgage interest and for other interest. It also provides a specific line for claiming a deduction for taxes and licenses.

Instead of deducting foreign taxes on Schedule C (or Schedule F), a sole proprietor may choose to claim a foreign tax credit. If foreign taxes are $300 or less (or $600 or less if the self-employed person files a joint return) and result from passive income, an election can be made to claim the credit directly on Form 1040. Otherwise, the credit must be figured on Form 1116, Computation for Foreign Tax Credit.

Partnerships and LLCs

In general, the partnership and LLC deducts taxes and interest on Form 1065. Separate lines are provided for deducting interest and for deducting taxes and licenses. These items are part of the business's operating expenses and figure into its income or loss passed through to partners or LLC members on Schedule K-1 and then reported on the owner's Schedule E. These items are not separately reported to partners or LLC members on Schedule K-1 for special treatment on an owner's individual income tax return.

However, interest that may be classified as investment interest is separately stated in Schedule K-1, since it is subject to an investment interest limitation on the partner's or member's individual income tax return.

Also, foreign taxes are separately stated items on Schedule K-1 to allow the owner to decide whether to take a deduction or credit on his or her individual return. Partners and LLC members treat foreign taxes in the same manner as self-employed individuals, explained above.

S Corporations

In general, the S corporation deducts taxes and interest on Form 1120S. Separate lines are provided for deducting interest and for deducting taxes and licenses. These items are part of the business's operating expenses and figure into its income or loss passed through to shareholders on Schedule K-1 and then reported on the owner's Schedule E. These items are not separately reported to shareholders on Schedule K-1 for special treatment on an owner's individual income tax return.

However, interest that may be classified as investment interest is separately stated in Schedule K-1, since it is subject to an investment interest limitation on the shareholder's individual income tax return.

Also, foreign taxes are separately stated items on Schedule K-1 to allow the shareholder to decide whether to take a deduction or credit on his or her individual return. S corporation shareholders treat foreign taxes in the same manner as self-employed individuals, explained above.

C Corporations

C corporations deduct taxes and interest on Form 1120. Separate lines are provided for deducting interest and for deducting taxes and licenses.

The foreign tax credit is figured on Form 1118.

CHAPTER 12

Depreciation, Amortization, and Depletion

Depreciation is a special type of deduction. It is an allowance for a portion of the cost of equipment or other property owned by you and used in your business. It is claimed over the life of the property, although it may be accelerated, with a greater amount claimed in the early years of ownership. The thinking behind depreciation is that equipment wears out. In theory, if you were to put into a separate fund the amount you claim each year as a depreciation allowance, when your equipment reaches the end of its usefulness you will have sufficient funds to buy a replacement (of course, the replacement may not cost the same as the old equipment). To claim a depreciation deduction, you do not necessarily have to spend any money. If you have already bought equipment, future depreciation deductions do not require any additional out-of-pocket expenditures.

Amortization is conceptually similar to depreciation. It is an allowance for the cost of certain capital expenditures, such as goodwill and trademarks, acquired in the purchase of a business. Amortization can be claimed only if it is specifically allowed by the tax law. It is always deducted ratably over the life of the property. As you will see, amortization is also allowed as an election for some types of expenditures that would otherwise not be deductible. Depletion is a deduction allowed for certain natural resources. The tax law carefully controls the limits of this deduction.

In this chapter you will learn about:

- General rules for depreciation
- MACRS depreciation
- First-year expensing
- Limitations on listed property
- Amortization
- Depletion
- Where to claim depreciation, amortization, and depletion

For a further discussion of depreciation, amortization, and depletion, see IRS Publication 463, Travel, Entertainment, Gifts, and Car Expenses; IRS Publication 534, Depreciating Property Placed in Service Before 1987; and Publication 946, How to Depreciate Property.

GENERAL RULES FOR DEPRECIATION

Depreciable Property

Depreciation is a deduction allowed for certain property used in your business. It is designed to offset the cost of acquiring it, so you cannot depreciate property you lease. To be depreciable, the property must be the kind that wears out, decays, gets used up, becomes obsolete, or loses value from natural causes. The property must have a determinable useful life that is longer than one year. Antiques, for example, generally cannot be depreciated because they do not have a determinable useful life; they can be expected to last indefinitely. The same is true for goodwill you build up in your business (though if you buy a business and pay for its goodwill, you may be able to amortize the cost, as explained later in this chapter).

Land is not depreciable because it, too, can be expected to last indefinitely. Land includes not only the cost of the acreage but also the cost of clearing, grading, planting, and landscaping. However, some land preparation costs can be depreciated if they are closely associated with a building on the land rather than the land itself. For example, shrubs around the entry to a building may be depreciated; trees planted on the perimeter of the property are nondepreciable land costs. Also, the cost of the minerals on the land may not be depreciated but may be subject to depletion.

When you own a building, you must allocate the basis of the property between the building and the land, since only the building portion is depreciable.

> **Definition** *Basis* Generally, the amount you pay for property. It does not matter whether you finance your purchase or pay cash. You add to basis sales taxes and other related expenses (such as nondeductible closing costs if you get a mortgage, or attorney's fees).

There is no special rule for making an allocation of basis. Obviously you would prefer to allocate as much as possible to the building and as little as possible to the land. However, the allocation must have some logical basis. It should be based on the relative value of each portion. What is the land worth? What is the building worth? You may want to use the services of an appraiser to help you derive a fair yet favorable allocation that will withstand IRS scrutiny.

Property that can be expected to last for one year or less is simply deducted in full as some other type of deduction. For example, if you buy stationery that will be used up within the year, you simply deduct the cost of the stationery as "supplies."

Depreciable property may be tangible or intangible. Tangible property is property you can touch—office furniture, a machine, or a telephone, for example. Tangible property may be personal property (a machine) or real property (a factory). "Personal property" does not mean you use the property for personal purposes; it is a legal term for tangible property that is not real property. Intangible property is property you cannot touch, such as copyrights, patents, and franchises.

If you use property for both business and personal purposes, you must make an allocation. You can claim depreciation only on the business portion of the property. Thus, for example, if you use your car 75 percent for business and 25 percent for personal purposes (including commuting), you can claim depreciation on only 75 percent of the property.

Certain property can never be depreciated. You cannot depreciate your inventory. Inventory is property held primarily for sale to customers in the ordinary course of your business. Sometimes you may question whether an asset is really part of your inventory or is a separate asset that can be depreciated. For example, containers generally are treated as part of the cost of your inventory and cannot be separately depreciated. However, containers used to ship products can be depreciated if your invoice treats them as separate items, whether your sales contract shows that you retain title to the containers and whether your records properly state your basis in the containers.

In order to claim depreciation, you must be the owner of the property. If you lease property, say an office, you cannot depreciate it; only the owner can, since it is the owner who suffers the wear and tear on his or her investment.

When to Claim Depreciation

You claim depreciation beginning with the year in which the property is placed in service.

> **Definition** *Placed in service* Ready and available for a specific use, whether or not the item is actually used.

You continue to claim depreciation throughout the life of the asset. The life of the asset is also called its "recovery period." Different types of assets are assigned to different recovery periods. The length of the recovery period has nothing to do with how durable a particular item may be. You simply check the classifications of property to find the recovery period for a particular item.

You stop claiming depreciation on the earlier of when the property's cost has been fully depreciated or when the property is retired from service. Property is retired from service when it is permanently withdrawn from use, by selling or exchanging it, abandoning it, or destroying it.

EXAMPLE: A machine with a five-year recovery period is no longer needed after three years for the task for which it was purchased. The machine is sold to another company that still has a use for it. Once the machine is sold, it has been permanently removed from your service. You cannot claim depreciation after this occurs.

The amount of depreciation you can claim in the year in which property is placed in service or retired from service is limited and is discussed later in this chapter.

Even if you do not actually claim depreciation, you are treated as having done so for purposes of figuring the basis of property when you dispose of it.

EXAMPLE: You place a piece of machinery in service in 1999 and claim a depreciation deduction on your 1999 return. In 2000 your revenues are low and you forget to report your depreciation deduction on your 2000 return. In 2001 you sell the machine. In calculating gain or loss on the sale, you must adjust basis for the depreciation you actually claimed in 1999 and the depreciation you should have claimed in 2000.

If you failed to claim depreciation in the past, file an amended return to fix the error if the tax year is still open (the statute of limitation on amending the return has not expired). Alternatively, you can correct the underdepreciation (even for a closed tax year) by filing for a change in accounting method on Form 3115. Under a special IRS procedure, you simply adjust your income in the current year. Be sure to write on Form 3115 "Automatic Method Change under Rev. Proc. 98-60."

MACRS DEPRECIATION

MACRS is a depreciation system that went into effect for tangible property placed in service after 1986. It is composed of two systems: a basic system, called the General Depreciation System (GDS), and an alternate system, called the Alternative Depreciation System (ADS). The difference between the two systems is the recovery period over which you claim depreciation and the method for calculating depreciation. You use the basic system unless the alternate system is required or you make a special election to use the alternate system. You cannot use either system for certain property: intangible property (patents, copyrights, etc.), motion picture films or videotapes, sound recordings, and property you elect to exclude from MACRS so that you can use a depreciation method based on some other measuring rod than a term of years (these other methods are not discussed in this book).

Basic System (GDS)

You can use the basic system to depreciate any tangible property unless you are required to use the alternate system, elect to use the alternate system, or are required to use some other depreciation method. To calculate your depreciation deduction, you need to know:

- The property's basis. If you purchase property, basis is your cost. If you acquire property in some other way (get it by gift, inheritance, or in a tax-free exchange), basis is figured in another way. For example, if your corporation acquires property from you upon its formation in a tax-free incorporation, then the corporation steps into your shoes for purposes of basis.

  EXAMPLE: You form a corporation (C or S) and contribute cash plus a computer. In exchange you receive all of the stock of the corporation. Your basis for the computer was $4,000. The corporation assumes your basis—$4,000.

  A similar rule applies to property you contribute to a partnership or LLC upon its formation. If you are a sole proprietor or an employee and convert property from personal use to business use, your basis for depreciation is the lesser of the fair market value on the date of conversion to business use or the adjusted basis of the property on that date.

  The cost of property includes sales taxes. If you hire an architect to design a building, the fees are added to the basis of the property and recovered through depreciation.

- The property's recovery period. Recovery periods are fixed according to the claim in which a property falls. These periods are listed below.

- The date the property is placed in service. Remember, this is the date the property is ready and available for its specific use.

- The applicable convention. These are special rules that govern the timing of deductions, as explained later in this chapter.

- The depreciation method. MACRS has five different depreciation methods, as explained below.

Recovery Periods

The class assigned to a property is designed to match the period over which the basis of property is recovered (for example, cost is deducted). Five-year property allows the cost of certain equipment to be deducted over five years (subject to adjustment for conventions discussed later).

3-year property   This includes taxis, tractor units for use over the road, racehorses over two years old when placed in service, any other horse over 12 years old when placed in service, breeding hogs, certain handling devices for manufacturing food and beverages, and special tools for manufacturing rubber products. Computer software purchased separately from a computer can be amortized over a period of 36 months (unless such software has a life of less than one year and, thus, can be deducted in full in the year it is placed in service).

5-year property   This includes cars, buses, trucks, airplanes, trailers and trailer containers, computers and peripheral equipment, some office machinery (calculators, copiers, typewriters), assets used in construction, logging equipment, assets used to manufacture organic and inorganic chemicals, and property used in research and experimentation. It also includes breeding and dairy cattle and breeding and dairy goats.

7-year property   This includes office fixtures and furniture (chairs, desks, files); communications equipment (fax machines); breeding and workhorses; assets used in printing; recreational assets (miniature golf courses, billiard establishments, concert halls); assets used to produce jewelry; musical instruments; toys; sporting goods; and motion picture and television films and tapes. This class is also the catchall for other property. It includes any property not assigned to another class.

10-year property   This includes barges, tugs, vessels, and similar water transportation equipment; single-purpose agricultural or horticultural structures placed in service after 1988; and trees or vines bearing fruits or nuts.

15-year property   This includes certain depreciable improvements made to land (bridges, fences, roads, shrubbery).

20-year property   This includes farm buildings (other than single-purpose agricultural or horticultural structures) and any municipal sewers.

Residential rental realty (rental buildings where 80 percent or more of the gross rental is from dwelling units)   The recovery period is 27.5 years.

Nonresidential realty   This class applies to factories, office buildings, and any other realty other than residential rental realty. The recovery period is 39 years (31.5 years for property placed in service before May 13, 1993). If you begin to use a portion of your home for business (a home office, for example), use the recovery period applicable on the date of conversion. For example, if you begin to use a home office in 1999, depreciate that portion of your home using a 39-year recovery period, even if you bought your home in 1990.

Improvements   In general, improvements or additions to property are treated as separate property and are depreciated separately from the property itself. The recovery period for improvements begins on the later of the date the improvements are placed in service or the date the property to which the improvements are made is placed in service. Use the same recovery period for the improvements that you would for the underlying property.

Conventions

There are three conventions that affect the timing of depreciation deductions. Two apply to property other than residential or nonresidential real property (essentially personal property such as equipment); the other applies to residential or nonresidential real property (rental units, offices, and factories).

Half-year convention   The half-year convention applies to all property (other than residential or nonresidential real property) unless superseded by the mid-quarter convention (explained below). Under the half-year convention, property is treated as if you placed it in service in the middle of the year. You are allowed to deduct only one-half of the depreciation allowance for the first year. This is so even if you place the property in service on the first day of the year.

Under this convention, property is treated as disposed of in the middle of the year, regardless of the actual date of disposition.

The half-year convention means that property held for its entire recovery period will have an additional year for claiming depreciation deductions. Only one-half of the first year's depreciation deduction is claimed in the first year; the balance of depreciation is claimed in the year following the last year of the recovery period.

EXAMPLE: A desk (7-year property) is placed in service on January 1, 1999. One-half of the depreciation deduction that would otherwise be claimed in the first year is allowed. Normal depreciation is claimed in years two through seven. The remaining depreciation is claimed in the eighth year (see table for depreciation rates, below).

Mid-quarter convention   Under the mid-quarter convention, all property placed in service during the year (or disposed of during the year) is treated as placed in service (or disposed of) in the middle of the applicable quarter. The mid-quarter convention applies (and the half-year convention does not) if the total bases of all property placed in service during the last three months of the year (the final quarter) exceeds 40 percent of the total bases of property placed in service during the entire year. In making this determination, do not take into consideration residential or nonresidential real property or property placed in service and then disposed of in the same year.

EXAMPLE: You are on a calendar year. In January 1999 you place in service machine A, costing $3,000. In November 1999 you place in service another machine, machine B, costing $10,000. You must use the mid-quarter convention to calculate depreciation for both machines. This is because more than 40 percent of all property placed in service during the year ($13,000) was placed in service in the final quarter of the year ($10,000). (Actually, 77 percent of all property placed in service in the year was placed in service in the final quarter of the year.)

EXAMPLE: The situation is the same as above, except machine B is placed in service in January and machine A is placed in service in November. In this instance, the mid-quarter convention does not apply because only 23 percent of all property placed in service in 1999 was placed in service in the final quarter of the year.

Mid-month convention   This convention applies only to real property. You must treat all real property as if it were placed in service or disposed of in the middle of the month. The mid-month convention is taken into account in the depreciation tables from which you can take your deduction. Simply look at the table for the type of realty (residential or nonresidential) you own. Then look in the table for the month in which the property is placed in service.

Depreciation Methods

There are five ways to depreciate property: the 200-percent declining balance rate, the 150-percent declining balance rate, the straight-line election, the 150-percent election, and the ADS method. Both 200-percent and 150-percent declining balance rates are referred to as accelerated rates.

You may use the 200-percent rate for 3-year, 5-year, 7-year, and 10-year property over the GDS recovery period. The half-year or mid-quarter convention must be applied. The 200-percent declining balance method is calculated by dividing 100 by the recovery period and then doubling it. However, as a practical matter you do not have to compute the rates. They are provided for you in special tables, which take into account the half-year or mid-quarter conventions:

MACRS RATES—HALF-YEAR CONVENTION

Year	3-year property	5-year property	7-year property
1	33.33%	20.00%	14.29%
2	44.45	32.00	24.49
3	14.81	19.20	17.49
4	7.81	11.52	12.49
5		11.52	8.93
6		5.76	8.92
7			8.93
8			4.46

MACRS RATES—MID-QUARTER CONVENTION—200% RATE THREE-YEAR PROPERTY

Year	1st quarter	2nd quarter	3rd quarter	4th quarter
1	58.33%	41.67%	25.00%	8.33%
2	27.78	38.89	50.00	61.11
3	12.35	14.14	16.677	20.37
4	1.54	5.30	8.33	10.19

FIVE-YEAR PROPERTY

Year	1st quarter	2nd quarter	3rd quarter	4th quarter
1	35.00%	25.00%	15.00%	5.00%
2	26.00	30.00	34.00	38.00
3	15.60	18.00	20.40	22.80
4	11.01	11.37	12.24	13.68
5	11.01	11.37	11.30	10.94
6	1.38	4.26	7.06	9.58

SEVEN-YEAR PROPERTY

Year	1st quarter	2nd quarter	3rd quarter	4th quarter
1	25.00%	17.85%	10.71%	3.57%
2	21.43	23.47	25.51	27.55
3	15.31	16.76	18.22	19.68
4	10.93	11.97	13.02	14.06
5	8.75	8.87	9.30	10.04
6	8.74	8.87	8.85	8.73
7	8.75	8.87	8.86	8.73
8	1.09	3.33	5.53	7.64

If the 200-percent declining balance rate is used, you can switch to the straight line when it provides a deduction for the year of value equal to or greater than the accelerated rate. Of course, total depreciation can never be more than 100 percent of the property's basis. The following table shows you when it becomes advantageous to switch to the straight-line rate.

WHEN TO CHANGE TO STRAIGHT-LINE METHOD

Class	Changeover year
3-year property	3rd
5-year property	4th
7-year property	5th
10-year property	7th
15-year property	7th
20-year property	9th

You use the 150-percent rate for 15- and 20-year property over the GDS recovery period. Again, you must also apply the half-year or mid-quarter convention. You change over to the straight-line method when it provides a greater deduction. Tables for this rate may be found in IRS Publication 946, How to Depreciate Property.

Residential and nonresidential realty must use the straight-line rate. Straight line is simply the cost of the property divided by the life of the property. However, you begin depreciation with the month in which the property is placed in service. This makes the rate vary slightly over the years. The tables following can be used to calculate depreciation for residential and nonresidential real property using basic depreciation (GDS). If you place nonresidential realty in service in 1999, be sure to use the 39-year table. For all tables, find your annual depreciation rate by looking in the column for the month in which the property was placed in service (for example, for calendar-year businesses, March is 3; August is 8). Then look at the year of ownership you are in (e.g., for the year in which you place property in service, look at year 1).

EXAMPLE: You are on a calendar year and placed in service a factory in April 1996. In 1999 your depreciation rate is 2.564 percent. You found this rate by looking at the table below for 39-year nonresidential property under month 4, year 4.

(Tables for depreciation for residential and nonresidential real property using ADS as well as years after year 9 for residential and pre–May 13, 1993, nonresidential realty may be found in Appendix A of IRS Publication 946, How to Depreciate Property.)

RATES FOR RESIDENTIAL REALTY YEARS—STRAIGHT LINE—MID-MONTH CONVENTION

	Month in the First Recovery Year the Property Is Placed in Service					
Year	1	2	3	4	5	6
1	3.485%	3.182%	2.879%	2.576%	2.273%	1.970%
2–9	3.636	3.636	3.636	3.636	3.636	3.636

	Month in the First Recovery Year the Property Is Placed in Service					
Year	7	8	9	10	11	12
1	1.667%	1.364%	1.061%	0.758%	0.455%	0.152%
2–9	3.636	3.636	3.636	3.636	3.636	3.636

RATES FOR NONRESIDENTIAL REALTY YEARS—31.5 YEARS—STRAIGHT LINE—MID-MONTH CONVENTION

	Month in the First Recovery Year the Property Is Placed in Service					
Year	1	2	3	4	5	6
1	3.042%	2.778%	2.513%	2.249%	1.984%	1.720%
2–7	3.175	3.175	3.175	3.175	3.175	3.175
8	3.175	3.174	3.175	3.174	3.175	3.174
9	3.174	3.175	3.174	3.175	3.174	3.175

	Month in the First Recovery Year the Property Is Placed in Service					
Year	7	8	9	10	11	12
1	1.455%	1.190%	0.926%	0.661%	0.397%	0.132%
2–7	3.175	3.175	3.175	3.175	3.175	3.175
8	3.175	3.175	3.175	3.175	3.175	3.175
9	3.174	3.175	3.174	3.175	3.174	3.175

RATES FOR NONRESIDENTIAL REALTY YEARS—39 YEARS— STRAIGHT LINE—MID-MONTH CONVENTION

	Month in the First Recovery Year the Property Is Placed in Service					
Year	1	2	3	4	5	6
1	2.461%	2.247%	2.033%	1.819%	1.605%	1.391%
2–39	2.564	2.564	2.564	2.564	2.564	2.564

	Month in the First Recovery Year the Property Is Placed in Service					
Year	7	8	9	10	11	12
1	1.177%	0.963%	0.749%	0.535%	0.321%	0.107%
2–39	2.564	2.564	2.564	2.564	2.564	2.564

You can elect to use the 150-percent rate for properties eligible for the 200-percent rate. If the election is made, the 150-percent rate is used over the ADS recovery period. Again, a half-year or mid-quarter convention is applied and there is a changeover to the straight-line method when it provides a greater deduction. The election may be advisable if you do not think you will have sufficient income to offset larger depreciation deductions. It may also be advisable to lessen or avoid the alternative minimum tax.

Note: Once you make the election to use the 150-percent rate over the ADS recovery period, you cannot change your mind.

The fifth method is the ADS method, discussed below.

Alternative Depreciation System (ADS)
You must use the alternative system (and not the basic system, GDS) for the following property:

- Listed property not used more than 50 percent for business. Listed property includes cars and other transportation vehicles, computers and peripherals (unless used only at a regular business establishment), and cellular telephones.

- Tangible property used predominantly outside the United States

- Tax-exempt use property

- Tax-exempt bond-financed property

- Imported property covered by an executive order of the president of the United States

- Property used predominantly in farming and placed in service during any year in which you elect not to apply the uniform capitalization rules to certain farming costs

The Alternative Depreciation System (ADS) requires depreciation to be calculated using the straight-line method. This is done by dividing the cost of the property by the alternate recovery period. In some cases, the recovery period is the same as for the basic system; in others, it is longer.

Recovery Periods Under ADS

Cars, computers, light-duty trucks	5 years
Furniture and fixtures	10 years
Personal property with no class life	12 years
Nonresidential/residential real estate	40 years

You can elect to use ADS for other property in order to claim more gradual depreciation. The election applies to all property within the same class placed in service during the year (other than real estate). For residential rental and nonresidential real property, you can make the election to use ADS on a property-by-property basis.

An election to use ADS may be helpful, for example, if you are first starting out and do not have sufficient income to offset large depreciation deductions. Use of ADS can help to avoid alternative minimum tax and the special depreciation computations required for alternative minimum tax.

For property placed in service after December 31, 1999, you can calculate depreciation for regular tax purposes using the same recovery periods as required for alternative minimum tax purposes. This eliminates the need to make any adjustments for alternative minimum tax and to keep separate records of depreciation taken for regular and alternative minimum tax purposes.

Recapture of Depreciation

If you sell or otherwise dispose of depreciable or amortizable property at a gain, you may have to report all or some of your gain as ordinary income. The treatment of what would otherwise have been capital gain as ordinary income is called recapture. Since this book is concerned primarily with deductions, the details of recapture rules will not be explained. It is important, however, to recognize that some of the tax benefit you enjoy from the deduction may be offset later on by recapture.

Recordkeeping for Depreciation

Since depreciation deductions go on for a number of years, it is important to keep good records of prior deductions. It is also necessary to maintain records since depreciation deductions may differ for regular income tax purposes and the alternative minimum tax. Recordkeeping is explained in Chapter 4.

FIRST-YEAR EXPENSING

Instead of depreciating the cost of tangible personal property over a number of years, you may be able to write off the entire cost in the first year. This is called first-year expensing or a Section 179 deduction (named after the section in the Internal Revenue Code that governs the deduction). A first-year expense deduction may be claimed whether you pay for the item with cash or credit. Thus, if you buy on credit, the first-year expense deduction can be used to enhance your cash flow position (you claim an immediate tax deduction but pay for the item over time).

You can elect to deduct up to a set dollar amount of the cost of tangible personal property used in your business. The dollar amount is:

Year	Dollar Amount
1999	$19,000
2000	20,000
2001–2002	24,000
2003 and later	25,000

LEGISLATIVE ALERT

Congress is considering an increase in the dollar amount to $30,000 starting in 2000.

The property must be acquired by purchase. If you inherit property, for example, and use in it your business, you cannot claim a first-year expense deduction. If you acquire property in whole or in part by means of a trade, you cannot claim a first-year expense deduction for the portion of the property acquired by trade.

EXAMPLE: You buy a new car that is used 100 percent for business. You pay cash and trade in your old car. You cannot compute the first-year expense deduction for the portion of the new car's basis that includes the adjusted basis of the car you traded in.

However, if you buy property on credit, you can still use the first-year expense deduction even though you are not yet out-of-pocket for the purchase price. A purchase on credit that entitles you a first-year expense deduction is a strategy for aiding your cash flow (i.e., you gain a tax deduction even though you have not expended the cash).

The property must have been acquired for business. If you buy property for personal purposes and later convert it to business use, you cannot claim a first-year expense deduction. If you are an employee, be prepared to show the property you expense was acquired for business (not personal) purposes. In one case, a sales manager was allowed to expense the cost of a home computer where she convinced the Tax Court that its use was entirely for her job. She had a heavy workload, could access company information via a modem, and was not allowed entry to her office after business hours.

Generally, the first-year expense deduction does not apply to property you lease to others. (There is no restriction on leased property by corporations.) However, a first-year expense deduction is allowed for leased property you manufactured and leased if the term of the lease is less than half of the property's class life and, for the first 12 months the property is transferred to the lessee, the total business deductions for the property are more than 15 percent of the rental income for the property.

Limits on First-Year Expensing

Three limits apply for first-year expensing: a dollar limit, an investment limit, and a taxable income limit.

Dollar limit   You cannot deduct more than the applicable dollar amount in any one year. (There is an additional first-year expense limit in the case of certain property placed in service in an empowerment zone designated by HUD or on an Indian reservation.) This dollar limit applies on a per-taxpayer basis. Thus, if an individual owns more than one business, he or she must aggregate first-year expense deductions from all businesses and deduct no more than a total of $19,000 in 1999. Married persons are treated as one taxpayer. They are allowed only one $19,000 deduction regardless of which spouse placed the property in service. If they file separate returns, each can claim only one-half of the $19,000 limit ($9,500).

Note: A special dollar limit for cars used in business supersedes the first-year expense deduction limit. See Chapter 7 for more details on deducting the costs of business cars. No first-year expense deduction can be claimed for listed property unless it is used more than 50 percent for business (see below).

Investment limit   The first-year expense deduction is really designed for small businesses. This is because every dollar of investments in equipment over $200,000 reduces the dollar limit.

EXAMPLE: In 1999 you buy equipment costing $210,000. Your first-year expense deduction is limited to $9,000 ($19,000 – $10,000).

If, in 1999, a business buys equipment costing $219,000, the deduction limit is fully phased out, so no first-year expense deduction is allowed.

Taxable income limit   The total first-year expense deduction cannot exceed taxable income from the active conduct of a business. You are treated as actively conducting a business if you participate in a meaningful way in the management or operations of a business.

Taxable income for purposes of this limit has a special meaning. Start with your net income (or loss) from all businesses that you actively conduct. If you are married and file jointly, add your spouse's net income (or loss). This includes certain gains and losses called Section 1231 gains and losses and interest from working capital in your business. It also includes salary, wages, and other compensation earned as an employee, so even though a moonlighting business that bought the equipment has little or no income, you may still be eligible for a full first-year expense deduction if your salary from your day job is sufficient. Reduce your net income (or loss) by any first-year expense deduction, the deduction for one-half of self-employment tax, and net operating loss carrybacks or carryforwards. This, then, is your taxable income for purposes of the taxable income limitation.

If your taxable income limits your deduction, any unused deduction can be carried forward and used in a future year.

EXAMPLE: Your taxable income (without regard to a first-year expense deduction) is $12,000. You place in service in 1999 a machine costing $14,000. Your first-year expense deduction is limited to $12,000. You can carry forward the additional $2,000 to next year.

Carryforwards of unused first-year expense deductions can be used if there is sufficient taxable income in the next year. You can choose the properties for which costs will be carried forward. You can allocate the portion of the costs to these properties as long as the allocation is reflected on your books and records.

Special Rules for Partnerships, Limited Liability Companies, and S Corporations
The dollar limit, investment limit, and taxable income limit apply at both the entity and owner levels. This means that partnerships as well as their partners and S corporations as well as their shareholders must apply all the limits. The same is true for limited liability companies and members.

EXAMPLE: You are a 50-percent shareholder in an S corporation that claims a first-year expense deduction in 1999 of $19,000. Your allocable share as reported on your Schedule K-1 is $9,500. You also own a business that you run as a sole proprietor. You place in service a machine costing $10,000. (Assume sufficient taxable income by the S corporation and for your sole proprietorship.) Your first-year expense deduction for this machine is limited to $9,500. The balance of the cost of the machine, $500, cannot be expensed in the current year because of the dollar limit.

Dispositions of First-Year Expense Property
If you sell or otherwise dispose of property for which a first-year expense deduction was claimed, or cease using the property for business, there may be recapture of your deduction. This means that you must include in your

income a portion of the deduction you previously claimed. The amount you must recapture depends on when you dispose of the property. The longer you hold it, the less recapture you have. If you sell property at a gain, recapture is not additional income; it is merely a reclassification of income. If you realize gain on the sale of first-year expense property, instead of treating the gain as capital gain, the recapture amount is characterized as ordinary income.

Recapture is calculated by comparing your first-year expense deduction with the deduction you would have claimed had you instead taken ordinary depreciation.

EXAMPLE: In 1996 you placed in service office furniture (7-year property) costing $10,000, which you fully expensed. In 1999 you used the property only 40 percent for business (and 60 percent for personal purposes). You calculate your recapture as follows:

First-year expense deduction		$10,000
Allowable depreciation		
$10,000 × 14.29%*	$1,429	
$10,000 × 24.49%	2,449	
$10,000 × 17.49%	1,749	
$10,000 × 12.49% × 40%	500	$ 6,127
Recapture amount		$ 3,873

*MACRS percentages from page 252.

If you transfer first-year expense property in a transaction that does not require recognition of gain or loss (for example, if you make a tax-free exchange or contribute the property to a corporation in a tax-free incorporation), an adjustment is made in the basis of the property. The adjusted basis of the property is increased before the disposition by the amount of the first-year expense deduction that is disallowed. The new owner cannot claim a first-year expense deduction with respect to this disallowed portion.

LIMITATIONS ON LISTED PROPERTY

Certain property is called listed property and is subject to special depreciation limits. Listed property includes:

- Cars

- Other transportation vehicles (including boats)

- Computers and peripherals, unless used only at a regular business establishment owned or leased by the person operating the establishment. A home office is treated as a business establishment.

- Cellular telephones (or similar telecommunication equipment)

These are the only items of listed property because they have been specified as such in the tax law. For example, fax machines and noncellular telephones are not treated as listed property.

It is advisable to keep a log or other record for the use of listed property. This will help you show that business use is more than 50 percent. However, if you use listed property, such as a computer, in a home office whose expenses are deductible, the Tax Court says you do not need records. The reason: Recordkeeping for business use does not apply to computers used at a place of business (which includes a home office that is the principal place of business and that is used regularly and exclusively for that business).

If business use of listed property is not more than 50 percent during the year, the basic depreciation system cannot be used. In this case, you must use the alternate depreciation system. Under this system, depreciation can be calculated only with the straight-line method. Divide the cost of the property by the alternative recovery period. For cars, computers, and other listed property, the alternative recovery period happens to be the same as the basic recovery period—five years.

Use of the alternative depreciation system means that instead of accelerating depreciation deductions to the earlier years of ownership, depreciation deductions will be spread evenly over the recovery period of the property.

Note: Weigh carefully an election to use ADS. If you make the election to use ADS, you cannot later change your mind.

AMORTIZATION

Certain capital expenditures can be deducted over a term of years. This is called amortization. The deduction is taken evenly over a prescribed period. Amortization applies only to the following expenditures:

- Intangibles acquired on the purchase of a business

- Business start-up costs and organizational expenses

- Construction period interest and taxes

- Research and experimentation costs

- Bond premiums

- Reforestation costs

- Pollution control facilities

- Costs of acquiring a lease

Intangibles Acquired on the Purchase of a Business

If you buy a business, a portion of your cost may be allocated to certain intangible items:

- Goodwill

- Going concern value

- Workforce in place

- Patents, copyrights, formulas, processes, designs, patterns, and know-how

- Customer-based intangibles

- Supplier-based intangibles

- Licenses, permits, and other rights granted by a governmental unit or agency

- Covenants not to compete

- Franchises, trademarks, or tradenames

These items are called "Section 197 intangibles," named after a section in the Internal Revenue Code. You may deduct the portion of the cost allocated to these items over a period of 15 years.

Section 197 intangibles do not include interests in a corporation, partnership, trust or estate, or sports franchise, interests in land, certain computer software, and certain other excluded items. Also, you cannot amortize the cost of self-created items. Thus, if you generate your own customer list, you cannot claim an amortization deduction.

Anti-churning rules   If you already own a business with goodwill and other intangibles, you cannot convert these into Section 197 intangibles, for which an amortization deduction would be allowed, by engaging in a transaction solely for this purpose. Special "anti-churning rules" prevent amortization for intangibles acquired in transactions designed to create an acquisition date after August 10, 1993 (the date on which Section 197 intangibles came into being).

Dispositions

If a Section 197 intangible is sold at a loss but other such intangibles are still owned, no loss can be taken on the sale. Instead the bases of the remaining Section 197 intangibles are reduced by the unclaimed loss. The same rule applies if a Section 197 intangible becomes worthless or is abandoned. No loss is recognized on the worthlessness or abandonment. Instead, the bases of remaining Section 197 are increased by the unrecognized loss.

Business Start-Up Costs and Organizational Expenses

When you start up a business, you may incur a variety of expenses. Ordinarily these are capital expenditures that are not currently deductible. They are expenses incurred to acquire a capital asset, namely, your business. However, the tax law allows amortization for certain business start-up costs. More specifically, you can elect to deduct these costs ratably over a period of 60 months or more. If you later sell your business before the end of the amortization period, you can deduct the unamortized amount in your final year.

Business start-up costs   These include amounts paid to investigate *whether* to start or purchase a business and *which* business to start or purchase. Expenses related to these activities are treated as start-up expenses. Examples of start-up costs include:

- A survey of potential markets

- An analysis of available facilities, labor, and supplies

- Advertisements for the opening of the business

- Travel and other expenses incurred to get prospective distributors, suppliers, or customers

- Salaries and fees for consultants and executives, and fees for professional services

Other similar expenses are amortizable if they would have been deductible if paid or incurred to operate a going business and were actually paid or incurred prior to the commencement of business operations. Thus, for example legal fees to prepare contracts for the purchase of a business are no longer start-up fees but, rather, are expenses that must be added to the cost of the business.

Organizational costs for a corporation   If you set up a corporation (C or S), certain expenses unique to this form of business can be amortized. These expenses include the cost of:

- Temporary directors

- Organizational meetings

- State incorporation fees

- Accounting services for setting up the corporation

- Legal services to draft the charter, bylaws, terms of the original stock certificates, and minutes of organizational meetings

You can deduct any other organizational costs if they are incident to the creation of a corporation, they are chargeable to the capital account, and the cost could have been amortized over the life of the corporation if the corporation had a fixed life.

You cannot amortize expenses related to selling stock, such as commissions, professional fees, and printing costs.

Organizational costs of a partnership   If you set up a partnership, certain expenses unique to this form of business can be amortized. As in the case of corporate organizational costs, partnership organizational costs include those that are incident to the creation of a partnership, are chargeable to the capital account, and would have been amortizable over the life of the partnership if the partnership had a fixed life.

Syndication costs to sell partnership interests are not treated as amortizable organizational costs. These nonamortizable costs include commissions, professional fees, and printing costs related to the issuing and marketing of partnership interests.

Construction Period Interest and Taxes

Interest and property taxes related to the construction of real property cannot be deducted in the year in which they are paid or accrued. Instead, they must be capitalized.

Research and Experimentation Costs

If you have research and experimentation costs, you have a choice of ways to deduct them. You can claim a current deduction for amounts paid or incurred in the year.

Alternatively, you can elect to amortize them over a period of not less than 60 months. Where you do not have current income to offset the deduction, it may be advisable to elect amortization.

You may be able to claim a tax credit for increasing your research and experimentation program. For further information on this credit, see instructions for Form 6765, Credit for Increasing Research Activities.

LEGISLATIVE ALERT

The credit (which is not discussed further in the book) expired on June 30, 1999, but Congress was considering a retroactive extension. If enacted, the credit would run through June 30, 2004.

Bond Premiums

If you pay a premium to buy bonds (a cost above the face amount of the bonds), you may be required to—or can elect to—amortize the premium.

For taxable bonds, there is an election. You can amortize the bond premium or instead treat the unamortized premium as part of the basis of the bond. The bond premium is calculated with reference to the amount that the bond issuer will pay at maturity or the earlier call date if it results in a smaller amortizable bond premium attributable to the period ending on the call date. Do not take into account any premium paid for a conversion feature. (Dealers in taxable bonds cannot deduct the amortizable bond premium.)

For tax-exempt bonds you must amortize the premium. However, you do not deduct the amortizable premium in calculating taxable income.

If you are required or elect to amortize the bond premium, decrease the basis of the bond by the amortizable premium.

Reforestation Costs

If you spend money on forestation or reforestation—planting and seeding, site preparation, and the costs of seeds, tools, and labor—you can elect to amortize these costs over a period of 84 months. Only a limited annual amount qualifies for amortization. The annual cap on amortizable costs is $10,000 per year ($5,000 for married persons filing separate returns).

Pollution Control Facilities

If you set up a pollution control facility for a plant or other property in operation before 1976, you can elect to amortize your costs over a period of 60 months. A certified pollution control facility is depreciable property that is a new identifiable treatment facility used to abate or control water or atmospheric pollution or contamination by removing, altering, disposing of, storing, or preventing the creation or emission of pollutants, contaminants, wastes, or heat. It must be certified by state and federal certifying authorities. The amortizable cost cannot include amounts recovered through its operation, such as through sales of recovered wastes. The certifying authorities will note this fact and limit the amortizable costs accordingly.

Costs of Acquiring a Lease

If you pay a fee to obtain a lease, you can amortize the cost over the term of the lease. The lease term includes all renewal options if less than 75 percent of the cost is attributable to the term of the lease remaining on the acquisition date. The remaining term of the lease on the acquisition date does not include any period for which the lease may be subsequently renewed, extended, or continued under an option exercisable by the lessee.

Year 2000 Upgrading

Many computers use two digits, rather than four, to represent the year in a date field (for example, "99" to represent 1999). The two-digit field may not recognize years after 1999 being after that date (for example, "00" may mean 1900 to a computer). This has come to be known as the Year 2000 problem (or Y2K). If you need to upgrade your computer and software to recognize dates in the next millennium, you may incur "year 2000 costs" to manually convert existing software, develop new software to replace existing software, buy software to replace existing software, or buy, lease, or develop software tools to assist your system in converting existing software to be year 2000 compliant. Here are your options on how to treat your Year 2000 costs:

- Buying new software must be amortized over 36 months (or less if you can show its life is less than 36 months). Amortization can begin with the month in which the software is placed in service.

- Developing software, including converted software, can be currently expensed as a research and development cost. Except in extraordinary cases, you may not claim a research credit for these development costs.

- Leasing software is deductible as a rental expense (as explained in Chapter 10).

DEPLETION

Depletion is a deduction allowed for certain mineral properties or timber to compensate the owner for the use of these resources. Mineral properties include oil and gas wells, mines, other natural deposits, and standing timber. In order to claim depletion, you must be an owner or operator with an economic interest in the mineral deposits or standing timber. This means that you are adversely affected economically when mineral properties or standing timber is mined or cut. Depletion is claimed separately for each mineral property, which is each mineral deposit in each separate tract or parcel of land. Timber property is each tract or block representing a separate timber account.

Note: Claiming depletion may result in alternative minimum tax (AMT) both for individuals and C corporations (not otherwise exempt from AMT).

Methods of Depletion

There are two ways to calculate depletion: cost depletion and percentage depletion.

Cost depletion is determined by dividing the adjusted basis of the mineral property by the total number of recoverable units in the property's natural deposit (as determined by engineering reports). Then this figure is multiplied by the number of units sold if you use the accrual method of accounting, or the number of units sold and paid for if you use the cash method. Cost depletion is the only method allowed for timber. The depletion deduction is calculated when the quantity of cut timber is first accurately measured in the process of exploitation. Special rules are used to determine depletion for timber. The depletion deduction is taken when standing timber is cut.

Percentage depletion is determined by applying a percentage, fixed by tax law according to each type of mineral, to your gross income from the property during the tax year.

PERCENTAGE FOR MINERAL PROPERTIES

Type of property	Percentage
Oil and gas—small producers	15%
Sulfur, uranium, and U.S. asbestos, lead, zinc, nickel, mica, and certain other ores and minerals	22
Gold, silver, copper and iron ore, and certain U.S. oil shale	15
Coal, lignite, sodium chloride	10
Clay and shale used for sewer pipe	7.5
Clay used for flowerpots, etc., gravel, sand, stone	5
Most other minerals and metallic ores	14

The deduction for percentage depletion is limited to no more than 50 percent (100 percent for oil and gas properties allowed to use percentage depletion) of taxable income from the property calculated without the depletion deduction and certain other adjustments. Only small producers are allowed to use percentage depletion for oil and gas properties. If you use percentage depletion for mineral properties but it is less than cost depletion for the year, you must use cost depletion.

Partnership Oil and Gas Properties
The depletion allowance, whether cost depletion or percentage depletion, must be calculated separately for each partner and not by the partnership. Each partner can decide on the depletion method. The partnership simply allocates to the partner his or her proportionate share of the adjusted basis of each oil and gas property. Each partner must keep this information separately. In separate records the partner must reduce the share of the adjusted basis of each property by the depletion taken on the property each year by that partner. The partner will use this reduced adjusted basis to figure gain or loss if the partnership later disposes of the property. (This partnership rule also applies to members in limited liability companies.)

S Corporation Oil and Gas Properties
The depletion allowance, whether cost depletion or percentage depletion, must be computed separately by each shareholder and not by the S corporation. The same rules apply to S corporations that apply to partnerships, with some modifications. To enable a shareholder to calculate cost depletion, the S corporation must allocate to each shareholder his or her adjusted basis of each oil and gas property held by the S corporation. This allocation is made on the date the corporation acquires the property. The shareholder's share of the adjusted basis of each oil and gas property is adjusted by the S corporation for any capital expenditures made for each property. Again, each shareholder must separately keep records of his or her pro rata share of the adjusted basis of each property and must reduce that share by depletion taken on the property. The reduced adjusted basis is used by the shareholder to determine gain or loss on the disposition of the property by the S corporation.

WHERE TO CLAIM DEPRECIATION, AMORTIZATION, AND DEPLETION

In general, depreciation, including any first-year expense deduction, is computed on Form 4562, Depreciation and Amortization, regardless of your form of business organization. However, special rules apply to different entities, as noted below.

If an election is made to use the 150-percent rate for property that could have used the 200-percent rate, you make the election by entering "150DB" in column (f) of Part II of Form 4562.

An election to use ADS is made by completing line 15 of Part II of Form 4562.

If depletion is taken for timber, you must attach Form T to your return.

In general, recapture of the depreciation and the first-year expense deduction is computed on Form 4797, Sales of Business Property, regardless of your form of business organization.

On pages 274–276 there are a completed Form 4562 and an accompanying worksheet to show depreciation for a florist shop business that placed equipment in service in both the current year and in prior years.

Employees

You complete Form 4562 only if you place depreciable property in service in the current year, are claiming depreciation on a car (regardless of when it was placed in service), or have amortization costs that begin in the current year. Thus, for example, if you buy a laptop computer this year that you use for your work and you want to claim a first-year expense deduction, you must file Form 4562. You do not have to complete Form 4562 if you are deducting job-related car expenses using either the standard mileage rate or actual mileage rate; you need only complete Form 2106, Employee Business Expenses, or Form 2106-EZ, Unreimbursed Employee Business Expenses. Your deductions are then entered on Schedule A as miscellaneous itemized deductions subject to the 2-percent-of adjusted-gross-income floor.

Self-Employed

You complete Form 4562 only if you place depreciable property in service in the current year, are claiming depreciation on a car (regardless of when it was placed in service), claim a deduction for any car reported on Schedule C or Schedule C-EZ (or Schedule F for farming operations), or have amortization costs that begin in the current year. Your deductions are then entered on Part II of Schedule C or Schedule C-EZ (or Schedule F). Depreciation and first-year expensing not included in Part II of Schedule C (for cost of goods sold) are entered on a specific line in Part I of Schedule C or as part of total expenses on Schedule C-EZ.

Partnerships and LLCs

You complete Form 4562 only if you place depreciable property in service in the current year, are claiming depreciation on a car (regardless of when it was placed in service), or have amortization costs that begin in the current year. The partnership or LLC decides on the depreciation method and whether to claim a first-year expense deduction. Ordinary depreciation is then entered on Form 1065 and is taken into account in calculating a partnership's or LLC's ordinary income or loss. Depreciation is reported on a specific line on Form 1065 and is reduced by depreciation included in the cost of goods sold. Similarly, depletion (other than on oil and gas properties) is part of a partnership's or LLC's ordinary income or loss and is reported on the specific line provided for depletion.

Amortization items, such as a deduction for organizational expenses, are part of "other deductions." An explanation for these items is included in a separate statement attached to the return.

First-year expense deduction is a separately stated item reported on Schedule K, and the allocable portion is passed through separately to partners or members on Schedule K-1.

Depletion of oil and gas properties is also a separately stated item reported on Schedule K. The allocable portion is passed through separately to partners/members on Schedule K-1.

S Corporations

You complete Form 4562 only if the corporation placed depreciable property in service in the current year, is claiming depreciation on a car (regardless of when it was placed in service), or has amortization costs that begin in the current year. The S corporation decides on the depreciation method and whether to claim a first-year expense deduction. Ordinary depreciation is then entered on Form 1120S and is taken into account in calculating an S corporation's ordinary income or loss. Depreciation is reported on a specific line on Form 1120S and is reduced by depreciation included in the cost

Sample Form 4562

Form **4562**	**Depreciation and Amortization** **(Including Information on Listed Property)**	OMB No. 1545-0172 **1999**
Department of the Treasury Internal Revenue Service (99)	▶ See separate instructions. ▶ Attach this form to your return.	Attachment Sequence No. **67**

Name(s) shown on return Field of Flowers	Business or activity to which this form relates Retail Florist	Identifying number 10-1787889

Part I   **Election To Expense Certain Tangible Property (Section 179) (Note:** *If you have any "listed property," complete Part V before you complete Part I.)*

1	Maximum dollar limitation. If an enterprise zone business, see page 2 of the instructions . .	**1**	$19,000
2	Total cost of section 179 property placed in service. See page 2 of the instructions	**2**	30,645
3	Threshold cost of section 179 property before reduction in limitation	**3**	$200,000
4	Reduction in limitation. Subtract line 3 from line 2. If zero or less, enter -0-	**4**	- 0 -
5	Dollar limitation for tax year. Subtract line 4 from line 1. If zero or less, enter -0-. If married filing separately, see page 2 of the instructions	**5**	19,000

	(a) Description of property	(b) Cost (business use only)	(c) Elected cost	
6				

7	Listed property. Enter amount from line 27. . . . . **7** 19,000		
8	Total elected cost of section 179 property. Add amounts in column (c), lines 6 and 7 . . .	**8**	19,000
9	Tentative deduction. Enter the smaller of line 5 or line 8	**9**	19,000
10	Carryover of disallowed deduction from 1998. See page 3 of the instructions	**10**	- 0 -
11	Business income limitation. Enter the smaller of business income (not less than zero) or line 5 (see instructions)	**11**	19,000
12	Section 179 expense deduction. Add lines 9 and 10, but do not enter more than line 11 . .	**12**	19,000
13	Carryover of disallowed deduction to 2000. Add lines 9 and 10, less line 12 ▶	**13**	

Note: *Do not use Part II or Part III below for listed property (automobiles, certain other vehicles, cellular telephones, certain computers, or property used for entertainment, recreation, or amusement). Instead, use Part V for listed property.*

Part II   **MACRS Depreciation For Assets Placed in Service ONLY During Your 1999 Tax Year (Do Not Include Listed Property.)**

Section A—General Asset Account Election

14   If you are making the election under section 168(i)(4) to group any assets placed in service during the tax year into one or more general asset accounts, check this box. See page 3 of the instructions . . . . ▶ ☐

Section B—General Depreciation System (GDS) (See page 3 of the instructions.)

(a) Classification of property	(b) Month and year placed in service	(c) Basis for depreciation (business/investment use only—see instructions)	(d) Recovery period	(e) Convention	(f) Method	(g) Depreciation deduction
15a 3-year property						
b 5-year property		3,000	5 yrs	MQ	200 DB	750.00
c 7-year property						
d 10-year property						
e 15-year property						
f 20-year property						
g 25-year property			25 yrs.		S/L	
h Residential rental property			27.5 yrs.	MM	S/L	
			27.5 yrs.	MM	S/L	
i Nonresidential real property			39 yrs.	MM	S/L	
				MM	S/L	

Section C—Alternative Depreciation System (ADS) (See page 5 of the instructions.)

16a Class life		2,345			S/L	43.80
b 12-year			12 yrs.		S/L	
c 40-year			40 yrs.	MM	S/L	

Part III   **Other Depreciation (Do Not Include Listed Property.)** (See page 6 of the instructions.)

17	GDS and ADS deductions for assets placed in service in tax years beginning before 1999 .	**17**	4,813.32
18	Property subject to section 168(f)(1) election	**18**	
19	ACRS and other depreciation	**19**	

Part IV   **Summary** (See page 6 of the instructions.)

20	Listed property. Enter amount from line 26.	**20**	315.00
21	**Total.** Add deductions on line 12, lines 15 and 16 in column (g), and lines 17 through 20. Enter here and on the appropriate lines of your return. Partnerships and S corporations—see instructions .	**21**	24,922.12
22	For assets shown above and placed in service during the current year, enter the portion of the basis attributable to section 263A costs . . **22** - 0 -		

For Paperwork Reduction Act Notice, see the separate instructions.   Cat. No. 12906N   Form **4562** (1999)

Form 4562 (1999)   Page **2**

Part V **Listed Property—Automobiles, Certain Other Vehicles, Cellular Telephones, Certain Computers, and Property Used for Entertainment, Recreation, or Amusement**

Note: *For any vehicle for which you are using the standard mileage rate or deducting lease expense, complete only 23a, 23b, columns (a) through (c) of Section A, all of Section B, and Section C if applicable.*

Section A—Depreciation and Other Information (Caution: *See page 8 of the instructions for limits for passenger automobiles.)*

23a Do you have evidence to support the business/investment use claimed? ☐ **Yes** ☐ **No**   **23b** If "Yes," is the evidence written? ☐ **Yes** ☐ **No**

(a) Type of property (list vehicles first)	(b) Date placed in service	(c) Business/ investment use percentage	(d) Cost or other basis	(e) Basis for depreciation (business/investment use only)	(f) Recovery period	(g) Method/ Convention	(h) Depreciation deduction	(i) Elected section 179 cost
24 Property used more than 50% in a qualified business use (See page 7 of the instructions.):								
USA 280F Van	11-16-99	100 %	25,300	6,300	5	200 DB/MQ	315.00	19,000
		%						
		%						
25 Property used 50% or less in a qualified business use (See page 7 of the instructions.):								
		%				S/L –		
		%				S/L –		
		%				S/L –		

26 Add amounts in column (h). Enter the total here and on line 20, page 1 . . . . .   **26**   315.00

27 Add amounts in column (i). Enter the total here and on line 7, page 1 . . . .   **27**   19,000

Section B—Information on Use of Vehicles

Complete this section for vehicles used by a sole proprietor, partner, or other "more than 5% owner," or related person.

If you provided vehicles to your employees, first answer the questions in Section C to see if you meet an exception to completing this section for those vehicles.

	(a) Vehicle 1		(b) Vehicle 2		(c) Vehicle 3		(d) Vehicle 4		(e) Vehicle 5		(f) Vehicle 6	
28 Total business/investment miles driven during the year (DO NOT include commuting miles)												
29 Total commuting miles driven during the year												
30 Total other personal (noncommuting) miles driven												
31 Total miles driven during the year. Add lines 28 through 30												
	Yes	No	Yes	No	Yes	No	Yes	No	Yes	No	Yes	No
32 Was the vehicle available for personal use during off-duty hours?												
33 Was the vehicle used primarily by a more than 5% owner or related person?												
34 Is another vehicle available for personal use?												

Section C—Questions for Employers Who Provide Vehicles for Use by Their Employees

Answer these questions to determine if you meet an exception to completing Section B for vehicles used by employees who **are not** *more than 5% owners or related persons.*

		Yes	No
35	Do you maintain a written policy statement that prohibits all personal use of vehicles, including commuting, by your employees?		
36	Do you maintain a written policy statement that prohibits personal use of vehicles, except commuting, by your employees? See page 9 of the instructions for vehicles used by corporate officers, directors, or 1% or more owners		
37	Do you treat all use of vehicles by employees as personal use?		
38	Do you provide more than five vehicles to your employees, obtain information from your employees about the use of the vehicles, and retain the information received?		
39	Do you meet the requirements concerning qualified automobile demonstration use? See page 9 of the instructions . .		

Note: *If your answer to 35, 36, 37, 38, or 39 is "Yes," you need not complete Section B for the covered vehicles.*

Part VI **Amortization**

(a) Description of costs	(b) Date amortization begins	(c) Amortizable amount	(d) Code section	(e) Amortization period or percentage	(f) Amortization for this year
40 Amortization of costs that begins during your 1999 tax year:					
41 Amortization of costs that began before 1999			**41**	
42 **Total.** Enter here and on "Other Deductions" or "Other Expenses" line of your return . . .			**42**	

✪

Depreciation Worksheet

Description of Property	Date Placed in Service	Cost or Other Basis	Business/ Investment Use %	Section 179 Deduction	Depreciation Prior Years	Basis for Depreciation	Method/ Convention	Recovery Period	Rate or Table %	Depreciation Deduction
Building	2-2-96	$65,000	100%		$4,793.75	$65,000	SL/MM	GDS 39	2.564%	$1,666.60
Desk and Chair	2-2-96	600	100%	$600	-0-	-0-				-0-
Refrigeration equipment	2-2-96	4,500	100%		3,204.00	4,500	200DB/HY	GDS/5	11.52%	518.40
Work tables	2-2-96	1,200	100%		854.40	1,200	200DB/HY	GDS/5	11.52%	138.24
Cash register	2-2-96	270	100%		192.24	270	200DB/HY	GDS/5	11.52%	31.10
Subtotal -- 1996 Property										2,354.34
Delivery truck	4-16-97	31,500	100%	18,000	5,467.50	13,500	150DB/HY	ADS/5	17.85%	2,409.75
Typewriter	7-3-97	300	100%		103.14	300	150DB/HY	ADS/6	16.41%	49.23
Subtotal -- 1997 Property										2,458.98
Computer	6-21-99	3,000	100%		-0-	3,000	200DB/MQ	GDS/5	25.00%	750.00
File cabinets*	9-9-99	475	100%		-0-	475	SL/MQ	ADS/10	3.75%	17.81
Store counters*	11-1-99	1,870	100%		-0-	1,870	SL/MQ	ADS/9	1.39%	25.99
Van	11-16-99	25,300	100%	19,000	-0-	6,300	200DB/MQ	GDS/5	5.00%	340.00
Subtotal -- 1999 Property				19,000						1,133.80
Grand Total -- 1999				19,000						5,947.12
Schedule of property subject to ADS, line 16a of Form 4562										
File cabinets						$ 475.81	SL/MQ	ADS/10		$ 17.81
Store counters						1,870.00	SL/MQ	ADS/9		25.99
Amount to be entered on line 16a						$ 2,345.00				$ 43.80

*

of goods sold. Similarly, depletion (other than of oil and gas properties) is part of an S corporation's ordinary income or loss and is reported on the specific line provided for depletion.

Amortization items, such as a deduction for organizational expenses, are part of "other deductions." An explanation for these items is included in a separate statement attached to the return.

The first-year expense deduction is a separately stated item reported on Schedule K, and the allocable portion is passed through separately to shareholders on Schedule K-1.

Depletion of oil and gas properties is also a separately stated item reported on Schedule K. The allocable portion is passed through separately to shareholders on Schedule K-1.

C Corporations

Form 4562 must be completed if any depreciation is claimed (regardless of the year in which the property is placed in service) or if amortization of costs begins in the current year. The depreciation deduction is then entered on Form 1120 on the specific line provided for depreciation. This deduction must be reduced by depreciation claimed in the cost of goods sold or elsewhere on the return. Depletion is entered on the specific line provided for depletion. Amortization is part of "other deductions," an explanation of which must be attached to the return.

CHAPTER 13

Advertising Expenses

You may run advertisements in newspapers, on the radio or television, or in magazines or trade journals to sell your products or services. You can deduct these costs, as well as the costs of other promotional activities. In this chapter you will learn about:

- Ordinary advertising expenses
- Promotion of goodwill
- Prizes, contests, and other promotional activities
- Help-wanted ads
- Where to deduct advertising expenses

At the same time, you will discover that some costs cannot be deducted or that certain costs need to be deducted as another type of business expense.

ORDINARY ADVERTISING EXPENSES

Like all other business expenses, advertising costs must be ordinary and necessary business expenses in order to be deductible. They must have a reasonable relationship to your business activities, and they must be reasonable in amount. However, there are no guidelines on what is "reasonable" in amount.

Deductible advertising expenses include the costs of:

- Business cards

- Ads in print or the media (such as newspaper or magazine advertisements, radio or television spots, or on-line computer messages). Also deductible as advertising expenses are the cost of listing your business in a charitable organization publication.

- Ads in telephone directories (such as Yellow Page listings)

- Web site costs—for example, monthly fees to America Online or a point-to-point protocol (PPP) account to provide access to the Internet

- Billboards (rental fees are an advertising expense)

- Signs with a useful life of not more than one year. Signs expected to last longer than a year can be depreciated, as explained in Chapter 12.

     EXAMPLE: The cost of metal or plastic signs with a life of more than one year have to be capitalized. The cost of restaurant menu folders are currently deductible, since the folders have a life of not more than one year.

- Package design costs that are part of an advertising campaign

PROMOTION OF GOODWILL

Expenses designed to create goodwill in the public's eye rather than to obtain immediate sales are also deductible. In fact, the advertising program can be of a long-term nature and still result in an immediate deduction. The IRS has ruled that the ordinary costs of advertising are currently deductible despite the fact that they produce a long-term benefit. And the Tax Court has agreed with this position, allowing graphic design costs to be currently deductible as advertising expenses, even though they may produce future patronage or goodwill.

EXAMPLE: The costs of installing window treatments in model homes as part of an advertising campaign are currently deductible. The costs are incurred to promote the name of the business.

The cost of distributing a company's samples can be deducted as an advertising expense where the distribution is designed to engender goodwill.

Creating and maintaining a Web site is another key way to keep your company name before the public. While there have not yet been any cases or rulings on the extent to which Web site–related expenses are deductible, it can certainly be argued that these expenses relate to creating goodwill for the company.

Another type of advertising involves sponsorships of teams. Your business may, for example, sponsor a bowling team or a Little League team. In return for the sponsorship, your company's name is displayed on the team uniform and may also be a part of the team's name. In these circumstances the costs of sponsorship are deductible as advertising expenses.

Free services provided to generate goodwill cannot be deducted as an advertising expense. For example, in one case a doctor provided free medical services and deducted as an advertising expense the value of his uncompensated services. The Tax Court disallowed the deduction because the doctor's labor was not an expense (it was not an amount paid or incurred).

Personal Versus Business Expenses

Expenses that smack of a personal nature may still constitute deductible advertising costs where it can be shown that the expenses were incurred primarily for business purposes. The following examples demonstrate when expenses may be considered primarily for business and when they may not:

EXAMPLE: A restaurant chain owner who maintained show horses for the purpose of advertising the company's name was allowed a current deduction. But an owner who bought a horse, named it after himself, and entered it in shows was not allowed a deduction when he failed to show there was any connection between the horse and his business.

EXAMPLE: A business owner who invited customers to his child's wedding reception could not deduct the cost for these guests as advertising. The nature of the expense was just too personal and the business aspect of the expense just too attenuated to make the cost a deductible advertising expense.

EXAMPLE: An attorney was not allowed to deduct the cost of new suits as an advertising expense. He claimed he needed to look good to attract new clients. Again, the expense was personal in nature and so was not deductible.

EXAMPLE: Costs of car racing by an officer of a computer research and design corporation were not deductible. Again, the expenses were personal in nature. In comparison, a meat processor that sponsored a race car could deduct expenses. The sponsorship allowed the company to display its logo on the car, and track announcers mentioned the car's sponsor during the race.

Lobbying Expenses

In general, the costs of advertising to influence legislation at the federal, state, or even local level are not deductible. Nondeductible expenses include:

- The costs of participating or intervening in any political campaign for or against any candidate in public office.

- The costs of attempting to influence the general public or segments of the public about elections, legislative matters, or referendums.

- The costs of communicating directly with certain executive branch officials in any attempt to influence the official actions or positions of such officials. These executives include the president, vice president, any officer or employee of the White House Office of the Executive Office of the President and the two most senior officers of each of the other agencies in the Executive Office, and certain other individuals.

- The costs of research, preparation, planning, or coordinating any of the activities already mentioned.

Not all lobbying expenses are nondeductible. You can still claim a deduction for de minimis in-house lobbying expenses. These are expenses not exceeding $2,000 per year to influence legislation or communicate directly with a specified executive branch official. There is also an exception for expenses to influence local legislation, such as decisions by a local council.

And, of course, professional lobbyists are entitled to deduct their own business expenses even though payments to them are not deductible.

Some types of goodwill activities may constitute deductible entertainment expenses. See Chapter 6.

PRIZES, CONTESTS, AND OTHER PROMOTIONAL ACTIVITIES

Amounts paid for prizes, contests, and other promotional activities may be deducted as advertising expenses where you can show that the expenses have a relationship to your business. The amounts expended must be reasonable. They must not be out of proportion to the amount of business expected to be obtained as a result of the prize, contest, or other promotional activity.

EXAMPLE: A restaurant owner gave away a car to the holder of a lucky-number ticket. These tickets had been distributed to patrons. The cost of the car was a deductible business expense.

Sponsorships of teams and other events can be deducted as advertising expenses. For example, sponsorship of a tennis match or golf tournament may be a deductible advertising expense.

Prizes and other awards given to employees are not treated as advertising costs. Instead, they are part of compensation. See Chapter 5.

HELP-WANTED ADS

Most advertising is designed to sell products or services. However, you also may advertise when trying to fill a position in your company. The cost of running help-wanted ads in newspapers and trade magazines is deductible as an ordinary and necessary business expense. It is not an advertising cost.

If you are out of work and take out an ad in a newspaper to seek a position, again, the cost may be deductible, but not as an advertising expense. Instead, it may be deducted as a cost of finding a job. For a further discussion on deducting job-hunting costs, see Chapter 19.

WHERE TO DEDUCT EXPENSES

Employees

An employee generally will not have any advertising expenses. He or she is only in the business of being an employee and need not promote that activity. When an employee takes out an ad in a newspaper or trade journal expressing availability for a new position, this expense may be deductible as a job-hunting expense. Deductible job-hunting expenses are explained in Chapter 19.

Self-Employed

Advertising costs are deductible on Schedule C. There is a specific line for this type of expense. If you are eligible to file Schedule C-EZ, you claim advertising costs along with other deductible expenses.

Partnerships and LLCs

Advertising costs are trade or business expenses that are taken into account in determining the profit or loss of the partnership or LLC on Form 1065. They are entered in the category of "Other Deductions" on Form 1065. A schedule is attached to the return explaining the deductions claimed in this category. They are not separately stated items passed through to partners and members. Therefore partners and members in LLCs report their net income or loss from the business on Schedule E; they do not deduct advertising costs on their individual tax returns.

S Corporations

Advertising costs are trade or business expenses that are taken into account in determining the profit or loss of the S corporation. They are reported on the specific line provided for advertising on Form 1120S. They are not separately stated items passed through to shareholders. Therefore shareholders report their net income or loss from the business on Schedule E; they do not deduct advertising costs on their individual tax returns.

C Corporations

Advertising costs are trade or business expenses that are taken into account in determining the profit or loss of the C corporation. They are reported on the specific line provided for advertising on Form 1120. The corporation then pays tax on its net profit or loss. Shareholders do not report any income (or loss) from the corporation.

CHAPTER 14

Retirement Plans

The Social Security benefits you may expect to receive will make up only a portion of your retirement income. In order to help you save for your own retirement and to encourage employers to provide retirement benefits to employees, the tax laws contain special incentives for retirement savings. Broadly speaking, if a retirement plan conforms to special requirements, then contributions are deductible while earnings are not currently taxable. What is more, employees covered by such plans are not immediately charged with income. If you have employees, setting up retirement plans to benefit them not only gives you a current deduction for contributions you make to the plan but also provides your staff with benefits. This helps to foster employee goodwill and may aid in recruiting new employees.

The type of plan you set up governs both the amount you can deduct and the time when you claim the deduction. Certain plans offer special tax incentives designed to encourage employers to help with employee retirement benefits. Even though you may be an employer, if you are self-employed (a sole proprietor, partner, or LLC member), you are treated as an employee for purposes of participating in these plans.

In this chapter you will learn about:

- Qualified retirement plans

- Added costs for retirement plans

- Retirement plans for self-employed individuals: Keogh plans, SEPs, and SIMPLE plans

- Salary reduction arrangements

- Individual Retirement Accounts (IRAs), including Roth IRAs

- Comparison of qualified retirement plans

- Nonqualified retirement plans

- Glossary of terms for retirement plans

- Where to claim deductions for retirement plans

For further information about retirement plans, see IRS Publication 560, Retirement Plans for Small Businesses (SEP, Keogh and SIMPLE Plans).

QUALIFIED RETIREMENT PLANS

Qualified retirement plans are plans that provide retirement benefits and meet stringent requirements under federal law. Some of these laws fall under the jurisdiction of the Treasury Department and the IRS; others fall under the Department of Labor. Qualified plans allow employees to defer reporting income from benefits until retirement while at the same time allowing employers to claim a current deduction for contributions to the plans.

Income earned by the plan is not currently taxed. Eventually it is taxed to employees when distributed to them as part of their benefits.

Types of Retirement Plans
There are two main categories of plans: defined benefit plans and defined contribution plans.

Defined benefit plans predict what an employee will receive in benefits upon retirement. This prediction is based on the employee's compensation, age, and anticipated age of retirement. It is also based on an estimation of what the plan can earn over the years. Then an actuary determines the amount that an employer must contribute each year in order to be sure that funds will be there when the employee retires. The employer takes a deduction for the actuarially determined contribution. There are, however, variations of defined benefit plans. For example, in a cash balance defined benefit plan, benefits payable upon retirement depend in part to plan performance.

Defined contribution plans are more like savings accounts. The employer contributes to an account for each employee. The contribution is based on a defined formula, such as a percentage of the employee's compensation. The account may not really be a separate account. In corporate plans it is a bookkeeping notation of the benefits that belong to each employee. The benefits that are ultimately paid to an employee are based on what the contributions actually earn over the years.

There is a variety of plans under the umbrella of defined contribution plans. The most common is the profit-sharing plan. Under this plan the employer agrees to contribute a percentage of employee compensation to the plan. The allocation is usually based purely on employees' relative compensation (but other factors, such as age, can be taken into account). Another common plan is a money purchase plan. Under this plan the employer also agrees to contribute a fixed percentage of compensation each year. Perhaps the most popular type of defined contribution plan today is the 401(k) plan (also called a cash and deferred compensation arrangement). The reason for its popularity: Contributions are made by employees through salary reduction arrangements that let them fund their retirement plan with pre-tax dollars. Employers often match to some extent employee contributions as a way of encouraging participation and providing additional benefits to employees.

Regardless of the plan selected, all plans have the same requirements designed to ensure that they do not benefit only owners and top executives but also ordinary workers. Many of these requirements are highly technical. They are explained here so that you will recognize how complicated the use of qualified plans can become. It may be helpful to discuss your retirement plans or anticipated plans with a retirement plan expert.

Corporations that do not want to become involved with the complexities of qualified plans can use simplified employee pensions (SEPs) or savings incentive match plans for employees (SIMPLEs), discussed later in this chapter in connection with plans for self-employed persons.

Covering Employees

A plan will be treated as "qualified" only if it allows employees who meet certain requirements to participate and receive benefits under it. In general, the plan must satisfy one of three tests. The first stipulates that the plan must cover at least 70 percent of all "nonhighly compensated employees." This is called the percentage test.

> **Definition** *Nonhighly compensated employees* All employees who are not treated as highly compensated employees. These essentially are rank-and-file employees.

> **Definition** *Highly compensated employees* These include owners and highly paid employees earning specified amounts. These amounts are adjusted annually for inflation. Thus, the coverage test needs to be checked annually.

Alternatively, the plan must cover a percentage of nonhighly compensated employees that is at least 70 percent of the percentage of highly compensated employees. This is called the "ratio test." The third alternative is called the "average benefit percentage test," or ABP test. This test also looks at the percentage of nonhighly compensated employees to be sure that there is no discrimination against them.

Participation

Participation is the right of an employee to be covered by a plan after meeting certain participation requirements (age and service requirements are discussed below). In order to be qualified, the plan must not only meet a coverage test but also meet a participation test. The plan must benefit the lesser of 50 employees or 40 percent or more of all employees. If an employer maintains more than one plan, participation must be satisfied by each plan individually. The plans cannot be grouped together (aggregated) for this purpose.

There are also age and service requirements. The plan can defer participation until the later of the employee attaining the age of 21 or completing one year of service. A two-year service requirement can be used if there is immediate and full vesting (vesting is discussed below).

Starting in 1999, 401(k) plans can rely on a safe harbor to ensure that coverage and participation requirements are satisfied. Employers must contribute 3 percent of compensation (whether or not employees contribute to the plan). Alternatively, they can match 100 percent of employee elective deferrals, up to 3 percent of compensation, and 50 percent of the deferral in excess of 3 percent up to 5 percent of compensation (effectively 4 percent of compensation).

Vesting

While the plan must permit certain employees to participate and have contributions made on their behalf, employers can, if they choose, require a certain number of years in the plan before benefits will belong absolutely to the participants. This delay in absolute ownership of benefits is called vesting. In order for plans to be qualified, employers cannot defer vesting beyond set limits.

A plan can provide for "cliff vesting." Under this type of vesting, there is no ownership of benefits before the completion of five years in the plan. At the end of five years, all benefits are fully owned.

The other vesting schedule is called "seven-year graded vesting." This permits vesting of 20 percent of benefits after three years of service, with an additional 20 percent vesting for each year thereafter. Under this vesting schedule, there is full vesting after seven years of participation in the plan.

If a plan is weighted toward owners and highly compensated employees, it may be treated as a "top-heavy plan" even though it satisfies the coverage and participation tests discussed earlier. A top-heavy plan requires more rapid vesting for participants. Cliff vesting must result after three years of participation. Alternatively, there is a six-year graded vesting schedule.

Permitted Disparity

An employer can reduce the cost of covering employees by "integrating" the plan with Social Security. This means that the employer can take into account the employer contribution to Social Security for each participant. In effect, the employer's contribution to Social Security is treated as the plan contribution so the employer saves the cost of having to make this contribution a second time to a qualified plan. (The employer payment of Social Security tax for each participant is deducted as taxes, not as a pension plan contribution.)

Ordinarily the disparity in contributions to employees is viewed as discriminatory. But integrating Social Security contributions with plan contributions is viewed as permitted disparity (i.e., is not discriminatory). The rules for permitted disparity are highly complex, and different rules apply to defined benefit plans and defined contribution plans.

Obtaining Plan Approval

Remember that your plan must be qualified. Only the IRS can tell you if your plan falls within this category. You can use a master or prototype plan for setting up your retirement plan. Plans following these prototypes generally meet IRS requirements, although they are not deemed to have automatic IRS approval. If you design your own plan (or have a professional design one for you), in order to be qualified, the plan must obtain IRS approval. This approval is granted on the basis of how the plan is written and how it will operate. There is no requirement that you obtain approval prior to operating a plan, but it is a good idea to get it. The process is complicated, and the use of a tax or pension professional is advisable.

Compensation Limit

Benefits and contributions are based on a participant's taxable compensation reported on an employee's W-2 form. It does not include tax-free fringe benefits or other excludable wages.

The law limits the amount of compensation that can be taken into account. For 1999 there is a $160,000 limit. This means that even if an employee earns $175,000, only the first $160,000 is used to compute benefits and contributions.

Where both spouses work for the same employer, each can receive a contribution based on his or her respective compensation (up to the compensation limit). A prior rule that had treated spouses working for the same employer as one unit has been repealed.

Contribution Limit

The contribution limit depends on the type of plan involved. For a profit-sharing plan, the 1999 limit is the lesser of 15 percent of compensation or $30,000. For other defined contribution plans, such as money purchase plans, the limit is the lesser of 25 percent of compensation or $30,000. These percentages are the top limits. Plans can adopt lesser percentages for contributions.

For defined benefit plans, there is no specific limit on contributions. Rather, the limit is placed on the benefits that can be provided under the plan. Then contributions are actuarially determined to provide these benefits. The plan cannot provide benefits exceeding $90,000 per year, adjusted annually for inflation. The 1999 limit after adjustment for inflation is $130,000. In other words, this is the amount used to calculate the maximum 1999 contributions to defined benefit plans.

Making Contributions

Contributions to defined benefit plans must be made on a quarterly basis. In order to avoid a special interest charge, contributions made in quarterly installments must be at least 90 percent of contributions for the current year or 100 percent of contributions for the prior year. If contributions are based on the current year, the balance of the contributions may be made as late as the due date for the employer's return, including extensions.

Contributions for defined contribution plans can be made at any time up to the due date of the employer's return, including extensions. In fact, contributions can be made even after the employer's tax return is filed as long as they do not exceed the return's due date.

EXAMPLE: An employer's return is due March 15, 2000. The employer files the return on March 1, 2000. Contributions for defined contribution plans can be made until March 15, 2000.

The only way to extend the time for making contributions is to obtain a valid filing extension. For example, an owner of a professional corporation on a calendar year who wants to extend the time for making contributions must obtain an extension of time to file Form 1120, the return for that corporation. To do this, Form 7004, Application for Automatic Extension of Time to File Corporation Income Tax Return, must be filed no later than March 15, the due date for Form 1120 for calendar-year corporations. Filing Form 7004 gives the professional corporation an automatic six-month filing extension, to September 15. The corporation then has until September 15 to make its contributions to the plan.

Contributions generally must be made in cash. Where cash flow is insufficient to meet contribution requirements, employers may be forced to borrow to make contributions on time. In some instances, contributions can be made by using employer stock.

Borrowing from the Plan

Owners in corporate plans may be able to borrow from the plan without adverse tax consequences. The plan must limit loans to the lesser of:

(a) $50,000, or

(b) The greater of one-half your accrued benefit or $10,000.

The loan must be amortized over a period of no more than five years (except for loans that are used to buy personal residences) and charge a reasonable rate of interest. As an owner, you cannot deduct interest on the loan.

The plan must also allow rank-and-file employees the opportunity to borrow from the plan on the same basis as owners and top executives.

ADDED COSTS FOR RETIREMENT PLANS

In addition to the contributions you make to the plan, there may be other costs to consider. The type of plan you have affects the nature and amount of these added costs.

Whether you have a defined contribution or a defined benefit plan, you may be required to maintain a bond for yourself or someone else who acts as a fiduciary in your plan. You also must update your plan documents so that they reflect the latest law changes.

If you are approaching retirement age and want to obtain the maximum retirement benefits for your contributions (the biggest bang for your buck), you may want to adopt a defined benefit plan. Before doing so, it is important to recognize that these types of plans entail two additional costs not associated with defined contribution plans.

Bonding Requirement

To ensure that you will not run off with the funds in your company retirement plan, leaving participants high and dry, you are required to be bonded if you have any control over the plan or its assets. This includes, for example, authority to transfer funds or make disbursements from the plan. The bond must be at least 10 percent of the amount over which you have control. The bond cannot be less than $1,000, but it need not exceed $500,000.

No bond is required if the plan covers only you as the owner (a self-employed person or a single shareholder-employee) or only partners and their spouses.

Plan Amendments

You are required to keep your plan up to date and operate it in accordance with law changes that are enacted from time to time. You have until the last day of the plan year starting after December 31, 1999 to incorporate law changes made since 1994 if you have not already done so. But you must operate your plan as if these changes have already been made to your plan documents.

You may incur professional fees for updating plan documents. If your plan is a prototype plan provided by a brokerage firm or mutual fund, however, there may be no charge for required updates.

If you discover errors in your plan (either in how it is written or how it is being operated), you can correct the errors and avoid or minimize penalties. If you do not take the initiative and the IRS discovers the problems, you can be subject to greater penalties, interest, and even plan disqualification. To correct problems, you can use the IRS's Employee Plans Compliance Resolution System (see Rev. Proc. 98-22 for details).

Actuarial Costs for Defined Benefit Plans

If you have a defined benefit plan, you must use the services of an enrolled actuary to determine your annual contributions. Thus you must expect to pay for this service year after year.

Pension Benefit Guaranty Corporation Premiums for Defined Benefit Plans

The Pension Benefit Guaranty Corporation (PBGC) is a quasi-federal agency designed to protect employee pension plans in the event that the employer goes under. In order to provide this protection, the PBGC charges annual premiums for each participant in the plan. First, there is a flat-rate premium of $19 per participant. Then, for underfunded plans only, there is a variable-rate premium of nine-tenths of 1 percent of underfunding. (Underfunding means that the employer has not contributed sufficient amounts to pay all anticipated pensions.)

RETIREMENT PLANS FOR SELF-EMPLOYED INDIVIDUALS: KEOGH PLANS, SEPS, AND SIMPLE PLANS

Self-employed individuals have three main options in retirement plans. First, they can set up qualified retirement plans, called Keogh plans. Keogh plans may be known by other names. They have been called H.R.10 plans, reflecting the number of the bill in Congress under which Keoghs were created. They may also be called "Basic Plans" or some other name created by a bank, brokerage firm, insurance company, or other financial institution offering Keogh plan investments. Another option in retirement plans for self-employed individuals is simplified employee pension plans, or SEPs, discussed below. A third option in retirement plans is savings incentive match plan for employees, or SIMPLEs, also discussed below.

Keogh Plans in General

Keogh plans are simply qualified plans for self-employed individuals. They are subject to the same requirements as qualified plans for corporations, discussed earlier. (Banks, brokerage firms, mutual funds, and insurance companies offering plans for self-employed individuals generally do not denominate them as Keoghs but simply by the type of plan established, such as a profit-sharing plan.) Like qualified plans, Keoghs must cover employees of a self-employed person on a nondiscriminatory basis. Also like qualified plans, they are limited in the amount that can be contributed and deducted.

There are two important distinctions between Keogh plans and qualified plans for corporations: the way in which contributions are calculated on behalf of owner-employees and restrictions on loans from the plan.

Contributions to Keogh Plans

Contributions to all retirement plans are based on compensation. For qualified plans covering employees of corporations, this is simply W-2 taxable wages. For self-employed individuals under Keogh plans, the basis for contributions is a little more complicated. Essentially, the basis for contributions on behalf of owner-employees is net earnings from self-employment. But this is not merely the net profit from your business on which self-employment tax is paid. Net earnings from self-employment must be further reduced by the deduction for one-half of the self-employment tax.

Calculating compensation of owner-employee on which contribution is based   Start with the profit amount from Schedule C or Schedule C-EZ (or Schedule F in the case of farming) or the net earnings from self-employment on Schedule K-1 of Form 1065. For partners this is essentially your distributive share of partnership income plus any "guaranteed payments." Net earnings from self-employment from various activities are totaled on Schedule SE, Self-Employment Tax.

After you have your "compensation," subtract from this amount one-half of self-employment tax computed on Schedule SE. This net amount is the figure upon which contributions to qualified retirement plans are based.

In order to make contributions on your own behalf, you must have net earnings from self-employment derived from your personal services. If you merely invest capital in a partnership while your personal services are not a material income-producing factor, you cannot make a Keogh contribution. If you are a limited partner, you cannot base a Keogh contribution on your distributive share of partnership income. Similar rules apply to members in limited liability companies. Income received from property, such as rents, interest, or dividends, is not treated as net earnings from self-employment.

Calculating your contribution rate   For self-employed individuals, the contribution rate must be adjusted for the employer deduction on behalf of yourself. This is a roundabout way of saying that the base percentage rate you use to determine contributions on behalf of employees, if any, must be adjusted for determining contributions on your own behalf. To arrive at this reduced percentage rate, divide the contribution rate, expressed as a decimal number, by 1 plus the contribution rate.

EXAMPLE: Your contribution rate for your profit-sharing plan is 15 percent. You divide 0.15 by 1.15 to arrive at the contribution rate on your behalf: 13.0435 percent.

EXAMPLE: Your contribution rate for your money purchase plan is 5 percent. You divide 0.05 by 1.05 to arrive at the contribution rate on your behalf: 4.7619 percent.

Remember, the maximum contribution cannot exceed the lesser of $30,000 or, in 1998, $160,000 times your contribution rate.

EXAMPLE: You maintain a 15-percent profit-sharing plan for your sole proprietorship, of which you are the only worker. In 1999 your net profit reported on Schedule C is $200,000. Your net earnings from self-employment for purposes of calculating Keogh contributions are $192,820.65 ($200,000 − $7,179.35 [one-half self-employment tax]). Your contribution is limited to $20,869.60 (13.0435 percent of $160,000). You cannot base your contribution on your full net earnings from self-employment because of the $160,000 limit. And you cannot obtain the full $30,000 contribution limit because of the 15-percent limit, adjusted for self-employed individuals as explained below.

Increasing Keogh Deductions

If you have a profit-sharing plan, the maximum contribution in 1999 is limited to $20,869.60 (13.0435 percent of $160,000). This is because no more than $160,000 of compensation can be taken into account in calculating contributions and benefits. If you earn a sizable amount and want to increase your contribution (and the deduction for your contribution), you should consider adopting a money purchase plan to complement your profit-sharing plan. You can provide that your money purchase plan make contributions at the rate of 6 percent, which adjusts to 5.6604 percent. This would give you an additional $9,056.64 in contributions and put you at the limit of contributions, which is $29,926.24 per year ($20,869.60 + $9,056.64).

Remember that increasing your contributions on your own behalf also means you must increase contributions for your employees, if any. Take this additional cost into account when deciding to increase contribution rates.

Loan Restrictions on Borrowing from Keogh Plans

Qualified plans allow participants to borrow against their retirement accounts within certain limits. Owner-employees generally cannot borrow against their Keogh accounts. If they do borrow, they may be subject to penalties on what are called prohibited transactions.

Simplified Employee Pensions (SEPs) in General

Simplified employee pensions, or SEPs, are another type of retirement plan that self-employed individuals can use to save for retirement on a tax-advantaged basis. (Corporations can use SEPs as well.) As the name implies, they do not entail all the administrative costs and complications associated with other qualified retirement plans. There are no annual reporting requirements, as is the case for Keogh plans and qualified corporate retirement plans.

SEPs are individual retirement accounts set up by employees to which an employer makes contributions, then deducts them. The contributions are a fixed percentage of each employee's compensation. To set up a SEP, an employer need only sign a form establishing the percentage rate for making contributions and for setting eligibility requirements. This is a one-page form, Form 5305-SEP, Simplified Employee Pension—IRA Contribution Agreement.

The form is not filed with the IRS. Instead, it serves merely as an agreement under which the employer makes contributions. The employer then instructs employees where to set up SEP-IRAs to receive employer contributions. Banks, brokerage firms, and insurance companies generally have prototype plans designed for this purpose.

The maximum contribution under a SEP is essentially the same as that for a profit-sharing plan: 15 percent of compensation or $30,000, whichever is less. For contributions made on behalf of owner-employees, this percentage works out to 13.0435 percent. As with other qualified plans, no more than $160,000 of compensation in 1999 can be taken into account in computing contributions.

Covering Employees

You must cover all employees who meet an age and service test. The SEP must cover employees who are 21 or older, earn over $400 in 1999, and have worked for you at any time in at least three out of five years. You can provide for more favorable coverage (for example, you can cover employees at age 18). The compensation requirement of $400 is adjusted annually for inflation in $50 increments.

Employees over the age of $70\frac{1}{2}$ can continue to participate in a SEP and receive employer contributions. However, required minimum distributions must also be made to these employees.

SEPs and Other Retirement Plans

SEPs can be combined with other qualified plans to provide greater benefits. If a SEP is combined with a profit-sharing plan, the maximum profit-sharing plan contribution of 15 percent must be reduced by the percentage contributed to a SEP. If the SEP is combined with another type of qualified plan, it is treated as a separate profit-sharing plan. Thus, for example, if a SEP is combined with a money purchase plan, the maximum money purchase plan contribution of 25 percent must be reduced by the percentage contributed to the SEP.

If an employer contributes to a SEP to which elective deferrals have been made (see salary reduction arrangements, below), the total contributions cannot exceed the lesser of 15 percent of compensation or $30,000.

Form for Adopting a SEP

Form **5305-SEP** (Rev. January 1997) Department of the Treasury Internal Revenue Service	**Simplified Employee Pension-Individual** **Retirement Accounts Contribution Agreement** (Under section 408(k) of the Internal Revenue Code)	OMB No. 1545-0499 **DO NOT File With** **the Internal** **Revenue Service**

_____ makes the following agreement under section 408(k) of the
(Name of employer)
Internal Revenue Code and the instructions to this form.

Article I—Eligibility Requirements (Check appropriate boxes—see **Instructions**.)

The employer agrees to provide for discretionary contributions in each calendar year to the individual retirement account or individual retirement annuity (IRA) of all employees who are at least _____ years old (not to exceed 21 years old) and have performed services for the employer in at least _____ years (not to exceed 3 years) of the immediately preceding 5 years. This simplified employee pension (SEP) ☐ includes ☐ does not include employees covered under a collective bargaining agreement, ☐ includes ☐ does not include certain nonresident aliens, and ☐ includes ☐ does not include employees whose total compensation during the year is less than $400*.

Article II—SEP Requirements (See **Instructions**.)

The employer agrees that contributions made on behalf of each eligible employee will be:
A. Based only on the first $160,000* of compensation.
B. Made in an amount that is the same percentage of compensation for every employee.
C. Limited annually to the smaller of $30,000* **or** 15% of compensation.
D. Paid to the employee's IRA trustee, custodian, or insurance company (for an annuity contract).

Employer's signature and date	Name and title

Paperwork Reduction Act Notice

You are not required to provide the information requested on a form that is subject to the Paperwork Reduction Act unless the form displays a valid OMB control number. Books or records relating to a form or its instructions must be retained as long as their contents may become material in the administration of any Internal Revenue law. Generally, tax returns and return information are confidential, as required by Code section 6103.

The time needed to complete this form will vary depending on individual circumstances. The estimated average time is:
Recordkeeping . . . . 1 hr., 40 min.
Learning about the
law or the form . . . . 1 hr., 35 min.
Preparing the form . . . 1 hr., 41 min.

If you have comments concerning the accuracy of these time estimates or suggestions for making this form simpler, we would be happy to hear from you. You can write to the Tax Forms Committee, Western Area Distribution Center, Rancho Cordova, CA 95743-0001. **DO NOT** send this form to this address. Instead, keep it for your records.

Instructions

Section references are to the Internal Revenue Code unless otherwise noted.

Purpose of Form

Form 5305-SEP (Model SEP) is used by an employer to make an agreement to provide benefits to all eligible employees under a SEP described in section 408(k). **Do not** file this form with the IRS. See **Pub. 560**, Retirement Plans for the Self-Employed, and **Pub. 590**, Individual Retirement Arrangements (IRAs).

Instructions to the Employer

Simplified Employee Pension.—A SEP is a written arrangement (a plan) that provides you with a simplified way to make contributions toward your employees' retirement income. Under a SEP, you can contribute to an employee's individual retirement account or annuity (IRA). You make contributions directly to an IRA set up by or for each employee with a bank, insurance company, or other qualified financial institution. When using Form 5305-SEP to establish a SEP, the IRA must be a Model IRA established on an IRS form or a master or prototype IRA for which the IRS has issued a favorable opinion letter. Making the agreement on Form 5305-SEP does not establish an employer IRA described in section 408(c).

When Not To Use Form 5305-SEP.—Do not use this form if you:

1. Currently maintain any other qualified retirement plan. This does not prevent you from maintaining another SEP.

2. Previously maintained a defined benefit plan that is now terminated.

3. Have any eligible employees for whom IRAs have not been established.

4. Use the services of leased employees (described in section 414(n)).

5. Are a member of an affiliated service group (described in section 414(m)), a controlled group of corporations (described in section 414(b)), or trades or businesses under common control (described in sections 414(c) and 414(o)), unless all eligible employees of all the members of such groups, trades, or businesses, participate in the SEP.

6. Will not pay the cost of the SEP contributions. Do not use Form 5305-SEP for a SEP that provides for elective employee

contributions even if the contributions are made under a salary reduction agreement.

Use Form 5305A-SEP, or a nonmodel SEP if you permit elective deferrals to a SEP.

Note: _SEPs permitting elective deferrals cannot be established after 1996._

Eligible Employees.—All eligible employees must be allowed to participate in the SEP. An eligible employee is any employee who: **(1)** is at least 21 years old, and **(2)** has performed "service" for you in at least 3 of the immediately preceding 5 years.

Note: _You can establish less restrictive eligibility requirements, but not more restrictive ones._

Service is any work performed for you for any period of time, however short. If you are a member of an affiliated service group, a controlled group of corporations, or trades or businesses under common control, service includes any work performed for any period of time for any other member of such group, trades, or businesses.

Excludable Employees.—The following employees do not have to be covered by the SEP: **(1)** employees covered by a collective bargaining agreement whose retirement benefits were bargained for in good faith by you and their union, **(2)** nonresident alien employees who did not earn U.S. source income from you, and **(3)** employees who received less than $400* in compensation during the year.

Contribution Limits.—The SEP rules permit you to make an annual contribution of up to 15% of the employee's compensation or $30,000*, whichever is less. Compensation, for this purpose, does not include employer contributions to the SEP or the employee's compensation in excess of $160,000*. If you also maintain a Model Elective SEP or any

* _This amount reflects the cost-of-living increase effective January 1, 1997. The amount is adjusted annually._
The IRS announces the increase, if any, in a news release and in the Internal Revenue Bulletin.

Cat. No. 11825J   Form **5305-SEP** (Rev. 1-97)

Salary Reduction Arrangements

Before 1997 a SEP of a small employer (with no more than 25 employees who were eligible to participate in the SEP at any time during the prior year) could be designed so that employees funded all or part of their own retirement plans. Employees agreed to reduce their compensation by a set amount. That amount, called an elective deferral, was then contributed to the SEP. Employees were treated as not having received the amount by which their salary was reduced so that they did not pay income taxes on that amount. Salary reduction arrangements in SEPs, called SARSEPs, were repealed for 1997 and later years. However, employers that had SARSEPs before 1997 can continue these plans, and employees hired after 1996 may participate in these plans. So, for example, if you had a SARSEP plan in 1996, you can continue to fund it in 1999.

Savings Incentive Match Plans for Employees (SIMPLEs)

Self-employed individuals have another retirement plan alternative: Savings Incentive Match Plans for Employees, or SIMPLE plans. These plans are open to small employers who want to avoid complicated nondiscrimination rules and reporting requirements. SIMPLE plans can be used by corporations as well as by self-employed business owners.

Definition   *Small employers*   Those with 100 or fewer employees who received at least $5,000 in compensation in the preceding year.

SIMPLE plans may be set up as either IRAs or 401(k) plans. The rules for both types of SIMPLE plans are similar but not identical. Employees can contribute to the plans on a salary reduction basis up to $6,000 in 1999. (The $6,000 limit is indexed for inflation after 1997 but remained unchanged for 1999.) Self-employed individuals can make similar contributions based on earned income.

Employers satisfy nondiscrimination rules simply by making required contributions.

Employers have a choice of contribution formulas:

- **Matching contributions (dollar-for-dollar) up to 3 percent of employee's compensation for the year.** For example, in 1999, if an employee earning $35,000 makes the maximum salary reduction contribution of $6,000, the employer must contribute $1,050

(3 percent of $35,000). The maximum matching contribution per employee in 1999 to a SIMPLE 401(k) is $4,800 (100 percent of the matching employee contribution, which is up to 3 percent of $160,000). However, there is no limit on compensation taken into account for employer matching contributions to a SIMPLE IRA.

Note: An employer can elect a lower matching rate under certain conditions.

- Nonelective contributions of 2 percent of compensation (regardless of whether the employee makes any contributions) for any employee earning at least $5,000. For example, in 1999, if an employee's compensation is $25,000, the employer's contribution is $500 (2 percent of $25,000). The maximum contribution per employee in 1999 is $3,200 (2 percent of $160,000, the maximum compensation that can be used to determine contributions).

Self-employed persons can make employer contributions to SIMPLE-IRAs on their own behalf as well as make their own contributions. In effect, they are treated as both employer and employee.

Employee and employer contributions vest immediately. This means that employees can withdraw contributions at any time (although withdrawals prior to age 59½ are subject to a 25-percent penalty if taken within the first two years of beginning participation, and 10 percent if taken after that period.)

Employers who want to let employees choose their own financial institutions can adopt SIMPLE plans merely by completing Form 5304—SIMPLE (pictured on the next page). Employers who want to choose the financial institutions for their employees use Form 5305—SIMPLE. Whichever option is chosen, the form is not filed with the IRS but is kept with the employer's records. This form has the necessary notification to eligible employees and a model salary reduction agreement that can be used by employees to specify their salary reduction contributions. Employers who use SIMPLE plans cannot maintain any other type of qualified retirement plan.

IRAs as a Plan Alternative

If the cost of covering employees is prohibitive for a self-employed individual, neither a Keogh, a SEP, nor a SIMPLE plan may be the answer. Instead, the self-employed individual may want to use an IRA. In this case,

Form Used to Adopt a SIMPLE Plan

Form **5304-SIMPLE** (December 1996) Department of the Treasury Internal Revenue Service	**Savings Incentive Match Plan for Employees of Small Employers (SIMPLE)** (Not Subject to the Designated Financial Institution Rules)	OMB No. 1545-1502 **DO NOT File with the Internal Revenue Service**

_____ establishes the following SIMPLE

_____ Name of Employer

plan under section 408(p) of the Internal Revenue Code and pursuant to the instructions contained in this form.

Article I—Employee Eligibility Requirements (Complete appropriate box(es) and blanks—see instructions.)

1 General Eligibility Requirements. The Employer agrees to permit salary reduction contributions to be made in each calendar year to the SIMPLE IRA established by each employee who meets the following requirements (select either **1a** or **1b**):

a ☐ **Full Eligibility.** All employees are eligible.

b ☐ **Limited Eligibility.** Eligibility is limited to employees who are described in both **(i)** and **(ii)** below:

　(i) Current compensation. Employees who are reasonably expected to receive at least $ _____ in compensation (not to exceed $5,000) for the calendar year.

　(ii) Prior compensation. Employees who have received at least $ _____ in compensation (not to exceed $5,000) during any _____ calendar year(s) (insert 0, 1, or 2) preceding the calendar year.

2 Excludable Employees (OPTIONAL)

　☐ The Employer elects to exclude employees covered under a collective bargaining agreement for which retirement benefits were the subject of good faith bargaining.

Article II—Salary Reduction Agreements (Complete the box and blank, if appropriate—see instructions.)

1 Salary Reduction Election. An eligible employee may make a salary reduction election to have his or her compensation for each pay period reduced by a percentage. The total amount of the reduction in the employee's compensation cannot exceed $6,000* for any calendar year.

2 Timing of Salary Reduction Elections

a For a calendar year, an eligible employee may make or modify a salary reduction election during the 60-day period immediately preceding January 1 of that year. However, for the year in which the employee becomes eligible to make salary reduction contributions, the period during which the employee may make or modify the election is a 60-day period that includes either the date the employee becomes eligible or the day before.

b In addition to the election periods in **2a,** eligible employees may make salary reduction elections or modify prior elections _____ _____ (If the Employer chooses this option, insert a period or periods (e.g. semi-annually, quarterly, monthly, or daily) that will apply uniformly to all eligible employees.)

c No salary reduction election may apply to compensation that an employee received, or had a right to immediately receive, before execution of the salary reduction election.

d An employee may terminate a salary reduction election at any time during the calendar year. ☐ If this box is checked, an employee who terminates a salary reduction election not in accordance with **2b** may not resume salary reduction contributions during the calendar year.

Article III—Contributions (Complete the blank, if appropriate—see instructions.)

1 Salary Reduction Contributions. The amount by which the employee agrees to reduce his or her compensation will be contributed by the Employer to the employee's SIMPLE IRA.

2 Other Contributions

a Matching Contributions

　(i) For each calendar year, the Employer will contribute a matching contribution to each eligible employee's SIMPLE IRA equal to the employee's salary reduction contributions up to a limit of 3% of the employee's compensation for the calendar year.

　(ii) The Employer may reduce the 3% limit for the calendar year in **(i)** only if:

　　(1) The limit is not reduced below 1%; **(2)** The limit is not reduced for more than 2 calendar years during the 5-year period ending with the calendar year the reduction is effective; and **(3)** Each employee is notified of the reduced limit within a reasonable period of time before the employees' 60-day election period for the calendar year (described in **Article II, item 2a**).

b Nonelective Contributions

　(i) For any calendar year, instead of making matching contributions, the Employer may make nonelective contributions equal to 2% of compensation for the calendar year to the SIMPLE IRA of each eligible employee who has at least $ _____ (not more than $5,000) in compensation for the calendar year. No more than $160,000* in compensation can be taken into account in determining the nonelective contribution for each eligible employee.

　(ii) For any calendar year, the Employer may make 2% nonelective contributions instead of matching contributions only if:

　　(1) Each eligible employee is notified that a 2% nonelective contribution will be made instead of a matching contribution; and

　　(2) This notification is provided within a reasonable period of time before the employees' 60-day election period for the calendar year (described in **Article II, item 2a**).

3 Time and Manner of Contributions

a The Employer will make the salary reduction contributions (described in **1** above) for each eligible employee to the SIMPLE IRA established at the financial institution selected by that employee no later than 30 days after the end of the month in which the money is withheld from the employee's pay. See instructions.

b The Employer will make the matching or nonelective contributions (described in **2a** and **2b** above) for each eligible employee to the SIMPLE IRA established at the financial institution selected by that employee no later than the due date for filing the Employer's tax return, including extensions, for the taxable year that includes the last day of the calendar year for which the contributions are made.

For Paperwork Reduction Act Notice, see Instructions. 　　Cat. No. 23377W 　　Form **5304-SIMPLE** (12-96) the maximum that can be deducted is $2,000. However, if a self-employed's spouse is a participant in a qualified plan, the self-employed person may deduct $2,000 only if the couple's combined adjusted gross income does not exceed $150,000. The $2,000 deduction phases out as the couple's AGI reaches $160,000. IRAs are discussed later in this chapter. If a self-employed individual contributes $2,000 to a Roth IRA, he or she cannot make deductible contributions to an IRA.

SALARY REDUCTION ARRANGEMENTS

Salary reduction arrangements are not limited to SIMPLE plans. Perhaps the most common form of salary reduction arrangement is elective deferrals to regular 401(k) plans. In fact, these plans have become the most popular form of retirement plans in recent years.

These plans allow employers to offer retirement benefits to employees that are largely funded by the employees themselves. To encourage employees to participate in the plans (employers cannot force employees to make contributions), employers may offer matching contributions. For example, an employer may match each dollar of employee deferral with a dollar of employer contributions or some other ratio. Employers who offer 401(k) plans must be careful that stringent nondiscrimination rules are satisfied.

Essentially, these rules require that a sufficient number of rank-and-file employees participate in the plan and make contributions. If the nondiscrimination rules are not satisfied, the plan will not be treated as a qualified plan and tax benefits are not available. Explaining the advantages of participating to rank-and-file employees and offering matching contributions are two ways to attract the necessary participation.

Employees who take advantage of elective deferral options cannot deduct their contributions to the 401(k) plan. They have already received a tax benefit by virtue of the fact that deferrals are excluded from taxable income for income tax purposes. They are still treated as part of compensation for purposes of FICA and FUTA.

From an employer perspective, using 401(k) plans can shift the investment responsibility to employees. Instead of making all investment decisions, the employer simply has to offer a menu of investment options to employees. Then the employees decide how they want their funds invested. Employees can be as conservative or as aggressive as they choose. Treasury and Department of Labor regulations detail the number and types of investment options that must be offered and what must be communicated to employees about these investment options.

There is a dollar limit on the elective deferral. In 1998 the elective deferral cannot exceed $10,000. This amount is adjusted annually for inflation in $500 increments. This means that the dollar amount will not be adjusted until the adjustment exceeds $500.

Those who work for certain tax-exempt organizations—schools, hospitals, and religious organizations—may be able to make elective deferrals used to buy tax-deferred annuities, called 403(b) annuities. The limit on elective deferrals to these plans is $10,000.

Loans from 401(k) Plans

The rules governing loans from 401(k) plans are the same as those discussed earlier in connection with loans from corporate plans. However, it should be noted that all participants, not just owners, are prohibited from deducting interest on plan loans. But the interest is really being paid to the participant's own account, so the loss of a deduction is not so important.

INDIVIDUAL RETIREMENT ACCOUNTS (IRAs)

Another retirement plan option to consider is an IRA. There are now three types of personal IRAs to consider for retirement savings: traditional deductible IRAs, traditional nondeductible IRAs, and the new Roth IRAs. The maximum amount that can be contributed each year is $2,000 (or taxable earned income if less than $2,000). If you have a nonworking spouse, the contribution limit is $2,000 for each spouse (as long as you have earned income of at least $4,000). Therefore the limit is considerably lower than the limit for other retirement plans.

If you are self-employed and have more than one business, you must aggregate your business income to determine compensation for purposes of calculating contributions. You cannot base an IRA contribution on a pension or annuity income or income received from property, such as rents, interest, or dividends. (A special rule allows alimony to be treated as compensation for purposes of IRA contributions.)

However, if you are in business and set up an IRA for yourself, you need not cover your employees. For some, this factor alone may dictate in favor of an IRA.

If you are age 70½ and have a business, you cannot make contributions to a deductible or traditional nondeductible IRA. In this instance, you may want to explore other retirement plans, such as the new Roth IRAs.

IRAs and Other Retirement Plans

Whether you can make deductible contributions to both an IRA and another retirement plan depends on your overall income. Individuals who are considered "active participants" in qualified retirement plans cannot deduct contributions to an IRA if adjusted gross income exceeds certain amounts. More specifically, in 1999 no deduction can be claimed by an active participant when adjusted gross income exceeds $41,000 in the case of single individuals, $61,000 for married persons filing jointly and surviving spouses, or $10,000 for married persons filing separate returns. The deduction is phased out for adjusted gross income of up to $10,000 less than the phase-out limit ($31,000 for singles; $51,000 for married persons filing joint returns). The phase-out limits will increase until they reach $50,000–$60,000 for singles in 2005, and $80,000–$100,000 for married persons filing jointly in 2007.

You are considered an active participant if, at any time during the year, either you or your spouse is covered by an employer retirement plan. An employer retirement plan includes all of the following plans:

- Qualified pension, profit-sharing, or stock bonus plan
- Keogh plan
- SEP plan
- SIMPLE plan
- Qualified annuity plan
- Tax-sheltered annuity
- A plan established by the federal, state, or political subdivision for its employees (other than a state Section 457 plan)

If you are an active participant (or your spouse is an active participant) and your AGI is over the limit for your filing status, you can make a traditional nondeductible IRA contribution. There is no AGI limit on making this type of IRA contribution.

Alternatively, you may want to make contributions to a Roth IRA. Contributions must be based on compensation (just as they are for traditional IRAs), but there are some important differences between the new Roth and traditional IRAs. First, contributions to a Roth can be made regardless of your age. So, for example, if you have a consulting business and you're 75 years old, you can still fund a Roth IRA. Second, there are no required lifetime minimum distributions, as there are from traditional IRAs commencing at age 70½. Third, contributions can be made regardless of whether you (or your spouse) are an active participant in a qualified retirement plan. Fourth, and most significantly, if funds remain in the Roth IRA for at least five years, withdrawals after age 59½, or because of disability, or to pay first-time home-buying expenses (up to $10,000 in a lifetime) are completely free from income tax.

The five-year period starts on the first day of the year in which contributions are made (or to which they relate). So, for example, if you make a 1999 contribution to a Roth IRA on April 17, 2000 (the due date of your 1999 return), the five-year holding period commences on January 1, 1999, the year to which the first contribution relates. However, you can make Roth IRA contributions only if your AGI is no more than $95,000, or $150,000 on a joint return. (The contribution limit is reduced if your AGI is between $95,000 and $110,000 if you are single, or $150,000 and $160,000 on a joint return).

In planning to maximize your retirement funds, you may want to convert your traditional IRAs to a Roth IRA if you did not do so in 1998. You can convert if your AGI is no more than $100,000 (regardless of whether you are single or married as long as you do not file a separate return if married). This will allow you to build up a tax-free retirement nest egg (provided the funds remain in the Roth IRA at least five years and are not withdrawn unless you meet a withdrawal condition). The price of conversion is that you must report all the income that would have resulted had you simply taken a distribution from your IRAs.

In deciding to use a traditional IRA, be aware of certain restrictions designed to encourage savings and prevent dissipation of the account prior to retirement. First, you generally cannot withdraw IRA contributions, or earnings on those contributions, before age 59½. Doing so may result in a 10 percent early distribution penalty. There are a number of exceptions to the early distribution penalty:

- Disability

- Withdrawals taken ratably over your life expectancy

- Distributions to pay medical expenses in excess of 7.5 percent of adjusted gross income

- Distributions to pay health insurance premiums by those who are unemployed (self-employed can be treated as unemployed for this purpose)

- Distributions to pay qualified higher education costs

- Distributions for first-time home-buying expenses (up to $10,000 in a lifetime)

After 1999 no penalty will apply to IRAs levied upon by the IRS to satisfy back taxes (although the Tax Court has refused to apply the penalty to such involuntary withdrawals).

Second, you must begin withdrawals from traditional IRAs no later than April 1 of the year following the year of attaining age 70$^{1}/_{2}$. The failure to take certain minimum distributions designed to exhaust the account over your life expectancy results in a 50-percent penalty tax. The minimum distribution requirement applies as well to qualified retirement plans, Keogh plans, SEP-IRAs, and SIMPLE plans.

COMPARISON OF QUALIFIED RETIREMENT PLANS

The different choices of qualified retirement plans have been discussed at length. But how do you know which plan is best for you? There are several factors to consider:

- How much money do you have to set aside in a retirement plan? If your business is continually profitable you may want to commit to a type of plan that requires contributions without regard to profits. If your business is good in some years but bad in others, you may want to use a profit-sharing-type plan that does not require contributions in poor years.

- How much will it cost to cover employees? Where there are few or no employees, then the choice of plan is largely a question of what will be the most beneficial to you. When a great number of employees will have to be covered, the cost may be too prohibitive to provide substantial retirement benefits. However, if your competitors offer plans to their employees, you may be forced to offer similar benefits as a means of attracting or retaining employees.

- How soon do you expect to retire? The closer you are to retirement, the more inclined you may be to use a defined benefit plan to sock away as much as possible.

- Also consider the costs of administration, the amount of entanglement with the IRS, and your financial sophistication and comfort level with more exotic arrangements.

COMPARISON OF RETIREMENT PLANS

Type of plan	Maximum contribution	Last date for contribution
IRA	$2,000 or taxable compensation, whichever is smaller	Due date of your return (without extensions)
SIMPLE plan	$6,000* (not to exceed taxable compensation), plus employer contributions	Due date of employer's return (including extensions)
SEP-IRA	$30,000* or 15 percent of participant's taxable compensation, whichever is smaller (including extensions)	Due date of employer's return
Qualified plan	Profit-sharing plan—smaller of $30,000* or 15 percent of compensation (13.0435 percent of self-employed's income) Money purchase plan—smaller of $30,000* or 25 percent of compensation (20 percent of self-employed's income)	Due date of employer's return (including extensions) **Note:** *Plan must be set up no later than the last day of the employer's tax year.*

Type of plan	Maximum contribution	Last date for contribution
	Defined benefit plan—amount needed to provide retirement benefit no larger than the lesser of $130,000* or 100 percent of the participant's average taxable compensation for highest three consecutive years	

*Amount subject to adjustment for inflation.

Defined Benefit Plans Versus Defined Contribution Plans

Defined benefit plans offer owners the opportunity to slant more contributions to their own benefit, especially if they are older than their employees. However, most small employers are moving away from defined benefit plans because of the complexities and costs of administration. Defined benefit plans are by far more costly to administer than defined contribution plans. First, there are the costs of plan design. Defined benefit plans may be specially tailored to each employer, whereas defined contribution plans generally use prototypes readily available. Second, there is the cost of the actuary to determine contributions necessary to fund the promised benefits. Third, there are annual premiums paid to the Pension Benefit Guaranty Corporation, a federal agency designed to provide some measure of protection for employees (somewhat akin to FDIC insurance for bank accounts). These premiums are calculated on a per-participant basis, with an additional premium for underfunded plans (as discussed earlier in this chapter).

Another factor to consider in deciding between defined benefit and defined contribution plans is the timing of making contributions. Contributions to defined contribution plans can be made at any time during the year to which they relate but can also be made as late as the due date for the employer's return, including extensions. In the case of defined benefit plans, contributions must be made more rapidly than those to defined contribution plans. Defined benefit plans have quarterly contribution requirements, and the failure to make sufficient contributions quarterly can result in penalties.

Keogh Versus SEP

If you use a profit-sharing plan, the contribution limit is the same for both Keogh plans and SEPs. However, there are some reasons for using one or the other type of retirement plan.

A Keogh plan offers one main advantage over SEPs. Distributions from Keogh plans are eligible for special averaging treatment. In contrast, all distributions from SEPs are treated as ordinary income. However, after 1999 special averaging treatment can no longer be used (other than by those who were born before 1936).

A SEP offers a couple of advantages over Keogh plans. A Keogh plan must be set up no later than the last day of your tax year, even though contributions can be made up to the due date of the return, including extensions. In contrast, a SEP can be set up as late as the date for making contributions, which is also the due date of your return, including extensions. There is less paperwork involved in a SEP than in a Keogh plan. While Keoghs must file annual information returns with the IRS, SEPs have no similar annual reporting requirements.

SIMPLE-IRA Versus Keogh or SEP

Business owners with modest earnings may be able to put *more* into a SIMPLE-IRA than a Keogh plan. The reason: The employee contribution (which a self-employed individual can also make) to a SIMPLE-IRA is not based on a percentage of income but rather a dollar amount up to $6,000 in 1999. (The 25-percent annual compensation limit applies to employee contributions to SIMPLE-401(k)s.) For example, assume a self-employed individual's net earnings from self-employment are $25,000. The top contribution to a SIMPLE-IRA is $6,750 ($6,000 salary reduction contribution, plus $750 employer matching contribution). In contrast, the contribution limit to a profit-sharing Keogh plan or SEP is only $3,031, less than half that allowed for a SIMPLE-IRA. The top contribution for a money-purchase Keogh is still only $4,647, considerably less than the contribution limit to a SIMPLE-IRA.

The bottom line is that business owners who want to maximize their retirement plan contributions need to run the numbers to determine which plan is preferable.

NONQUALIFIED RETIREMENT PLANS

If you have a business and want to provide retirement benefits without the limitations and requirements imposed on qualified plans, you can use nonqualified plans. These plans have been growing in popularity in recent years because of restrictions and costs associated with qualified plans. Nonqualified plans are simply plans you design yourself to provide you and/or your employees with whatever benefits you desire. Benefits under the plan are not taxed to the employees until they receive them and include them in their income.

There are no nondiscrimination rules to comply with. You can cover only those employees you want to give additional retirement benefits, and this can be limited to owners or key executives. There are no minimum or maximum contributions to make to the plan. However, because nonqualified plans give you all the flexibility you need to tailor benefits as you see fit, the law prevents you, as the employer, from enjoying certain tax benefits. You cannot deduct now amounts you will pay in the future to employees under the plan. Your deduction usually cannot be claimed until benefits are actually paid to employees. However, there is one circumstance under which you can deduct these amounts. If you segregate the amounts from the general assets of your business so that they are not available to meet the claims of your general creditors, the amounts become immediately taxable to the employees and thus deductible by you.

How a Nonqualified Plan Works

Suppose you want to allow your key employees the opportunity to defer bonuses or a portion of their compensation until retirement. To do this, you set up a nonqualified plan. The plan allows key employees to defer specified amounts until termination, retirement, or some other time or event. The employees in the plan must agree to defer the compensation before it is earned. They generally have no guarantee that the funds they agree to defer will, in fact, be there for them upon retirement. If your business goes under, they must stand in line along with all your other creditors. Employees should be made to understand the risk of a deferred compensation arrangement.

Once you set up the terms of the plan, you simply set up a bookkeeping entry to record the amount of deferred compensation. You may also want to credit each employee's deferred compensation account with an amount representing interest. In the past there had been some controversy on the tax treatment of this interest. One court had allowed a current deduction for the interest. The IRS, on the other hand, had maintained that no deduction for the interest could be claimed until it, along with the compensation, was paid out to employees and included in their income. However, that court changed its view and now agrees with the IRS. As long as receipt of the interest is deferred, so, too, is your deduction for the interest.

Rabbi Trusts

These is a special kind of nonqualified deferred compensation that got its name from the original employees covered by the plan—rabbis. The plans provide a measure of security for employees without triggering current taxation on contributions under the plan. Employers are still prevented from claiming a current deduction. These plans have now been standardized, and the IRS even provides model rabbi trust forms to be used on setting them up.

GLOSSARY OF TERMS FOR RETIREMENT PLANS

The following terms have been used throughout this chapter in connection with retirement plans:

Compensation   The amount upon which contributions and benefits are calculated. Compensation for employees is taxable wages reported on Form W-2. Compensation for self-employed individuals is net profit from a sole proprietorship or net self-employment income reported to a partner or limited liability member on Schedule K-1.

Coverage   Qualified plans must include a certain percentage of rank-and-file employees.

Defined benefit plans   Pension plans in which benefits are fixed according to an employee's compensation, years of participation in the plan, and age upon retirement. Contributions are actuarially determined to provide sufficient funds to cover promised pension amounts.

Defined contribution plans   Retirement plans in which benefits are determined by annual contributions on behalf of each participant, the amount these contributions can earn, and the length of time the participant is in the plan.

Elective deferrals   A portion of salary that is contributed to a retirement plan on a pretax basis. Elective deferrals apply in the case of 401(k) plans, 403(b) annuities, SARSEPs (established before 1997), and SIMPLE plans.

Excess contribution penalty   A 6-percent cumulative penalty imposed on an employer for making contributions in excess of contribution limits.

Funding   In the case of defined benefit plans, the amount of assets required to be in the plan in order to meet plan liabilities (current and future pension obligations).

Highly compensated employees   Owners and employees earning compensation over certain limits that are adjusted annually for inflation.

Keogh plans   Qualified retirement plans for self-employed individuals; also called H.R.10 plans. In general, Keogh plans are no different from qualified retirement plans for corporations.

Master and prototype plans   Plans typically designed by banks and other institutions to be used for qualified retirement plans.

Money purchase plans   Defined contribution plans in which the annual contribution percentage is fixed without regard to whether the business has profits.

Nondiscrimination   Requirements to provide benefits for rank-and-file employees and not simply to favor owners and highly paid employees.

Participation   The right of an employee to be a member of the plan and have benefits and contributions made on his or her behalf.

Pension Benefit Guaranty Corporation (PBGC)   A federal agency that will pay a minimum pension to participants of defined benefit plans in companies that have not made sufficient contributions to fund their pension liabilities.

Premature distribution penalty   A 50-percent penalty imposed on a participant for receiving benefits before age $59\frac{1}{2}$ or some other qualifying event.

Profit-sharing plan   A defined contribution plan with contributions based on a fixed percentage of compensation.

Prohibited transactions   Dealings between employers and the plan, such as loans, sales, and other transactions between these parties. Prohibited transactions result in penalties and can even result in plan disqualification.

Required distributions   Plans must begin to distribute benefits to employees at a certain time. Generally, benefits must begin to be paid out no later than April 1 following the year in which a participant attains age

$70^1/_2$. Failure to receive required minimum distributions results in a 50-percent penalty on the participant.

Roth IRAs Nondeductible IRAs that permit tax-free withdrawals if certain holding period requirements are met.

Salary reduction arrangements Arrangements to make contributions to qualified plans from an employee's compensation on a pretax basis. In general, salary reduction arrangements relate to 401(k) plans, 403(b) annuities, SARSEPs in existence before 1997, and SIMPLE plans.

Savings incentive match plans of employees IRA- or 401(k)-type plans that permit modest employee contributions via salary reduction and require modest employer contributions. SIMPLE plans are easy to set up and administer.

Simplified employee pensions IRAs set up by employees to which an employer makes contributions based on a percentage of income.

Stock bonus plans Defined contribution plans that give participants shares of stock in the employer rather than cash.

Top-heavy plans Qualified retirement plans that provide more than a certain amount of benefits or contributions to owners and/or highly paid employees. Top-heavy plans have special vesting schedules.

Vesting The right of an employee to own his or her pension benefits. Vesting schedules are set by law, although employers can provide for faster vesting.

WHERE TO CLAIM DEDUCTIONS FOR RETIREMENT PLANS

Employees

If you contribute to an IRA and are entitled to a deduction, you claim it on page 1 of Form 1040 as an adjustment to gross income. If you contribute to a salary reduction plan (such as a SIMPLE or a 401(k) plan), you cannot deduct your contribution.

Self-Employed

Contributions you make to qualified retirement plans (Keoghs, SEPs, or SIMPLEs) on behalf of your employees are entered on Schedule C (or Schedule F for farming operations) on the specific line provided on the form called "pension and profit-sharing plans." Contributions you make on your own behalf are claimed on page 1 of Form 1040 as an adjustment to gross income. Contributions you make to an IRA are also claimed on page 1 of Form 1040 as an adjustment to gross income.

Partnerships and LLCs

Deductions for contributions to qualified plans on behalf of employees are part of the partnership's or LLC's ordinary trade or business income on Form 1065. The deductions are entered on the line provided for "retirement plans."

The entity does not make contributions on behalf of partners or members. Partners and members can set up their own retirement plans based on their self-employment income. Thus, if partners and members set up Keogh plans, they claim deductions for their contributions on page 1 of Form 1040.

As a practical matter, small partnerships and LLCs generally do not establish qualified plans for employees, since the partners and members do not get any direct benefit.

S Corporations

Deductions for contributions to qualified plans on behalf of employees other than more-than-2-percent employees are taken by the corporation as part of its ordinary trade or business income on Form 1120S. Enter the deduction on the line provided for "pension, profit-sharing, etc. plans." This line includes contributions to nonqualified plans if the corporation is entitled to claim a current deduction for such contributions.

More-than-2-percent owners can set up their own retirement plans. If they do, contributions are deducted on page 1 of Form 1040.

C Corporations

C corporations deduct contributions to retirement plans on Form 1120. The deduction is entered on the line provided for "pension, profit-sharing, etc. plans." This line includes contributions to nonqualified plans if the corporation is entitled to claim a current deduction for such contributions.

Other Reporting Requirements for All Taxpayers

Qualified plans entail annual reporting requirements. If you maintain a qualified plan, you must file certain information returns with the IRS each year to report on the amount of plan assets, contributions, number of employees, and such. There are penalties for failure to file these returns on time and for overstating the pension plan deduction.

Plans with fewer than 100 participants must file Form 5500 C/R, Return/Report of Employee Benefit Plan with Fewer than 100 Participants, each year. The return is due by the last day of the seventh month following the close of the plan year (July 31 of a calendar-year plan).

Those with one-person plans (and their spouses) can use a simplified information return, Form 5500-EZ, Annual Return of One Participant (Owners and Their Spouses) Pension Benefit Plan. This form need not be filed if plan assets as of the end of the year do not exceed $100,000. However, if the plan assets exceeded $100,000 in any year beginning on or after January 1, 1994, Form 5500-EZ must be filed even though plan assets dipped below $100,000.

EXAMPLE: You maintain a Keogh plan on a calendar-year basis. In 1999 your plan has $105,000 in assets. In 2000, due to fluctuations in the stock market, your plan assets are only $95,000. You must still file Form 5500-EZ for 2000, because plan assets exceeded $100,000 in a year beginning on or after January 1, 1994.

The return is due by the last day of the seventh month following the close of the plan year. Thus, if the plan is on a calendar year, the return is due no later than July 31 of the following year. Obtaining an extension to file an income tax return does not extend the time for filing these returns. However, if you do obtain a filing extension for your individual return to August 15, you still have to calculate your retirement plan contribution earlier than that so you can file Form 5500-EZ by July 31.

Note: There are no special annual reporting requirements for IRA plans, SEPs, or SIMPLE-IRAs. Other plans with 100 or more participants must complete Form 5500.

Annual Information Return

Form **5500-EZ**

Department of the Treasury
Internal Revenue Service

Please type or print

**Annual Return of One-Par ticipant
(Owners and Their Spouses) Retirement Plan**

This form is required to be filed under
section 6058(a) of the Internal Revenue Code.

▶ See separate instructions.

OMB No. 1545-0956

19**98**

This Form Is Open
to Public Inspection

For the calendar plan year 1998 or fiscal plan year beginning , 1998, and ending , 19

This return is: *(i)* ☐ the first return filed *(ii)* ☐ an amended return *(iii)* ☐ the final return *(iv)* ☐ a short plan year (less than 12 mos.)

Check here if you filed an extension of time to file and attach a copy of the approved extension . . . . ▶ ☐

Use IRS label. Other-wise, please type or print.	**1a** Name of employer	**1b Employer identification number**
	Number, street, and room or suite no. (If a P.O. box, see instructions for line 1a.)	**1c** Telephone number of employer
		1d Business activity code (new codes—see page 6 of instr.)
	City or town, state, and ZIP code	**1e** If plan year has changed since last return, check here . . . . ▶ ☐

2a Is the employer also the plan administrator? ☐ Yes ☐ No (If "No," see instructions.)

2c Date plan first became effective
Month   Day   Year

2b *(i)* Name of plan ▶ ....

2d Enter three-digit plan number

(ii) ☐ Check if name of plan has changed since last return

3 Type of plan: **a** ☐ Defined benefit pension plan (attach Schedule B (Form 5500)) **b** ☐ Money purchase pension plan (see instructions)
c ☐ Profit-sharing plan   **d** ☐ Stock bonus plan   **e** ☐ ESOP plan (attach Schedule E (Form 5500))

4a If this is a master/prototype, or regional prototype plan, enter the opinion/notification letter number . .

b Check if this plan covers: *(i)* ☐ Self-employed individuals, *(ii)* ☐ Partner(s) in a partnership, or *(iii)* ☐ 100% owner of corporation

5a Enter the number of qualified pension benefit plans maintained by the employer (including this plan). .

b Check here if you have more than one plan and the total assets of all plans are more than $100,000 (see instructions) . . . . ▶ ☐

6 Enter the number of participants in each category listed below:

		Number
a Under age 59½ at the end of the plan year .	**6a**	
b Age 59½ or older at the end of the plan year, but under age 70½ at the beginning of the plan year	**6b**	
c Age 70½ or older at the beginning of the plan year	**6c**	

7a *(i)* Is this a fully insured pension plan which is funded entirely by insurance or annuity contracts? . . ▶ ☐ Yes ☐ No

If "Yes," complete lines 7a(ii) through 7f and skip lines 7g through 9d.

(ii) If 7a(i) is "Yes," are the insurance contracts held: . . . . ▶ ☐ under a trust ☐ with no trust

b Cash contributions received by the plan for this plan year	**7b**	
c Noncash contributions received by the plan for this plan year	**7c**	
d Total plan distributions to participants or beneficiaries	**7d**	
e Total nontaxable plan distributions to participants or beneficiaries	**7e**	
f Transfers to other plans.	**7f**	
g Amounts received by the plan other than from contributions	**7g**	
h Plan expenses other than distributions	**7h**	
8a Total plan assets at the end of the year	**8a**	
b Total plan liabilities at the end of the year	**8b**	

9 Check "Yes" and enter amount involved if any of the following transactions took place between the plan and a disqualified person during this plan year. Otherwise, check "No."

	Yes	No	Amount
a Sale, exchange, or lease of property	**9a**		
b Payment by the plan for services	**9b**		
c Acquisition or holding of employer securities	**9c**		
d Loan or extension of credit	**9d**		

If 10a is "No," do not complete line 10b and line 10c. See the specific instructions for line 10b and line 10c.

		Yes	No
10a Does your business have any employees other than you and your spouse (and your partners and their spouses)? ▶	**10a**		
b Total number of employees (including you and your spouse and your partners and their spouses) ▶ _____ .			
c Does this plan meet the coverage requirements of Code section 410(b)? . . . . ▶	**10c**		
11a Did the plan distribute any annuity contracts this plan year? . . . . ▶	**11a**		
b During this plan year, did the plan make distributions to a married participant in a form other than a qualified joint and survivor annuity or were any distributions on account of the death of a married participant made to beneficiaries other than the spouse of that participant? . . . . ▶	**11b**		
c During this plan year, did the plan make loans to married participants? . . . . ▶	**11c**		

Under penalties of perjury and other penalties set forth in the instructions, I declare that I have examined this return, including accompanying schedules and statements, and to the best of my knowledge and belief, it is true, correct, and complete.

Signature of employer (owner) or plan administrator ▶   Date ▶

For Paperwork Reduction Act Notice, see the instructions to Form 5500-EZ.   Cat. No. 63263R   Form **5500-EZ** (1998)

CHAPTER 15

Losses on Property

The focus of this book has been on deductions for various types of expenses. Deductions alone are not the only way to reduce your taxes. You are also allowed to subtract from your other income certain losses you sustain on business property. If you own business property and dispose of it for an amount that is less than your basis in the property, you may realize a loss. The tax law recognizes different kinds of losses for different types of property. In this chapter you will learn about:

- Capital losses

- Section 1231 losses

- Section 1244 losses

- Worthless securities

- Where to deduct losses on property

Casualty and theft losses are discussed in Chapter 16.

For further information on losses on property, see IRS Publication 544, Sales and Other Dispositions of Assets.

CAPITAL LOSSES

If you own property used in or owned by your business other than Section 1231 property (defined below) or Section 1244 stock (also defined below), loss on the sale or other disposition of the property generally is treated as a capital loss. Capital losses are losses that are taken on capital assets.

Definition *Capital assets* Most property is treated as capital assets. Thus, for example, your interest in a partnership or stocks and securities is treated as capital assets.

Excluded from the definition of capital assets are:

- Property held for sale to customers or property that will physically become part of merchandise for sale to customers (inventory)

- Accounts or notes receivable generated by your business (for example, accounts receivable from the sale of inventory)

- Depreciable property used in your business, even if already fully depreciated (for example, your telephones)

- Real property used in your business (for example, your factory)

- A copyright; literary, musical, or artistic composition; a letter or memorandum; or other similar property (for example, photographs, tapes, manuscripts) created by your personal efforts or acquired from the creator by gift or in another transaction entitling you to use the creator's basis

- U.S. government publications

Determining the Amount of Your Loss

The difference between the amount received for your property on a sale, exchange, or other disposition and your adjusted basis in the property is your gain or loss.

> **Definition** *Amount received*   The cash, fair market value of property, and relief of liability you get when you dispose of your property. You own a computer system for your business. You upgrade with a new system and sell your old system to another business. You receive $5,000 cash, plus the buyer agrees to pay off the remaining balance of $2,000 on a bank loan you took to buy the system. Your amount received is $7,000 ($5,000 cash, plus $2,000 liability relieved).

> **Definition** *Adjusted basis*   This is your basis in the property, adjusted for certain items. Start with your original cost if you bought the property (the cash and other property you paid to acquire it). Even if the cash did not come out of your pocket—for example, if you took a loan—the cash you turn over to the seller is part of your basis. Then adjust the basis by reducing it for any depreciation claimed (or that could have been claimed) and any casualty loss you claimed with respect to the property. For example, if your original computer system cost you $10,000 and you claimed $2,000 depreciation, your adjusted basis is $8,000.

Where the adjusted basis exceeds the amount received, you have a loss. Where the amount received exceeds the adjusted basis, you have a gain.

Sale or Exchange Requirement

In order to obtain capital gain or loss treatment on the disposition of a capital asset, you must sell or exchange property. Typically, you sell your property, but other transactions may qualify for sale or exchange treatment. For example, if your corporation redeems some or all of your stock, you may be able to treat the redemption as a sale or exchange. Capital losses are subject to limitation on current deductibility as explained later in this chapter.

If you dispose of property in some way other than a sale or exchange, gain or loss generally is treated as ordinary gain or loss. For example, if you abandon business property, your loss is treated as ordinary loss, even though the property is a capital asset. However, if the property is foreclosed on or repossessed, your loss may be a capital loss. Ordinary losses are deductible without regard to the results from other transactions and can be used to offset various types of income (such as interest income).

In some cases, even if you sell or exchange property at a loss, you may not be permitted to deduct your loss. If you sell, exchange, or even abandon a Section 197 intangible (see Chapter 12 for a complete discussion of the amortization of Section 197 intangibles), you cannot deduct your loss if you still hold other Section 197 intangibles that you acquired in the same transaction. Instead, you increase the basis of the Section 197 intangibles that you still own. This means that instead of deducting your loss in the year you dispose of one Section 197 intangible, you will deduct a portion of the loss over the remaining recovery period for the Section 197 intangibles you still hold.

Similarly, you cannot deduct losses on sales or exchanges of property between related parties (defined below). This related party rule prevents you from deducting a loss if you sell a piece of equipment to your spouse. However, the party acquiring the property from you (the original transferee, or in this case, your spouse) can add to the basis the amount of loss you were not allowed to deduct in determining gain or loss on a subsequent disposition of the property.

EXAMPLE: You sell your partnership interest to your daughter for $7,500. Your basis in the interest is $10,000. You cannot deduct your $2,500 loss. However, if your daughter then sells the partnership interest for $12,000, her gain is minimized to the extent of your nondeductible loss. Her tentative gain is $4,500 ($12,000 amount received less basis of $7,500). The amount of gain she must report is $2,000 ($4,500 tentative gain less $2,500 nondeductible loss).

Related Parties

The tax law defines who is a related party. This includes not only certain close relatives (spouses, siblings, parents, children, grandparents, and grandchildren), but also certain businesses you control. A controlled entity is a corporation in which you own, directly or indirectly, more than 50 percent of the value of all outstanding stock or a partnership in which you own, directly or indirectly, more than 50 percent of the capital interest or profits interest. Businesses may be treated as related parties. These relationships include:

- A corporation and partnership if the same persons own more than 50 percent in the value of the outstanding stock of the corporation and more than 50 percent of the capital interest or profits interest in the partnership

- Two corporations that are members of the same controlled group (one corporation owns a certain percentage of the other, or owners own a certain percentage of each corporation)

- Two S corporations if the same persons own more than 50 percent in value of the outstanding stock in each corporation

- Two corporations, one of which is an S corporation, if the same person owns more than 50 percent in value of the outstanding stock of each corporation

Special rules are used to determine "control." These rules not only look at actual ownership but also take into account certain constructive ownership (ownership that is not actual but has the same effect in the eyes of the tax law). For example, for purposes of the related party rule, you are treated as constructively owning any stock owned by your spouse.

Special rules also apply to transactions between partners and their partnerships.

It is important to note that what you may view as a related party may not be treated as such for tax purposes. Thus, for example, your in-laws and cousins are not treated as related parties. If you sell property to an in-law or cousin at a loss, you are not prevented from deducting the loss.

Loss Limits on Individuals

You can deduct capital losses against capital gains without limit. Short-term losses from sales of assets held one year or less are first used to offset short-term gains otherwise taxed up to 39.6 percent. Similarly, long-term losses from sales of assets held more than one year offset long-term gains otherwise taxed as low as 20 percent (10 percent for those in the 15 percent tax bracket). Losses in excess of their category are then used to offset gains starting with those taxed at the highest rates. For example, short-term losses in excess of short-term capital gains can be used to offset long-term capital gains from the sale of qualified small business stock, 50 percent of such gain of which is otherwise taxed at 28 percent (for an effective tax rate of 14 percent). However, if your capital losses exceed your capital gains, you can deduct only $3,000 of losses against your other income (such as salaries, dividends, and interest income). If married persons file separate returns, the capital loss offset to other income is limited to $1,500. If you do not use up all of your capital losses, you can carry over any unused amount and claim it in future years. There is no limit on the carryover period for individuals.

Loss Limits on Corporations

If your corporation realizes capital losses, they are deductible only against capital gains. Any capital losses in excess of capital gains can be carried back for three years and then, if not used up, carried forward for up to five years. If they are not used within the five-year carryover period, they are lost forever.

The carryback may entitle your corporation to a refund of taxes from the carryback years. The corporation can apply for this refund by filing Form 1120X, Amended U.S. Corporation Income Tax Return. A corporation cannot choose to forego the carryback in order to simply carry foreword the unused capital losses.

Special rules apply in calculating the corporation's carryback and carryforward. You do not use any capital loss carried from another year when determining the corporation's capital loss deduction for the current year. If you have losses from more than one year carried to another year, you use the losses as follows: First, deduct the loss from the earliest year. After that is fully deducted, deduct the loss from the next earliest year. You cannot use a capital loss carried from another year to produce or increase a net operating loss in the year to which you carry it.

SECTION 1231 LOSSES

Certain assets used in business are granted special tax treatment. This treatment seeks to provide a win-win situation. If a sale or other disposition of these assets results in a net gain, the gain can be treated as capital gain. If a net loss results, the loss is an ordinary loss.

Definition *Section 1231 property*   Property held for more than one year and used in a business or held for the production or rents or royalties.

Examples of Section 1231 property include:

- Property held for sale to customers (inventory)
- Real property and depreciable personal property held for more than one year (such as equipment)
- Leaseholds held for more than one year
- Timber, coal, and iron ore

Losses (or gains) due to casualty, theft, or condemnation may also be treated as Section 1231 losses (or gains) if the property was held for more than one year.

Determining Section 1231 Losses (or Gains)

You must use a netting process to determine your Section 1231 losses (or gains). This means combining all gains and losses from the sale or other disposition of Section 1231 property. If your Section 1231 gains exceed your Section 1231 losses, then all of your gains and losses are treated as capital gains and losses. On the other hand, if your Section 1231 losses equal or exceed your Section 1231 gains, all of your gains and losses are treated as ordinary gains and losses.

However, the fact that your Section 1231 losses for the year equal or exceed Section 1231 gains does not automatically ensure ordinary gain and loss treatment. You must check to see whether a special recapture rule applies. Under the recapture rule, net Section 1231 gain is treated as ordinary income to the extent it does not exceed nonrecaptured net Section 1231 losses taken in prior years.

Definition *Nonrecaptured losses*   These are the total of net Section 1231 losses for the five most recent preceding tax years that have not been applied (recaptured) against any net Section 1231 gains in those years.

These recapture rules are extremely complex. They are designed to prevent you from being able to time gains and losses from year to year so that you take your gains as capital gains and your losses as ordinary losses. The recapture rules, in effect, treat your gains and losses as occurring in the same year so that what would ordinarily have been treated as capital gains is partially or fully treated as ordinary income.

EXAMPLE: You had a net Section 1231 loss of $8,000 in 1996 from the sale of a Section 1231 asset. In 1997 you had no Section 1231 gains or losses. In 1998 and 1999 you had net Section 1231 gains of $5,250 and $4,600, respectively. In 1998, $5,250 of the net Section 1231 losses claimed in 1996 are recaptured. This means that the gain of $5,250 is treated as ordinary income rather than as capital gain. For 1999 the balance of the 1996 nonrecaptured Section 1231 loss, $2,750, is recaptured ($8,000 net loss in 1996 less $5,250 recaptured in 1997). This means that of the $4,600 gain in 1999, $2,750 is treated as ordinary income, and the balance, $1,850, is treated as capital gain. There are no additional nonrecaptured losses to worry about in future years.

As you can see from the example, losses are recaptured beginning with the earliest year subject to recapture.

SECTION 1244 LOSSES

If you own stock in a company considered to be a small business (defined below) and you realize a loss on this stock, you may be able to treat the loss as an ordinary loss. This loss is referred to as a Section 1244 loss because of the section in the Internal Revenue Code that defines it. Ordinary loss treatment applies to both common stock issued at any time and preferred stock issued after July 18, 1984. You can claim an ordinary loss if you sell or exchange the stock or if it becomes worthless. This special tax rule for small business stock presents another win-win situation for owners. If the company does well and a disposition of the stock produces a gain, it is treated as capital gain. If the company does not do well and the disposition of the stock results in a loss, the loss is treated as ordinary loss, which is fully deductible against your other income (such as salary, dividends, and interest income).

Qualifying for Ordinary Loss Treatment

The corporation issuing the stock must be a small business. This means that it can have equity of no more than $1 million at the time the stock is issued. This equity is the amount of cash or other property invested in the company in exchange for the stock. The stock must be issued for cash and property other than stock and securities. This definition of small business stock applies only to the loss deduction under Section 1244. Other definitions of small business stock apply for other purposes under the tax law.

You must acquire the stock by purchase. The ordinary loss deduction is allowed only to the original purchaser of the stock. If you inherit stock in a small business, receive it as a gift, or you buy it from someone who was the original purchaser of the stock, you do not qualify for ordinary loss treatment.

Most important, the corporation must have derived over half its gross receipts during the five years preceding the year of your loss from business operations, and not from passive income. If the corporation is in business for less than five years, then only the years in which it is in business are considered. If the corporation's deductions (other than for dividends received and net operating losses) exceed gross income, the five-year requirement is waived.

Limit on Ordinary Loss Deduction

You can treat only the first $50,000 of your loss on small business stock as an ordinary loss. The limit is raised to $100,000 on a joint return, even if only one spouse owned the stock. However, losses in excess of these dollar limits can be treated as capital losses, as discussed earlier in this chapter.

The ordinary loss deduction can be claimed only by individuals. If a partnership owns Section 1244 stock and sustains a loss, an ordinary loss deduction can be claimed by individuals who were partners when the stock was issued. If the partnership distributes stock to partners and the partners then realize a loss on the stock, they cannot treat the loss as an ordinary loss.

If an S corporation owns Section 1244 stock and sustains a loss, it cannot pass the loss through to shareholders in the same way that partnerships can pass the loss through to their partners. Even though S corporation shareholders receive tax treatment similar to that of partners, one court that has considered this question concluded that the language of the tax law results in a difference in this instance. The denial of an ordinary loss deduction for Section 1244 stock is one important way in which the tax treatment differs between partnerships and S corporations.

WORTHLESS SECURITIES

If you buy stock or bonds (collectively called securities) in a corporation and the securities become worthless, special tax rules apply. In general, loss on a security that becomes worthless is treated as a capital loss. If the stock is Section 1244 stock, you can claim an ordinary loss deduction, as explained above.

To claim a deduction for worthless securities, you must be able to show that the securities are completely worthless. If they still have some value, you cannot claim the loss. To show complete worthlessness, you must show that there is no reasonable possibility of receiving repayment on a bond or any value for your stock. Insolvency of the corporation issuing the security is certainly indicative of worthlessness. However, even if a corporation is insolvent, there may still be some value to your securities. The corporation may be in a bankruptcy restructuring arrangement designed to make the corporation solvent again someday. In this instance, the securities are not considered to be worthless securities.

You can claim a deduction for worthless securities only in the year in which worthlessness occurs. Since it is difficult to pinpoint when worthlessness occurs, you have some flexibility. The tax law allows you seven years to go back and amend a prior return to claim a deduction for worthless securities.

EXAMPLE: In 2000 you learn that stock you owned in a business became worthless in 1996. In general, you have seven years from the due date of your 1996 return, or April 15, 2004, to amend your 1996 return to claim the loss deduction.

If you own stock in a publicly held corporation, it is advisable to check with a securities broker to see whether there has been some definite event to fix the time of worthlessness. If you are unsure whether a security actually became worthless in a particular year, consider claiming it anyway. You can renew your claim in a subsequent year if the facts show worthlessness did, in fact, occur in that subsequent year. If you fail to claim the loss in the earlier year and that year proves to be the year of worthlessness, your claim may be lost forever.

If you own stock in an S corporation that becomes worthless, you must first adjust the basis in the stock for your share of corporate items of income, loss, and deductions. If there is any excess basis remaining, you can then claim the excess as a loss on worthless securities.

For further information about claiming a deduction for worthless securities, see IRS Publication 550, Investment Interest and Expenses.

WHERE TO DEDUCT LOSSES ON PROPERTY

For All Taxpayers

Section 1231 gains and losses are reported on Form 4797, Sales of Business Property. Then the results from Form 4797 are carried over and reported on the business's tax return. For individuals, Form 4797 gains and losses are reported directly on Form 1040.

Employees

Employees may buy stock in their employer. The loss may be a capital loss or an ordinary loss on Section 1244 stock. Capital losses are reported on Schedule D and carried over to page 1 of Form 1040. An ordinary loss on Section 1244 stock is reported in Part II of Form 4797. The results of Form 4797 are then reported on page 1 of Form 1040.

If you need to amend a tax return to claim a deduction for worthless securities, file Form 1040X, Amended U.S Individual Income Tax Return.

Self-Employed

Losses on Section 1231 property are reported on Form 4797. The results are then carried over to page 1 of Form 1040. Do not enter the results on Schedule C (or on Schedule F in the case of farming operations).

If you need to amend a tax return to claim a deduction for worthless securities, file Form 1040X, Amended U.S. Individual Income Tax Return.

Partnerships and LLCs

Capital losses are separately stated items that are not taken into account in calculating ordinary business income or loss. They are entered on Schedule K, and the partners' or members' allocable share of the capital losses is reported to them on Schedule K-1. The net amount of capital losses (or gains) is computed by the business on its own Schedule D.

Section 1231 losses, on the other hand, are calculated on Form 4797 and then entered directly on Form 1065. These losses are part of the ordinary income or loss of the business.

S Corporations

Capital losses are separately stated items that are not taken into account in figuring the S corporation's ordinary income or loss. The net amount of capital losses (or gains) is calculated by the corporation on its own Schedule D. The capital losses are then entered on Schedule K; a shareholder's allocable share of capital losses from Schedule D is reported on Schedule K-1.

Section 1231 losses, on the other hand, are computed on Form 4797 and then entered directly on Form 1120S. These losses are part of the ordinary income or loss of the corporation. A shareholder's share of ordinary income or loss is reported on Schedule K-1.

C Corporations

Capital losses are reported on a corporation's Schedule D. The net amount of losses (or gains) is entered on Form 1120 on the line provided for "capital gain net income." The corporation must then apply its own limitations on capital losses, as explained in this chapter.

Section 1231 losses are computed on Form 4797 and then entered on Form 1120. Both capital losses and Section 1231 losses are part of the corporation's taxable income.

If the corporation discovers that it suffered a loss from worthless securities in a prior year and wants to file an amended return, use Form 1120X, Amended U.S. Corporation Income Tax Return.

CHAPTER 16

Casualty and Theft Losses

arthquakes in Montana, floods in North Dakota, droughts in New Jersey, hurricanes in Texas, ice storms in New York—these are just some examples of the types of weather-related events that can do severe damage to your business property. If you suffer casualty or theft losses to your business property, you can deduct the losses. You may also suffer a loss through condemnation or a sale under threat of condemnation. Again, the loss is deductible. Certain losses—those from events declared to be federal disasters—may even allow you to recover taxes you have already paid in an earlier year. But if you receive insurance proceeds or other property in return, you may have a gain rather than a loss. The law allows you to postpone reporting of the gain if certain steps are taken. In this chapter you will learn about:

- Casualty and theft
- Condemnation and threats of condemnation
- Disaster losses
- Postponing gain on casualties, thefts, and condemnations
- Deducting property insurance and other casualty/theft-related items
- Where to deduct casualty and theft losses and related items

For further information about deducting casualty and theft losses, see IRS Publication 547, Casualties, Disasters, and Thefts (Business and Nonbusiness).

CASUALTY AND THEFT

If you suffer a casualty or theft loss to business property, you can deduct the loss. There are no dollar limitations on these losses, as there are on personal losses. Nor are there adjusted gross income limitations on these losses, as there are on casualty and theft losses to personal losses.

Definition of Casualty

If your business property is damaged, destroyed, or lost because of a storm, earthquake, flood, or some other "sudden, unexpected or unusual event," you have experienced a casualty. For losses to nonbusiness property (such as your personal residence), the loss must fall squarely within the definition of a casualty loss. Losses to business property need not necessarily satisfy the same definition (as explained below).

The tax law spells out what is considered a "sudden, unexpected or unusual event." To be sudden, the event must be one that is swift, not one that is progressive or gradual. To be unexpected, the event must be unanticipated or unintentional on the part of the one who has suffered the loss. To be unusual, the event must be other than a day-to-day occurrence. It cannot be typical of the activity in which you are engaged.

Examples of casualties   Certain events in nature automatically are considered a casualty: earthquake, hurricane, tornado, cyclone, flood, storm, and volcanic eruption. Other events have also come to be known as casualties: sonic booms, mine cave-ins, shipwrecks, and acts of vandalism. Fires are considered casualties if you are not the one who started them (or did not pay someone to start them). Car or truck accidents are casualties provided they were not caused by willful negligence or a willful act. Progressive or gradual deterioration, such as rust or corrosion of property, is not considered a casualty.

Note: Business losses are deductible without having to establish that the cause of the loss was a casualty. Thus, if your equipment rusts or corrodes over time, you can deduct your loss even though it does not fit into the definition of a casualty loss (assuming you can fix the time of the loss). The reason for understanding the definition of the term "casualty" is that it determines where the loss is reported. It also comes into play in connection with deferring tax on gains from casualties, as discussed later in this chapter.

Proof of casualties   You must show that a specific casualty occurred and the time it occurred. You must also show that the casualty was the direct cause of the damage or destruction to your property. Finally, you must show that you were the owner of the property. If you leased property, you must show that you were contractually liable for damage so that you suffered a loss as a result of the casualty.

Definition of Theft

The taking of property must constitute a theft under the law in your state. Generally, theft involves taking or removing property with the intent to deprive the owner of its use. Typically, this includes robbery, larceny, and embezzlement.

If you are forced to pay extortion money or blackmail in the course of your business, the loss may be treated as a theft loss if your state law makes this type of taking illegal.

If you lose or misplace property, you cannot claim a theft loss unless you can show that the disappearance of the property was due to an accidental loss that was sudden, unexpected, or unusual. In other words, if you misplace property and cannot prove a theft loss occurred, you may be able to deduct a loss if you can establish a casualty was responsible for the loss.

Proof of theft   You must show when you discovered the property was missing. You must also show that a theft (as defined by your state's criminal law) took place. Finally, you must show that you were the owner of the property.

Determining a Casualty or Theft Loss

To calculate your loss, you must know your "adjusted basis" in the property.

Definition   *Adjusted basis*   This is generally your cost, plus any improvements made to it, less any depreciation claimed. Basis is also reduced by any prior casualty losses claimed with respect to the property.

You also need to know the fair market value of the property. If the property was not completely destroyed, you must know the extent of the damage. This is the difference between the fair market value of the property before and after the casualty.

EXAMPLE: Your business car is in an accident and you do not have collision insurance. The car's fair market value before the accident was $9,000. After the accident, the car is worth only $6,000. The decrease in the fair market value is $3,000 ($9,000 value before the loss, less $6,000 value after the loss).

How do you determine the decrease in fair market value? This is not based simply on your subjective opinion. In most cases, the decrease in value is based on an appraisal by a competent appraiser. If your property is located near an area affected by a casualty that causes your property value to decline, you cannot take this general decline in value into account. Only a direct loss of value may be considered. Presumably, a competent appraiser will be able to distinguish between a general market decline and a direct decline as a result of a casualty. The IRS looks at a number of factors to determine whether an appraiser is competent and his or her appraisal can be relied upon to establish fair market value. These factors include:

- Familiarity with your property both before and after the casualty

- Knowledge of sales of comparable property in your area

- Knowledge of conditions in the area of the casualty

- Method of appraisal

Remember that if the IRS questions the reliability of your appraiser, it may use its own appraiser to determine value. This may lead to legal wrangling and ultimately to litigation on the question of value. In order to avoid this problem and the costs entailed, it is advisable to use a reputable appraiser, even if this may seem costly to you.

Appraisals used to secure a loan or loan guarantee from the government under the Federal Emergency Management Agency (FEMA) are treated as proof of the amount of a disaster loss. Disaster losses are explained later in this chapter.

You may be able to establish value without the help of an appraiser in certain situations.

- If your car is damaged, you can use "blue book" value (the car's retail value, which is printed in a book used by car dealers). You can ask your local car dealer for your car's retail value reported in the blue book. You can then modify this value to reflect such things as mileage, options, and the car's condition before the casualty. Book values are not official, but the IRS has come to recognize that they are useful in fixing value. Of course, if your car is not listed in the blue book, you must find other means of establishing value. Value before the casualty can be established by a showing of comparable sales of similar cars in your area. According to the IRS, a dealer's offer for your car as a trade-in on a new car generally does not establish value.

- Repairs may be useful in showing the decrease in value. To use repairs as a measure of loss, you must show that the repairs are needed to restore the property to its pre-casualty condition and apply only to the damage that resulted from the casualty. You must also show that the cost of repairs is not excessive and that the repairs will not restore your property to a value greater than it had prior to the casualty. Making repairs to property damaged in a casualty can result in double deductions: one for the cost of repairs and the other for the casualty loss.

EXAMPLE: Severe flooding destroyed a business owner's property. He was not compensated by insurance. The IRS, in a memorandum to a district counsel, allowed him to claim a casualty loss for the damage as well as deducting the cost of repairs to the property where such repairs merely restored it to its pre-casualty condition.

The last piece of information necessary for determining a casualty or theft loss is the amount of insurance proceeds or other reimbursements, if any, you received or expect to receive as a result of the casualty or theft. While insurance proceeds are the most common reimbursement in the event of a casualty or theft, there are other types of reimbursements that are taken into account in the same way as insurance proceeds. These include:

- Court awards for damages as a result of suits based on casualty or theft. Your reimbursement is the net amount of the award—the award less attorney's fees to obtain the award.

- Payment from a bonding company for a theft loss

- Forgiveness of a federal disaster loan under the Disaster Relief and Emergency Assistance Act. Typically, these are given under the auspices of the Small Business Administration or the Farmers Home Administration. The part you do not have to repay is the amount of the reimbursement. Services provided by relief agencies for repairs, restoration, or cleanup are considered reimbursements that must be taken into account.

- Repairs made to your property by your lessee, or repayments in lieu of repairs

What happens if you have not received an insurance settlement by the time you must file your return? If there is a reasonable expectation that you will receive a settlement, you treat the anticipated settlement as if you had already received it. In other words, you take the expected insurance proceeds into account in calculating your loss. Should it later turn out that you received more or less than you anticipated, adjustments are required in the year you actually receive the insurance proceeds, as explained later in this chapter.

If the amount of insurance proceeds or other reimbursements is greater than the adjusted basis of your property, you do not have a loss. Instead, you have a gain as a result of your casualty or theft loss. How can this be, you might ask? Why should a loss of property turn out to be a gain for tax purposes? Remember that your adjusted basis for business property in many instances reflects deductions for depreciation. This brings your basis down. But your insurance may be based on the value of the property, not its basis to you. As such, if your basis has been adjusted downward for depreciation but the value of the property has remained constant or increased, your insurance proceeds may produce a gain for you. Gain and how to postpone it are discussed later in this chapter.

Calculating loss when property is completely destroyed or stolen Reduce your adjusted basis by any insurance proceeds received or expected to be received and any salvage value to the property. The result is your casualty loss deduction. The fair market value of the property does not enter into the computation.

EXAMPLE: Your machine is completely destroyed by a flood. You have no flood insurance, and the destroyed machine has no salvage value. The adjusted basis of the machine is $6,000. Your casualty loss is $6,000 (adjusted basis of the property [$6,000], less insurance proceeds [zero]).

If the casualty or theft involves more than one piece of property, you must determine the loss (or gain) for each item separately. If your reimbursement is paid in a lump sum and there is no allocation among the items, you must make an allocation. The allocation is based on the items' fair market value before the casualty.

Calculating loss when property is partially destroyed   Calculate the difference between the fair market value of the property before and after the casualty. Reduce this by any insurance proceeds. Then compare this figure with your adjusted basis in the property, less any insurance proceeds. Your casualty loss is the smaller of these two figures.

EXAMPLE: Your machine is damaged as a result of a flood. You do not have flood insurance. The machine is valued at $8,000 before the flood and $3,000 after it. Your adjusted basis in the machine is $6,000. Your loss is $5,000, the difference between the fair market value of the machine before and after the flood, which is smaller than your adjusted basis.

If you lease property from someone else (for example, if you lease a car used for business), your loss is limited to the difference between the insurance proceeds you receive, or expect to receive, and the amount you must pay to repair the property.

Inventory and Crops

You cannot deduct a loss with respect to inventory or crops damaged or destroyed by a casualty. Your inventory account is simply adjusted for the loss. In the case of crops, the cost of raising them has already been deducted, so no additional deduction is allowed if they are damaged or destroyed by a casualty.

Recovered Property

What happens if you deduct a loss for stolen property and the property is later recovered? Do you have to go back and amend the earlier return on which the theft loss was taken? The answer is no. Instead, you report the recovered property as income in the year of recovery.

But what if the property is not recovered in good shape or is only partially recovered? In this instance, you must recalculate your loss. You use the smaller of the property's adjusted basis or the decrease in the fair market value from the time it was stolen until you recovered it. This smaller amount is your recalculated loss. If your recalculated loss is less than the loss you deducted, you report the difference as income in the year of recovery. The amount of income that you must report is limited to the amount of loss that reduced your tax in the earlier year.

Insurance Received (or Not Received) in a Later Year

If you had anticipated the receipt of insurance proceeds or other property and took that anticipated amount into account in calculating your loss but later receive more (or less) than you anticipated, you must account for this discrepancy. As with recovered stolen property, you do not go back to the year of loss and make an adjustment. Instead, you take the insurance proceeds into account in the year of actual receipt.

If you receive more than you had expected (by way of insurance or otherwise), you report the extra amount as income in the year of receipt. You do not have to recalculate your original loss deduction. The additional amount is reported as ordinary income to the extent that the deduction in the earlier year produced a tax reduction. If the additional insurance or other reimbursement, when combined with what has already been received, exceeds the adjusted basis of your property, you now have a gain as a result of the casualty or theft. The gain is reported in the year you receive the additional reimbursement. However, you may be able to postpone reporting the gain, as discussed later in this chapter.

If you receive less than you had anticipated, you have an additional loss. The additional loss is claimed in the year in which you receive the additional amount.

EXAMPLE: In 1999 your business car was completely destroyed in an accident. Your adjusted basis in the car was $8,000. The car had a value of $10,000 before the accident and no value after the accident. You expected the driver responsible for the accident to pay for the damage. In fact, a jury awarded you the full extent of your loss. However, in 2000 you learn that the other driver will not pay the judgment and does not have any property against which you can enforce your judgment. In this instance, you have received less than you anticipated. You do not recalculate your 1999 taxes. Instead, you deduct your loss (limited to your adjusted basis of $8,000) in 2000.

Basis

If your property is partially destroyed in a casualty, you must adjust the basis of the property:

- Decrease basis by insurance proceeds or other reimbursements and loss deductions claimed

- Increase basis by improvements or repairs made to the property to rebuild or restore it

Year of the Loss

In general, the loss can be claimed only in the year in which the casualty or other event occurs. However, in the case of the theft, the loss is treated as having occurred in the year in which it is discovered.

CONDEMNATIONS AND THREATS OF CONDEMNATION

The government can take your property for a public use if it compensates you for your loss. The process by which the government exercises its right of eminent domain to take your property for public use is called condemnation. In a sense, you are being forced to sell your property at a price essentially fixed by the government. You usually can negotiate a price; sometimes you are forced to seek a court action and have the court fix the price paid to you. Typically, an owner is paid cash or receives other property upon condemnation of property.

Sometimes the probability of a condemnation becomes known through reports in a newspaper or other news medium or proposals at a town council meeting. For example, there may be talk of a new road or the widening of an existing road that will affect your property. If you do not voluntarily sell your property, the government will simply go through the process of condemnation.

Where there is a condemnation, you may also voluntarily sell other property. If the other property has an economic relationship to the condemned property, the voluntary sale can be treated as a condemnation.

Not every condemnation qualifies for special tax treatment. Where property is condemned because it is unsafe, this is not a taking of property for public use. It is simply a limitation on the use of the property by you.

For tax purposes, a condemnation or threat of condemnation of your business property is treated as a sale or exchange. You may have a gain or you may have a loss, depending upon the condemnation award or the proceeds you receive upon a forced sale. But there is something special in the tax law where condemnations are concerned. If you have a gain, you have an opportunity to avoid immediate tax on the gain. This postponement of reporting the gain is discussed later in this chapter.

Condemnation Award

The amount of the condemnation award determines your gain or loss for the event. The amount of money you receive or the value of property you receive for your condemned property is your condemnation award. Similarly, the amount you accept in exchange for your property in a sale motivated by the threat of condemnation is also treated as your condemnation award.

If you are in a dispute with the city, state, or federal government over the amount that should be paid to you and you go to court, the government may deposit an amount with the court. You are not considered to have received the award until you have an unrestricted right to it. This is usually after the court action is resolved and you are permitted to withdraw the funds for your own use.

Your award includes moneys withheld to pay your debts. For example, if the court withholds an amount to pay a lien holder or mortgagee, your condemnation award is the gross amount awarded to you, not the net amount paid to you.

The condemnation award does not include severance damages and special assessments.

Definition *Severance damages* Compensation paid to you if part of your property is condemned and the part not condemned suffers a reduction in value as a result of the condemnation. Severance damages may cover the loss in value of your remaining property or compensate you for certain improvements you must make to your remaining property (such as replacing fences, digging new wells or ditches, or planting trees or shrubs to restore the remaining property to its condition prior to the condemnation of your other property).

> **Definition** *Special assessments* Special assessments are charges against you for improvements that benefit the remaining property as a result of the condemnation of your other property (such as widening of the streets or installing sewers).

Treatment of severance damages Severance damages are not reported as income. Instead, they are used to reduce the basis of your remaining property. However, only net severance damages reduce basis. This means that you must first subtract from severance damages any expenses you incurred to obtain them. You also reduce severance damages by any special assessments levied against your remaining property if the special assessments were withheld from the award by the condemning authority. If the severance damages related only to a specific portion of your remaining property, then you reduce the basis of that portion of the property.

If the net severance damages are greater than your basis in the remaining property, you have a gain. However, you can postpone reporting the gain, as discussed later in this chapter.

Generally, you and the condemning authority will contractually agree on which portion of an award is for condemnation and which part, if any, is for severance damages or other awards. This allocation should be put in writing. You cannot simply go back after the transaction is completed and try to make an allocation. You may, however, be able to convince the IRS that the parties intended to make a certain allocation if the facts and circumstances support this argument. If there is no written allocation and you cannot convince the IRS otherwise, all of the amounts received will be treated as a condemnation award (and no part will be treated as severance damages).

Treatment of special assessments Special assessments serve to reduce the condemnation award. They must actually be withheld from the award itself; they cannot be levied after the award is made, even if it is in the same year.

If a condemnation award includes severance damages, then the special assessments are first used to reduce the severance damages. Any excess special assessments are then used to reduce the condemnation award.

DISASTER LOSSES

In the past several years, our country has experienced a large number of major disasters, including hurricanes, floods, fires, blizzards, and earthquakes. When large areas suffer sizable losses, the president may declare the areas eligible for special federal disaster relief. This disaster assistance comes in the form of disaster relief loans, special grants (money that does not have to be repaid), special unemployment benefits, and other types of assistance. Still, despite all these efforts by the federal government, as well as state, local, and private agencies, you may experience serious disruption to your business and loss to your business property. The tax law provides a special rule for certain disaster losses that will give you up-front cash to help you get back on your feet.

Typically, you deduct your loss in the year in which it occurred. However, you may make a special election to deduct your loss on a prior year's return. This can result in a tax refund that may provide you with needed cash flow.

EXAMPLE: In January 2000 you suffer an uninsured disaster loss of $25,000. You may, of course, deduct the loss on your 2000 return, which is filed in 2001 (assuming you are on a calendar-year basis). Alternatively, you may elect to deduct your loss on your 1999 return.

If your loss occurs later in the year, after you have already filed your tax return for the prior year, you can still get a tax refund by filing an amended return for the prior year. For example, if in the example above your loss occurred in December 2000 (after you filed your 1999 return), you can file an amended return for 1999 to claim the disaster loss.

You must make the election to claim the loss on the prior year's return by the later of:

- The due date (including extensions) for filing your income tax return for the year in which the disaster occurred, or

- The due date (including extensions) for the preceding year's return.

Not all seeming disasters qualify for this special tax election. To be treated as a disaster, your loss must have resulted from a casualty in an area declared by the president to be eligible for federal disaster assistance.

If you suffer a loss in your inventory due to a disaster, you need not account for your loss simply by a reduction in the cost of goods sold. Instead, you can claim a deduction for your loss. The loss can be claimed on the return for the year of the disaster or on a return (or amended return) for the preceding year. If you choose to deduct your inventory loss, then you must also reduce your opening inventory for the year of the loss so that the loss is not also reflected in the inventory; you cannot get a double benefit for the loss.

POSTPONING GAIN ON CASUALTIES, THEFTS, AND CONDEMNATIONS

Casualties, thefts, and condemnations are called involuntary conversions. The law recognizes that when you suffer an involuntary conversion, you generally have some economic loss even though you may have a gain for tax purposes. The law allows you to avoid having to report the gain immediately. You can postpone reporting the gain (and the tax on that gain) by purchasing replacement property within set time limits.

> **Definition** *Replacement property* This is either property that is similar or related in service or use to the destroyed or condemned property, or at least an 80-percent interest in a corporation owning such property. For property destroyed in a federally declared disaster area, it is any tangible property held for productive use in a business.

You can either buy or construct replacement property. Replacement property is explained more fully below. To fully postpone reporting the gain, the cost of the replacement property must at least equal the amount you received for your old property.

Replacement Period

There are different replacement periods, depending upon the event that caused the gain.

Casualty and theft losses For a casualty or theft loss, the replacement period begins on the date that the property was damaged, destroyed, or stolen. The replacement period ends two years after the close of the first year in which you realize any part of the gain.

EXAMPLE: Your factory is burned to the ground on February 1, 1999. In November 1999 you receive an insurance settlement. You have until December 31, 2001 (two years after the close of 1999, the first year in which your realized your gain), to buy replacement property.

You may realize some gain even though you have not received the full extent of your gain. This can occur, for example, where your property is condemned and you are permitted to withdraw some deposits made in the court by the condemning authority. Once you realize any gain, your replacement period begins.

If you construct replacement property, the construction must be completed before the end of the replacement period. You cannot simply give the contractor an advance payment before the end of this period. If you cannot meet the replacement deadline, consider asking for an extension (as explained below).

Condemnations For a condemnation you are given an even longer replacement period. For gain realized on a condemnation, the replacement period begins on the earlier of the date on which you disposed of the condemned property or the date that the threat of condemnation began. The replacement period ends three years after the close of the first tax year in which any part of the gain on the condemnation is realized. However, a two-year period applies if your replacement property is the acquisition of control in a corporation that owns replacement property. The three-year replacement period applies only to the direct purchase of replacement property.

EXAMPLE: In February 1999 your factory is condemned to make room for a new highway through your city. In November 1999 you receive a condemnation award. You have until December 31, 2002, to buy replacement property. If you had received notice from the city or state in December 1998 that the property would be condemned, the replacement period would have begun in December 1998 even though the actual condemnation did not take place until February 1999.

If, after you receive notice that your property will be condemned, you acquire replacement property, you are treated as having made a timely replacement even though you bought the replacement property before the actual condemnation. However, if you buy property before there is a threat of condemnation, it cannot be treated as replacement property.

Extension of replacement period   If your replacement period is winding down and you do not think you can meet the deadline (if, for example, it looks as though closing on the purchase of replacement property will be delayed or construction of new property will not be completed), you can ask the IRS for an extension. The application for an extension must be made before the end of the replacement period; do not wait until your time expires and then apply. In making your application, include the details of why you need the extension. You must show that there is reasonable cause for the delay—it cannot simply be a matter of your not having gotten around to it. There must be circumstances beyond your control that prevented you from meeting the deadline.

Changing your mind   If you report gain and then decide to buy replacement property, you can undo the reporting of gain if the replacement is made within the replacement period. You simply file an amended return for the year in which the gain was reported. Explain that you originally paid tax on the gain but then acquired property of sufficient cost within the replacement period and you now wish to postpone gain.

Replacement Property

Replacement property generally must be property designed to substitute for the property that was destroyed, damaged, stolen, or condemned. You are not required to use the actual cash received. For example, if you received insurance proceeds for the destruction of your factory, you can buy another factory with a mortgage; you need not use the insurance proceeds. However, you must buy or build the replacement property (or buy a controlling interest in a corporation). You cannot treat property you acquire by gift or inheritance as replacement property. Also, qualified replacement property cannot be acquired from a "related party" (a close relative or a business that you control) where the amount of the gain is more than $100,000. For partnerships and S corporations, the $100,000 limit is applied at both the owner and business levels.

The property must be similar or related in service or use to the old property. This entails using property in the same business or for the same purpose. In most cases, similar use is rather obvious. There are, however, some situations where it is not clear whether the replacement property is similar or related in service or use. There have been numerous cases disputing whether replacement property meets this standard. It is advisable to make certain that your replacement property does not fall into an area of ambiguity that could lead to disputes with the IRS.

If you own property outright (through a fee simple), you can replace it with a leasehold interest that runs at least 15 years. The same is true for the reverse situation (acquiring a fee simple for a 15-year or more leasehold interest).

Special rule for property destroyed in a federally declared disaster   Business property compulsively or involuntarily converted as a result of an event in a federally declared disaster is treated as similar or related in service or use to any tangible property held for productive use in a business. This rule allows a business owner who is wiped out by a disaster to start anew. For example, if you own an ice-cream stand that is destroyed in a hurricane and the area is eligible for federal disaster relief, you can postpone gain on in-surance proceeds you receive for your stand if you buy a truck that you will use to start a lawn care business.

Special rule for condemned realty   If you have a gain as a result of the condemnation (or threat of condemnation) of real property used in your business, you can replace it with like-kind property. Like-kind property is an easier standard to meet than "similar or related in service or use"; it simply means any real property. The category covers both improved and unimproved property. It applies to easements, rights-of-way, leaseholds for a term of 30 years or more, perpetual water rights (if treated as real prop-erty under state law), and any similar continuing interests in real property. Like-kind property can also apply to outdoor advertising displays as long as a first-year expense deduction is not claimed for the displays.

Basis of Replacement Property

All along, the discussion has focused on postponing gain. So when do you have to report the gain? The answer is generally when you sell or otherwise dispose of the replacement property. The gain you postponed is taken into account in the basis of the replacement property.

The basis of the replacement property is generally the same as that for the old property. The basis of the old property, however, is adjusted upward and downward for certain items.

- Decrease basis by any money received that is not used to acquire the replacement property and by the amount of loss reported on your return.

- Increase basis by any additional money spent on the investment property over and above money you received and the amount of gain reported on your return.

Special rule for acquisition of a controlled corporation   If you buy a controlling interest in a corporation intended to replace your involuntarily converted property, you must reduce both the basis in your stock and the basis in the corporation's property that serves as replacement property.

EXAMPLE: An office building you own is destroyed in a flood. You use your insurance proceeds to buy 100 percent of the stock of X Corporation. The sole asset of X Corporation is an office building. You reduce the basis in your X stock and the basis of X's office building by the gain you postponed.

Death of an Owner

If an owner dies in the year in which gain is realized from a casualty, theft, or condemnation and before replacement property has been acquired, the owner's estate cannot then buy replacement property. All of the gain must be reported on the owner's final income tax return.

DEDUCTING PROPERTY INSURANCE AND OTHER CASUALTY/ THEFT-RELATED ITEMS

It is well and good that you can write off your casualty and theft losses. But as a practical matter, you should carry enough insurance to cover these situations so that you will not suffer any financial loss should these events befall your business. If you carry insurance to cover fire, theft, flood, or any other casualty related to your business, you can deduct your premiums.

If you maintain a home office, you must allocate the cost of your homeowner's policy and deduct only the portion allocated to the business use of your home as part of your home office deduction (as discussed in Chapter 17). Be sure to check your homeowner's policy to see that it covers your business use. You may have to obtain additional coverage if you use your home for certain types of business activities. For example, if you have clients or customers come to your home, it may be advisable to increase your liability coverage. The cost of additional coverage for business guests (which may be in the form of a rider to your policy) may be rather modest. Similarly, your homeowner's policy may not cover business equipment in your home office, such as your computer, fax, or copying machine. Again, a small rider may be necessary to protect you against lost.

If you are a manufacturer who includes business insurance as part of the cost of goods sold, no separate deduction can be taken for these insurance premiums.

If you self-insure to cover casualty or theft by putting funds aside, you cannot deduct the amount of your reserves. In this case, only actual losses are deductible, as explained earlier in this chapter. Self-insurance may be advisable to cover certain casualties that may not be covered by your policy. For example, your policy may not cover damage from civil riots. Self-insurance is also a good idea where you have a high deductible (for example, a state-prescribed deductible for flood insurance in a coastal area). Be sure to review carefully your policy's exclusions (the types of events not covered by your insurance).

Use and Occupancy Insurance

If you carry insurance to cover profits that are lost during a time you are forced to close down due to fire or other cause, you may deduct the premiums. If you then do shut down and collect on the insurance, you report the proceeds as ordinary income.

Car Insurance

The same rule that applies to business property insurance also applies to insurance for your car or other vehicle used in your business. This insurance covers liability, damages, and other losses in accidents involving your business car. However, if you use your car only partly for business, you must allocate your insurance premiums. Only the portion related to business use of your car is deductible. The portion related to personal use of your car is not deductible.

If you use the standard mileage allowance to deduct expenses for business use of a car, you cannot deduct any car insurance premiums. The standard mileage rate already takes into account an allowance for car insurance.

Deductions for various types of insurance are discussed in greater detail in Chapter 20.

Appraisals

If your property is damaged by a casualty and you pay a qualified appraiser to establish the fair market value of the property in order to prove your damage and the extent of your loss, you claim a separate deduction for appraisal fees. You do not take the appraisal fees into account in calculating your casualty loss deduction.

WHERE TO DEDUCT CASUALTY AND THEFT LOSSES AND RELATED ITEMS

Employees

Casualty and theft losses to business property are calculated in Section B of Form 4684, Casualty and Theft Worksheet for Individuals. Losses are then netted against gains and are entered on Form 4797, Sales of Business Property. Your losses are entered directly on page 1 of Form 1040. They are not taken on Schedule A, as are casualty and theft losses to personal property (such as your personal residence). Nor are they limited by the $100 per casualty or 10-percent-of-adjusted-gross-income limitation that applies to casualty and theft losses to nonbusiness property.

If the casualty or theft happened to property used for both business and personal purposes, you must make an allocation. Only the business portion of the loss is free from the $100/10-percent limitations. For example, if you use a car 75 percent for business and 25 percent for personal purposes and the car is totaled in an accident for which you do not have collision insurance, 75 percent of your loss (the business portion) is claimed without regard to the $100/10-percent limits; the other 25 percent of your loss (the personal portion) is subject to both the $100 and 10-percent limits.

Self-Employed

Casualty and theft losses to business property are calculated in Section B of Form 4684. Losses are then netted against gains and are entered on Form 4797. The net result is then entered on page 1 of Form 1040; you do not enter the amount on Schedule C.

Losses from involuntary conversions are netted against gains and losses from Section 1231 property. This is essentially depreciable property, used in a trade or business and held for more than one year, that is not held for inventory or for sale to customers in the ordinary course of business. (Certain livestock, crops, timber, coal, and domestic iron ore can also be Section 1231 property.) Thus, even if you have a casualty loss, you may not get the benefit of the loss if you have gains from the sale or exchange of Section 1231 property. However, losses to inventory are taken into account in the cost of goods sold.

If you elect to postpone gain on a casualty, theft, or condemnation, make your election on the return for the year in which you realized gain. If you acquired replacement property before filing your return, attach a statement to the return showing the amount realized, how you computed your gain, and any gain reported. If you have not yet acquired replacement property by the time you must file your return, simply attach a statement to your return showing the circumstances of the casualty, theft, or condemnation giving rise to the gain, how you calculated your gain, and that you intend to acquire replacement property within the replacement period. Then, when you do buy replacement property, attach another statement to the return for the year of the replacement purchase explaining the replacement.

If the replacement period expires before you acquire replacement property (and you do not obtain an extension for the replacement period), you must file an amended return for the year in which you realized gain. You report your full gain on this amended return. You must also file an amended return if you buy replacement property whose cost is not sufficient to postpone the reporting of all of your gain. You report the portion of the gain not covered by the replacement property on this amended return.

Once you have designated certain property as your replacement property, you cannot later substitute other property for it. However, if your replacement property is found to be unsuitable, you can then substitute other qualified property, provided the replacement period has not expired.

Partnerships and LLCs

The partnership or LLC reports income or loss from an involuntary conversion (casualty, theft, or condemnation) on Form 4797. The net gain or loss is taken into account in arriving at the total trade or business income or loss on Form 1065 on the specific line provided for net gain or loss from Form 4797. If there is a gain as a result of a casualty or theft to business property, the partnership or LLC must elect to defer the recognition of gain and buy the replacement property. The individual partners or LLC members cannot make a separate election. Each partner or LLC member reports his or her distributive share of business income or loss on his or her personal income tax return.

Even if you are a silent partner in an activity that is treated as a passive activity, casualty and theft losses are not subject to the passive loss limitations. You may claim these losses as long as they are not a recurrent part of the business.

S Corporations

If the S corporation has income or loss from an involuntary conversion (casualty, theft, or condemnation), it must file Form 4797. The net gain or loss is taken into account in arriving at the S corporation's total trade or business income or loss on Form 1120S. Net gain or loss from Form 4797 is reported on the specific line provided on Form 1120S for this purpose. If there is a gain as a result of a casualty or theft to business property, the S corporation must elect to defer the recognition of gain and buy the replacement property. The individual shareholders cannot make a separate election. Each shareholder reports his or her distributive share of S corporation income or loss on his or her personal income tax return.

Even if you are a "silent partner" in an activity that is treated as a passive activity (a shareholder who does not materially participate in the business), casualty and theft losses are not subject to the passive loss limitations. You may claim these losses as long as they are not a recurrent part of the business.

The election to postpone reporting of gain is made at the corporate level. Each shareholder cannot make a separate election.

C Corporations

C corporations report net gains or losses from involuntary conversions on Form 4797 and then use the net amount to arrive at taxable income on Form 1120. Net gains or losses from Form 4797 are reported on the specific line provided on Form 1120 for this purpose.

CHAPTER 17

Home Office Deductions

Today over 40 million Americans work at home at least some of the time, and the number is growing. Computers, faxes, modems, and the information highway make it easier and, in some cases, more profitable to operate a home office. As a general rule, the cost of owning or renting your home is a personal one and, except for certain specific expenses (such as mortgage interest, real estate taxes, and casualty losses), you cannot deduct personal expenses. However, if you use a portion of your home for business, you may be able to deduct a number of expenses, including rent or depreciation, mortgage and real estate taxes, maintenance, and utilities. These are collectively referred to as "home office deductions." They are claimed as a single deduction item. The deduction is allowed for both self-employed individuals and employees who meet special requirements. In this chapter you will learn about:

- Home office deductions in general
- Special requirements for employees
- Allocating the business part of home expenses
- Deduction limits
- Special business uses of a home
- Ancillary benefits of claiming home office deductions

- Implications of claiming home office deductions on home sales

- Where to deduct home office expenses

This chapter talks about home "office" expenses; however, you need not use your home as an office to claim this deduction. Home office is simply a name assigned to a category of deductible business expenses. For example, you may use your garage to do mechanical repairs, or a greenhouse to grow plants for sale. The expenses related to these uses may be treated as home office expenses.

It has long been thought that claiming a home office deduction is an automatic red flag for an audit. However, there are no statistics to show that this is true. If you meet the tests for claiming a home office deduction as explained in this chapter and you have proof of your expenses, you should have nothing to fear, even if your return is questioned.

For more information about home office deductions see IRS Publication 587, Business Use of Your Home.

HOME OFFICE DEDUCTIONS IN GENERAL

Whether you own your home or rent it, you may be able to deduct a portion of the costs of your home if you use it for business. This is so for both employees and self-employed individuals. However, the law is very strict on what constitutes business use of a home. First, you must use the portion of your home exclusively and regularly for business. Then you must meet one of three tests. The home office must be:

- Your principal place of business,

- A place to meet or deal with patients, clients, or customers in the normal course of your business, or

- A separate structure (not attached to your house or residence) that is used in connection with your business.

Exclusively and Regularly

Exclusive use of a home office means that it is used solely for your business activities and not for personal purposes, including investment activities. If you have a spare bedroom or a den that you have equipped with a computer, telephone, and perhaps a fax/modem, you cannot meet the exclusive use test for a home office if you also use that room as a guest room or family den.

The exclusive use test does not require you to set aside an entire room for business purposes. You can meet this test if you clearly delineate a portion of a room for business. It must be a separately identifiable space. However, you need not mark off this separate area by a permanent partition to satisfy the "separately identifiable" space requirement.

There are two important exceptions to the exclusive use requirement: day-care facilities and storage space. Each of these exceptions is discussed later in this chapter.

The home office must also be used on a regular basis for your business activity. This determination is based on all the facts and circumstances. Occasional or incidental use of a home office will not satisfy this requirement, even if such space is used exclusively for business purposes.

Principal Place of Business

Your home office is treated as your principal place of business if it is the place where you conduct your business. It may be your prime activity or a sideline business. As long as it is the main location for the particular activity, it is your principal place of business.

Your home office is considered to be your principal place of business if it is used for substantial managerial or administrative activities and there is no other fixed location for such activities.

EXAMPLE: You run an interior design business, seeing clients in their homes and offices. You use your home office to schedule appointments, keep your books and records, and order supplies. You can treat your home office as your principal place of business because you use it for substantial managerial or administrative activities and you do not have a store front or other office for such work.

Examples of substantial administrative or management activities include:

- Billing customers, clients, and patients
- Forwarding orders
- Keeping books and records
- Ordering supplies

- Reading professional or trade journals and papers
- Scheduling appointments
- Writing reports

Even if you perform administrative or management activities at places other than your home office, you can still take the home office deduction if you fall into one of the following categories:

- You do not conduct substantial administrative or management activities at a fixed location other than your home office, even if such activities are performed by other people at other locations. For example, another company handles your billing from its own place of business.

- You carry out administrative or management activities at sites that are not fixed locations of the business in addition to performing the activities at home. For example you do these tasks in your car or in a motel room while on the road.

- You conduct insubstantial amounts of administrative and management activities at a fixed location other than the home office. For example, you do minimal paperwork at an office—not your home office—once in a while.

- You conduct substantial *nonadministrative* and *nonmanagement* business activities at a fixed location other than a home office. For example, you meet with or provide services to customers, clients, or patients at a fixed location other than your home office.

- You have suitable space to conduct administrative or management activities outside your home but instead choose to use your home office for doing these activities.

  EXAMPLE: Same as the example above, but you schedule appointments for your interior design business from your car phone. Because your car is not considered a fixed location, you can still claim a home office deduction.

More than one business   If you are an employee and also conduct a sideline business from a home office, you may deduct your home office expenses for the sideline business. The business activity from the home office need not be your main activity; the home office simply must be the principal place of business for the sideline activity.

However, if you conduct more than one activity from a home office, be sure that each activity meets all home office requirements. Otherwise you may lose out on deductions. For example, if you are an employee and also have a business that you run from your home, if you use the home office for your employment-related activities (and not for the convenience of your employer, as explained below), then you fail the exclusive use test for the home-based business. You will not be able to deduct any home office expenses even though the home office is the principal place of business for the home-based activity.

Place to Meet or Deal with Patients, Clients, or Customers

If you meet with patients, clients, or customers in a home office, you can deduct home office expenses. The home office need not be your principal place of business. You can conduct business at another location, and your home office can be a satellite office. However, if you use your home office only to make or receive phone calls with patients, clients, and customers, you do not meet this test. While making or receiving phone calls can arguably be viewed as "dealing" with patients, clients, or customers, the IRS will not view it as such.

This test generally allows professionals—attorneys, doctors, accountants, architects, and others—to deduct home office expenses. Even though they have another office, they can still use a home office and deduct related expenses. Of course, the meeting or dealing with clients and others must be more than occasional; it must be on a "regular" basis. However, the home office must be used exclusively for business. You cannot use it for personal activities during the time when it is not used for business.

EXAMPLE: An attorney with an office in the city has a den in her home in the suburbs that she uses to meet with clients on weekends and in the evenings. If the den is also used by her family for recreation, then it cannot be treated as a home office because it fails the "exclusive use" test. However, if it is used only for regularly meeting with her clients, home office expenses are deductible.

Separate Structure

If you have a separate freestanding structure on your property, you can treat it as a home office if you use it exclusively and regularly for your home office activity. A separate structure may be a garage, a studio, a greenhouse, or even a barn. It need not be an office in order for expenses to be deducted as home office expenses. Nor need the separate structure be the principal place of your business activity. Further, it need not be a place to meet or deal with patients, clients, or customers in the normal course of your business. It simply must be used in connection with your business.

EXAMPLE: You own a flower shop in town. You have a greenhouse on your property in which you grow orchids. You can deduct the home office expenses of the greenhouse.

What constitutes a separate structure? The answer is not always clear. In one case, the Tax Court treated a separate structure in a taxpayer's backyard as part of the house itself because of the close relationship to it. If your local real estate law treats a separate structure as "appurtenant" to the house, then it is not a separate structure for purposes of the home office deduction rules.

Examples of separate structures that may qualify as home offices include an artist's studio, a florist's greenhouse, and a carpenter's workshop.

SPECIAL REQUIREMENTS FOR EMPLOYEES

If you use your home for business, you can deduct home office expenses if your use is for the convenience of your employer. However, this is not an easy standard to satisfy. There is no hard-and-fast rule for proving that your use of a home office is for the convenience of your employer. Neither the tax law nor regulations provide any guidelines. Your home office use is not treated as being for the convenience of your employer simply because it is appropriate or helpful to your job; there must be a real need on the part of your employer for you to use an office at home. In this age of computers, if your employer allows you to "telecommute" from a home office because it suits your schedule, this is not necessarily for your employer's convenience. As long as your employer provides you with an office, there must be some other compelling reason for you to use a home office for business. Simply getting a letter from your employer that the home office use is for the employer's convenience may not be enough to satisfy the IRS if your return is questioned. But if your employer has no office space for you to use so that telecommuting is the only arrangement feasible, then clearly such arrangement is for the convenience of the employer. Of course, there may be situations where it is not clear whether the arrangement if for the convenience of the employer. Then, factors such as office space, arrangements with other workers, and other factors must be considered.

If you employ your spouse, you may be able to deduct home office expenses by requiring your spouse to use the home office for your convenience. There have been no cases or rulings testing this arrangement, but if there is a real need on your part for it, the arrangement just might work.

You cannot claim a home office deduction if you rent a portion of your home to your employer and then perform services in it as an employee. If you do rent space to your employer, the rent is still taxable to you.

ALLOCATING THE BUSINESS PART OF HOME EXPENSES

Some expenses of the home office are directly related to business use. For example, if you paint your home office, the entire cost of the paint job is a business expense. Other expenses are indirectly related to business use of your home office; rather, they relate to your entire home. Indirect expenses include:

- Deductible mortgage interest
- Real estate taxes
- Depreciation
- Rent
- Utilities
- Insurance
- General repairs to the home (such as servicing the heating system)
- Security systems
- Snow removal
- Cleaning

Only the portion of indirect expenses related to the business use of your home is deductible. How do you make an allocation of expenses? If you have five rooms and use one for business, can you allocate one-fifth of expenses, or 20 percent, for business? The answer is yes if the rooms are more or less the same size. This is often not the case. If rooms are of unequal size, you allocate expenses based on the square footage of business use. Determine the size of your home; then determine the size of your home office. Divide the size of your home office by the size of your home to arrive at a percentage of business use.

EXAMPLE: Your home is 1,800 square feet. Your home office is 12 feet × 15 feet, or 180 square feet. Therefore, your home office use is 10 percent (180 divided by 1,800).

Once you have determined your business percentage, you apply this percentage against each indirect expense.

EXAMPLE: Your business percentage is 20 percent and your total real estate taxes for the year are $5,000. You may treat $1,000 ($5,000 × 20%) as part of your home office deduction. The balance of your real estate taxes continues to be deductible as an itemized deduction on Schedule A.

EXAMPLE: Your business percentage is 20 percent, and instead of owning your home you rent it. If your annual rent is $12,000, you may treat $2,400 ($12,000 × 20%) as part of your home office deduction. The balance of your rent is not deductible, since it is a personal expense.

You apply the business percentage against deductible mortgage interest. You can include a second mortgage and deductible points in this figure. Again, the portion of your mortgage interest not treated as part of your home office deduction continues to be deductible as an itemized deduction on Schedule A.

Casualty losses may be either an indirect or direct expense, depending upon the property affected by the casualty. If, for example, your home office is damaged in a storm and you are not fully compensated by insurance, you claim your loss as a direct expense. If, however, the damage is to your entire home (such as a roof leak), you treat the loss as an indirect expense. Remember that the limits on deducting casualty losses to nonbusiness property ($100 per incident/10-percent-of-adjusted-gross-income floor) do not apply to business casualties. See Chapter 16 for more information on deducting casualty losses.

If you rent your home, you can deduct the business portion of rent as an indirect expense. If you own your home, you cannot deduct the fair rental value of your home office. However, you can claim depreciation on your home office. See Chapter 12 for more information on depreciation.

Generally, utility expenses—for electricity, gas, oil, trash removal, and cleaning services—are treated as indirect expenses. The business portion is part of your home office deduction; the nonbusiness portion is not deductible. However, in some instances you may be able to deduct a greater portion of a utility expense. For example, if you can show that electrical use for your home office is greater than the allocable percentage of the whole bill, you can claim that additional amount as a direct expense.

The business portion of a homeowner's insurance policy is part of your home office deduction. It is an indirect expense. If you also pay additional coverage directly related to your home office, treat the additional coverage as a direct expense. You may, for example, carry special coverage for your home office equipment (computer, library, etc.). In fact, if you do not now maintain special coverage for home office equipment, you should check your homeowner's policy to see if damage or loss to your business equipment would be covered. You may think your computer is covered, but some homeowner policies may exclude business equipment. Also check whether your homeowner's policy covers personal liability for on-premises injury to patients, clients, and customers who visit your home office. Again, you may have to carry additional insurance for this type of liability.

Repairs may be direct or indirect expenses, depending on their nature. A repair to a furnace is an indirect expense; a repair to a window in the home office itself is a direct expense.

A home security system for your entire home can give rise to two types of write-offs. First, the business portion of your monthly monitoring fees is an indirect expense. Second, the business portion of the cost of the system itself may be depreciated. This depreciation also becomes part of your indirect expenses.

Telephone Expenses

Telephone expenses are not part of your home office deduction. They are separately deductible. However, if you maintain a home office, there is a special rule that limits a deduction for a telephone line: You may not deduct the basic monthly service charge for the first telephone line to your home as a business expense. You can, however, deduct business-related charges, such as long-distance calls for business or call answering, call waiting, and call forwarding. You can also deduct the entire phone bill of a second phone line used exclusively for business. You can deduct any additional lines used for business, such as dedicated fax lines.

Nondeductible Expenses

Not every home-related expense can be treated as a home office deduction. For example, the cost of landscaping and lawn care cannot be treated as a home office expense.

Deduction Limits

Home office deductions cannot exceed your gross income from the home office activity. For those who conduct their primary business from home, the gross income limit poses no problem. Income from the home office activity will more than exceed home office expenses. Thus, for example, if a dentist conducts his or her practice from a home office, there should be no problem in deducting all home office expenses. For those who use a home office for a sideline activity, however, the gross income limit may pose a problem.

What Is Gross Income?

For purposes of limiting home office deductions, gross income means income from the business activity conducted in the home office.

EXAMPLE: A teacher who teaches full-time at school conducts a retail business from a home office. For purposes of limiting home office deductions, gross income includes only the income from the retail business.

To calculate gross income, look to your profit reported on Schedule C if you are self-employed or the portion of your salary earned in the home office if you are an employee. You can adjust your Schedule C profit for certain items. If you sold your home, the portion of the gain related to the home office increases your gross income for purposes of limiting home office deductions. If you suffer a loss on the home office portion, you reduce your gross income.

If your gross income from your home office business activity is less than your total business expenses, your home office deduction is limited. Your deduction for otherwise nondeductible expenses (such as utilities or depreciation) cannot exceed gross income from the business activity, reduced by the business portion of otherwise deductible expenses (such as home mortgage interest or real estate taxes) and business expenses not attributable to business use of the home (such as salaries or supplies). This sounds rather complicated, but Form 8829, Expenses for Business Use of Your Home, incorporates this limitation. This rule merely orders the categories of deductions.

If, after applying this ordering of deductions, you still have unused home office deduction, you can carry forward the unused portion. The carryforward can be deducted in a future year when there is gross income from the same home office activity to offset it. There is no time limit on the carryforward. You can claim it even though you no longer live in the home in which the deduction arose, as long as there is gross income from the same activity to offset the deduction. Be sure to keep adequate records to support your carryforward deduction.

SPECIAL BUSINESS USES OF A HOME

There are two exceptions to the "exclusive use" requirement: day-care facilities and storage space. If either of these exceptions applies, you can deduct your home office expenses even though the space is also used for personal purposes.

Day-Care Facilities

If you use all or part of your home on a regular basis as a facility to provide day-care services, you may claim home office deductions if you meet certain tests.

- You must provide day care for children, elderly persons (age 65 and older), or persons who are physically or mentally unable to care for themselves.

- You must have a license, certificate, registration, or other approval as a day-care center or family or group day-care home under your state law. You can claim home office expenses if you have applied for approval and are awaiting it. You cannot claim home office expenses if your application has been rejected or your approval revoked.

Calculating your home office deduction   If you use a portion of your home exclusively for day-care services, you can deduct your expenses as described above for any other type of business use of a home. If, however, you use a portion of your home for day-care services but also use it for personal purposes, you must follow special allocation rules to determine your home office deduction. You must compare the business use of the space with the total use of the space. There are two methods for making this comparison:

- Compare the number of hours of business use in a week with the number of hours in a week (168 hours).

- Compare the number of hours of business use in the tax year with the number of hours in a tax year (8,760 in a 365-day year).

Then this percentage is applied to the business percentage of total space.

EXAMPLE: An individual uses her basement to provide day-care services. The basement represents 50 percent of her house's total square footage. She uses her basement for 12 hours per day, five days per week, 50 weeks per year, for day-care services. Her family uses the basement during the times it is not being used for day-care services. She uses her home for a total of 3,000 hours per year for business, or 34.25 percent of the total hours in the year (3,000 divided by 8,760). In calculating the amount of indirect expenses allocable to her business use, she can deduct 17.13 percent (34.25 percent of 50 percent).

If meals are provided as part of the day-care services, the cost of the meals is not included in a home office deduction. It is a separate expense. In calculating the deductible portion of the meal costs, 100 percent of the costs to day-care recipients is deductible. If you also provide meals to employees, only 50 percent of the cost of meals for them is deductible. No percentage of the cost of meals consumed by you or your family is deductible. If you receive reimbursements under the Child and Adult Food Care Program under the U.S. Department of Agriculture, you must include in income any reimbursements in excess of your expenses for eligible children.

Storage

If space is used on a regular basis for the storage of your inventory or sample products, you can deduct home office expenses even though you also use the space for personal purposes and thus fail the exclusive use test. The storage space that is deductible is only the actual space used. For example, if a portion of a basement is used for storage, only the expenses related to that portion are deductible even if the rest of the basement is not used for other purposes.

Expenses of storage space are deductible even though the exclusive use test is not satisfied if:

- The home is the fixed location of the business activity (you run the business from home)

- The business activity is selling goods wholesale or retail

- The space is used as a separately identifiable space suitable for storage

EXAMPLE: An individual in the gift basket business that she runs from home uses her family room to store sample gift baskets. She may deduct the portion of the family room used to store her samples even though the family room is also used for personal purposes.

ANCILLARY BENEFITS OF CLAIMING HOME OFFICE DEDUCTIONS

Claiming home office deductions means more, tax-wise, than simply deducting the expenses related to that office. It means additional tax benefits may be available.

Having a home office means that travel to and from the office for business is fully deductible (there is no such thing as "commuting" from a home office). So travel from your home to a customer's location and back again is a fully deductible business expense. Business use of your car is explained in Chapter 7.

Having a home office also means it is not necessary to keep a log of computer use. A computer used in a regular business establishment is not treated as listed property for which an owner must prove business use exceeds 50 percent in order to claim first-year expensing or accelerated depreciation. A home office for which a deduction is allowed is treated as a "regular business establishment." First-year expensing and depreciation are explained in Chapter 12.

IMPLICATIONS OF HOME OFFICE DEDUCTIONS ON HOME SALES

Claiming a home office deduction has important consequences when you sell your home. First, any depreciation you have claimed with respect to your home reduces the basis in the home. This, in turn, increases the gain.

However, if you used your home office for less three out of five years before the date of sale, you can still claim the home sale exclusion on your entire gain. (This is because you used the entire home as a principal residence for two out of five years before the date of sale.) The home sale exclusion is up to $250,000 ($500,000 on a joint return) of your gain.

If you qualify for the home sale exclusion for the entire home (e.g., you use the office for personal purposes for at least two years before the date of sale), the depreciation you have taken on a home office since May 6, 1997, is "recaptured" at the rate of 25 percent. This means you must report your total depreciation deductions related to home office use after this date and pay tax on the total amount at the rate of 25 percent. If you cannot use the exclusion for the home office portion (e.g., you do not meet the two-year rule), then all depreciation taken on the home office is recaptured at the rate of 25 percent.

WHERE TO DEDUCT HOME OFFICE EXPENSES

Employees

Employees do not compute their home office deduction on Form 8829, Expenses for Business Use of Your Home. Instead, use the special worksheet in IRS Publication 587, which largely follows Form 8829. You will find this worksheet on page 364.

Your home office deduction is entered on Form 2106, Employee Business Expenses, or Form 2106-EZ, Unreimbursed Employee Business Expenses, if you are otherwise allowed to use this form. Then the deductions from Form 2106 or 2106-EZ are entered on Schedule A as miscellaneous itemized deductions subject to the 2-percent-of-adjusted-gross-income floor discussed in Chapter 1.

Remember that if you lease your home to your corporation, you cannot take any home office deductions (other than the mortgage interest, real estate taxes, and casualty and theft losses allowed to all homeowners).

Self-Employed

Self-employed individuals compute home office deductions on Form 8829, Expenses for Business Use of Your Home. This form allows you to calculate the portion of your home used for business. This portion, or percentage, is then used to allocate your home-related expenses. You also use the form to calculate any carryover of unused home office expenses.

If you first begin to use your home office this year and you own your home, you must also complete Form 4562, Depreciation and Amortization, to calculate the depreciation deduction entered on Form 8829. Depreciation is explained in full in Chapter 12. Note that when you begin to use part of your home for business, it is depreciated as nonresidential realty over 39 years (31.5 years if you began home office use before May 13, 1993). You must determine the basis of your home office in order to calculate depreciation. Basis on the conversion of property from personal use to business use is the lesser of the fair market value of the office on the date you begin business use or the adjusted basis of the property on that date. If you are not sure about the fair market value of your home office, get an appraisal. Ask a local real estate agent to assist you in this task.

The home office deduction calculated on Form 8829 is entered on a specific line on Schedule C for expenses for business use of your home. You cannot use Schedule C-EZ, Net Profit From Business, if you claim a home office deduction.

Farmers

Self-employed farmers who file Schedule F instead of Schedule C do not compute home office deductions on Form 8829. Instead, they should calculate these deductions on the worksheet on page 364 in the same way as employees. Then the home office deduction is entered on Schedule F.

Partners and LLC Members

If you use a home office for your business, you figure your deductions in the same way as an employee. Use the worksheet on page 364 (do not use Form 8829 to figure your home office deduction).

Worksheet for Employees to Calculate the Home Office Deduction

Worksheet To Figure the Deduction for Business Use of Your Home

PART 1—Part of Your Home Used for Business:

1) Area of home used for business . . . .   1) _____

2) Total area of home . . . .   2) _____

3) Percentage of home used for business (divide line 1 by line 2 and show result as percentage) . . . .   3) _____ %

PART 2—Figure Your Allowable Deduction

4) Gross income from business (see instructions) . . . .   4) _____

		(a) Direct Expenses	(b) Indirect Expenses
5)	Casualty losses	5) _____	_____
6)	Deductible mortgage interest	6) _____	_____
7)	Real estate taxes	7) _____	_____
8)	Total of lines 5 through 7	8) _____	

9) Multiply line 8, column (b), by line 3 . . . .   9) _____

10) Add line 8, column (a), and line 9 . . . .   10) _____

11) Business expenses not from business use of home (see instructions) . . . . . .   11) _____

12) Add lines 10 and 11 . . . .   12) _____

13) Gross income limit. Subtract line 12 from line 4 . . . .   13) _____

14)	Excess mortgage interest	14) _____	_____
15)	Insurance	15) _____	_____
16)	Repairs and maintenance	16) _____	_____
17)	Utilities	17) _____	_____
18)	Other expenses	18) _____	_____
19)	Add lines 14 through 18	19) _____	_____

20) Multiply line 19, column (b) by line 3 . . . .   20) _____

21) Carryover of operating expenses from prior year (see Instructions) . . . . . .   21) _____

22) Add line 19, column (a), line 20, and line 21 . . . .   22) _____

23) Allowable operating expenses. Enter the **smaller** of line 13 or line 22 . . . .   23) _____

24) Limit on excess casualty losses and depreciation. Subtract line 23 from line 13 . . . . . .   24) _____

25) Excess casualty losses (see instructions) . . . .   25) _____

26) Depreciation of your home from line 38 below . . . .   26) _____

27) Carryover of excess casualty losses and depreciation from prior year (see instructions)   27) _____

28) Add lines 25 through 27 . . . .   28) _____

29) Allowable excess casualty losses and depreciation. Enter the **smaller** of line 24 or line 28 . . . . . .   29) _____

30) Add lines 10, 23, and 29 . . . .   30) _____

31) Casualty losses included on lines 10 and 29 (see instructions) . . . .   31) _____

32) Allowable expenses for business use of your home. (Subtract line 31 from line 30.) See instructions for where to enter on your return . . . .   32) _____

PART 3—Depreciation of Your Home

33) Smaller of adjusted basis or fair market value of home (see instructions) . . . .   33) _____

34) Basis of land . . . .   34) _____

35) Basis of building (subtract line 34 from line 33) . . . .   35) _____

36) Business basis of building (multiply line 35 by line 3) . . . .   36) _____

37) Depreciation percentage (from applicable table or method) . . . .   37) _____

38) Depreciation allowable (multiply line 36 by line 37) . . . .   38) _____

PART 4—Carryover of Unallowed Expenses to Next Year

39) Operating expenses. Subtract line 23 from line 22. If less than zero, enter -0- . . . .   39) _____

40) Excess casualty losses and depreciation. Subtract line 29 from line 28. If less than zero, enter -0- . . . .   40) _____

Form for Self-Employed Individuals to Calculate the Home Office Deduction

Form **8829**	**Expenses for Business Use of Your Home**	OMB No. 1545-1266
Department of the Treasury Internal Revenue Service	▶ **File only with Schedule C (Form 1040). Use a separate Form 8829 for each home you used for business during the year.** ▶ **See separate instructions.**	**19 99** Attachment Sequence No. **66**

Name(s) of proprietor(s) | Your social security number

Part I   Part of Your Home Used for Business

1	Area used regularly and exclusively for business, regularly for day care, or for storage of inventory or product samples. See instructions	1	
2	Total area of home	2	
3	Divide line 1 by line 2. Enter the result as a percentage	3	%

- For day-care facilities not used exclusively for business, also complete lines 4–6.
- All others, skip lines 4–6 and enter the amount from line 3 on line 7.

4	Multiply days used for day care during year by hours used per day	4	hr.
5	Total hours available for use during the year (365 days × 24 hours). See instructions	5	8,760 hr.
6	Divide line 4 by line 5. Enter the result as a decimal amount	6	.
7	Business percentage. For day-care facilities not used exclusively for business, multiply line 6 by line 3 (enter the result as a percentage). All others, enter the amount from line 3 ▶	7	%

Part II   Figure Your Allowable Deduction

8	Enter the amount from Schedule C, line 29, **plus** any net gain or (loss) derived from the business use of your home and shown on Schedule D or Form 4797. If more than one place of business, see instructions			8	

See instructions for columns (a) and (b) before completing lines 9–20.

		(a) Direct expenses	(b) Indirect expenses		
9	Casualty losses. See instructions	9			
10	Deductible mortgage interest. See instructions	10			
11	Real estate taxes. See instructions	11			
12	Add lines 9, 10, and 11	12			
13	Multiply line 12, column (b) by line 7		13		
14	Add line 12, column (a) and line 13			14	
15	Subtract line 14 from line 8. If zero or less, enter -0-			15	
16	Excess mortgage interest. See instructions	16			
17	Insurance	17			
18	Repairs and maintenance	18			
19	Utilities	19			
20	Other expenses. See instructions	20			
21	Add lines 16 through 20	21			
22	Multiply line 21, column (b) by line 7		22		
23	Carryover of operating expenses from 1998 Form 8829, line 41		23		
24	Add line 21 in column (a), line 22, and line 23			24	
25	Allowable operating expenses. Enter the **smaller** of line 15 or line 24			25	
26	Limit on excess casualty losses and depreciation. Subtract line 25 from line 15			26	
27	Excess casualty losses. See instructions		27		
28	Depreciation of your home from Part III below		28		
29	Carryover of excess casualty losses and depreciation from 1998 Form 8829, line 42		29		
30	Add lines 27 through 29			30	
31	Allowable excess casualty losses and depreciation. Enter the **smaller** of line 26 or line 30			31	
32	Add lines 14, 25, and 31			32	
33	Casualty loss portion, if any, from lines 14 and 31. Carry amount to **Form 4684**, Section B			33	
34	Allowable expenses for business use of your home. Subtract line 33 from line 32. Enter here and on Schedule C, line 30. If your home was used for more than one business, see instructions ▶			34	

Part III   Depreciation of Your Home

35	Enter the **smaller** of your home's adjusted basis or its fair market value. See instructions	35	
36	Value of land included on line 35	36	
37	Basis of building. Subtract line 36 from line 35	37	
38	Business basis of building. Multiply line 37 by line 7	38	
39	Depreciation percentage. See instructions	39	%
40	Depreciation allowable. Multiply line 38 by line 39. Enter here and on line 28 above. See instructions	40	

Part IV   Carryover of Unallowed Expenses to 2000

41	Operating expenses. Subtract line 25 from line 24. If less than zero, enter -0-	41	
42	Excess casualty losses and depreciation. Subtract line 31 from line 30. If less than zero, enter -0-	42	

For Paperwork Reduction Act Notice, see page 3 of separate instructions.   Cat. No. 13232M   Form **8829** (1999)

CHAPTER 18

Medical Coverage

Medical coverage is an expensive personal expense for most people. So, for many, a job that provides medical coverage offers an important benefit. For the small business owner there is often a need to obtain personal coverage. It may also be imperative to offer medical coverage as a benefit to attract and keep good employees. A deduction of all or a portion of the cost of medical coverage is a significant cost-saving feature of providing such coverage.

In this chapter you will learn about:

- Deducting medical insurance

- Deducting health insurance for self-employed persons and more-than-2-percent S corporation shareholders

- Using medical reimbursement plans

- Shifting the cost of coverage to employees

- Setting up medical savings accounts

- COBRA coverage

- Where to deduct health insurance

For more information about deducting medical coverage, see IRS Publication 535, Business Expenses, IRS Publication 553, Highlights of 1998 Tax Changes, and IRS Publication 969, Medical Savings Accounts.

DEDUCTING MEDICAL INSURANCE

You are not required to provide medical insurance for employees. If you choose to do so, you can deduct the cost of their group hospitalization and medical insurance. Deductible medical coverage includes premiums for long-term care insurance.

> **Definition** *Long-term care insurance* An insurance contract that provides coverage for long-term care services necessary for diagnostic, preventive, therapeutic, curing, treating, mitigating, and rehabilitative services, as well as maintenance or personal care services required by a chronically ill person and provided pursuant to a plan of care prescribed by a licensed health care practitioner.

Long-term care insurance must:

- Be guaranteed renewable.

- Not provide for a cash surrender value or other money that can be repaid, assigned, pledged, or borrowed.

- Provide that refunds of premiums, other than refunds on the death of the insured or complete surrender or cancellation of the contract, and dividends under the contract may be used to reduce future premiums or increase future benefits.

- Not pay or reimburse expenses incurred for services or items that would be reimbursed under Medicare, except where Medicare is a secondary payer or the contract makes per diem or other periodic payments without regard to expenses.

Medical coverage provided to employees is treated as a tax-free fringe benefit. According to the IRS, medical coverage provided to a domestic partner is taxable to the employee because a domestic partner is not a spouse under state law. However, an employer providing such medical coverage can still deduct it (since the employee is taxed on the cost of coverage for a domestic partner as additional compensation).

The value of long-term care insurance provided through a cafeteria plan or other flexible spending arrangement is not excludable from the employees' income.

You deduct medical premiums according to your method of accounting. If you use the cash method, you generally deduct premiums in the year you pay them. If you are on the accrual method, you generally deduct premiums in the year you incur the liability for them (whether or not you actually pay the bill at that time). The IRS maintains that premiums covering a period of more than one year cannot be deducted except for the portion of the premium that relates to the current year.

You cannot deduct amounts you set aside or put into reserve funds for self-insuring medical costs (see medical reimbursement plans below). However, your actual losses (when you pay for uninsured medical costs) are deductible.

Coverage for retirees.   You are not required to continue providing medical coverage for employees who retire (beyond COBRA requirements discussed below). If you choose to pay for such coverage, you may deduct it. You may terminate your obligation for this coverage as long as you retained the right to do so in any plan or agreement you made to provide the coverage (for example, in an employee's early retirement package).

Special Rules for Partnerships and S Corporations

The business may provide coverage not only for rank-and-file employees but for owners as well. Partnerships and S corporations follow special rules for health insurance coverage provided to owners.

First, partnerships deduct accident and health insurance for their partners as guaranteed payments made to partners. Alternatively, partnerships can choose to treat the payment of premiums on behalf of their partners as a reduction in distributions. In this alternative, the partnership cannot claim a deduction.

S corporations deduct accident and health insurance for its shareholder-employees in the same way as it does for other employees.

Payment of accident and health insurance for a shareholder means the premiums are not treated as wages for purposes of FICA (Social Security and Medicare taxes) if the insurance is provided under a plan or system for employees and their dependents. Of course, even where the payment is not treated as wages for FICA, it is still taxable to the shareholder for income tax purposes.

A partnership or S corporation must report the medical insurance that it provides to owners on the owners' Schedule K-1. This is picked up by the partners and S corporation shareholders as income (unless, in the case of the partnership, the partnership does not claim a deduction). Owners may be entitled to deduct a percentage of health insurance, as explained below.

DEDUCTING HEALTH COVERAGE BY SELF-EMPLOYED PERSONS AND MORE-THAN-2-PERCENT S CORPORATION SHAREHOLDERS

Self-employed persons (sole proprietors, partners, and LLC members), as well as more-than-2-percent S corporation shareholders, may be able to deduct a percentage of the cost of health insurance they buy directly or receive through their business. Health insurance for purposes of the deduction includes the cost of long-term care insurance.

The deductible percentage is:

Year	Percentage
1999–2001	60%
2002	70
2003 and later	100

LEGISLATIVE ALERT

Congress is considering acceleration of full deductibility of medical insurance for the self-employed. If enacted, the 100 percent deduction would apply starting in 2000.

The deduction is taken from gross income on page 1 of Form 1040. This means the deduction is allowed even if the self-employed person does not itemize deductions. (Amounts in excess of this deduction can be taken into account as an itemized medical expense deductible to the extent that medical expenses exceed 7.5 percent of adjusted gross income.)

The deduction cannot exceed the net earnings from the business in which the medical insurance plan is established. For S corporation shareholders, the deduction cannot be more than wages from the corporation (if this was the business in which the insurance plan was established).

You cannot take the deduction for any month if you were eligible to participate in any employer (including your spouse's) subsidized health plan at any time during the month. For example, suppose you are a single, self-employed individual and pay for your own health coverage. On July 1, 1999, you begin a job in which your employer provides you with health insurance. You can deduct the applicable percentage of your health insurance from January 1 through June 30, 1999 (the time you did not receive any subsidized health coverage).

In calculating self-employment tax, do not reduce net earnings from self-employment by your allowable medical insurance deduction.

USING MEDICAL REIMBURSEMENT PLANS

Businesses can set up special plans, called medical reimbursement plans, to pay for medical expenses not otherwise covered by insurance. For example, medical reimbursement plans can pay for the cost of eye care or cover co-payments and other out-of-pocket costs. Medical reimbursement plans are self-insured plans; they are not funded by insurance.

Medical reimbursement plans can cover only employees. These include owners of C corporations (but not S corporations). The plans cannot discriminate in favor of highly compensated employees, such as owners and officers.

The IRS has endorsed a way around the ban on deducting medical costs of self-employed owners. If the business has a medical reimbursement plan for employees and your spouse is an employee (nonowner), the medical reimbursement plan can cover the medical expenses of your spouse-employee and your employee's spouse (you) and dependents. In this way, your medical costs are deductible by the business and are not taxable to you.

Disadvantages

While self-insured medical reimbursement plans provide advantages to employers, there is a significant risk of substantial economic exposure (that claims will run higher than anticipated and planned for). This problem can be addressed by setting a dollar limit (such as $2,500) on medical reimbursements for the year.

Another disadvantage to this type of plan is the administration involved (reviewing and processing reimbursement claims). For a very small employer, however, this may not be significant.

SHIFTING THE COST OF COVERAGE TO EMPLOYEES

Health insurance is increasingly costly to employers. There are several ways in which business owners can reduce their costs without putting employees out in the cold.

Sharing the cost of premiums   Instead of employers paying the entire cost of insurance, employers can shift a portion of the cost to employees. For example, employers may provide free coverage for employees but shift the cost of spousal and dependent care coverage to employees.

Flexible spending arrangements (FSAs)   Businesses can set up these plans to allow employees to decide how much they want to pay for medical expenses. These arrangements allow employees to pay for medical expenses on a pretax basis. At the beginning of the year, they agree to a salary reduction amount that funds their FSA. Contributions to an FSA are not treated as taxable compensation (and are not subject to FICA). Employees then use the amount in their FSA to pay for most types of medical-related costs, such as medical premiums, orthodontia, or other expenses during the year not covered by medical insurance. FSAs cannot be used to pay for cosmetic surgery unless it is required for medical purposes (such as to correct a birth defect).

EXAMPLE: Employee A agrees to a monthly salary reduction amount of $100. This means that A has $1,200 during the year to spend on medical costs.

The downside to employers is that employees can use all of their promised contributions for the year whenever they submit proof of medical expenses. This means that if employees leave employment after taking funds out of their FSA but before they have fully funded them, the employer winds up paying the difference. So, for example, if an employee who promises to contribute $100 per month submits a bill for dental expenses of $1,200 on January 15 and leaves employment shortly thereafter, the employee has contributed only $100; the employer must bear the cost of the additional $1,100 submission.

Of course, the flip side benefits the employer. If employees fail to use up their FSA contributions before the end of the year (referred to as the "use it or lose it" rule), the employer keeps the difference. Nothing is refunded to the employees.

LEGISLATIVE ALERT

Congress is considering expansion of FSAs to include long-term care insurance. If enacted, the change would apply starting in 2001.

Cafeteria Plans

Employers can give employees a choice of benefits by setting up cafeteria plans. This makes sense for some employers, since cafeteria plans allow working couples to get the benefits they need without needless overlap. For example, if one spouse has health insurance coverage from his employer, the other spouse can select dependent care assistance or other benefits offered through a cafeteria plan. Cafeteria plans do not require employees to reduce salary or make contributions to pay for benefits. Benefits are paid by the employer.

Premium-Only Plans

In these plans, employees choose between health coverage or salary. If they select the coverage, it is paid by means of salary reduction. In effect, employees are paying for their own coverage, but with pre-tax dollars. The employer deducts the compensation (whether the employee chooses the coverage or takes the salary). The only cost to the employer under this type of plan is the cost of administering it. (Many payroll service companies will administer the plan for a modest charge.) Bonus: Both the employer and employee save on FICA if the medical coverage is chosen.

Note: Medical savings accounts (explained below) cannot be part of cafeteria plans.

SETTING UP MEDICAL SAVINGS ACCOUNTS

Employers can choose to provide the least costly medical insurance to employees (called "high deductible" insurance plans). They can then contribute to special savings accounts of employees to pay for needed medical expenses. Alternatively, they can simply let employees make their own contributions to MSAs.

Businesses that maintain "high-deductible" health insurance plans may contribute (within limits) to medical savings accounts for employees. These accounts are similar in concept to IRAs: They allow employees to save for medical expenses. Employees can use amounts in their MSAs as they see fit (to pay for uninsured medical costs or otherwise). Payments of uninsured medical expenses are tax-free; payments of other items are taxable. What is more, payments of other items by those under age 65 are subject to penalty.

Eligibility

MSAs are open only to small employers (those with 50 or fewer employees) and self-employed individuals with "high-deductible" plans. In 1999, they are health insurance plans with an annual deductible between $3,050 and $4,550 for family coverage, or $1,550 and $2,300 for single coverage. The health insurance must have an annual cost on out-of-pocket expenses of $5,600 or less for families, or $3,050 or less for singles.

Note: MSAs are a four-year pilot program open to a limited number of participants. It is set to expire at the end of 2000.

LEGISLATIVE ALERT

There has been a proposal in Congress to greatly expand the use of medical savings accounts. If enacted, MSAs would become permanent and could be offered as part of a cafeteria plan. Also, the deduction would be increased to 100 percent of the deductible under high-deductible plans starting in 2001.

Contributions

Employer contributions to MSAs for employees are not taxable to employees. Contributions are limited to 75 percent of the annual deductible for family coverage or 65 percent of the annual deductible for single coverage. Thus, the 1999 contribution ranges are $2,287 and $3,412 for family coverage and between $1007 to $1,495 for single coverage.

EXAMPLE: You maintain a high-deductible plan for your employees. The deductible under your insurance plan is $4,000 for family coverage and $2,000 for singles. Your contributions are limited to $3,000 ($4,000 × 75%) for employees with family coverage and $1,300 ($2,000 × 65%) for those with single coverage.

If a high-deductible plan is not in place for the entire year, the contribution is limited to the ratable portion of the annual deductible for the time the plan is in effect.

Note: These same contribution limits apply to employees and self-employed individuals who make contributions on their own behalf. Personal contributions within these limits are deductible.

Contributions to MSAs must be made in cash (they cannot be made in the form of stock or other property). The contributions must be made no later than the due date of the return (without regard to extensions).

Contributions can only be made on behalf of individuals who are under age 65. However, those 65 and older now have the option of selecting Medicare-MSAs under a Medicare+Choice coverage alternative to traditional Medicare (called "fee for service"). Medicare-MSAs are not funded by employers nor self-employed individuals; they are funded by contributions from the government. Thus, Medicare-MSAs will not generate any tax deductions for small businesses nor self-employed individuals.

COBRA COVERAGE

Employers who normally employ 20 or more employees and who provide coverage for employees must extend continuation coverage (referred to as COBRA—the initials for the law that created continuation coverage). COBRA entitles employees who are terminated (whether voluntarily or otherwise) to pay for continued coverage of what they received while employed. COBRA also covers families of deceased employees and former spouses of divorced employees. COBRA coverage generally applies for 18 months (36 months in some cases).

Employers can charge for COBRA coverage but only up to a set limit. This is the cost of the coverage to the employer plus an administrative fee. The limit on the total cost to the individual for COBRA coverage is 102 percent of the cost of the insurance.

Employers who fail to provide COBRA and/or to provide proper notice of COBRA can be subject to a substantial penalty.

Note: COBRA does not include the cost of long-term care insurance.

WHERE TO DEDUCT HEALTH INSURANCE

Employees

If you pay for your own health insurance, you can deduct premiums only as an itemized deduction on Schedule A. Premiums, along with other unreimbursed medical expenses, are deductible only to the extent they exceed 7.5 percent of adjusted gross income.

MSA contributions are treated separately from other medical expenses. If you make contributions to MSAs, they are deductible on page 1 of Form 1040 (regardless of whether you itemize your other deductibles). You must complete Form 8853 to claim a deduction for MSA contributions.

Self-Employed

Coverage provided to employees is fully deductible on Schedule C (or Schedule F for farming operations). The allowable percentage of coverage for the self-employed person is deducted on page 1 of Form 1040.

Contributions to MSAs on your own behalf are also deductible on page 1 of Form 1040. You must complete Form 8853 to claim a deduction for MSA contributions.

Partnerships and LLCs

Insurance paid by the partnership is deducted on Form 1065. Coverage for partners is included in guaranteed payments and reported to them on Schedule K-1. If the partnership chooses to treat the payment of insurance premiums for partners as a reduction in distributions, no deduction can be claimed.

The allowable percentage of coverage for partners is deducted on page 1 of their individual returns (Form 1040). You must complete Form 8853 to claim a deduction for MSA contributions.

S Corporations

Insurance paid by the S corporation is deducted on Form 1120S. Coverage for more-than-2-percent S corporation shareholders is reported to them on Schedule K-1.

The allowable percentage of coverage for more-than-2-percent S corporation shareholders is deducted on page 1 of their individual returns (Form 1040). You must complete Form 8853 to claim a deduction for MSA contributions.

C Corporations

Insurance paid by the corporation is deducted on Form 1120.

CHAPTER 19

Deductions for Farmers

B usiness owners engaged in farming activities may be entitled to special deductions not claimed by other businesses. These special deductions are in addition to the same types of deductions that other business owners enjoy. A "farm" includes stock, dairy, poultry, fish, fruit, and truck farms. Thus, it encompasses plantations, ranches, ranges, and orchards.

Farmers have been given these special rules in recognition of their unique business arrangements and to make their tax reporting easier. Some of these rules have been highlighted in other parts of this book. For example, farmers (other than farming syndicates) generally are allowed to use the cash method of accounting to report their income and expenses.

In this chapter you will learn about:

- Farm expenses

- Farm losses

- Farm-related tax credits

- Nondeductible farm-related expenses

For further information about deducting farming expenses, see IRS Publication 225, Farmer's Tax Guide.

FARM EXPENSES

Ordinary and necessary business expenses related to farming generally are deductible. The *timing* of the deduction generally is determined by your method of accounting (cash or accrual). However, in addition to the types of expenses claimed by nonfarm businesses, farmers may be able to claim deductions for expenses unique to farming activities and in ways more favorable than general tax rules would allow.

Prepaid Farm Supplies

If you are on the cash method of accounting, expenses generally are deductible when paid. However, if you prepay farm supplies, they must be deducted ratably over the period during which they will be used *unless* you qualify for an exception to this prepayment rule.

Prepaid farm supplies include amounts paid for:

- Feed, seed, fertilizer, and similar farming supplies not consumed during the year (other than what is on hand at the end of the year but would have been consumed had it not been for fire, storm, flood, drought, disease, or other casualty).

- Poultry bought for use in your farm business that would be deductible in the following year if you had capitalized the cost and deducted it ratably over the lesser of 12 months or the useful life of the poultry.

- Poultry bought for resale and not resold during the year.

Prepaid farm expenses are deductible to the extent they do not exceed 50 percent of other deductible farm expenses in the year (including depreciation and amortization). Any prepaid expenses in excess of this limit are deductible in the following year.

EXAMPLE: In 1999, you bought fertilizer ($4,500), feed ($1,500), and seed ($750) for use in the following year for a total of $6,750. Your other farm expenses in 1999 total $12,000. You can deduct prepaid expenses up to $6,000 (50% of $12,000). The excess $750 is deductible in 2000, the year in which such items will be consumed.

If you are a "farm-related taxpayer" (your main home is a farm, your principal business is farming, or a member of your family lives on the farm or has farming as his or her principal business), you are not subject to the 50 percent limit if:

- Your prepaid farm supplies expense is more than 50 percent of your other deductible farm expenses because of a change in business operations caused by unusual circumstances, or

- Your total prepaid farm supplies expense for the preceding three years is less than 50 percent of your total other deductible farm expenses for those three years.

Livestock Feed

Generally, even though you are on the cash basis, feed must be deducted in the year in which your livestock consumes it. However, if you meet all of the following three tests for the *advance payment of feed,* you can deduct in the year of payment the cost of feed your livestock will consume in a later year (subject to the prepaid farm supplies limit above):

- The expense is a payment for the purchase of feed and not a deposit. A binding contract for delivery shows this is *not* a deposit.

- The prepayment has a business purchase and is not merely a tax avoidance scheme. A business purpose would include securing more favorable payment terms and prices.

- The deduction of these costs does not result in a material distortion of income. For example, if this is your customary practice, then the deduction will have roughly the same impact on your income each year and will not produce a material distortion.

This limit on deducting the advance payment of feed does not apply to the purchase of commodity futures contracts.

Labor and Related Costs

You can deduct reasonable wages you pay for regular farm labor, piecework, contract labor, and other forms of labor hired to work your farm. This includes payments to your spouse or child as long as there is a true employer-employee relationship.

You can also deduct related costs including:

- The cost of maintaining houses and their furnishings for tenants or hired help (including heat, light, insurance, depreciation, and repairs).

- Insurance related to the workers (such as health insurance and workers compensation).

- Employer's share of FICA on farm wages.

You must reduce your deduction for wages by any employment tax credits you may be entitled to claim on such wages. These credits are explained in Chapter 5.

Breeding Fees

Cash method farmers may deduct breeding fees as a farm business expense. Accrual method farmers must capitalize such fees and allocate them to the cost basis of the calf, foal, and so on to which they relate.

Fertilizer and Lime

You have a choice on when to deduct the cost of fertilizer and lime used to enrich, neutralize, or enhance farm land:

- Deduct it in the year you paid or incurred the expense (subject to the prepaid farm supplies rule discussed earlier in this chapter) or

- If the benefit from the material lasts more than one year, you can capitalize the cost and deduct a part of it each year in which the benefit lasts.

After you make your choice, you cannot change your reporting method without IRS consent.

Depreciation

Property used in farming generally is subject to the same depreciation rules as property used in nonfarm businesses. The rules for depreciation are discussed in Chapter 12. However, certain farming property has special recovery periods. The following shows the recovery periods for property used in farming:

Type of property	General Depreciation System	Alternate Depreciation System
Agricultural structures (single purpose)	10	15
Airplanes and helicopters	5	6
Cattle (dairy or breeding)	5	7
Cotton-ginning assets	7	12
Drainage facilities	15	20
Farm building (other than single purpose)	20	25
Fences (agricultural)	7	10
Goats and sheep (breeding)	5	5
Grain bins	7	10
Hogs (breeding)	3	3
Horses (age when placed in service)		
Breeding and working (12 years or less)	7	10
Breeding and working (more than 12 years)	3	10
Race horses (more than 2 years)	3	12
Horticultural structures (single purpose)	10	15
Logging equipment and machinery	5	6
Machinery and equipment (nonlogging)	7	10
Tractor units (over-the-road)	3	4
Trees or vines bearing fruit or nuts	10	20

Type of property	General Depreciation System	Alternate Depreciation System
Truck		
Unloaded weight 13,000 lb. or more	5	6
Weight less than 13,000 lb.	5	5
Waterwells	15	20

Instead of depreciating certain farm-related property, you may claim a first-year expense deduction. The limit for 1999 is $19,000. In addition to equipment and machinery used in farming, this deduction can be taken with respect to single-purpose agricultural or horticultural structures, grain bins, and drainage facilities.

Soil and Water Conservation Expenses

Generally, soil and water conservation expenses must be capitalized. However, you can elect to deduct such expenses within limits. The deduction cannot be more than 25 percent of gross income from farming. Expenses must be consistent with a plan approved by the Natural Resources Conservation Service (NRCS) of the Department of Agriculture or a comparable state agency.

Expenses eligible for this special write-off include costs for:

- Treating or moving earth (e.g., leveling, conditioning, grading, terracing, contour furrowing, and restoration of soil fertility).

- Constructing, controlling, and protecting diversion channels, drainage or irrigation ditches, earthen dams, watercourses, outlets, and ponds.

- Eradicating brush.

- Planting windbreaks.

They also include assessments by conservation districts for any of these expenses (but not more than 10 percent of your deductible share plus $500 and subject to the total limitation).

Reforestation Expenses

You can elect to amortize qualified reforestation expenses over a period of up to 84 months. The election applies each year to property with a basis up to $10,000 ($5,000 if you are married and file separately). Expenses in excess of this amount are added to the basis of your property.

The top annual amortization deduction each year is $1,428.57 ($10,000 ÷ 7). However, for the first and eighth years, the deduction is one half of $1,428.57, or $714.29.

The election is made on Form 4562, Depreciation and Amortization. You also attach a statement to your return describing your reforestation expenses and the dates you incurred them.

Miscellaneous Expenses

Ordinary and necessary business expenses common to all businesses (for example, advertising cost or attorney's fees) are deductible. Other expenses specific to farming activities that may be deductible as ordinary and necessary expenses include:

- Chemicals

- Fuels and oil

- Freight and trucking

- Ginning

- Insect sprays and dusts

- Litter and bedding

- Livestock fees

- Storage and warehousing

- Tying materials and containers

- Veterinary fees and medicine

FARM LOSSES

If your deductible farm expenses exceed your farm income, you have a loss from the operation of your farm. The amount you can deduct of your farm loss may be limited by a number of rules. These rules are explained in greater detail in Chapter 3. However, consider here how these rules may especially impact on farming activities:

Passive activity rules Losses from an activity in which you do not materially participate and any rental activity cannot exceed your income from passive activities. Thus, if you own the farm but do not work it yourself, you may not be able to deduct your losses.

At-risk rules These rules, which limit your deduction for losses to your economic investment, apply to farming activities in the same way in which they apply to nonfarming activities.

Hobby loss rules If you are not engaged in the farming activity with a realistic profit motive, then your losses are not deductible. They do not carryover to another year; they are gone forever. There is considerable litigation each year involving "gentlemen farmers" and their success in deducting losses depends on demonstrating a profit motive.

Net Operating Losses

Farmers are subject to special rules for net operating loss carrybacks. For losses incurred in 1999, instead of the two-year carryback applicable to most other businesses, farmers can use a five-year carryback for farming losses. However, there is a three-year carryback for the part of the NOL attributable to a presidentially declared disaster or a casualty or theft loss.

You can choose to forego the carryback and simply carryforward the loss for up to 20 years. There is no special carryforward period for farmers.

For farms operated through a partnership or S corporation, the losses pass through to the owners who claim the NOLs on their individual returns.

Net operating losses—figuring them and claiming quick refunds—are discussed in greater detail in Chapter 20.

FARM-RELATED TAX CREDITS

Farmers may be entitled to claim the same tax credits available to other businesses. For example, if they pay wages to certain types of workers, they may be eligible to claim employment credits. These credits are discussed in Chapter 5.

Farm-Related Credits

In addition to credits available to nonfarm businesses, certain credits may be unique (or more relevant) to farmers. These include:

Credit for kerosene for household use   The credit is the amount of excise tax paid on kerosene used in your home for heating, lighting, and cooking.

Credit for federal tax paid on fuels   The credit is the amount of excise tax paid on gasoline, special motor fuels, and compressed natural gas used on a farm for farming purposes. Farmers may not claim a credit or refund for undyed diesel fuel or undyed kerosene. (The credit is allowed only to the ultimate vendor, a seller registered with the IRS to sell such fuel to the user of the fuel.)

Credit for fuels used in off-highway business use   The credit is for the amount of excise tax paid on fuels used in running stationery machines (such as generators), for cleaning purposes, or in other vehicles not registered for highway use. However, if undyed diesel fuel or undyed kerosene is used on a farm, the fuel is not considered as being used in a off-highway vehicle.

Claiming a Credit or Refund

You can claim the above credits for fuel-related excise taxes on your income tax return. The credits are claimed on Form 4136. Alternatively, you can claim a refund of the excise taxes you already paid. The claim for refund can be made for any quarter of your tax year for which you can claim $750 or more.

If for any quarter the excise tax paid on all fuels used for qualifying purposes is less than $750, you carry the amount over to the next quarter of your tax year to determine if you can claim at least $750 for that quarter. If you cannot claim at least $750 at the end of the fourth quarter of your tax year, you must claim a credit on your income tax return.

You can use Form 8849 to file a claim for refund. If you file Form 720, you can use the Schedule C portion of Form 720 for your claims, rather than Form 8849.

You must file a quarterly claim by the last day of the first quarter following the end of the last quarter included in the claim. If you do not file a timely refund claim for the fourth quarter of your tax year, you will have to claim a credit for that amount on your income tax return.

If you claimed taxes as an expense deduction that reduced your income, you must now include any credit or refund of excise taxes on fuels.

EXAMPLE: A cash basis farmer filed his 1998 return on April 15, 1999, on which he deducted gasoline that included $110 of excise tax. He then claimed a credit of $110 for excise tax paid on fuel. The $110 is reported as additional income in 1999.

Waiver of the Right to Claim a Credit or Refund

If fertilizer or pesticides are applied to your farm aerially or otherwise, you can waive your right to claim a credit or fund. The waiver allows the applicator to claim the credit or refund. (You may even be required to make the waiver as part of your contract with the applicator.)

To make a waiver, you must sign an irrevocable statement knowingly giving up your right to the credit or refund. The statement must clearly identify the period covered by the waiver. The waiver must be signed before the applicator files his or her return. A sample Waiver is reproduced on page 386.

Exemption from Excise Tax on Fuels

As a farmer, you can buy diesel fuel and kerosene excise tax free (and so are not eligible to claim any credit with respect to these fuels). To obtain tax exemption, you must provide the vendor with a signed certificate and keep a copy of it with your other business records. A sample Exemption Certificate is reproduced on page 387.

For more information about these special tax credits, see IRS Publication 378, Fuel Tax Credits and Refunds.

NONDEDUCTIBLE FARM-RELATED EXPENSES

Not every expense arising on the farm can be written off. Some expenses are personal in nature and are nondeductible. Other expenses may be subject to limitations. Nondeductible expenses include:

- Personal or living expenses (such as taxes, insurance, and repairs to the home) that do not produce farm income. If you pay expenses (such as electricity) that is used for both personal and farm purposes, you must allocate the expenses accordingly (and deduct only the farm portion). While personal expenses are not deductible, there

Sample Waiver

WAIVER OF RIGHT TO CREDIT OR REFUND

I hereby waive my right as owner, tenant, or operator of a farm located at:

_____

Address

to receive credit or refund for fuel used by:

_____

Name of Applicator

on the farm in connection with cultivating the soil, or the raising or harvesting of any agricultural or horticultural commodity. This waiver applies to fuel used during the period:

_____

Both Dates Inclusive

I understand that by signing this waiver, I give up my right to claim any credit or refund for fuel used by the aerial applicator or other applicator of fertilizer or other substances during the period indicated, and I acknowledge that I have not previously claimed any credit for that fuel.

_____

Signature

_____

Date

Sample Exemption Certificate

EXEMPTION CERTIFICATE

(To support vendor's claim for credit or payment under section 6427 of the Internal Revenue Code)

_____

Name, Address, and Employer Identification Number of Seller

The undersigned buyer ("Buyer") hereby certifies the following under penalties of perjury:

A. Buyer will use the diesel fuel to which this certificate relates either — (check one):

1. ☐ On a farm for farming purposes (as defined in §48.6420-4 of the Manufacturers and Retailers Excise Tax Regulations)(and Buyer is the owner, tenant, or operator of the farm on which the fuel will be used).

2. ☐ On a farm (as defined in §48.6420-4(c)) for any of the purposes described in ¶ (d) of that section (relating to cultivating, raising, or harvesting)(and Buyer is not the owner, tenant, or operator of the farm on which the fuel will be used).

B. This certificate applies to the following (complete as applicable):

1. If this is a single purchase certificate, check here ☐ and enter:

   a. Invoice or delivery ticket number _____

   b. Number of gallons _____

2. If this is a certificate covering all purchases under a specified account or order number, check here ☐ and enter:

   a. Effective date _____

   b. Expiration date _____
   (period not to exceed 1 year after effective date)

   c. Buyer account or order number _____

■ Buyer will provide a new certificate to the seller if any information in this certificate changes.

■ If Buyer uses the diesel fuel to which this certificate relates for a purpose other than stated in the certificate Buyer will be liable for any tax.

■ Buyer understands that the fraudulent use of this certificate may subject Buyer and all parties making such fraudulent use of this certificate to a fine or imprisonment, or both, together with the costs of prosecution.

_____

Signature and Date Signed

_____

Printed or Typed Name and Title of Person Signing

_____

Name, Address, and Employer Identification Number of Buyer is one exception. You may claim a tax credit for the excise tax on kerosene used in your home for heating, lighting, and cooking (discussed earlier in this chapter). Also, a portion of the home may qualify for a home office deduction as discussed in Chapter 17.

- Expenses of raising anything consumed by you and your family.

- The value of animals or crops you raised that died. The costs of raising the animals or crops were separately deductible (under the rules discussed throughout this chapter).

- Cost of raising unharvested crops sold with land owned more than one year if you sell both at the same time to the same person. Instead, add these costs to the basis of the land for purposes of determining your gain or loss on the sale. Similarly, the cost of unharvested crop you buy with land is added to the purchase price of the land. This cost is then taken into account to determine your profit (or loss) when you later sell the land.

- Fines and penalties. However, penalties you pay for exceeding marketing quotas are deductible. If such penalties are paid by the purchaser of your crop, you simply report the net amount you receive as income (you do not claim a separate deduction for the penalties).

WHERE TO DEDUCT FARMING EXPENSES

Self-Employed
Farming expenses are deductible in Part II of Schedule F. There are specific lines for various types of farming expenses. There is also a "catchall" line for reporting "other expenses." If there are more than six "other expenses," attach a statement to the return listing these other deductions.

Partnerships and LLCs
Farming expenses are deductible in Part II of Schedule F. There are specific lines for various types of farming expenses. There is also a "catchall" line for reporting "other expenses." Then Schedule F is attached to the partnership return, Form 1065.

Most expenses are not separately stated items passed through to partners and members. They are simply part of the entity's ordinary business income or loss. Therefore partners and members in LLCs report their net income or loss from the farm on Schedule E.

S Corporations

Farms operated as S corporations claim deductions on the corporation's return, Form 1120. Most expenses are not separately stated items passed through to shareholders. They are simply part of the corporation's ordinary business income or loss. Therefore shareholders report their net income or loss from the farm on Schedule E.

C Corporations

Farms operated as C corporations report their expenses on the corporation's return, Form 1120. This form contains separate lines for deducting certain costs. Other costs must be reported on the catchall line for "other deductions" with an explanation attached. Shareholders do not report any income (or loss) from the corporation.

All Taxpayers

The credit for federal tax on fuels is figured on Form 4136, Credit for Federal Tax Paid on Fuels.

Instead of claiming the credit on the current return, taxpayers may be entitled to a refund. The refund is claimed on Form 8849, Claim for Refund of Excise Taxes.

CHAPTER 20

Miscellaneous Business
Deductions

S ome miscellaneous business items defy classification. Still, you may
be able to deduct them. In this chapter you will learn about:

- Other business expenses in general

- Job-seeking expenses

- Moving expenses

- Educational expenses

- Charitable contributions made by your business

- Dues and subscriptions

- Legal and professional fees

- Supplies, materials, and uniforms

- Insurance

- Payments to directors and independent contractors

- Penalties, fines, and damages

- Expenses of disabled persons

- The dividends-received deduction

- Net operating losses

- Aborted business ventures

- Expenses of winding up a small business

- Checklists of deductible and nondeductible expenses

- Where to deduct miscellaneous business expenses

Some of these deductions apply only to individuals; others apply only to corporations. Review all of the categories to see which deductions may apply to you.

For more information on other business expenses, see IRS Publication 535, *Business Expenses*.

OTHER BUSINESS EXPENSES IN GENERAL

You generally can deduct any business expense if it is considered ordinary and necessary. It need not fit neatly into a specific category as long as it meets three tests:

- The expense must be related to the business you carry on (be it employment or a business you own).

- The expense cannot be a capital expenditure. Capital expenditures are costs related to the acquisition of a capital asset. For example, you cannot deduct the cost of improvements to property. These costs are capital in nature. However, some capital expenditures can be recovered through deductions for depreciation or amortization; see Chapter 8.

- The expense must be ordinary and necessary.

Definition   *Ordinary*   Common and accepted in your business.

Definition   *Necessary*   Helpful or appropriate to your business. To be necessary, an expense need not be indispensable. For example, if you send flowers to your employee in the hospital, you may deduct the cost of the flowers.

Another requirement that applies to all deductions in general is that the expenses must be reasonable in amount. What is reasonable is a question of fact based on the particular situation.

Checklists of various miscellaneous deductions related to your business status can be found toward the end of this chapter.

JOB-SEEKING EXPENSES

Being an employee is treated as a trade or business. It is considered to be the business of being an employee. Therefore certain expenses related to getting a job may be deductible as ordinary and necessary business expenses. These include:

- Cost of résumés

- Postage and telephone charges

- Travel costs for interviews

- Career counseling

- Advertising your availability in a newspaper or magazine

These costs are deductible if you are already in a job and are seeking a new one. If you lost your job because you quit, you were fired, or your company downsized, you can still deduct these expenses as long as you are still in the business of being an employee. You cannot deduct these expenses if you have been out of the job market for many years, because you are no longer considered to be in the business of being an employee. Thus, for example, women who return to the job market after a number of years of staying home to raise children cannot treat their job-hunting costs as deductible business expenses.

You cannot deduct the expenses of obtaining your first job. You are not yet in the business of being an employee.

If you are laid off and receive outplacement services from your former employer (such as office spouse and résumé counseling), you need not include this benefit in income. It is treated as a tax-free fringe benefit. If you pay for these services yourself, they are deductible.

If you receive reimbursement from a prospective employer for the costs of traveling to an interview, you cannot deduct your costs. But the good news is that you are not taxed on the reimbursement.

Employer Reimbursements and Outplacement Services

If you are an employer and reimburse a prospective employee for the costs of traveling to an interview, you can deduct the allowance as a business expense. You do not have to treat the reimbursement as wages or as payments subject to employment taxes.

If you provide outplacement services for discharged employees to help them find new employment, you can deduct your costs as a business expense. Some of your costs may fall into specific deduction categories. For example, if you rent a separate office for use by discharged employees looking for new employment, you treat the cost of the office as a rental deduction. Utilities related to the office are deducted along with other utility costs.

MOVING EXPENSES

If you move your business to another location (for example, you relocate your offices to larger quarters) or you move equipment to another location (for example, you move machinery from one plant to another), your moving costs are deductible. There is no requirement that your new location be any special distance from the old one.

In general, if you personally move from one home to another, you cannot deduct the cost of moving your furnishings and family, because these are personal expenses. However, if you relocate because of a change in jobs or a new business, you may be able to deduct your moving expenses. The tax law allows a deduction for moving expenses for certain job-related moves.

To claim deductible moving expenses, you must show three things:

- That your move was of a sufficient distance ("distance test")

- That you worked at your new location for the required length of time (or were prevented from doing so) ("time test")

- If you are an employee, that your expenses are not paid or reimbursed by your employer

Distance Test

The distance between your new job or business location and your former home must be at least 50 miles more than the distance between your old job or business location and your former home. If you move to another city or state, generally you have no difficulty in satisfying the distance test. Where you simply move across town, be sure that the move is of a sufficient distance to make your expenses deductible.

EXAMPLE: You take a job in the same metropolitan area, but way across town. You move to an apartment in the part of town in which your new job is located. The distance between your new job location and your former home is 57 miles. The distance between your old job location and your former home is 5 miles. The distance test is met because the difference is at least 50 miles (57 miles − 5 miles = 52 miles).

In calculating the distance test, use the most commonly traveled routes between locations. You need not measure distance "as the crow flies."

What if you have been out of work a long time or you are changing from part-time to full-time employment? In this case, the new job location must be at least 50 miles from your former home.

Usually the distance between your new home and job locations is not considered. However, if the distance between your new home and new job location is more than the distance between your old home and new job location, you may not be able to deduct your moving expenses. The only way to deduct moving expenses in this situation is to show that you are required to live in your new home as a condition of employment or the move results in an actual decrease in commuting time or expense.

Work in Your New Location ("Time Test")

If you are an employee, you must remain on the job at your new location for at least 39 weeks during the 12-month period that starts with your arrival at the new location. You need not stay with the same employer for all those weeks. You can get another job in the same location and deduct moving expenses as long as the total employment time is at least 39 weeks. In general, only full-time employment is used to satisfy the 39-week requirement, although there is a special rule for certain seasonal employment.

If you are laid off or fired from your employment without any willful misconduct on your part, the 39-week test is waived. The time test is also waived if you fail to meet the 39-week requirement because of circumstances beyond your control—strikes, temporary absences, illness, natural disasters, and such. The time is waived if you are transferred from your new job to another location for your employer's benefit. According to the IRS, this waiver does not apply if you request a transfer for your benefit.

The waiver does not apply if you resign, are fired for willful misconduct, or reach the mandatory retirement age of your new employment where you anticipated this retirement.

If you are self-employed or a partner or LLC member, there is a 78-week test. You must work full-time in your business for 78 weeks in a 24-month period beginning with the move to the new location. At least 39 weeks must occur within the first 12 months of arrival.

You need not wait out the time requirements before claiming the deduction for moving expenses. You can deduct your costs in the year of the move under the assumption that you will meet the time test. If you do not (for example, if you move again before the end of the 39 or 78 weeks), then you must report your deduction as income in the subsequent year. Alternatively, you can amend the earlier return to delete the deduction for moving expenses.

If you are not sure whether you will meet the time test, you can instead file your return for the year of the move without the deduction and then amend it after the time test has been satisfied.

Change in employment status   If you change your employment status to that of an employee (for example, if you shut down your business and find a job in your new location), you need only meet the 39-week test. If you change your employment status from employee to self-employed person before satisfying the 39-week test, you must meet the 78-week test to deduct moving expenses.

Deductible Moving Expenses

Only certain moving expenses are deductible. You may deduct the actual cost of moving your household goods and personal effects. What constitutes a "personal effect" has been rather liberally interpreted. For example, one taxpayer was able to deduct moving costs for a sailboat. The cost of packing, crating, and transporting furniture, the related insurance, and some storage costs are examples of deductible expenses.

You can also deduct the travel costs for you and members of your household. You need not all travel together. For example, you may relocate immediately and your family may follow when your old home is sold or when the school year ends. Keep track of all transportation expenses for you and members of your household.

Travel costs include transportation and lodging to get from your old home to your new one. If you travel by your car, you can use a standard mileage allowance of 10 cents per mile, plus tolls and parking. Alternatively, you can deduct your actual expenses for gas, oil, and repairs on the trip, plus tolls and parking. You cannot deduct the cost of meals on the trip from your old home to your new home.

If your employer pays your moving expenses or you receive reimbursement from your employer, you cannot deduct your costs. Your employer will not include the reimbursements in your income if the employer believes that you would have been entitled to a deduction had you not received reimbursement.

EDUCATIONAL EXPENSES

If you take educational courses, you may be able deduct their cost as a business expense (or you may qualify for new tax credits, explained below under personal education incentives). The tax law clearly states what types of educational courses are deductible and what types are not.

You can deduct education courses that are primarily undertaken to:

- **Maintain or improve skills required in your employment or in your business.** If you have been away from the job market for some time, you may no longer be considered in a business (the business of being an employee). In this case, education costs are not deductible.

- **Meet the requirements of an employer or applicable law or regulations imposed as a condition of retaining your salary, status, or employment.** For example, continuing professional education courses are deductible as business expenses.

You cannot deduct education courses designed to:

- **Meet minimum educational requirements.** This precludes you from deducting the cost of obtaining any professional degree in law, accounting, medicine, or dentistry. The fact that you may already be performing service in an employment status within the profession does not necessarily mean that you have met the minimum education requirements. For example, if a second-year law student is hired to do research, the cost of the third year of law school is not a deductible education expense since the student has not yet met the minimum education requirements to practice law (three years of law school and admission to the bar). If new minimum requirements are imposed after you have met old minimum requirements, however, the cost of taking the additional courses is deductible.

- **Qualify you for a new business.** A mere change in duties is not treated as a new business if it involves the same general type of work. For example, all teaching and related duties are treated as the same general type of work. However, if the education qualifies you for a new business, you cannot deduct courses even though you intend to remain in your old line of work. For example, a CPA who attends law school at night cannot deduct the cost of courses, since this leads to a new line of work—law. This is so even if the CPA never plans to practice law. A bookkeeper who takes courses to get a B.A. in accounting cannot deduct education expenses because the courses lead to a new business of being an accountant. However, a practicing attorney who takes courses toward an LL.M. can deduct expenses because the courses do not lead to a new line of work.

- **Relate to something that does not pertain directly to your business.** For example, an attorney could not deduct the cost of an English course that he argued would help him write better briefs. The courses were not directly related to his business of law even though they were helpful to his work.

Note: You cannot deduct your education costs if you claim an education credit for the same expenses, as explained below.

Deductible Expenses

If education costs are deductible, the following types of expenses may be deducted:

- Tuition and fees

- Books

- Travel costs to and from school. This includes the cost of going to or from home to school, as well as travel between work and school. If you attend a seminar at a resort, see Chapter 6 to determine whether or to what extent you may deduct your education-related travel costs.

However, you may not deduct the cost of travel as a form of education. Thus, for example, an architect cannot deduct the cost of a trip to Rome to look at ancient Roman architecture as an educational expense.

Employer-Paid Education

If your employer pays for the cost of your courses, you cannot also take a deduction. Employer-provided education may be a tax-free fringe benefit on which you are not taxed. Such benefits are discussed in Chapter 5. If you have a C corporation and the corporation pays your education costs, the corporation can deduct the costs whether or not you are taxed on the benefits.

Personal Education Incentives

There are a number of personal tax incentives designed to encourage higher education. Here are some to consider:

- **Hope scholarship credit** There is a credit of up to $1,500 per student for the cost of tuition and fees for the first two years of college (100 percent of the first $1,000 of tuition, plus 50 percent of the next $1,000 of tuition). The full credit can be claimed for the taxpayer, spouse, or dependents, but only if adjusted gross income is below threshold amounts ($40,000 for singles or $80,000 for married persons filing jointly). The credit phases out for adjusted gross income between $40,000 and $50,000 for singles ($80,000 and

$100,000 on a joint return). No credit can be claimed if adjusted gross income is over $50,000 for singles (or $100,000 on a joint return). No credit can be claimed by a married person who files a separate return.

- **Lifetime learning credit** There is a credit of up to $1,000 (20 percent of up to $5,000; 20 percent of up to $10,000 beginning in 2003 for a top credit of $2,000) per return for the cost of tuition and fees for any college, graduate school, or vocational training. Like the Hope scholarship, the lifetime learning credit can be claimed for the taxpayer, spouse, or dependents, but only if adjusted gross income is below those same threshold amounts. Unlike the Hope scholarship, there is no limit on the number of years you can claim this credit. This credit cannot be claimed if the Hope credit is elected for any student (but you can claim the credit for any other eligible student). For example, if your child begins college and you take a graduate course, you can elect the Hope credit for your child and the lifetime learning credit for yourself if your AGI is below the threshold amount.

- **Interest on student loans** In 1999, interest of up to $1,500 on student loans is deductible as an adjustment to gross income on page 1 of Form 1040 (it is deductible whether or not you itemize your other personal deductions). The deduction limit is scheduled to increase in $500 increments until it reaches $2,500 in 2001. Qualified interest is interest paid on the loan during the first 60 months in which interest payments are required. The full deduction can only be claimed if your adjusted gross income is below a threshold amount ($40,000 for singles or $60,000 on a joint return). The deduction phases out over the next $15,000 of adjusted gross income, so that no deduction can be claimed once adjusted gross income exceeds $55,000 for singles or $75,000 on a joint return.

LEGISLATIVE ALERT

Congress is considering elimination of the 60-month limit on student loan interest deductions. If enacted, this change will be effective starting in 2000.

- **Penalty-free IRA withdrawals**   Withdrawals from IRAs used to pay qualified higher education costs by those under age $59^{1}/_{2}$ are not subject to the 10 percent premature distribution penalty. However, using IRA funds for education is still costly since the distribution is subject to regular income tax and you lose the opportunity for tax-free compounding.

CHARITABLE CONTRIBUTIONS MADE BY YOUR BUSINESS

Your business may contribute cash or property to various charities. In general, the amount of your charitable contribution is deductible, but there are certain limits and requirements that must be followed.

Individuals can deduct charitable contributions only as itemized deductions. For example, if you are a partner and the partnership makes a charitable contribution, the contribution is passed through to you as a separately stated item and you then deduct it on your Schedule A as an itemized deduction. The same is true for members of limited liability companies and shareholders in S corporations. Self-employed individuals who file Schedule C do not take business-related charitable contributions as a business expense. Charitable contributions are deducted on Schedule A. Similarly, an employee who makes a charitable contribution at work (for example, amounts are withheld from pay as contributions to the United Fund or another charity) deducts the contribution on Schedule A as a charitable contribution (not as an employee business expense). Charitable contributions by individuals are subject to certain adjusted gross income limits.

Donations of property by a partnership, limited liability company, or S corporation can affect the owner's basis in his or her business interest. For example, suppose a partnership owned equally by two individuals donates a painting worth $80,000 that the partnership bought for $50,000. Each partner can deduct $40,000 on his or her individual return (50 percent of $80,000). However, each partner must also reduce the basis in the partnership interest by $25,000 (50 percent of the property's basis).

Sometimes it is not clear whether an expense is a charitable contribution or some other business expense. For example, if you pay to run an ad in a journal of a tax-exempt organization, the expense may be an advertising expense rather than a charitable contribution.

Corporations

Corporations may make charitable contributions and deduct them on their returns. The contributions must be made to public charities. The corporation cannot take a deduction if the organization receiving the contribution benefits any private shareholder or individual.

The corporation's accounting method may affect the timing of the deduction for a contribution. Cash method corporations deduct the contribution only in the year it is actually made. Corporations on the accrual method can choose to deduct contributions made within two-and-a-half months after the close of its year as having been made in the prior year. To do this, the board of directors of the corporation must authorize the payment of the contribution within two-and-a-half months after the close of the year. This authorization should be reflected in the corporate minutes.

A corporation can deduct only charitable contributions that total no more than 10 percent of its taxable income. Taxable income for purposes of this limitation does not include the deduction for contributions, the deduction for dividends received and dividends paid, net operating loss carrybacks, and capital loss carrybacks.

Contributions in excess of the 10-percent limit can be carried forward for up to five years. If the corporation makes contributions in the carryforward years, the current deductions are taken into account before the carryforwards. Carryovers of excess charitable contributions cannot be deducted in a subsequent year if they increase a net operating loss carryover.

Corporations cannot claim a charitable contribution deduction for amounts given to an organization that conducts lobbying activities on matters of direct financial interest to their business.

Inventory

If you donate items from your inventory, the deduction is limited to the fair market value of the property on the date of the contribution, reduced by any gain that would have been realized if you had sold the property at its fair market value instead of donating it. Be sure to remove from opening inventory any contributions you make (namely, the costs for the donated property included in prior years). These costs are not part of the cost of goods sold for the year in which the contribution is made.

However, if a C corporation donates items from inventory to a public charity or an operating foundation where the inventory will be used for the care of the ill, the needy, or infants, add to the deduction 50 percent of the difference between the basis and the fair market value of the inventory (but not more than 200 percent of the basis of the property). This special inventory rule does not apply to S corporations.

Scientific Property Used for Research

A C corporation can claim a larger deduction than ordinarily allowed if it contributes certain scientific property used for research to an institution of higher education. This special rule allows the corporation to increase its deduction by 50 percent of the difference between its basis and the fair market value of the property (but not more than 200 percent of the basis of the property). This special deduction is not allowed for S corporations, personal holding companies, or service organizations.

Computer Equipment

C corporations can receive an increased contribution deduction for donations of computers, software, and peripheral equipment no more than two years old to schools (grades K–12). The deduction is the cost (basis) in the equipment plus one-half of the amount of ordinary income that would have been realized if the property had been sold. The deduction cannot exceed twice the basis of the donated property. This enhanced charitable deduction is set to expire at the end of 2000.

DUES AND SUBSCRIPTIONS

Dues

Certain dues are deductible; others are not. Dues paid to unions are deductible. If you pay dues to professional, business, or civic organizations, they, too, are deductible, as are dues to the following organizations:

- American Bar Association, American Institute of CPA, American Medical Association, and other professional associations

- Chambers of commerce, business leagues, trade associations, boards of trade, real estate boards, and business lunch clubs

- Civitan, Rotary, Lions, and other civic organizations

However, no deduction is allowed for dues to other types of clubs, such as athletic, sporting, airline, hotel, or other recreational clubs, even though membership is for business.

Subscriptions

The cost of subscriptions to business or professional publications is deductible. However, if you are on the cash basis and prepay subscriptions—that is, your subscription covers a period of more than one year—your deduction may be limited to the cost related to one year. Then you can deduct an allocable portion of the subscription cost in each succeeding year.

EXAMPLE: In January 1999 you pay for a three-year subscription to a trade magazine. Your total cost is $150. (Assume you are on a calendar year for reporting your income and deductions.) In 1999 you can deduct $50 (one-third of your total cost). In 2000 and again in 2001, you can deduct $50, the remaining portion of your subscription cost.

Legal and Professional Fees

Legal and professional fees related to your business are deductible. Professional fees may include, for example, not only legal fees but also accounting fees, actuarial fees, systems analyst fees, and appraisal fees.

Legal Fees

Legal fees for business matters generally are deductible. Fees related to wrongful discharge actions are also deductible, as are legal fees incurred by a corporate director to defend against stockholder allegations of misconduct. Other deductible legal fees are those for tax advice or to obtain an IRS ruling.

Limits on Deducting Legal Fees

If legal fees are incurred to acquire a capital asset, they are not separately deductible. Instead, they are added to the basis of the asset. For example, if you pay attorney's fees to handle the closing when you buy your office building, the fees cannot be currently deducted. They are part of the basis of your office building and are recovered through depreciation.

Legal fees that are personal in nature cannot be deducted at all. For example, legal fees to pursue a personal injury action are not deductible even if the injury occurred on a business trip. Also, legal fees to prepare your will are not deductible even if your will provides for the disposition of your business upon your death. Similarly, legal fees for divorce are not deductible even though they relate to preserving your interest in a business.

However, if part of the fees deals with tax issues, you can deduct the allocable portion of the fees for tax advice.

Legal fees to incorporate your business are part of incorporation fees that may be amortized. Amortization of incorporation fees is discussed in Chapter 12.

Accounting Fees

If you pay an accountant to show you how to set up your books or to keep your books for you, the accounting fees are deductible. Also deductible are fees for accounting advice, such as advice on whether to change your method of accounting or your method of inventory.

Tax Preparation Fees

If you pay a preparer to complete your tax return for your business (Form 1065, Form 1120, or Form 1120S), the cost is fully deductible on the appropriate return. If you are self-employed, the allocable cost of preparing Schedule C is a deductible business expense that can be claimed on Schedule C. The balance of tax preparation fees is deductible as a miscellaneous itemized expense on Schedule A, subject to the 2-percent-of-adjusted-gross-income floor.

Accounting fees incurred in investigating whether to buy a business are not currently deductible but may qualify as start-up expenses that can be amortized over a period of up to 60 months. Amortization of start-up costs is discussed in Chapter 12.

The same rule applies to tax assistance fees paid to contest a tax deficiency. The portion related to business income is deductible on Schedule C; the portion related to nonbusiness income is deductible on Schedule A.

Recovering Legal Fees and Other Costs from the Government

If you are involved in a tax dispute with the IRS and you win, you may be able to make the government pay any reasonable costs of your tax contest. You must have exhausted your administrative remedies and have substantially prevailed in your tax dispute. Then the IRS has the burden of proving that its position in going after you was substantially justified. If the IRS did not follow published regulations, revenue rulings, revenue procedures, information releases, notices or announcements, private letter rulings, determination letters, or technical advice memoranda issued to you, then there is a rebuttable presumption that the IRS's position was not substantially justified. Also, the fact that the IRS has lost in other appellate courts on substantially similar issues must be taken into account in determining whether the IRS's position was not substantially justified. If you succeed, you can recover attorney's fees at the rate of $130 per hour. In limited circumstances, a higher award may be possible. This dollar limit will be adjusted for inflation after 1999.

If you are successful in your claim to recover costs from the government (for example, if the IRS fails to prove that it was substantially justified in its position), you cannot also take a deduction for these costs. If you have already taken a deduction for your costs, you must include the government's award in your income.

The opportunity to recover legal fees from the government is limited to individuals with a net worth below $2 million per individual. In the case of businesses, the net worth requirement is below $7 million and fewer than 500 employees.

Lobbying Costs
Fees paid to professional lobbyists to influence legislation on the federal, state, or local level are not deductible. However, in-house lobbying costs up to $2,000 are deductible.

SUPPLIES, MATERIALS, AND UNIFORMS
The cost of incidental supplies and materials used in your business are deductible as ordinary and necessary business expenses. However, if you are on the cash basis and order such large quantities that the supplies or materials will last you more than a year, you can deduct only the portion of the cost related to supplies or materials expected to be used within the year.

Postage
The costs of postage, overnight delivery charges, and other mailing and shipping costs are deductible.

Books, Software, and Equipment
Books, software, and professional equipment that normally have a life of less than a year can be deducted. For example, if you buy a business book that is updated annually, you can deduct its cost. By the same token, if you

buy tax return preparation software that applies to one tax year, you can deduct its cost. However, if you buy a professional library or other equipment that can be expected to last for more than a year, its cost must be depreciated. See Chapter 12 for depreciation rules.

Uniforms and Clothing

The cost of uniforms required by the job generally is deductible. Thus, for example, the cost of nurse's uniforms is deductible. However, clothing that is adaptable to ordinary street use is not deductible even if used solely in business.

EXAMPLE: An actor who buys a tuxedo for a role cannot deduct the cost because the tuxedo is adaptable to street use—in other words, it can be used in other ways than on-the-job uses.

Nondeductible clothing costs cannot be transformed into deductible costs by calling the clothing something else. For example, an attorney cannot deduct the cost of business suits by claiming they are an advertising expense, even though a prosperous look is a way of attracting new clients.

If the cost of the clothes is deductible as a business expense, then the cost of cleaning the clothes is also deductible.

INSURANCE

The cost of most types of business-related insurance is deductible. Examples of deductible insurance include:

- Casualty insurance to cover flood, fire, storm, and other casualty destruction to property. Casualty insurance may include coverage for data recovery necessitated by destruction or damage to a computer system. This may be a separate policy or part of a comprehensive casualty insurance policy. Casualty insurance also covers loss of property by theft. Check to make sure your policy covers theft of laptop computers. If the policy does not provide this specific coverage, you can obtain a separate policy for this purpose.

- Accident and health insurance (including long-term care insurance). The business can deduct this coverage for its employees, spouses, and dependents. Employees can exclude this benefit from their income (with a limited exclusion for long-term care insurance).

Self-employed individuals (partners, LLC members, and more-than-2-percent S corporation shareholders) cannot enjoy this tax-free fringe benefit. Instead, self-employed persons and more-than-2-percent S corporation shareholders can deduct a percentage of their health insurance costs on their individual returns. Deducting medical coverage is explained more fully in Chapter 18.

- Errors and omissions insurance to provide protection for doing or failing to do something in the line of work (similar to professional liability coverage but for nonprofessionals). Self-employed individuals can carry the coverage to protect themselves. Businesses can carry the coverage to protect themselves with respect to the acts of their employees.

- Employer practices liability (EPL), a relatively new type of coverage that protects employers from claims by employees based on sexual harassment, age discrimination, wrongful termination, or other similar work-related claims.

- Group-term life insurance for employees. This type of coverage allows employees to name the beneficiaries who will receive the proceeds. What is more, up to $50,000 of coverage is not taxable to employees if the coverage is provided on a nondiscriminatory basis (coverage does not favor owners and top executives at the expense of rank-and-file employees). This type of coverage is discussed in more detail in Chapter 5.

- Key-person life insurance for employees. This type of coverage protects the business from the loss of a key employee. The proceeds are payable to the business, allowing it to look for replacement help and to cover losses in the interim.

- Credit insurance to cover nonpayment of debts owed to the business.

- Overhead insurance to cover the costs of rent, salaries, and other overhead expenses during periods of illness by the owner.

- Business interruption coverage. Like overhead insurance, this type of coverage provides payment during a period in which a business is forced to close, such as during a natural disaster or a civil riot.

- Worker's compensation. Businesses are required to provide coverage for employees.

- Automobile insurance on business cars.

- Professional liability coverage to provide protection from malpractice claims. However, premiums paid to physician-owned carriers may not be deductible unless most of the policyholders are not economically related to one another and none of them owns a controlling interest in the insuring company.

- Product liability coverage to provide protection from claims that products you manufacture or sell are defective and have caused injury to the public.

- Performance bonds to ensure the faithful performance of employees, and bonds to ensure a company's performance on a contract. These are also called surety bonds.

- Fidelity bonds to protect clients and customers against theft or embezzlement by company employees.

- PBGC premiums for defined benefit plans to provide a minimum retirement benefit to employees if the plan goes under.

Disability insurance you pay for your employees is deductible. But if you buy insurance coverage for yourself, you cannot deduct your premiums even though the insurance relates to your work. Of course, if you receive benefits under a policy you took for yourself (in which premiums were nondeductible), you are not taxed on the benefits.

In most cases, insurance premiums are currently deductible in full. However, if you are on the cash basis and your premium covers a period of more than one year, you may deduct only the premiums related to the current year. The balance of the premiums is deductible over the period to which they relate.

If you are a business owner and enter into a cross-purchase buy-sell agreement with other owners to acquire the interests of an owner who dies, the agreement may be funded with life insurance. In this instance, the cost of the premiums is not deductible. The reason: No deduction is allowed for premiums paid on life insurance if you are, directly or indirectly, the policy beneficiary.

EXAMPLE: A and B are partners in the AB Partnership. They have a buy-sell agreement that requires A to buy B's interest in the event of B's death, and vice versa. A takes out life insurance on B and will use the proceeds of the policy to buy out B's interest if B dies before A. Similarly, B takes out life insurance on A. Neither A nor B may deduct the premiums on this life insurance arrangement even though there is a business reason for the purchase.

Interest on life insurance policies   If you take a loan on a life insurance policy covering the life of anyone in whom you have an insurable interest, you may not deduct the interest on the loan. So, if you borrow on a policy maintained to fund a buy-sell agreement, you may not deduct the interest. Corporations (and other nonnatural persons) generally may not deduct a portion of interest on any of their outstanding loans to the extent of any "unborrowed policy cash value" (cash surrender value of the policy reduced by any loans). This interest deduction rule, however, does not apply if the business owns a policy covering only one individual who owns at least 20 percent of the business or is an employee, officer, or director of the company.

PAYMENTS TO DIRECTORS AND INDEPENDENT CONTRACTORS

Payments to directors and independent contractors are not treated as compensation. Rather, they are miscellaneous payments that are deductible as a business expense. Since they are not compensation, they are not subject to employment taxes.

Individuals who work for their corporations and also serve as directors receive both salary (as an employee) and self-employment income (as a director). Such individuals may be able to reduce the tax on directors' fees by setting up retirement plans based on this self-employment income.

For a discussion of whether a worker is an employee or an independent contractor, see Business Organization, Chapter 1.

PENALTIES, FINES, AND DAMAGES

If you contract to perform work and are subject to penalty for noncompletion or lateness, you can deduct the penalty.

EXAMPLE: You contract to remodel a kitchen. The contract calls for a penalty if the job is not completed within a month. You do not bring the job in on time and must pay a penalty for each day beyond the month. You can deduct this penalty.

You can also deduct compensatory damages paid to the government. However, you cannot deduct nonconformance penalties imposed by the Environmental Protection Agency for failing to meet certain emission standards.

If you lose a business lawsuit and must pay damages, you deduct your outlays. For example, if you lose a malpractice case and your insurance carrier pays 95 percent of the damages while you pay 5 percent, you can deduct your payment.

If you are subject to governmental fines or penalties because you violated the law, no deduction is allowed. Such penalties include:

- Amounts paid as penalties to plead no contest or to plead guilty to a criminal offense

- Penalties imposed by federal, state, or local law (e.g., additions to tax imposed by the Internal Revenue Code)

- Payments to settle actual or possible civil or criminal litigation

- Fines for violation of housing codes

- Fines by truckers for violating state highway maximum weight limits or air quality laws

- Civil penalties for violating federal laws on mine safety or discharge into navigable waters

Nongovernment fines or penalties are deductible. For example, one broker who was fined by the Chicago Mercantile Exchange for violating trading limitations was allowed by the Tax Court to deduct his payment.

Treble Damages for Antitrust Violations

One-third of the treble damages for antitrust violations is deductible; the balance is treated as a nondeductible penalty.

Restitution Payments

These payments generally are regarded as fines and are deductible. However, if restitution payments are made in lieu of a prison sentence, they are viewed as a nondeductible governmental penalty even though the funds go to a private person rather than to the government.

Related Expenses

Certain expenses related to nondeductible fines or penalties may themselves be deductible. For example, legal fees to defend your business against prosecution or civil action for a violation of a law imposing a fine or civil penalty are deductible.

EXPENSES OF DISABLED PERSONS

Individuals with handicaps or disabilities may incur certain expenses to enable them to work. For example, a blind individual may hire a reader. In general, the cost of work-related expenses of disabled persons is deductible.

Sometimes it may be difficult to decide whether the expense is a personal medical expense that is subject to a 7.5-percent-of-adjusted-gross-income floor or a business expense. If the expense is required for the individual to perform his or her job and the goods or services are not used primarily for personal purposes, the expense can be treated as a business expense. For example, attendant care services at the office generally are treated as business expenses. You must show a physical or mental handicap that results in a functional limitation to employment, such as blindness or deafness.

Work-related business expenses of handicapped persons are itemized deductions that are not subject to the 2-percent floor. If the handicapped person is self-employed, the expenses are deductible as any other business expense on Schedule C.

If you, as an employer, incur special costs because of compliance with the Americans with Disabilities Act, you may deduct these costs as ordinary and necessary business expenses. If they are capital in nature, you may be able to claim a special deduction or credit, as explained in Chapter 8.

THE DIVIDENDS-RECEIVED DEDUCTION

C corporations may be able to claim a special deduction for a percentage of certain stock dividends they receive. This is called a dividends-received deduction. Other taxpayers—individuals, partnerships, limited liability companies, and S corporations—cannot claim this deduction.

Percentages of the Dividends-Received Deduction

The percentage of the dividend that can be deducted depends on the amount of stock your corporation owns and the type of company paying the dividends. Other factors may operate to further limit the percentage.

70-percent deduction   If your corporation owns less than 20 percent of the stock of the dividend-paying corporation, your dividends-received deduction is 70 percent of the dividends you receive from that corporation.

80-percent deduction   If your corporation owns at least 20 percent of the stock of the dividend-paying corporation, your dividends-received deduction is 80 percent of the dividends you receive from that corporation.

100-percent deduction   If your corporation and the dividend-paying corporation are members of an affiliated group, all of the dividends received are deductible. The full deduction also applies to small business investment companies that received dividends from domestic corporations.

42-percent deduction   If your corporation owns less than 20 percent of the preferred stock issued before October 1992 of a taxable public utility, your dividends-received deduction is limited to 42 percent of the dividends received from that public utility. If your corporation owns more than 20 percent of the utility, the dividends-received deduction increases to 48 percent.

Other Limits on the Dividends-Received Deduction

In addition to the percentage limitation, other limits may apply to reduce or eliminate entirely the deduction.

Limit for debt-financed portfolios   If your corporation borrows to buy or carry a stock portfolio, the 70-percent and 80-percent dividends-received deductions must be reduced by the percentage related to the amount of debt.

Overall limit   There is an overall limit on the deduction for dividends received. This limit is calculated on Schedule C of Form 1120.

No deduction allowed   Certain types of deductions do not qualify for the dividends-received deduction. These include dividends from:

- Foreign corporations. However, in some cases a limited deduction is allowed for foreign corporations that are more than 10-percent domestically owned.

- Real estate investment trusts.

- Corporations whose stock has been held for only 45 days or less during the 90-day period beginning on the date that is 45 days before the date on which the shares become ex-dividend.

- Corporations whose stock has been held for 90 days or less during the 180-day period beginning on the date that is 90 days before the date on which the shares became ex-dividend, if the stock has preference as to dividends and the dividends received on it are attributable to a period of more than 365 days.

- Tax-exempt corporations.

- Corporations to which your corporation is obligated (pursuant to a short sale or otherwise) to make related payments for positions in substantially similar or related property.

NET OPERATING LOSSES

If deductions and losses from your business exceed your income, you may be able to use the losses to offset income in other years. Net losses from the conduct of your business are called net operating losses (NOLs).

Net operating losses are not an additional loss deduction. Rather, they are the result of your deductions exceeding the income from your business. The excess deductions are not lost; they are simply used in certain other years.

You have a net operating loss if you have deductions from a trade or business, deductions from your work as an employee, or deductions from casualty and theft losses.

Only individuals and C corporations can claim net operating losses. Partnerships, limited liability companies, and S corporations cannot have NOLs, since their income and losses pass through to owners. Partners, LLC members, and S corporation shareholders can have NOLs on their individual returns. These NOLs are created by their share of the business's operating losses.

Calculating NOLs

After you have completed your tax return for the year, you may find that you have an NOL. If you are an individual, you may have an NOL if your adjusted gross income, reduced by itemized deductions or the standard deduction (but before personal exemptions), is a negative figure. C corporations may have an NOL if taxable income is a negative figure. This negative figure merely indicates a possibility of an NOL; then you must determine whether, in fact, there actually is one. This is because certain adjustments must be made to that negative figure in arriving at an NOL. Individuals and corporations calculate NOLs slightly differently.

Individuals

An NOL does not include personal exemptions, net capital losses, nonbusiness losses, or nonbusiness deductions. The NOL can be computed on Schedule A of Form 1045. This form adds back to taxable income any of these items claimed on the return and makes other adjustments required to compute the NOL. For example, individuals must add back to taxable income any deductions for IRA contributions, alimony, the standard deduction, and charitable contributions. More specifically, nonbusiness deductions in excess of nonbusiness income get added back. Do not add back business-related deductions for:

- One-half of self-employment tax

- Moving expenses

- State income tax on business profits

- Interest and litigation expenses on state or federal income taxes related to business

- Payments by a federal employee to buy sick leave

- Loss on rental property

- Loss on the sale or exchange of business real estate or depreciable business property

- Loss on the sale of accounts receivable if you are on the accrual method

- Loss on the sale or exchange of stock in a small business company or small business investment company if the loss is treated as an ordinary loss (such as loss on Section 1244)

Corporations

The NOL for corporations generally is calculated by reducing gross income by deductions. Special rules then apply to adjust the NOL.

- A full dividends-received deduction is taken into account in calculating the NOL. For example, the 70-percent or 80-percent limit is ignored.

- NOLs from other years are not taken into account in calculating a current NOL.

- Losses that fall under the passive activity rules cannot be used to calculate an NOL.

If a corporation's ownership changes hands, limits apply on the use of NOL carryforwards. The tax law does not want one corporation to acquire another for the purpose of using NOLs of the target corporation to offset the income of the acquiring corporation. These rules are highly complex.

Carrybacks and Carryovers

Net operating losses may be carried back and, if not used up, carried forward for a certain number of years. The carryback and carryforward periods depend on the year in which the NOL arose.

For NOLs arising in tax years beginning before August 6, 1997, the carryback period is three years and the carryforward period is 15 years. You first carry the loss back to a year that is three years before the year in which the NOL arose (the NOL year). If it is not used up in this year, you carry it back to a year that is two years earlier. If it is not used up in this year, carry it to the year before the NOL year. If the NOL is still not used up, you can begin to carry it forward (with modifications explained below). However, if it is not used up after carrying it forward for 15 years, it is lost forever.

For NOLs arising in tax years beginning after August 5, 1997 (which means 1998 calendar years), generally there is a two-year carryback and a 20-year carryforward period. However, for small businesses (those with average annual gross receipts of $5 million or less during a three-year period), the three-year carryback continues to apply to net operating losses arising from government-declared disasters (for farmers and ranchers, there is a five-year carryback for all NOLs). There is a 10-year carryback in the case of NOLs arising from product liability.

Be sure to keep track of both categories of net operating losses. For example, do not lump your carryforwards together.

Caution

Personal service corporations are not allowed to carry back an NOL to any year in which there is a Section 444 election in effect to use a tax year other than a required tax year.

If your business is struggling, you can use an NOL carryback to generate quick cash flow. The carryback will offset income in the carryback years, and you will receive a refund of taxes paid in those years.

Individuals can file Form 1045, Application by Taxpayers Other than Corporations for Tentative Refund, to obtain a relatively quick refund. The IRS generally will act on the refund within 90 days of the filing of the form. When you carry back an NOL, you may have to recalculate certain deductions in the carryback years. These are deductions based on adjusted gross income. Remember that the NOL will lower your adjusted gross income in the carryback years and therefore allow for greater itemized deductions that have an adjusted-gross-income floor. You may also have to recalculate alternative minimum tax.

If your marital status in the carryback or carryover years differs from your status in the NOL year, only the spouse who has the NOL can claim it. If you file a joint return, the NOL deduction is limited to the income of the spouse who had the NOL.

EXAMPLE: In 1998 you divorce after many years of marriage. In 1999 you have an NOL. If you do not forgo the two-year carryback, the NOL carryback is applied only against your income on the 1997 return, which were joint returns (in 1998 you were divorced by the end of the year and your filing status was single). After you deduct the NOL calculated with reference to your taxable income, you then apply the tax rates for married filing jointly.

If your NOL is greater than the taxable income for the year to which you carried it, you must make certain modifications to taxable income to see how much of the NOL is used up in that carryback/carryover year and how much is still available as a carryover. The carryover is the excess of the NOL deduction over modified taxable income for the carryback/carryforward year. Modified taxable income means taxable income without regard to the NOL and with no deduction for net capital losses or personal exemptions. Also, you must recalculate items affected by a change in adjusted gross income. Your modified taxable income cannot be less than zero. You can determine your modified taxable income using Schedule B of Form 1045 for any carryback years and for carryovers from those years.

If you have carryovers from more than one year, you use the carryovers in the order in which they were incurred.

Corporations can expedite a refund from an NOL carryback by using a special form, Form 1139, Corporation Application for Tentative Refund from Carryback of Net Operating Losses and Unused Investment Credit, to obtain a quick refund. This form cannot be filed before the income tax return for the NOL year is filed. It must be filed no later than one year after the NOL year. What is more, if a corporation expects to have an NOL in the current year, it can delay filing the income tax return for the prior year with the knowledge that the tax on the prior year's return will be fully or partially offset by the NOL.

You can also claim an NOL on an amended return, Form 1040X or Form 1120X. Individuals who carry back NOLs cannot recalculate self-employment tax and get a refund of this tax. The NOL applies only to income tax purposes.

Election to Forgo Carryback

Instead of carrying a 1999 net operating loss back two years and then forward, you can elect to forgo the carryback and just carry forward the loss for 20 years. You make this election in the NOL year by attaching a statement to your return if you are an individual or by checking the appropriate box on the corporate return for C corporations. Once the election is made, it cannot be changed. If you incur another NOL in a subsequent year, you must make a separate election if you also want to forgo the carryback.

Some taxpayers prefer to forgo the carryback because they are afraid of calling attention to prior tax years and risking an audit. While this is certainly a possibility, claiming a carryback will not necessarily result in an audit of a prior year.

The election to forgo the NOL carryback applies not only to regular income tax purposes but also to alternative minimum tax purposes.

ABORTED BUSINESS VENTURES

What happens if you investigate the purchase of a business or the start of a venture but the deal never goes through? Or you hire an architect to design a building but never get town approval for the construction? The costs of starting up and organizing a business are not immediately deductible in full (but may be amortized, as explained in Chapter 12). However, the costs of an aborted business venture are immediately deductible.

To deduct your costs, you must have proceeded beyond a general search. Once you focus on a particular business and the deal falls through, you can deduct your expenses. Mere investigatory expenses are not deductible; only those related to a specific business are. Thus, for example, if you travel to look at various business opportunities, you cannot deduct your travel costs. But once you select one particular business and begin drawing up contracts, your legal costs for the contracts are deductible even if they never get signed.

EXPENSES OF WINDING UP A SMALL BUSINESS

Unfortunately, the cold statistics show that many small businesses fail. Some last longer than others, but a large number of ventures will reach a point where they are so unprofitable that the owners must simply give up.

Certain expenses relate to the winding up of a small business. They are deductible business expenses.

Unamortized Costs

If you have been amortizing certain items, such as organizational or incorporation fees, you can deduct the unamortized amounts on a final return for the business. For example, say the business elected to amortize organizational costs over 60 months, but it goes under after only 36 months. You can deduct $24/60$ of your organizational costs on the final return, in addition to any of the amortization allowed for the final year of the return.

Other Expenses

You may incur special costs for going out of business. For example, a corporation may have to pay a special fee to the state corporation or franchise department when terminating. There may also be additional legal and accounting fees for winding up a business. Again, these costs are deductible business expenses.

CHECKLISTS OF DEDUCTIBLE AND NONDEDUCTIBLE EXPENSES

Checklist of Deductions for Self-Employed Individuals

abandonment of assets, loss for
accounting fees
acquiring a lease, cost of
actuary fees for defined benefit
  plans
advertising
agreement not to compete
air transportation taxes
allowances and returns
amortization of acquired
  intangibles
association dues
attorney's fees
automobiles (see cars)
bad debts
bank fees
Black Lung benefit trust
  contributions
bond premium
bonuses to employees
breach of contract damages
bribes
buildings, demolition of
business conventions
business interruption insurance

capital losses
cars
casualty insurance
casualty losses
cellular phones
commissions paid to
  independent contractors
computers
conventions
copyrights
cruise ship, conventions on
dependent care
depreciation
dues for professionals
education expenses
employee compensation
employment taxes
entertainment expenses
equipment
excise taxes
experimental costs
fax machines
fines
first-year expensing of
  equipment

franchise fees
franchise taxes
freight
fuel taxes
FUTA tax for employees
gifts
going concern value
goodwill
handicapped, improvements for
health insurance for employees
home office expenses
insurance
    business interruption
    car
    casualty
    errors and omissions
    health
    liability
    long-term care
    malpractice
    overhead
    workers' compensation for
    employees
intangible drilling costs
interest
Internet-related fees
involuntary conversions
journals
Keogh plan contributions
kickbacks
labor costs
lease payments
legal fees
liability insurance
libraries
license fees

maintenance costs (repairs)
malpractice insurance
materials
medical insurance
medical reimbursement plans
meals for business
mortgages
moving expenses
net operating losses
office in home
oil and gas wells
organizational expenses
outplacement services for
    employees
overhead insurance
pagers
patents
penalties
pension plans
pollution control facilities
postage
qualified retirement plan
    contributions
real estate taxes
reforestation expenses
registration fees
removal of architectural barriers
rent
research costs
retirement plan contributions
royalty payments
sales tax
Section 197 intangibles
self-employment tax
SEP-IRAs
sick pay to employees

SIMPLE plan contributions
software
start-up costs
subscriptions
supplemental unemployment
  benefits for employees
supplies
tax return preparation fees
thefts
timber
tools
tradenames
trademarks
transportation expenses

travel expenses
trucks (see cars)
unemployment payments to
  state compensation fund for
  employees
uniforms
use tax
utilities
vandalism
wages for employees
work clothes
workers' compensation for
  employees

Checklist of Deductions for Employees

advances for travel and
  entertainment expenses
association dues
automobiles (see cars)
bad debts
breach of contract damages
breakage charges
business conventions
cars
cellular phones
cleaning costs for deductible
  uniforms
computers
conventions
cruise ships, conventions on
dependent care
depreciation
dues for professional
  associations/unions

education expenses
entertainment expenses
equipment
fax machines
first-year expensing of
  equipment
gifts
home office expenses
impairment-related job expenses
insurance for business, car
interview expenses
IRAs
job-hunting expenses
journals
jury fees returned to employer
lease payments for business
  property
legal fees
license fees

materials and supplies
meals for business
moving expenses
nonbusiness bad debts
office in home
performing artist expenses
résumés
Section 1244 losses
small tools
subscriptions
supplies

tax return preparation fees
telephone
tools
transportation expenses
travel expenses
trucks (see cars)
uniforms
union dues
utilities in a home office
work clothes

Checklist of Deductions for Small Corporations

abandonment of assets, loss for
accident and health plans,
    contributions to
accounting fees
acquiring a lease, cost of
actuary fees for defined benefit
    plans
advances for travel and enter-
    tainment expenses
advertising agreement not to
    compete
air transportation taxes
allowances and returns
amortization of acquired intan-
    gibles
amortization of premium on
    bonds
appraisal fees
association dues
attorney's fees
automobiles (see cars)
awards and prizes to employees

bad debts
bank fees
Black Lung benefit trust
    contributions
bond premiums
bonuses
breach of contract damages
bribes
buildings, demolition of
business conventions
business interruption insurance
capital losses
cars
casualty insurance
casualty losses
cellular phones
charitable contributions
commissions paid to indepen-
    dent contractors
compensation
computers
conventions

copyrights
cruise ships, conventions on
dependent care
depreciation
disability insurance
dividends-received deduction
education expenses
employee benefit plans
employee compensation
employment taxes
entertainment expenses
equipment
excise taxes
experimental costs
fax machines
FICA
fines
first-year expensing of
   equipment
foreign taxes
franchise fees
franchise taxes
freight
fringe benefits
fuel taxes
FUTA tax for employees
gifts
going concern value
goodwill
group term life insurance
handicapped, improvements for
health plans, contributions to
incorporation fees
insurance
      business interruption
      car

      casualty
      employer practices liability
      errors and omissions
      group term
      health
      key person life
      liability
      life
      long-term care
      malpractice
      overhead
      workers' compensation
intangible drilling costs
interest
Internet-related fees
involuntary conversions
journals
kickbacks
labor costs
lease payments
legal fees
liability insurance
libraries
license fees
life insurance
maintenance costs (repairs)
malpractice insurance
materials
meals for business
medical insurance
medical reimbursement plans
medical savings account (MSA)
   contributions
Medicare tax
mortgages
moving expenses

Checklist of Deductions Not Allowed

anticipated liabilities

architect's fees (generally capitalized)

at-risk, losses in excess of

bad debt deduction for income not reported

bar examination fees

car used for commuting

club dues for recreational, social, and athletic clubs

commuting expenses

containers treated as part of inventory

demolition of entire buildings

disability insurance for yourself

dividend payments

educational costs to meet minimum job requirements

embezzlement losses of income not yet reported

estimated tax penalties

federal income tax

FICA by employees

fines

401(k) contributions by employees

gifts to business clients or customers over $25

hobby losses

interest on life insurance policy loans funding buy-sell agreements

inventory

IRA contributions by participants in qualified plans with AGI over set limit

IRA rollovers

job-hunting costs for a first job

land costs

lobbying expenses (other than de minimus in-house)

not-for-profit activity losses

passive activity losses in excess of passive activity limits

penalties paid to the government

political contributions

reimbursed expenses (payments received by employees under accountable plans)

related parties, losses on sales to

salary reduction contributions to retirement plans

self-insurance reserve funds

spousal travel costs

state and local income taxes on self-employment income

tax penalties

travel costs as a form of education

treble damage awards— two-thirds

WHERE TO DEDUCT MISCELLANEOUS BUSINESS EXPENSES

Employees

In general, employee business expenses are deductible as itemized expenses on Schedule A, subject to the 2-percent-of-adjusted-gross-income floor discussed in Chapter 1.

Special rule for performing artists   Expenses are fully deductible from gross income if you meet certain tests:

- You must perform services as a performing artist as an employee for at least two employers.

- Your business deductions must exceed 10 percent of your gross income from the performance of services.

- Your adjusted gross income without regard to these business deductions must not exceed $16,000.

If you meet these tests to fully deduct your expenses, they are not claimed as itemized deductions on Schedule A but rather as an adjustment to gross income on page 1 of Form 1040. Be sure to write "QPA" next to your deduction.

Handicapped persons   Business-related expenses of disabled or handicapped individuals are itemized deductions that are not subject to the 2-percent floor.

Moving expenses   Moving expenses that are not reimbursed by an employer are deductible from gross income on page 1 of Form 1040. They are deductible regardless of whether other deductions are itemized. The moving expense deduction is not subject to the 2-percent floor. Complete Form 3903, Moving Expenses, to determine your deductible moving expenses.

Education credits   The Hope scholarship and lifetime learning credits are figured on Form 8863, Education Credits, the amount of which is then entered on page 2 of Form 1040.

Net operating losses   Net operating losses are computed on Form 1045, Applications by Taxpayers Other than Corporations for Tentative Refund. You use this form or Form 1040X to claim a net operating loss carryback. If you are carrying forward an NOL, you claim the loss as a negative amount entered on Form 1040 as "other income."

Self-Employed

Certain items discussed in this chapter are itemized on Schedule C. These include commissions and fees, insurance, and legal and professional services. Other miscellaneous business expenses discussed in this chapter are grouped together and deducted as "other expenses" on Schedule C. "Other expenses" are separately listed and explained in Part V of Schedule C. You can use Schedule C-EZ only if total business expenses do not exceed $2,500.

For self-employed farmers, certain expenses discussed in this chapter, such as insurance, are itemized on Schedule F. Other miscellaneous business expenses discussed in this chapter, such as legal and accounting fees, are grouped together and deducted as "other expenses" on Schedule F. Farming expenses are explained in Chapter 19.

Moving expenses are a personal expense claimed directly on your Form 1040 rather than on Schedule C. You figure your deductible moving costs on Form 3903 and then enter the deduction on page 1 of Form 1040 as an adjustment to gross income.

Education credits (the Hope scholarship and lifetime learning credits) are personal credits claimed directly on your Form 1040. You figure your credits on Form 8863, Education Credits, and then enter the credit amount on page 2 of Form 1040.

Net operating losses are computed on Form 1045, as discussed above under "Employees."

Partnerships and LLCs

All of the miscellaneous business expenses discussed in this chapter to which a partnership or limited liability company is entitled are entered on Form 1065 as "other expenses." Attach a schedule to the return, itemizing these expenses.

One of the expenses discussed in this chapter is subject to special limitations at the partner/member level and so is a separately treated item reported on Schedule K and passed through to partners/members on Schedule K-1. This separately treated item is charitable contributions by the partnership/LLC. It is separately stated because it is subject to limitation at the owner level. Partners/members report their net income or loss from the business on Schedule E. However, separately stated items are reported on the owner's personal return in the appropriate space. For example, charitable contribution deductions are reported on the owner's Schedule A.

Partners and LLC members who have deductible moving expenses claim them on page 1 of their Form 1040. Partners and LLC members who are eligible for education credits claim them on page 2 of their Form 1040. For details, see "Employees" above.

If the partnership or LLC passes through losses to the partners/members, they may be able to claim a net operating loss deduction. See the discussion under "Employees," above.

S Corporations

All of the miscellaneous business expenses discussed in this chapter to which the S corporation is entitled are entered on Form 1120S as "other deductions." Attach a statement to the return explaining these deductions.

However, deductions that are subject to special limitations at the shareholder level are separately treated items reported on Schedule K and passed through to shareholders on Schedule K-1. For example, charitable contributions by the S corporation are separately stated items because they are subject to limitation at the shareholder level. Shareholders report their net income or loss from the business on Schedule E. Separately stated items are reported on the shareholder's personal return in the appropriate space. For example, charitable contribution deductions are reported on the owner's Schedule A.

Shareholders who are also employees of their S corporations and who have unreimbursed moving expenses compute them on Form 3903 and then enter the deduction on page 1 of Form 1040 as an adjustment to gross income.

If the S corporation passes through losses to the shareholders, it may be able to claim a net operating loss deduction. See the discussion under "Employees," above.

C Corporations

Miscellaneous business expenses are taken into account in determining the profit or loss of the C corporation on Form 1120. The corporation then pays tax on its net profit or loss. Shareholders do not report any income (or loss) from the corporation.

Charitable contributions by the corporation, as well as net operating losses and special deductions for dividends received, are listed separately on Form 1120. All other miscellaneous deductions are grouped together and reported as "other deductions." Attach a schedule to the return explaining these deductions.

If a corporation claims a dividends-received deduction, it must also complete Schedule C, Dividends and Special Deductions, of Form 1120. The net amount of the dividends-received deduction is then entered on page 1 of Form 1120 after any net operating loss has been taken. The dividends-received deduction is not part of the "other deductions" reported on this form.

Net operating losses carried from other years to the current year are deducted on the specific line provided for this item on Form 1120. If a corporation has a net operating loss for the current year, it can obtain a quick refund by filing Form 1139, Corporation.

Application for Tentative Refund from Carryback of Net Operating Loss and Unused Investment Credit. If it expects to have an NOL in the current year and will be able to offset tax in the prior year, it can delay the filing of the prior year's return by filing Form 1138, Statement of Purpose for an Extension of Time for Payment of Taxes by a Corporation Expecting a Net Operating Loss Carryback. On this form you explain why a loss is expected. The extension is in effect until the end of the month in which the return for the NOL year is due, including extensions. If a corporation wants to forgo the carryback, it must indicate this election by checking the appropriate box in Schedule K, Other Information, of Form 1120.

All Businesses

If your business makes payments of more than $600 to independent contractors for services during the year, you may be required to file an annual information return, Form 1099—Miscellaneous Income. Report the payments as nonemployee compensation in the appropriate box on the form.

Also use this form to report payments to corporate directors.

Form 1099-MISC must be furnished to independent contractors and corporate directors no later than January 31 of the year following that in which payments were made. Copies of Form 1099 must also be sent to the IRS, along with a transmittal form, Form 1096, Annual Summary and Transmittal of U.S. Information Returns. This must be done by February 29 of the year following the year in which payments were made. (Although the date generally is February 28, year 2000 is a leap year.) However, for information returns required to be filed after December 31, 1999, you have until March 31 if you file electronically.

CHAPTER 21

Deductions for AMT

Reducing regular tax is only half the battle that a small business owner wages to increase after-tax returns. Minimizing or avoiding alternative minimum tax where applicable is a second important front that must be addressed. Some business owners may find themselves subject to AMT if they have certain substantial deductions and/or credits.

In this chapter you will learn about:

- AMT basics
- Exemption for small corporations
- Deduction limits for AMT

AMT BASICS

Alternative minimum tax, or AMT as it is called, is designed to ensure that all taxpayers pay at least some tax. Years ago, with tax shelters and other loopholes, wealthy individuals and corporations often paid little or no tax. In an effort to make all taxpayers share the tax burden, an alternative minimum tax was imposed. The AMT is a separate tax system, with its own deductions and tax rates. A business owner computes his or her regular income tax as well as a tentative AMT. The extent to which the tentative AMT exceeds regular tax liability is reported as AMT. AMT liability can be reduced by a limited foreign tax credit.

> **LEGISLATIVE ALERT**
>
> There has been a proposal in Congress to let personal tax credits be utilized against the regular tax without causing any AMT liability.

There are two different AMT structures: one for C corporations and another for other taxpayers.

C corporations pay AMT at the rate of 20 percent. This rate is applied to alternative minimum taxable income (AMTI) reduced by an exemption amount of $40,000 (reduced by 25 percent of the amount by which AMTI exceeds $150,000). Alternative minimum taxable income includes an "ACE adjustment" (which stands for adjusted current earnings). This adjustment is designed to measure income tax on as broad a basis as it is for financial reporting purposes.

Business owners have a two-tier AMT rate structure of 26 percent on the first $175,000 of income subject to AMT, plus 28 percent on any excess amount. The amount subject to these tax rates is reduced by an exemption amount of $45,000 on a joint return, $33,750 for singles, and $22,500 for married filing separately. This exemption amount is phased out for high-income taxpayers (for example, no exemption may be claimed on a joint return when AMT income exceeds $330,000).

Who is subject to AMT? Potentially all businesses are subject to AMT. However, starting in 1998, small C corporations may be exempt, as explained later in this chapter. Owners of pass-through entities (partnerships, LLCs, and S corporations) figure AMT on their individual returns. They include business items passed through to them and identidμud as AMT items on their Schedule K-1.

EXEMPTION FOR SMALL CORPORATIONS

Before 1998 all C corporations were required to figure AMT liability. Now "small corporations" are entirely exempt from AMT.

> **Definition** *Small corporation*   A corporation with average gross receipts of $5 million or less for the three tax years beginning after December 31, 1993, and ending before the year in which the exemption is claimed.

EXAMPLE: X, Inc., a C corporation, had average gross receipts of $275,000 for the three-year period that included 1996, 1997, and 1998. For 1999, X is a small corporation and, therefore is exempt from AMT.

New C corporations (those with the first tax year being 1999), other than those aggregated with other corporations, are exempt from AMT in 1999 without regard to gross receipts. The tax law simply assumes that start-ups are small corporations.

Once your business is established as a "small corporation," it retains that status (and is exempt from AMT) as long as its average gross receipts for the prior three-year period do not exceed $7.5 million. The first year of small corporation status is ignored for purposes of this three-year period.

Note: While a C corporation generally can claim a tax credit with respect to AMT liability incurred in a prior year, a small corporation can claim only a limited AMT credit.

Loss of small corporation status   If your business succeeds to the extent that it loses its small corporation status, special AMT rules continue to apply to "formerly small corporations." These rules simplify AMT for such corporations. In general, these corporations start fresh for certain AMT items and never have to make certain AMT adjustments.

DEDUCTION LIMITS FOR AMT

Certain deductions that were allowed for regular tax purposes may be disallowed or modified for AMT. The following deductions that were claimed on individual returns may not be deducted for AMT purposes:

- Personal exemptions
- Any addition to the standard deduction
- Itemized deduction for taxes
- Itemized deduction for miscellaneous expenses

The following deductions that were claimed on individual returns must be modified for AMT purposes:

- Investment interest

- Itemized deduction for medical expenses (only expenses in excess of 10 percent of adjusted gross income are deductible for AMT purposes, while those in excess of 7.5 percent of AGI are deductible for regular tax purposes)

- Itemized deduction for home mortgage interest (only interest to buy, build, or substantially improve a principal residence or second home is deductible for AMT purposes, while interest on home equity loans used for other purposes may be deductible for regular tax purposes)

- Depreciation, as explained below

- Net operating losses, as explained below

- Mining exploration and development costs (the regular tax deduction must be amortized over 10 years)

- Research and experimentation expenditures (costs most be amortized over 10 years if you are not a material participant in the business)

- Passive activity losses from nonfarming activities (losses are adjusted for items not deductible for AMT purposes)

Adjustments for depreciation   The depreciation method that you use for regular tax purposes may require that an adjustment be made for AMT purposes. For AMT purposes you are allowed only a limited depreciation deduction. If you claimed more for regular tax purposes, you must adjust your AMT income accordingly.

For property (other than real property) acquired after 1986, your AMT depreciation is limited to the 150-percent declining balance method, switching to straight line when a larger depreciation deduction results.

For real property acquired after 1986, your AMT depreciation is limited to straight line over 40 years.

Note: Different adjustments apply to property placed in service before 1987. Follow the instructions to Form 6251.

For real property placed in service after December 31, 1998, an AMT adjustment is no longer required. For personal property placed in service after this date, a depreciation election can be made to use the same depreciation method for regular and AMT purposes so that an AMT adjustment is avoided. By making this election, depreciation is figured using the 150-percent declining balance method over the regular tax recovery period (instead of the 200-percent declining balance method). For an explanation of these depreciation methods, see Chapter 12.

Net operating losses   The NOL deduction for regular tax purposes must be adjusted for AMT. This is because only a limited NOL deduction is allowed for AMT purposes. The NOL for AMT purposes is the regular tax NOL except that the nonbusiness deduction adjustment includes only AMT itemized deductions (i.e., state and local taxes and certain other deductions cannot be used to figure the NOL deduction).

You may be able to eliminate your AMT liability because of your NOL deduction. However, the NOL deduction cannot be more than 90 percent of AMT income (without regard to the NOL deduction). If you cannot use all of your NOL because of the 90-percent limit, you may carry it back and forward under the applicable carryback/carryforward periods (explained in Chapter 19). However, the carryback and carryforward NOLs are also subject to the 90-percent limit.

Note: Special rules not discussed here apply to NOL carryforwards from years after 1982 and before 1987. Also, if you claim an NOL carryforward from a tax year before 1983 and your AMT for that year was deferred because of the NOL, you may be liable for a special tax of 15 percent of the NOL carryforward deducted in 1999.

Other adjustments and preferences   In figuring AMT income on which AMT tax is imposed, certain income items are also given special treatment. These include incentive stock options, long-term contracts, tax-exempt interest on private activity bonds, and basis adjustments for AMT gain or loss.

WHERE TO FIGURE AMT

Self-Employed

If you have any adjustments or preference items, you must complete Form 6251, Alternative Minimum Tax—Individuals. You may or may not have any AMT liability.

Partnerships and LLCs

The business reports an owner's share of AMT items on Schedule K-1. As an owner, you must complete Form 6251 to see if you owe any AMT.

S Corporations

The business reports an owner's share of AMT items on Schedule K-1. As an owner, you must complete Form 6251 to see if you owe any AMT.

C Corporations

Small corporations exempt from AMT are not required to complete any special forms. C corporations not exempt from AMT figure their AMT liability on Form 4626, Alternative Minimum Tax—Corporations.

CHAPTER 22

Tax Deduction Strategies

U nderstanding what the various business deductions are all about is only half the job. You must also know when to claim certain deductions and when not to claim them. You should also be aware of the common traps that business owners often fall into with deductions.

In this chapter you will learn about:

- Tax-saving tips

- Common errors in claiming deductions, and how to avoid them

Finally, it is important to recognize that you should not always go it alone. You may need to get the assistance of tax professionals or additional information from the IRS. You need to know how to obtain referrals to tax professionals. You also need to know some important IRS telephone numbers to call for assistance. This information is included for your convenience.

TAX-SAVING TIPS

Tax-Planning Decisions

Some deductions are under your control, in the sense that you decide whether to incur the expenditure. Also, sometimes you are permitted to make tax elections on when to claim write-offs. Here are some pointers that can help you maximize your deductions. Or you can follow the reverse strategy if you already have losses for the year and want to accelerate income to offset those losses (and defer deductions).

- **Cash-basis businesses.** If you account for your expenses and income on a cash basis, you can influence when you claim deductions for year-end expenses. For example, you can stock up on supplies and pay off outstanding accounts payable to build up your deductions. At the same time, you can delay billing out for services or merchandise so that payment will be received in the following year. This will allow you to defer your income while accelerating your deductions.

  However, in accelerating deductions, do not prepay expenses that relate to items extending beyond one year. For example, if you pay a three-year subscription to a trade magazine, you can deduct only the portion of the subscription (one-third) that relates to the current year; the balance is deductible in future years as allocated.

  In deferring income for services or goods sold, do not delay billing where collection may be in jeopardy.

- **Accrual method businesses.** The board of directors of an accrual-basis corporation can authorize a charitable contribution and make note of it in the corporate minutes. A current deduction can be claimed even if the contribution is paid after the end of the year (as long as it is paid no later than two-and-a-half months after the close of the year). Charitable contributions are discussed in Chapter 20.

- **Owner participation.** If you own a business, be sure that your level of participation is sufficient to allow you to deduct all your losses under the passive loss limitation rules. Increase your level of participation and keep records of how and when you participated in the business. Passive loss rules and the various participation tests under these rules are discussed in Chapter 3.

- **Increase basis to fully utilize losses.** If you are an owner in a pass-through entity, your share of losses generally is deductible only to the extent of your basis in the business. Explore ways in which to increase your basis so that the losses can be fully utilized. Basis rules and their impact on loss deductions are discussed in Chapter 3.

- **Minimize FICA.** Owners who work for their corporations may be able to extract distributions on a FICA-free basis by arranging loans or rentals to the business and taking payments in the form of interest or rents. Of course, these arrangements must be bona fide. However, S corporation shareholders who perform substantial services for their corporation should not erroneously characterize compensation as dividends.

- **Review qualified plan selection.** If you are self-employed and use an IRA, Keogh, SEP, or SIMPLE plan to save for retirement, review your choice of plan annually to see if it optimizes your benefits while keeping costs down. Similarly, corporations should review existing plans to see whether terminations or other courses of action are warranted as cost-cutting measures. If you want to terminate one plan and begin another, do not do so without consulting a pension expert. You must be sure that your old plan is in full compliance before it is terminated.

- **Carry medical coverage for yourself and employees.** Buy the kind of coverage you can afford. The business picks up the expense for your personal insurance protection. Even if you cannot receive this benefit on a tax-free basis (if, for example, you are a partner or S corporation shareholder who must include business-paid insurance in your income), you can deduct a percentage of the coverage on your individual return. You can reduce the cost of coverage to the business by buying a "high-deductible" plan that allows employees to contribute to medical savings accounts on a tax-deductible basis. Alternatively, you can make deductible contributions to MSAs on behalf of your employees. You can shift most of the cost of coverage to employees by adopting a premium-only cafeteria plan. If you have a C corporation and are a shareholder-employee, you can institute a medical reimbursement plan to cover out-of-pocket medical costs not otherwise covered by insurance (such as dental expenses, eye care, or prescription drugs). Medical coverage strategies are discussed in Chapter 18.

- **Institute other employee benefit plans.** If you have a C corporation and are a shareholder-employee, you may be able to turn your non-deductible personal expenses into deductible business expenses. For example, you can have the corporation institute a group term life insurance plan for employees and obtain tax-free coverage up to

$50,000. Of course, in weighing the advantages and disadvantages of employee benefit plans, be sure to consider the cost of covering rank-and-file employees, since most benefit plans have strict non-discrimination rules. Also take into account the fact that employer-paid educational assistance and adoption plans cannot give more than 5 percent of benefits to shareholders owning more than 5 percent of the stock, making such plans undesirable for such closely held corporations. Employee benefits are discussed in Chapter 5.

- **Reimbursement arrangements.** If your company reimburses you for travel and entertainment costs, be sure that the arrangement is treated as an "accountable plan." This will ensure that you are not taxed on reimbursements, since your offsetting deductions would be subject to the 2-percent-of-adjusted-gross-income floor. With an accountable plan, the company deducts the expenses and no income is reported to you. Reimbursement arrangements are discussed in Chapter 6.

- **Take optimum write-offs for business equipment purchases.** Where the business can benefit from a larger deduction, instead of depreciating the cost of equipment over the life of the property, consider electing first-year expensing (e.g., a deduction of up to $19,000 in 1999). Alternatively, where the business cannot benefit from a current depreciation deduction because it does not have sufficient income to offset the deduction, consider electing alternative depreciation to spread deductions over future years. Time business equipment purchases carefully in view of the mid-quarter convention. Depreciation and expensing are discussed in Chapter 12.

- **Abandonment versus selling of property.** If you have property that simply is of no value to the business, you may want to abandon it rather than sell it for a nominal amount. This will allow the business to take an ordinary loss deduction rather than a capital loss on a sale. A sale of Section 1231 property may result in a capital or ordinary loss, depending upon other Section 1231 transactions for the current year and prior Section 1231 losses. Abandonment of property and Section 1231 property are discussed in Chapter 15.

- **Disaster losses.** If you suffer a disaster loss to business property in an area declared by the president to be eligible for federal disaster assistance, consider claiming the deduction on a return for the year preceding the year of the loss if this will give you needed cash flow or result in a greater benefit from the deduction. Disaster losses are discussed in Chapter 16.

- **Elect to forgo a net operating loss carryback.** If the business has a net operating loss in 1999, it can generally carry the loss back two years (three years for small business disaster losses; five years for farmers and ranchers; 10 years for product liability) and forward for 20 years. Alternatively, it can elect to forgo the carryback and simply carry the loss forward. Where a corporation was in a low tax bracket in prior years but is in a higher tax bracket now (and expects to remain in a high bracket in the future), it may be advisable to elect to forgo the carryback. If the business simply does not have any prior income to offset by a net operating loss, do not make an election; simply carry the loss forward. By not making the election, you preserve the right to carry back the net operating loss if the IRS subsequently audits an earlier return and income results. Net operating losses are discussed in Chapter 20.

- **Review the business structure.** Changes in the business climate, in tax law, and in state law may warrant a change in the form of business organization. For example, you may start out your business as a sole proprietor; later you may want to incorporate in order to take advantage of certain employee benefit plans. Review the options that will afford tax reduction and other benefits. Business organization is discussed in Chapter 1.

- **Do year-end planning.** Businesses have an opportunity to save on taxes with year-end planning. Well-timed deductions may prove advantageous. Begin year-end planning well before the end of the year in order to have time to implement your decisions.

Audit-Proofing Your Return

Your goal should be to claim all the deductions to which you are entitled in order to minimize your business income. At the same time, you want to "audit-proof" your return to avoid confrontations with the IRS. The following are some tips you can use to ensure that your write-offs will be allowed.

- **Keep good records.** You want to be able to back up your deductions with proof of when the expense was paid or incurred, the amount of the expense, and why you think it is deductible. If you develop good recordkeeping practices, you will automatically be assured of the necessary evidence to support your deductions. For example, if you want to claim deductions for travel and entertainment expenses, you must have certain proof of expenditures. Using a computer to keep your books and records can simplify both recordkeeping requirements and tax return preparation. Recordkeeping is explained in detail in Chapter 4.

- **Formalize agreements between corporations and shareholders.** If loans are made to or from shareholders, be sure that the interest rate, terms of repayment, and other particulars of the loans are written down. Have the note signed by the parties. Formal agreements should also be made if property is leased by a shareholder to the corporation.

- **Supply all necessary information.** In completing business returns, be sure to fill out all forms and schedules required. Also include all required information for claiming certain deductions. For example, if you have a bad debt, you cannot simply deduct the loss. You must attach a statement to the return detailing the nature and extent of the bad debt.

- **Review the IRS audit guide for your industry (if such a guide has been released).** This guide is used by IRS personnel to review returns of businesses within an industry and thus provides key information about what the IRS is on the lookout for. Currently more than two dozen guides are available free from the IRS web site at www.irs.ustreas.gov/plan/bus_info/index.html.

- **Ask for the IRS's opinion.** If you are planning a novel transaction or want to take a deduction about which you are unsure, you may be able to get the IRS's view on the situation. You may want to request a private letter ruling. If the ruling is favorable, you can be confident of your position. If it is unfavorable, you may be able to modify the situation as the ruling suggests. The IRS charges a user fee for issuing letter rulings (the amounts vary). Before asking for a ruling, though, it may be better to discuss the situation with a tax professional who can research existing precedent and help you prepare a ruling request.

- **File on time.** If you delay filing, you face not only penalties and interest but also the loss of deductions. For example, you must claim a deduction for contributions to a Keogh plan no later than the due date of your return. If you cannot meet the filing deadline, be sure to ask for a filing extension in a timely manner. File the correct form for claiming a filing extension appropriate to your business return. Also, check state income tax rules for filing extensions that may require a separate form.

FORMS FOR FILING EXTENSIONS

If you file:	Ask for an extension on:
Schedule A, Form 1040, for employees	Form 4868
Schedule C, Form 1040, for sole proprietors	Form 4868
Schedule F, Form 1040, for farmers	Form 4868
Form 1065, for partnerships and LLCs	Form 8736
Form 1120, for C corporations	Form 7004
Form 1120S, for S corporations	Form 7004

- **Get good advice.** If you are unsure of whether you are entitled to claim a particular deduction, ask a tax professional. Be sure to understand the protection you receive from attorney-client privilege. This privilege applies to accountants and other federally authorized tax practitioners with respect to federal civil tax matters. But it does not apply to mere tax return preparation, state tax matters (unless your state extends similar protection), or other federal non-tax matters (such as securities matters).

COMMON ERRORS IN CLAIMING DEDUCTIONS, AND HOW TO AVOID THEM

The IRS has compiled a list of errors that arise with great frequency on business returns in connection with deductions. By being forewarned of these errors, you should be able to avoid them.

Salary of Corporate Officers

Some corporations have been claiming deductions for management or consulting fees paid to the corporation's owners. At the same time, these corporations have not claimed deductions for salary. This leads the IRS to conclude that the corporations are misclassifying payments to corporate officers as fees rather than compensation in order to avoid payroll taxes. Corporations may be liable for penalties for failing to withhold and deposit payroll taxes and for failing to file required payroll tax returns. Of course, sometimes payments to shareholders may very well be management or consulting fees for occasional outside assistance. But where these individuals conduct the actual business of the corporation—perform the services for which the corporation was organized or provide management services on a full-time or consistent basis—the payments look more like compensation.

S corporations especially may also fail to deduct compensation paid to owner-employees and instead call distributions to them "dividends." The rationale for this strategy is to reduce the corporation's liability for payroll taxes. Again, the IRS has identified this strategy as a common error and has imposed penalties on S corporations that have followed it. If an owner-employee performs substantial services for the S corporation, some reasonable amount of payment for services must be treated as deductible compensation subject to payroll taxes.

Below-Market Loans

Loans from shareholders to their corporations that bear an interest rate lower than the applicable federal rate (a rate set monthly by the IRS, which varies with the term of the loan) result in phantom or "imputed" interest. Shareholders must report this interest; corporations can deduct the imputed interest. If the corporation fails to take an interest deduction, the IRS may conclude that the shareholder has not really made a loan but rather a contribution to the capital of the corporation, and no deduction for the corporation will be allowed.

Loans to shareholders from their corporations may also present tax deduction problems. Shareholders are entitled to deduct imputed interest in this case (as business or investment interest), with the corporation picking up the imputed interest as interest income. Unfortunately, some corporations are failing to report the income, but they are still showing the loan on their balance sheets. This is an unnecessary error for corporations to make. If the shareholders are also employees of the corporation, then the corporation can claim a deduction for compensation to the shareholder-employees to offset the imputed interest income. If, however, the shareholders are not employees of the corporation, the payments to them must be treated as dividends, which are not deductible by the corporation.

Travel and Entertainment Deductions

Some businesses claim a full deduction for business meals and entertainment. They do not correctly apply the 50-percent limit on these deductions. This problem commonly occurs for meals and entertainment away from home.

Bad Debt Deductions

Some individuals are claiming bad debt deductions as ordinary losses rather than short-term capital losses. In other words, they are classifying the bad debt as a business bad debt when, in fact, it may be a nonbusiness bad debt. For example, if a shareholder has a bad debt for a loan to the corporation, the loan should be treated as a nonbusiness bad debt because it is not incurred in a trade or business; rather, it is made to protect one's investment as a shareholder.

Casualty Losses

Some businesses fail to reduce deductions for casualty losses by any insurance reimbursements received. This results in an overstatement of casualty losses.

Claiming Losses in General

Some taxpayers claim losses in excess of amounts that are otherwise allowed. They fail to observe the passive loss limitation rules that limit loss deductions for activities in which there is no material participation. Just because someone owns stock in an S corporation, for example, does not mean that he or she is a material participant in the business. The shareholder must meet special material participation tests to deduct losses in excess of passive income.

Other taxpayers may be deducting hobby losses in excess of income from this type of activity. While income from a hobby-type activity is fully taxable, losses are deductible only to the extent of income from the activity.

Also, some shareholders in S corporations claim losses in excess of their basis in the corporation. Losses are deductible only to the extent of a shareholder's basis in stock and loans to the corporation. Basis is adjusted annually for various transactions—shareholder's distributive share of S corporation income that is taxable to the shareholder, distributions by the corporation, and losses claimed. Losses in excess of basis are not lost. They can be carried forward and used in a subsequent year when there is sufficient basis to offset them.

TAX ASSISTANCE

Your primary focus should be on running your business and making it profitable. This may leave you little or no time to attend to tax matters. It may be cost effective to use the services of a tax professional to maintain your books and records, file your returns, and provide needed tax advice.

There are many different types of tax professionals to choose from. The particular type of counsel you seek depends in part on your needs and what you can afford to pay for the services provided. The types of tax professionals you can consult include:

- Accountants
- Enrolled agents
- CPAs
- Tax attorneys

Storefront tax return preparation services may provide assistance with filing your returns. They generally are not staffed to provide tax guidance.

Keep in mind that information you disclose to an attorney is completely confidential. The extension of attorney-client privilege to other federally authorized tax practitioners (such as accountants) in civil tax matters does not apply to mere return preparation and in other situations described earlier in this chapter.

If you do not know the name of a specific individual to help you, ask business acquaintances for referrals. Another source of references is the Yellow Pages of your phone book. Then, if you wish to check whether a particular CPA is licensed as claimed, you can call your state Society of CPAs. Similarly, if you want to check on a particular attorney, call your state Bar Association. Do not hesitate to ask the professional what he or she charges for the services to be provided.

Help from the IRS

The IRS provides a number of publications, some of which have been mentioned throughout the book, that can give you important information on tax deductions to which you may be entitled. These publications include:

Publication #	Title
15	Circular E, Employer's Tax Guide
15-A	Employer's Supplemental Tax Guide
51	Circular A, Agricultural Employer's Tax Guide
225	Farmer's Tax Guide
334	Tax Guide for Small Business (for Individuals Who Use Schedule C or C-EZ)
349	Federal Highway Use Tax on Heavy Vehicles
378	Fuel Tax Credits and Refunds
463	Travel, Entertainment, Gift, and Car Expenses
521	Moving Expenses
526	Charitable Contributions
533	Self-Employment Tax
534	Depreciating Property Placed in Service Before 1987
535	Business Expenses

Publication #	Title
969	Medical Savings Accounts
1220	Specifications for Filing Forms 1098, 1099, 5498, and W-2G Magnetically or Electronically
1542	Per Diem Rates

These publications are available directly from the IRS by calling 1-800-829-3676 or by visiting your local IRS office, post office, or library. You can also download them from the IRS's Web site at www.irs.ustreas.gov. Forms are also available by fax by dialing 1-703-321-8020 (a toll call).

Another valuable source of assistance is the instructions for particular tax returns. For example, if your business is an S corporation, you can obtain guidance on claiming various tax deductions from the instructions for Form 1120S.

You may want to attend a free IRS seminar offered to new business owners. Topics covered in these seminars include recordkeeping, tax filing requirements, employment taxes, and federal tax deposit rules. There are also special seminars for different types of businesses (e.g., S corporations). To find out about a seminar in your area, call the IRS's Taxpayer Education Coordinator (listed in the Blue Pages of your local phone book and available through the IRS's general number, 1-800-829-1040).

If you have questions, you may direct them to the IRS. However, do not simply rely on statements made to you by someone in the your local IRS office or over the telephone. If you want to rely on IRS advice, be sure to get it in writing. The IRS is not bound by oral advice, but it is bound by any written advice it may give you.

If you have a thorny tax issue involving substantial dollars and are not sure how the IRS will rule on the subject, you may want to obtain a special ruling. You can ask for a private letter ruling without the assistance of a tax professional, but this may not be the best course of action. You need to frame your question appropriately. Also, you need to supply a great deal of information to the IRS before it will take any action. A tax professional can ensure that your request will receive the attention you desire. The procedure entails the payment of a user fee that must accompany your ruling request.

If you have a problem with the IRS and cannot seem to get a satisfactory answer, you may want to ask the IRS to direct your question to its Problem Resolution section.

Help from the Small Business Administration

The Small Business Administration has teamed up with the IRS to provide tax assistance to small business owners. Small business tax forms and publications are now available at all 73 of the SBA's Business Information Centers (BICs) and One-Stop Capital Shops. IRS technical specialists are also available at BICs in Atlanta, Boston, Chicago, and Los Angeles one day per week to provide seminars, workshops, and one-on-one assistance (but not with tax preparation).

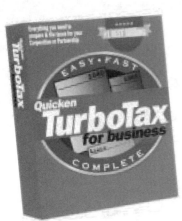
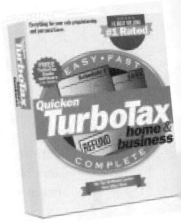

Index

Symbols

2-percent rule, 21
3-year property, 249, 252
5-year property, 249, 252-253
7-year property, 249, 252-253
10-year property, 249
15-year property, 249
20-year property, 249
150-percent declining balance rate, 254-256
200-percent declining balance rate, 252-253
401(k) retirement plans, 286
  loans from, 302
941TeleFile system, 101-102

A

aborted business ventures, 418
above-market loans, 237-238
accelerated depreciation, 162
accountable plans, 146-147
  for business use of car, 183-184
accountants, 445
accounting fees, 404

accounting methods, 25, 34-39
  accrual, 36-39
  cash, 34-36
  installment, 39
  uniform capitalization rules, 40-41
accounting periods, 25, 30-34
  business purpose for fiscal year, 32
  limits on use of fiscal year, 31-32
  seasonal businesses, 31
  Section 444 election for fiscal year, 32-33
accrual accounting method, 25, 36-39
active participation, 49
actual expense method, 159-173
  depreciation and, 161-173
  recordkeeping, 184
  and sale of car, 172
  versus standard mileage allowance, 159-160, 174
ADA (American with Disabilities Act), 194-195
adjusted basis, 318
adjusted gross income, 21
adoption assistance, as statutory employee benefit, 78

ADS (Alternative Depreciation System), 247, 256-257
advertising expenses, 278-283
  contests and, 282
  goodwill promotions, 279-282
  help-wanted ads, 282
  lobbying deductions, 281-282
  ordinary, 278-279
  personal versus business expenses, 280-281
  prizes and, 282
  where to deduct, 282-283
airfare, 104, 107
Alabama
  as high-cost area for high-low method, 148
  per diem meal allowances, 108
all events test, 36
Alternative Depreciation System (ADS), 247, 256-257
alternative minimum tax (AMT), 430-435
  deduction limits, 432-434
  depreciation adjustments, 433-434
  exemption for small corporations, 431-432